THE SONY TAPE GUIDE TO
WHO'S WHO IN THE 1984 OLYMPICS

THE SONY TAPE GUIDE TO
WHO'S WHO
IN THE 1984
OLYMPICS

EDITED BY DAVID EMERY

PELHAM BOOKS

First published in Great Britain by
Pelham Books Ltd
44 Bedford Square
London WC1B 3DU
1984

Sony Tape Guide to Who's Who in the 1984 Olympics.
    1. Olympic Games *(23rd: 1984: Los Angeles)*
    2. Athletes — Biography
    I. Emery, David
    796.4'8'0922   GV722

    ISBN 0-7207-1519-9

Designed, edited and produced by First Editions
319 City Road, London EC1V 1L J

Typeset by Presentia Arts, Horsham
Origination by D.S. Colour International
Printed by Redwood Burn, Trowbridge, England

Contents

Foreword by Brendan Foster

The attraction of the Olympic Games is as diverse as the 23 sports that make up this year's event in Los Angeles.

For the media they represent the biggest global happening of them all, demanding the longest, most saturated coverage of any international event.

For the sporting public they are the greatest show on earth, three weeks of pride and patriotism, disappointment and delight.

For the athletes they are the fruition of four years' hard work and hope, the supreme test that has inspired them through many a dark, lonely night. Thousands of the world's fittest, strongest young people will be putting their dreams under the public microscope.

Ordinary men and women with extraordinary talent have been transformed into superstars overnight; cities have been bankrupted; commercial fortunes made and lost; international friendships forged or ruined.

All for the sake of some 200 lumps of gold-plated metal that hang from ribbons round necks.

It is true that the Olympic creed is all about the honour of taking part. And so it is for the many thousands of sportsmen and women who will congregate in Los Angeles in July. Among them, however, will be an elite who have come not just to take part — but to take part *to win*.

This outstanding book is about them — the leading medal hopes in each sport. It gives a unique insight into the past records, current form and human characteristics of these athletes. With this book by your side you will be able to form you own opinion of the likely medal winners as you follow the elation and despair of this momentous event on your TV.

The Sony Tape Guide to Video Recording

The 1984 Olympics. Without a doubt, the world's biggest spectator event, where even the intensity of worldwide competition is overshadowed by the intensity of international interest. And an event where your video recorder really comes into its own to let you watch at a time to suit you, and allow medal-winning triumphs to be enjoyed over and over again . . .

Yet the blank videotape you choose for your recordings can be just as important to your eventual viewing pleasure as the machine you are using.

Since producing the first magnetic recording tape in Japan well over 30 years ago, Sony have constantly been developing tape technology resulting in the range of advanced audio and video recorders and high quality tapes that we see today.

Whatever video recorder you possess and whichever format you have chosen, you can rely on Sony Videotape to assure you of absolute performance and quality. And of course you can choose the right length for your needs, from 30 minutes to 215 minutes. So whether you're recording a series of sprints, middle-distance events, or even a complete marathon, there's a length that's just right. And you can work out what length you'll need with the help of the finishing times given throughout this book.

THE SONY VIDEO TAPE RANGE

BETA DYNAMICRON

L-125	30 min
L-250	65 min
L-370	95 min
L-500	130 min
L-750	195 min
L-830	215 min

BETA DYNAMICRON HG

L-500HG	130min
L-750HG	195min

VHS DYNAMICRON

E-120	2 hour
E-180	3 hour

V2000 DYNAMICRON

VCC 240	2 hour
VCC 360	3 hour
VCC 480	4 hour

The best tape formulation for most purposes is Dynamicron, a high quality tape which combines highly-efficient recording performance with long-lasting qualities. However, for those recordings you are particularly anxious to preserve for posterity, such as the highlights of the Olympics, choose from the High Grade Dynamicron range, offering improved, top quality performance and even longer recording life.

To ensure a consistently high standard of recording for your videotape collection, there are several things you can do to help. To keep a recording intact, make sure you snap off the security tab on the back of the cassette, which prevents recording over an existing programme. To re-record subsequently, simply cover the slot with sticky tape. If you identify your tapes with the labelling stickers provided, peel off the old one and clean the surface before attaching an updated label.

Store your cassette in conditions which are not dusty or damp, not in sunlight or near direct heat. Also remember not to place them close to anything magnetic, such as a loudspeaker, as this can effectively wipe the tape clean!

Follow these guidelines and you will build a fine series of recordings which will do justice to your own video collection, and will let you savour the highlights of the 1984 Olympics for years to come.

9

Data compiled and researched by: Ivan Berenyi (*Gymnastics, Boxing, Judo, Weightlifting and Wrestling*); Pat Besford (*Swimming*); Tim Glover (*Equestrianism*); John Goodbody (*Judo*); Stan Greenberg (*Athletics*); Richard Hills (*Fencing*); Ray Moore (*Swimming*); John Morris (*Boxing*); Ian Morrison (*Gymnastics, Boxing, Archery, Fencing, Modern Pentathlon, Shooting, Judo, Weightlifting, Wrestling, Canoeing, Yachting and Rowing*); Randall Northam (*Athletics*); Mike Price (*Cycling*); Keir Radnedge (*Team Sports*); Pat Rowley (*Team Sports*); John Wilkinson (*Cycling*).

All photographs by Allsport/Tony Duffy except for the following:
Terry Beckett (*pp 134, 137, 145*), Coloursport (*pp 136, 138, 139, 140, 142, 149, 154, 156, 157, 158, 164, 168, 170*), Karina Hoskyns (*pp 165, 166, 168, 170*), George Kirkley (*pp 150, 153, 156, 159*), Photosport (*pp 162, 179, 180, 181, 182*), Sporting Pictures (UK) (*pp 134, 141, 143, 149, 151, 174, 180*).

Additional design by Tristram Woolston, Woolston Design Associates

5

The Olympic Games evolved from the mythological conflicts of Ancient Greek gods. **1)** Sites date back to 300 BC. **2)** The games were revived in Athens in 1896. **3)** London saw the resumption of the Olympics after World War II in 1948.

4 and **5)** Los Angeles has already played host to the Games: in 1932 the opening ceremony took place in the Coliseum where the 1984 ceremony will be held. Over 1½ million people saw the 1932 Olympics and the Games made a million dollar profit.

Athletics: Track events

The track events of the first of the modern Olympic Games were held in the stadium of Herodes, which dates back to 300 BC. Now a major tourist attraction in the centre of bustling Athens, it was sadly in need of restoration when Baron Pierre de Coubertin decided to revive the 'Games'.

Charles Perry, the groundsman at Stamford Bridge, then the home of English athletics, now the home of Chelsea football club, was called in but even he could do nothing about a track which measured 333.3 metres (364½ yd) and had such tight turns that the organizers decided against holding a 200 metres race.

Britain gained two golds when Edwin Flack won the 800 metres and 1500 metres, although these were later credited to Australia, because Flack was, after all, an Australian studying accountancy in London. Typical of the casual way the Olympics were treated in those days was the fact that Flack fitted them in with a month's holiday in Athens. He also took part in, but dropped out of, the marathon, which provided the most warming story of the first Olympic running events. The race from Marathon, the scene of a Greek victory over the Persians in 490 BC, was 40km (some 24 miles long), not the precisely measured 42,195m (26 miles 385 yards) it is today. Nor were countries restricted to three men per event, as they are today. The Greeks were always likely to provide the winner if only because they had 21 starters. The race was supposed to commemorate the feat of Pheidippides, who is alleged to have run from Marathon to Athens with news of the battle and then died with the word 'victory' on his lips.

Having been defeated in the discus, the Greek speciality, the locals, then as now, desperately needed a victory, and when Spiridon Louis, trotted into the stadium, Athens went wild. His winning margin of 7 min 13 sec remains the greatest in Olympic Marathon history. He was followed in by a band, women threw jewellery at him, Greek royalty jogged alongside him and he was made for life. He was even given a plot of land, known as 'Field of Marathon'.

Greece looked as though they would also get the bronze; but Velokas, of Greece, who finished in third position, admitted accepting a lift and was disqualified – the first of the Olympic cheating stories.

The Olympics were not yet established as a major sporting event and were lucky to survive the Paris Games of 1900. That competition lasted five months, the track in the Bois de Boulogne was poor and there was a mixture of amateur and professional events. Even so some of the track events were worthwhile. It was decided in 1900 to hold a 60 metres for men and this was won by Alvin Kraenzlein of the USA who also took the 110 and 200 metres hurdles plus the long jump.

Britain's tiny team of five brought home three gold medals. Charles Bennett, of Finchley Harriers, won the 1500 metres in 4:06.2, a world record, and Frank Tysoe won the 800 metres. Both combined to help Britain take the 5000 metres team event.

As in Paris four years earlier the 1904 Games at St Louis were once again held in conjunction with a world's fair and once again Britain's team was minute. The 60 metres was staged for the second and last time and won by Archie Hahn of the USA who also took the 100 and 200 metres.

Another American, James Lightbody, won the 800,.1500 and 2500 metres steeplechase but the standard was not as high as it should have been and once again there was a cheating story in the marathon. This time Fred Lorz, of the USA, gave up after 15 kilometres, accepted a lift to 8 kilometres from the stadium finish, and entered the stadium some eight minutes ahead of fellow American Thomas Hicks. The AAU banned him for life, although Lorz, a New Yorker, claimed he had been joking.

The Olympics were again staged in Athens in 1906, but these Games were not counted numerically in the records. Hahn won the 100 metres again and is, in fact, the only man to have won the event twice.

American Melvin Sheppard wins the 1908 1500 metres at White City, London, with Britain's Harold Wilson second

Italy's Dorando Pietri is helped across the line, and subsequently disqualified, in the 1908 Marathon

The next proper Games were held in London at White City in 1908. This was the first time athletics were regarded seriously by most nations.

The British and Americans argued fiercely, particularly over the 400 metres which Wyndham Halswelle of Britain won with a walk over. Halswelle, who started favourite, having set a British 440-yard record of 48.6 in Glasgow only three weeks before, had set a new Olympic record of 48.4 in winning his semi-final. But the final was not run in lanes and with only the home straight left Robbins of the USA was leading. Halswelle and John Carpenter, another American, moved out to pass and Carpenter, on Halswelle's left, ran diagonally, giving the British runner no chance to overtake, and slowed down before the line. It was decided that Carpenter be disqualified and that the final should be run in 'strings' — taped lanes. But the Americans boycotted the re-run and Halswelle ran the distance solo in 50 seconds.

On the track the 800 and 1500 metres were won by Melvin Sheppard of America, whose 1:52.8 was a world record for the 800 — not a two lap race because the track was 536.45 metres (586 yd 2½ ft). He also helped the USA to victory in the medley relay.

Once again the marathon provided the sensation. Italy's Dorando Pietri entered the stadium first but in a clearly disorientated condition. He turned right at first instead of left, and although he was redirected he collapsed. He was assisted to his feet but fell over four more times and was helped over the finish.

The Americans, whose John Hayes finished second, rightly protested and Pietri was disqualified. Such was the wave of public sympathy, though, that the Italian was given a replica of the gold cup awarded to Hayes.

This was the first time the marathon had been held over 26 miles 385 yards (approx 41 kilometres), 'the classic' distance that remains to this day. The original race was to be an exact 26 miles from Windsor Castle to White City, but 385 yards (352 metres) was tacked on so it could finish in front of the Royal Box.

With the Olympics now firmly established as a four year cycle, Stockholm was the next city to stage the spectacle, with Charles Perry being asked to construct another track, this time of 383 metres (419 yards). The stadium was built like a medieval castle and remains one of the most picturesque on the international circuit.

In 1912 the USA was the major power once again, winning the 100, 200, 400 and 800 metres, with Ted Meredith setting a world record for the 800 metres. But in the 1500 metres Britain's Arnold Strode Jackson won by the narrowest margin possible in those days, one tenth of a second.

This was the year that established the Finnish distance running tradition. Hannes Kolehmainen won the 5000 metres and 10000 metres as well as the 8000 metres cross country. In the 5000 metres both he and Jean Bouin, of France, broke the world record. But Kolehmainen had to wear Russian colours because Finland was not then independent. He had his compensation in 1920 and 40 years later when he helped Paavo Nurmi light the Olympic flame in the Helsinki stadium.

The 1920 Olympics were held in Antwerp after the great war had wiped out the 1916 games planned for Berlin. Now for the first time the track was 400 metres.

Kolehmainen made his mark again with victory in the marathon in 2h 32:35.8 but his 12.8 sec margin of victory over Juri Lossman, of Estonia, is still the narrowest in Olympic history. This time he wrapped himself in the Finnish blue and white flag.

Finnish great Hannes Kolehmainen wins 1912 5000 metres.

This was also the occasion of Paavo Nurmi's Olympic debut. Nurmi, who won 12 medals in three Games, won the 10000 metres and cross country, plus another gold in the cross country team and finished second in the 5000 metres. Great as that feat was it was to be bettered in 1924.

The record machine . . . Paavo Nurmi, 12 medals from three Olympics

The Americans were not so dominant this time and Bevil Rudd, of South Africa, took the 400 metres, with 31-year-old Albert Hill of Britain, who had served three years in the Army in France, winner of the 800 metres and 1500 metres within three days.

1924 was 'Chariots of Fire' year. Anyone who has seen that memorable film will be familiar with the story behind two British gold medals, Harold Abrahams in the 100 metres and Eric Liddell in the 400 metres. The story has been adapted to give dramatic emphasis. Abrahams, it is true, did incur the displeasure of the autocratic authorities by engaging a professional coach, Sam Mussabini, although some of his advice is questionable these days. But it is not true that Liddell decided just beforehand that he would not run in the 100 metres because the heats were on a Sunday. Liddell, later to become a missionary in China, knew that he would not run when the timetable was published some months beforehand. True the officials tried to persuade him to change his mind but he was adamant. Had he run the 100 metres he might well have won. As it was the Edinburgh University divinity student, who had represented Scotland on the rugby field, won the 400 metres.

Another British winner was Douglas Lowe, like Abrahams a Cambridge University student, and at only 21 he took the 800 metres.

But the story of the games concerns Nurmi: in just an hour and a quarter the man who was dubbed the Flying Finn won the 1500 metres and the 5000 metres. He also won the 3000 metre team race, the 10000 metres cross country, and with his team medal this gave him five golds, a record for one Games. It would have been six but individual medals were not given in the 3000 metres team race.

Nurmi carried on to 1928 and Amsterdam, taking the 10,000 metres gold and taking silver in the 5000 metres and 3000 metres steeplechase.

The Amsterdam Olympics saw an innovation – women's events. The first woman Olympic winner was Anni Holdman of Germany who won the first 100 metres heat.

Britain's Lord Burghley wins the 400 metres hurdles at the 1928 Amsterdam Olympics with America's Frank Cuhel second

Percy Williams, of Canada, the 'perfect' physical specimen according to Dutch doctors, who tested 3000 Olympic competitors, won the 100 metres and 200 metres while the USA's only gold on the track came in the 400 metres through Barbuti.

Douglas Lowe retained the 800 metres title and Lord Burghley, later the Marquis of Exeter and President of the IAAF, won the 400 metres hurdles.

The Finns dominated the track from 1500 metres up: Larva took the 1500 metres, Ritola the 5000 metres, Nurmi the 10000 metres, and Loukola the steeplechase. In all they won nine of the 12 medals on offer.

Nurmi wanted to run in Los Angeles in 1932 but the IAAF suspended him for alleged professionalism. However, the Finns still provided winners in the distance races: Lehtinen won the 5000 metres and Volmari Iso-Hollo the 3400 metres steeplechase. (It should have been 3000 metres but the field ran one lap too many!) But the Finns were upstaged by the Americans, with Eddie Tolan winning the 100/200 metres double. The new photo finish equipment was called into action in the 100 metres when Tolan just pipped his team-mate Ralph Metcalfe. Then in the 200 metres Tolan won again, although later Metcalfe's lane was found to have been 1.50 metres too long.

In the 400 metres Bill Carr set a new world record of 46.2 beating his great rival Ben Eastman who had established a world best of 46.4 only five months before. Tommy Hampson continued Britain's dominance of the 800 metres following Hill and Lowe (twice). His time of 1:49.7 was the first time anybody had ducked under 1:50. Britain also won the 50,000 metres walk with Tommy Green, who at 39 years 120 days is the oldest man to win an Olympic walk.

Emil Zatopek, triple gold medallist in Helsinki 1952, heads Britain's Gordon Pirie

The women came into their own in Los Angeles with Stanislawa Walasiewicz of Poland, better known as Stella Walsh, winning the 100 metres in a world record 11.9. There was speculation after her death in 1980 that she would have failed a sex test had she been competing today.

Babe Didrikson, only 18, won the 80 metres hurdles (and javelin) in world record time. She later became better known as the best woman golfer in the world.

The 1936 Games in Berlin belonged to Jesse Owens. Adolf Hitler had intended that the Berlin Games would celebrate what he saw as the superiority of the Aryan race — Owens saw to it that they were remembered for his superb ability.

The black sprinter/long jumper was already a superstar having set six world records in little over an hour the previous year. Now he was to win the 100 metres, 200 metres and long jump and help the American team to a 4 x 100 metres relay victory.

His 100 metres time of 10.3 would have been a world record but for wind assistance, his 200 metres time of 20.7 was the best around a full turn, while his long jump of 8.06m (26ft 5½in) had been bettered only by himself. The American time of 39.8 in the relay was the first time any quartet had gone under 40 seconds.

The most celebrated track victory though belonged to Jack Lovelock of New Zealand, an Oxford University student, whose scientific training methods had become a byword. Lovelock timed his victory to perfection in 3:47.8, a world record.

Britain won the 50000 metres walk again, this time through Harold Whitlock. But the 800 metres went to Woodruff of the USA.

There were no Olympics during World War II, so London, just recovering from the hostilities, staged the next Games in 1948. These saw the entry of Emil Zatopek onto the Olympic stage. The Czech whose style was characterised by an exaggerated roll of the head won the 10,000 metres and finished second in the 5000 metres and brought good humour and grace to a world still shocked by the savagery of war.

Jesse Owens at the 1936 Berlin Olympics where he collected four gold medals

◄ *'Chariots of Fire' Harold Abrahams makes his famous dip to gold in the 1924 100 metres in Paris*

15

The shock of the track events came in the 100 metres when Harrison Dillard of the USA won gold. Earlier in the year Dillard had broken the world 110 metres hurdles record and was a sure favourite for that event. But then, as now, the Americans had a sudden death trial and Dillard had fallen in the final. He opted for the flat 100 metres and proved he 'could run some too'.

The 400 metres, though, provided the spectacle of the Games, a duel between two Jamaicans, Arthur Wint and Herb McKenley. McKenley was the favourite and he spurted away leaving the tall Wint apparently beaten. But McKenley had gone off too quickly and Wint hauled him in to clock 46.2 and equal the Olympic record.

In the women's events, the orange-knickered Fanny Blankers-Koen made it a benefit event, winning the 100 metres and 200 metres, the 80 metres hurdles and anchoring the Dutch sprint relay team, the most golds by a woman at any one Games.

Fanny Blankers-Koen of Holland sprints to one of her four gold medals in 1948

Emil Zatopek had given notice at Wembley that he was an Olympic star, now at Helsinki in 1952 he shone brightest of them all. He achieved a treble gold medal haul never before managed, the gruelling 5000 metres, 10,000 metres and then the marathon. A truly remarkable feat.

He later dismissed his triumph by insisting *'The other runners said "After you Mr Zatopek" and so I made my own pace. It is not like that today'.* But this genuinely modest man ought to accept more credit. Zatopek had not run a marathon before and padding along with Jim Peters, the Englishman who revolutionised marathon running, he asked *'Are we going fast enough?'. 'No',* said Jim, gritting his teeth and forcing the pace. But he had to drop out with cramp and Zatopek, head rolling, shoulders shrugging and what looked like a grin on his face, strode on to win by two and a half minutes.

Herb McKenley got his gold medal in the relay, after losing the 100 metres on a photo finish and being beaten by fellow Jamaican George Rhoden in the individual 400 metres.

Harrison Dillard returned to his 'proper' event the 110 metres hurdles to win another gold medal.

Britain had found gold medals on the track hard to win, taking none at all at Wembley or Helsinki. Then in Melbourne in 1956 they had a first man home — Chris Brasher in the steeplechase — only to find he was disqualified for pushing Ernst Larsen of Norway. Hungary's Sandor Rozsnyoi was given the gold, but after a protest Brasher was reinstated, the jury of appeal deciding the contact had been accidental, after both men had said their rhythm was not affected.

The likeliest British gold medal seemed to lie with Gordon Pirie in the 10000 metres. but Pirie was destroyed by Vladimir Kuts of the Soviet Union, who also won the 5000 metres.

Bobby-Joe Morrow took a sprint double and gold from the 4 x 100 metres relay while Jenkins of the USA took the 400 metres and Courtney, also USA, the 800 metres.

American dominance on the track did not extend to the 1500 metres where Ireland's Ron Delaney sprinted over the last 200 metres to victory. Zatopek, recovering from illness, finished sixth in the marathon, behind Alain Mimoun trying the distance for the first time.

The woman star was Australian Betty Cuthbert, with 100-metre, 200-metre and sprint relay golds.

Herb Elliott, Otis Davis, Abebe Bikila, Wilma Rudolph... take your pick of great champions from Rome in 1960. Elliott won the 1500 metres in a world record 3:35.6 — four tenths faster than his own record — Davis won an epic 400 metres in a world record 44.9 while Rudolph, only 19, took the 100 metres and 200 metres, and a sprint relay gold. Dorothy Hyman of Britain was second in the 100 metres and third in the 200 metres but Britain's only gold came in the 50000 metres walk through Don Thompson. The 'Mighty Mouse' as he was instantly dubbed prepared for the Roman weather by spending as much time as possible in a steam bath.

Wilma Rudolph . . . sprint double in 1960

But for many Bikila's victory was the most memorable and the most significant. He padded down the Appian Way in bare feet, effortlessly reeling off the miles of the marathon, although an undisciplined scooter rider almost knocked him over 50 yards from home. The inscrutable member of the Ethiopian Imperial Guard thus became the first black African to win a gold medal. He was not to be the last.

Tokyo 1964 — rain and at last British success with gold medals for Lynn Davies in the men's long jump and Mary Rand in the women's. Gold also in the 20000 metres walk for Ken Matthews and the women's 800 metres for Ann Packer plus seven silvers. But the Games will be chiefly remembered for Bikila, later to suffer horrible injuries in a car crash, becoming the first man to retain the marathon title, for Peter Snell becoming the first man in forty-four years to take the 800 metres and 1500 metres double, and for the awesome power of Bob Hayes in the 100 metres and sprint relay.

Most of all perhaps, they will be remembered for the defeat of Ron Clarke in the 10,000 metres. Clarke was the greatest distance runner against the clock of all time. But the Australian, now working in London, could not win a major title and an unknown, Billy Mills from America, a country which had never won at 10,000 metres or 5000 metres, pipped him. A shocked Clarke could only finish third.

In the women's events Wyomia Tyus won the 100 metres equalling Rudolph's world record of 11.2 in the semi-final. Betty Cuthbert brought her gold medal total to four by taking the 400 metres while Ann Packer's 2:01.1 in only her eighth race at the distance was an 'official' world record. But Shin Keum Dan of North Korea had twice gone under two minutes, although her achievements were unrecognised by the IAAF.

*Golden boys and girls of 1964 . . . Lynn Davies and Mary Rand provided a long jump double
for Britain; New Zealand's Peter Snell struck double gold all by himself, in the 800 and 1500 metres*

Ann Packer, who was to marry men's team captain Robbie Brightwell, also took silver in the 400 metres.

The thin air of Mexico City made a nonsense of the track events in 1968. There were suggestions that people might die in running events such as the 10,000 metres and while no one did, the fact that the Games were held 2240 metres (7350 feet) above sea level gave an advantage to the Africans in particular.

Those taking part in events up to and including 800 metres loved it. There were world records for the men's 100, 200, 400, 800 metres, 400 metres hurdles and both relays. . In the women's events new world marks were set at 100 metres, 200 metres and sprint relays. . One of the world records, David Hemery's 48.12 in the 400 metres hurdles brought Britain her solitary gold medal, her fancied distance runners being victims of altitude. The records of men like Jim Hines in the 100 metres and Tommie Smith in the 200 metres lasted for years. Lee Evans' 43.86 in the 400 metres is still a record.

Yet at the other end of the scale Kip Keino's 1500 metres time was 3:34.9, 1.8 outside the then world record. The 5000 metres time, set by

Ann Packer with a victory smile made in Japan

Mohammed Gammoudi was 14:05 although the world best was 13:16.6. The 10000 took 29:27.4 compared with 27:39.4, a mockery of fair and equal competition and a disaster for Ron Clarke, robbed again of gold. He needed oxygen after the race.

Politics reared its head at the 200 metres medal ceremony when Tommie Smith, the winner, and third placed Juan Carlos stood with fists raised in a black power salute. To prove that all wounds heal in the end Carlos is now working for the Los Angeles Olympic Committee.

In the women's events Wyomia Tyus successfully defended her 100 metre title — the only woman to do so. In the final she clocked the first official 11 seconds by a women (11.08 automatic timing).

Britain's favourite for a woman's gold, Lillian Board was pipped on the line by a little known French girl Colette Besson.

Lillian Board

At Munich in 1972 some remarkable track performances were overshadowed by a classic gaffe by the Americans. Sprinters Eddie Hart and Rey Robinson, who had equalled the world record of 9.9 for the 100 metres when finishing first and second in the US trials, were lying on their beds in the Olympic village watching the events on television when Robinson said *'That's our race'.* The American track coach Stan Wright was working with an old timetable and so the two missed the second round. They were scratched but the third American, Robert Taylor, was dashed to the start and without any warm up finished second behind Valeri Borzov. Taylor also finished second to Borzov in the final. The powerfully built Soviet completed a sprint double by taking the 200 metres in 20 seconds dead.

Britain's big gold medal hope, Dave Bedford, was vanquished in both the 5000 metres and 10,000 metres by Lasse Viren and it was left to Ian Stewart with a bronze to salvage some British pride at 5000 metres. The look on his face after the medal ceremony showed the disdain with which he regarded the medal. In the 10,000 metres Viren tumbled over Gammoudi but although he lost two seconds he recovered to surge away over the final 600 metres. Jim Ryun, the world 1500 metres record holder was not so lucky. He fell in the heats and failed to qualify.

David Hemery's attempt to regain the 400 metres hurdles title was in vain with John Akii-Bua in first place breaking the world record. Hemery was third and ever the modest realist he said: *'How can you complain. It was fantastic running'.*

Twenty-two year old German student Nobert Sudhaus 'won' the marathon and he covered almost a lap in the stadium before officials became suspicious of his fresh face and clean kit. A few minutes later the real winner, American Frank Shorter, returning to his birth place, took the crowd's applause. Shorter's victory is generally considered to have sparked the enormous American and now world running boom.

Renate Stecher, of the GDR, took the women's sprint double, and East Germany collected other track golds through Monika Zehrt (400 metres) and Annelie Ehrhardt (100 metres hurdles). A new event for women, the 1500 metres, was won by Ludmilla Bragina of the USSR. Amazingly she broke the world record in the heat, then in the second round and then again in the final. By the end of the games she had sliced more than six seconds off her previous best, the old record.

The African boycott robbed the 1976 Montreal Olympics of many fascinating clashes, notably the world 1500 metres record holder Filbert Bayi against the world mile record holder John Walker, Miruts Yifter against Lasse Viren, John Akii-Bua against Ed Moses. But it did not prevent Montreal from throwing up some startling performances. Walker duly won the 1500 metres while Viren became the only man to defend the 5000 metres and 10000 metres titles successfully. Viren recalled the Flying Finns of the 1920s by running in the marathon and finishing fifth. There were rumours in Montreal of blood doping but Viren was a great champion.

But the greatest in Montreal was not Viren, nor Ed Moses who won the 400 metres hurdles, nor Don Quarrie who took the 200 metres — it was surely Alberto Juantorena, who collected the first 400 and 800 metres double.

Juantorena, from Cuba, had two nicknames — 'The Horse' and 'White Lightning'. He was dubbed 'The Horse' because he was tall and strong and he took time to get going, but when he was in full stride he was 'white lightning'. He won the 800 metres in a world record, 1:43.5, in his ninth race at the distance, then he took the 400 metres gold in 44.26, the fastest time ever achieved at sea level. In the 4 x 400 metres relay he tried the impossible and was timed at the 200 metres mark at an incredible 20.1. Not unnaturally he could not keep up that pace.

Tatyana Kazankina, small, introverted and pale as a ghost, was the female star, winning the 800 metres in a world record 1:54.9 and then the 1500 metres, again a first double of its kind. But the sentimental champion was Irena Szewinska of Poland who won the 400 metres in a world record, in her fourth Olympics.

In Moscow in 1980 there was another boycott, this time more serious in that the Americans, West Germans and Japanese stayed away. The Soviet invasion of Afghanistan had far reaching consequences on the track, several 1980 Olympic champions will always wonder what might have been, and some must know that gold would not have been theirs had everyone been in contention.

It would be wrong to suggest that Britain's Allan Wells would not have won the 100 metres especially as he beat most of the Americans on the European circuit after Moscow. But it is true that Wells's winning

Lasse Viren of Finland wins the 5000 metres at Montreal ahead of New Zealand's Dick Quax and West Germany's Klaus-Peter Hildenbrand

Bronislaw Malinowski of Poland touches down in front of Filbert Bayi (Tanzania) in the Moscow steeplechase

time of 10.25 was the slowest since Armin Hary in 1960. Nevertheless it was a thrilling race. Wells, a huge powerful Scot, was in lane eight with his chief rival, the smooth striding Cuban, Silvio Leonard, in lane one. They may have been separated by six lanes but at the end they were so close together that each thought he had won. Then the scoreboard showed an action replay and Wells was convinced. He swooped around on a lap of honour, the track marshals, who had been instructed not to allow any celebratory laps, unwilling to get in the way of such a large and fast man.

Wells had gone to Moscow expecting to do well in the 200 metres but he had to be content with silver, and there can be few who will doubt that Pietro Mennea would have won had the Americans been there. The Italian's winning time of 20.19 was faster than any other except for the altitude assisted 19.83 of Tommie Smith in Mexico City. Once again Wells relied on power, Mennea on stealth. While the Scot blasted out and hung on, Mennea controlled his race, accelerating to take Wells as the big man buckled in the last few strides.

But would Victor Markin have won had the Americans been in contention? Not as open to doubt as the hurdles, but although the unknown Markin's winning time of 44.60 was a European record it was slower than Juantorena in 1976 and only marginally faster than Vince Matthews in Munich.

None of the Americans would have made much difference to the 800 metres or the 1500 metres, both British victories although they went to the 'wrong' people. Sebastian Coe, the world 800 metres record holder was expected to win the two lap race, but he ran like a novice, and Steve Ovett had an easy victory which must have surprised him. America's Don Paige might have made a difference but only to the third place. With little love lost between Coe and Ovett the return match at 1500 metres was eagerly awaited. Ovett was the favourite. After all he was the world record holder, the European champion and the better tactician. Coe, although fast, did not have a background at the event. But fate in the shape of East Germany's Jurgen Straub took a hand. After a

funereal first half Straub took off, making the race, in effect an 800 metres. Coe was able to stretch his legs and run free and although Ovett got onto his shoulder coming into the straight Coe kicked again and was home. His relief showed in the way he kissed the track.

It is unlikely that any of the Americans would have made a difference although Thomas Wessinghage of West Germany might have been able to intervene, but not in those final coruscating two laps.

Incidentally, finishing eighth on this occasion and wondering what had hit him was a blond, curly haired 19-year-old from Jarrow. It was Steve Cram gaining invaluable experience.

Would the Americans or Germans have made any difference to Miruts Yifter in the 5000 metres and 10000 metres? The balding Ethiopian air force officer of indeterminate age missed the 5000 metres in Munich because he arrived late. He could not run in Montreal because of the African boycott, but in Moscow, helped by the Ethiopian game plan which involved the other team members setting up the race for him, Yifter the Shifter was dominant. Even though the running boom had taken off in the States it is unlikely that even Craig Virgin could have stopped Yifter from winning.

The marathon was a different story. Without the Americans and the Japanese the race was not a true reflection of world strength. But can anyone deny that Waldemar Cierpinski was a worthy champion? His time of 2h 11:03.0 was more than a minute outside his Montreal winning time, but respectable on a hot humid day.

Where the American absence did have a marked effect was in the two hurdles races. Of course things can go wrong, but Renaldo Nehemiah and Ed Moses were the nearest thing to certainties that you can get in athletics. Nehemiah had taken the world record down to 13.00 (automatic timing). In 1981 he was to record 12.93, a record which still stands. He was far and away the best hurdler of his generation and Greg Foster, another American, was the closest to him. So when East Germany's Thomas Munkelt won the race in 13.39 it was the slowest winning time since 1964. When he takes out his gold medal to show his grandchildren Munkelt must surely say 'however, Renaldo Nehemiah was not there'.

Likewise Volker Beck, another East German, must tell his descendants the story of Ed Moses. Beck's time of 48.70 was the slowest since 1964 and it is reasonable to assume that Moses could have been at least a second faster and that the European record holder, Harald Schmid, could also have beaten that time.

The Americans would probably not have altered the story of the steeplechase, the best race of the Games. Here Filbert Bayi, denied a chance to win the 1500 metres four years earlier, set off by himself. But Bronislaw Malinowski, of Polish and Scottish parentage, bided his time, reeled in the Tanzanian like a big game fisherman, and strode to victory. Sadly the Pole was to die in a car crash.

The American women would have made little difference to the results. Evelyn Ashford would undoubtedly have been among the medallists in the sprints but the power in women's athletics lies chiefly behind the iron curtain, where they take the female side of the sport much more seriously and scientifically.

As it was the 100 metres was a surprise victory for Ludmilla Kondratyeva of the Soviet Union over the world record holder Marlies Gohr of the GDR. But East Germany reasserted itself in the 200 metres when Barbel Wockel repeated her 1976 victory the first time the 200 metres title had been successfully defended. The tall German who had a baby between the Montreal and Moscow Olympics went on to win gold in the 4 x 100 metres relay and her total of four Olympic golds equals the record held by Fanny Blankers-Koen and Betty Cuthbert.

East Germany won the 400 metres too, through world record holder Marita Koch, but at 800 metres the Soviets were back with what must rank as the leading performance of the 1980 women's track events. Nadyezhda Olizarenko had broken Tatyana Kazankina's world record with a time of 1:54.85 six weeks before the Games. In the Lenin stadium she led all the way to finish in 1:53.43. The Soviet Union captured all three medals.

Kazankina did not contest the 800 metres, prefering to concentrate on the 1500 metres which she won in 3:56.6, the third fastest run ever. Twelve days later in Zurich she took 2.5 off her own world record with one of the greatest performances of all time, 3:52.47, which was faster than Paavo Nurmi's 1924 world record.

Jose Abascal (ESP)
1500 metres
Born: March 17, 1958, Madrid, Spain.
Height: 182cm/5ft 11½in.
Weight 67kg/147lb.
Career Highlights
World Championships: *1500* fifth 1983.
European Championships: *1500* bronze 1982.

In another era, Abascal would be a champion, but the tall Spaniard has had to make do with a position as an also ran on the European circuit, although in 1982, when Seb Coe and Steve Ovett were missing he got a European bronze in Athens.

Valeriy Abramov (URS)
5000 metres
Born: August 22, 1956, Ertsevo, Arkhangelsk, USSR.
Height: 173cm/5ft 8in.
Weight: 61kg/134.5lb.
Career Highlights
World Championships: *5000* eleventh 1983.
European Championships: *5000* sixth 1982.
World Cup: *5000* fourth 1981, silver 1979.
European Cup: *1500* fourth 1979; *5000* silver 1981.
World Student Games: *1500* ninth 1977.

Abramov has never been really able to make the transition from 1500 to 5000 metres or fulfill his undoubted promise.

Said Aouita (MOR)
1500 metres
Born: November 2, 1960, Rabat, Morocco.
Height: 175cm/5ft 8in.
Weight: 64kg/141lb.
Career Highlights
World Championships: *1500* bronze 1983.
World Student Games: *1500* gold 1981; *800* seventh 1981.
African Championships: *1500* silver 1982, ninth 1979; *800* bronze 1982.

The middle distance sensation of 1983, Aouita managed to recreate his brilliant early season form to take third place in the World Championships in Helsinki.

He first came to the fore in the 1981 World Student Games but burst into world class early in 1983 and sensibly was not tempted to over-race.

Going into Helsinki he led the world rankings with 3:32.54. But the big boys quickly worked out his tactics and he can expect a harder time in 1984.

Vasiliy Arkhipenko (URS)
400 metres hurdles
Born: January 28, 1957, Nikolayevka, Donetsk, USSR.
Height: 178cm/5ft 10in.
Weight: 68kg/149.6lb.
Career Highlights
Olympic Games: *400h* silver 1980.
European Championships: *400h* fourth 1982, bronze 1978.
World Cup: *400h* fourth 1981, bronze 1979.
European Cup: *400h* silver 1979.
World Student Games: *400h* silver 1979, fourth 1977.

One of Europe's most consistent performers recently, he holds the Soviet record with 48.34, even though he has given way as number one to Alexander Kharlov, the Helsinki bronze medallist.

He was lucky though to win silver in Moscow with the Americans absent.

▲
The Man from the Kazbah, Said Aouita of Morocco, third in the Helsinki 1500

◄
Soviet record holder over 400 metres hurdles, Vasiliy Arkhipenko

Kebede Balcha (ETH)
Marathon
Born: September 9, 1951, Rift
    Valley, Ethiopa.
Height: 166cm/5ft 5in.
Weight: 49kg/108lb.
Career Highlights
World Championships: *marathon*
    silver 1983.

After failing to finish in the 1980 Olympics, Balcha kept Ethiopia's distance running tradition alive with their only medal in Helsinki.

He won the Montreal marathon three times, and was fourth in the London marathon in 1983.

Dick Beardsley (USA)
Marathon
Born: March 21, 1956, Excelsior,
    Minnesota, USA.
Height: 175cm/5ft 9in.
Weight: 59kg/123.8lb.
Career Highlights
London *marathon* joint winner
    1981.

Beardsley was the joint winner of the first London marathon in 1981, clasping hands with Norway's Inge Simonsen to cross the line.

He went on to record 2:08.53 when chasing Alberto Salazar home in Boston, but a leg injury put paid to his World Championship hopes. If he can stay injury-free he will be a contender.

Uwe Becker (FRG)
800/1500 metres
Born: December 10, 1955,
    Rosche, West Germany.
Height: 188cm/6ft 2in.
Weight: 70kg/154lb.
Career Highlights
World Championships: *1500*
    eleventh 1983.
European Championships: *1500*
    sixth 1982.

A chemistry student who has always threatened to break through, Becker, like everybody else in the 1500 metres, has suffered because of the excellence of Coe and Ovett.

Olaf Beyer (GDR)
800/1500 metres
Born: August 4, 1957, Grimma,
    East Germany.
Height: 186cm/6ft 1in.
Weight: 69kg/152lb.
Career Highlights
European Championships: *800*
    seventh 1982, gold 1978;
    1500 ninth 1978.
World Cup: *800* fourth 1979,
    seventh 1977; *1500* bronze
    1979.
European Cup: *800* bronze 1981,
    fifth 1979, silver 1977; *1500*
    gold 1981.

Olaf Beyer's victory in the 1978 European Championships was one of the biggest shocks of the decade. Everyone except the East Germans expected Coe and Ovett to contest the gold, but after Coe made the pace, Ovett swept past, relaxed and could not counter when Beyer came through like a train. The East German's failure to even qualify for the final in Moscow raised suspicions as to how Beyer's Prague victory was achieved. When he won the European Cup 1500 metres in 1981, it seemed his future might lie at that distance.

Mike Boit (KEN)
800/1500 metres
Born: January 1, 1949, Nandi,
    Kenya.
Height: 180cm/5ft 11in.
Weight: 68kg/149lb.
Career Highlights
Olympic Games: *800* bronze
    1972; *1500* fourth 1972.
World Championships: *1500*
    twelfth 1983.
Commonwealth Games: *800* gold
    1978, silver 1974; *1500*
    bronze 1982, sixth 1974.
World Cup: *800* 1979 silver; *1500*
    fifth 1977.
Records
African *800* (1:43.57 1976)
African *mile* (3:49.45 1981).

◄
Ageless Mike Boit of Kenya will still be a man they need to watch in Los Angeles

Who knows what Boit would have achieved at Olympic level had Kenya not pulled out of Montreal and Moscow. As it is, Boit, now studying for a PhD at Oregon University in Eugene, had to make do with a bronze at that level.

But his durability is shown by the fact that he reached the final of the 1500 metres in Helsinki, although he faded to twelfth. In 1981 he twice chased Sebastian Coe home in his two world mile record races, and in 1982 was still able to lift a medal in the Commonwealth 1500 metres.

◄◄
Dick Beardsley of America, joint winner of the first London Marathon

Peter Bourke (AUS)
800 metres
Born: April 23, 1958, South
   Canfield, Victoria, Australia.
Height: 182cm/5ft 11½in.
Weight: 73kg/161lb.
Career Highlights
Commonwealth Games: *800* gold
   1982.

Bourke had more reason than
most to be grateful for the absence
of Sebastian Coe and Steve Ovett
in Brisbane at the Commonwealth
Games. He took the gold but the
clerk could not sustain his form
into 1983, when a virus infection
affected his running.

*Australia's Peter Bourke,
Commonwealth 800
metres champion* ▶

*Tom Byers, the rabbit who
hared away with a shock
1500 metre triumph over
Ovett and Co. in Oslo* ▶▶

Arto Brygarre (FIN)
110 metres hurdles
Born: May 26, 1958, Kouvola,
   Finland.
Height: 191cm/6ft 3in.
Weight: 88kg/194lb.
Career Highlights
Olympic Games: *110h* sixth 1980.
World Championships: *110h* silver
   1983.
European Championships: *110h*
   bronze 1982, 1978.
World Student Games: *110h* sixth
   1981.
European Cup: *110h* fourth 1977.

Brygarre became a national hero
when he became the first Finn to
win a medal in the 1983 World
Championships. He competed like
a man inspired, but the bronze
medals in two European Championships perhaps better indicate
his true worth.
   This economics student will be
hard put to split the Americans in
Los Angeles.

Andreas Busse (GDR)
800/1500 metres
Born: May 6, 1959, Dresden, East
   Germany.
Height: 185cm/6ft 0½in.
Weight: 70kg/154lb.
Career Highlights
Olympic Games: *800* fifth 1980;
   1500 fourth 1980.
World Championships: *1500*
   seventh 1983.
European Championships: *800*
   sixth 1978; *1500* eleventh
   1982.
European Cup: *1500* silver 1983.

A millwright, Busse, like most East
German middle distance runners,
could have done with a few outings
on the European circuit. His placings in major events show that with
a little more experience of fast
pace he could have done better.
   Now Busse has turned to 1500
metes to the exclusion of the 800
metres, he is likely to provide the
Eastern bloc's best bet for winning
a medal in the Los Angeles 1500
metres.

Tom Byers (USA)
1500 metres
Born: April 12, 1955, Eugene,
   USA.
Height: 186cm/6ft 1in.
Weight: 71kg/157lb.
Career Highlight
Bislett Games: *1500* first 1982.

Tom Byers was second in the
American Championships 1500
metres in 1974. Injury kept him
out of the headlines until 1981,
then he hit the limelight in Oslo as
the rabbit who won. He was in the
1500 metres at the Bislett
Stadium as pacemaker for a Steve
Ovett world record attempt. But
the field didn't go with him and
Byers hung on to win and at last
justify his talent.

▲
Bert Cameron of Jamaica, aiming for 400 metres gold and a sea level world record

Bert Cameron (JAM)
400 metres
Born: November 16, 1959, Spanish Town, Jamaica.
Height: 188cm/6ft 2in.
Weight: 79kg/174lb.
Career Highlights
World Championships: *400* gold 1983.
Commonwealth Games: *400* gold 1982.
World Cup: *400* bronze 1981.

No one can deny that the genial Jamaican is the greatest one-lap runner in the world. His big ambition, apart from the Los Angeles Olympic title, is to record the fastest time at sea level. In 1982 he won his third NCAAA title in 44.62, which was the fastest in the world that year. He has just finished at University of Texas in El Paso, USA.

Tonie Campbell (USA)
110 metres hurdles
Born: June 14, 1960, Los Angeles, USA.
Height: 188cm/6ft 2in.
Weight: 73kg/161lb.
Career Highlight
World Student Games: fourth 1981.

Nobody has won the Olympic Marathon three times in a row. East Germany's Waldemar Cierpinski is two thirds of the way there ► ►

Tonie Campbell's failure to take one of the top three places in the 1983 American trials cost him a place in Helsinki.

He is reckoned by statisticians to be the 'best' athlete who did not go to the World Championships. Instead, he hit the European circuit, gunning for fellow-American Sam Turner, whom he beat convincingly in the AAA championships.

Ernesto Canto (MEX)
20 kilometre walk
Born: October 18, 1959, Mexico City, Mexico.
Height: 170cm/5ft 7in.
Weight: 58kg/128lb.
Career Highlights
World Championships: *20k* gold 1983.
Lugano Cup: *20k* gold 1981, sixth 1979.

Canto was a PE teacher who was given a 'sabbatical' of three years which enables him to train for seven to eight hours a day.

Waldemar Cierpinski (GDR)
Marathon
Born: August 3, 1950, Nuegattersleben, East Germany.
Height: 170cm/5ft 7in.
Weight: 59kg/130lb.

Career Highlights
Olympic Games: *marathon* gold 1980, 1976.
World Championships: *marathon* bronze 1983.
European Championships: *marathon* sixth 1982, fourth 1978; *10000* nineteenth 1978.
European Cup: *marathon* silver 1981; *3000s/chase* sixth 1973.
Records
Olympic *marathon* (2:09.55 1976).

Cierpinski was an international steeplechaser with a respectable 8:32.4 before he switched to marathon running. A sports lecturer, he made his marathon debut of 2:20.29 in 1974, and even though he took seventh in the 1975 Kosice marathon there was no suggestion that he might devastate the field in Montreal and take two minutes off Abebe Bikila's Olympic record.

In between Olympics he managed a fastest of 2:12.20 when finishing fourth in the Prague Europeans, but he emulated Bikila's feat of retaining the Olympic title with 2:11.03, the second fastest time of his life. A bronze in Helsinki showed that he cannot be ruled out of contention for a third Olympic title in Los Angeles.

Darren Clark (AUS)

400 metres
Born: September 6, 1965, Sydney,
    Australia.
Height: 178cm/5ft 10in.
Weight: 76kg/167.5lb.
Career Highlight
World Championships: *400*
    semi-final 1983.

This muscular young Australian won the AAA Championships in 45.05 at 17, which was a world best for his age. But his inexperience showed in Helsinki and he failed to make the final. Repeating his AAA's time in Helsinki would have brought him a share of the gold.

He was originally more interested in Rugby League but gave that up for fear of injury when he decided to concentrate on the track. He was coached by Alan Hawes, to a clean sweep of the 1983 Australian Junior titles, winning the 100, 200 and 400 metres.

Sebastian Coe (GBR)

800/1500 metres
Born: September 29, 1956,
    London, England.
Height: 177cm/5ft 9½in.
Weight: 56kg/123lb.
Career Highlights
Olympic Games: *800* silver 1980;
    1500 gold 1980.
European Championships: *800*
    silver 1982, bronze 1978.
World Cup: *800* gold 1981.
European Cup: *800* gold 1979,
    1981, fourth 1977.
Records
World *800* 1981 (1:41.73), 1979
    (1:42.4); *1500* 1979
    (3:32.03); *mile* 1981
    (3:48.53) (3:47.33); *1000*
    1981 (2:12.18), 1980
    (2:13.4).
World best indoors: *800* 1983
    (1:44.91), *1000* 1983
    (2:18.58).

Sebastian Coe spent last winter wondering whether he would be able to compete in the Los Angeles Olympics, after a lymph gland infection wiped out his World Championship chances. The same glandular problem cost Coe the gold in the Athens European Championships, and if he cannot get fit for Los Angeles he will remain as the greatest 800 metres runner in the world against the clock, but one who could not win a major title. His 1981 world record of 1:41.73 is way in front of his contemporaries. No-one else has bettered 1:43, let alone 1:42. Coe's record up to

1979 did not suggest he would become a phenomenon. He won bronze in the Prague European Championships, and his front running style seemed tailor-made for kickers like Ovett. But in 44 days in 1979 he rewrote the record books, taking the 800, 1500 metres and mile, and becoming the first man to hold all three.

In 1980 Coe broke the 1000 metres record going into Moscow. So highly regarded was he that he flew in to hold a packed press conference in the Olympic press centre, something afforded to no other athlete. But in the 800 metres he ran in a way described by the influential French sports newspaper *L'Equipe* as 'naive'. He sprinted in to win the silver, but Ovett was far and away in front. Coe got his revenge in the 1500 metres, when helped by the surge of Jurgen Straub from half way, he was able to run fast and free to gold. So relieved was he that he bent on his knees to kiss the Lenin Stadium track.

Coe continued in 1981 in the same rich form, lowering his 800

metres record, as well as his 1000 metres, and twice breaking the mile best. The only one that evaded him was the 1500 metres. But a stress fracture at the start of 1982, followed by his glandular problem led to defeat by Germany's Hans Peter Ferner in Athens, and Coe had to opt out of the Commonwealth Games.

He seemed to have cracked the problem in 1983 when he created new indoor bests over 800 and 1000 metres, but defeats at 1500 metres and a mile, plus the final crushing blow of finishing fourth in the 800 metres at Gateshead shortly before the team was due to leave for Helsinki, led him to withdraw from the World Championships and put his future career in doubt.

Sebastian Coe, fighting a desperate battle against time to challenge for his rightful recognition as the world's best 800 metre runner
◄

▲
Muscular Darren Clark is the Australian find of the Eighties

Eamonn Coghlan (IRL)

5000 metres
Born: November 21, 1952, Dublin,
    Republic of Ireland.
Height: 177cm/5ft 9¾in.
Weight: 63kg/159lb.
Career Highlights
Olympic Games: *5000* fourth
    1980; *1500* fourth 1976.
World Championships: *5000* gold
    1983.
European Championships: *1500*
    silver 1978.
World Cup: *500* 1981 gold.

Eamonn Coghlan's delight at winning gold in Helsinki was understandable. After many years of trying, the personable Irishman, once employed by his country's tourist board, had at last finished first in a major championship. In the States the Dubliner is known as king of the boards and is the only man to have run under 3:50 for the mile indoors. A broken right leg in January stopped him running indoors last winter but he expected to be back in time for Los Angeles. Since leaving the mile and 1500 metres just before the Moscow Olympics, he has run thirteen times at 5000 metres and lost only once, in the Moscow final.

Garry Cook (GBR)

800 metres
Born: January 10, 1958, Walsall,
    England.
Height: 185cm/6ft 1in.
Weight: 72kg/158.5lb.
Career Highlights
European Championships: *800*
    fourth 1982.
Commonwealth Games: *800* fifth
    1978.
World Student Games: silver 1979.

Although he finished fourth in the 1982 European Championships — when more self assertiveness might have got him a medal — Cook fell in the Commonwealth semi-final.

One of the friendliest men in athletics, he is married to sprinter Kathy Cook, who will be in the British Women's team competing in Los Angeles.

Alberto Cova (ITA)

5000/10000 metres
Born: December 1, 1958, Inverigo,
    Como, Italy.
Height: 176cm/5ft 9in.
Weight: 58kg/128lb.
Career Highlights
World Championships: *10,000*
    gold 1983.
European Championships: *10,000*
    gold 1982.
European Cup: *10000* silver 1983;
    5000 bronze 1983, sixth 1981.

The doleful-looking Italian never shares the pace, never shapes the destiny of the race, but Cova is a master at snatching victory in the last few strides.

He will be a favourite for the 10,000 metres in Los Angeles.

*Garry Cook, another of
Britain's fine half milers*
◄ ◄

*Alberto Cova, the little
Italian with an eye for big
titles, wins the World
Championship 10000
metres*
◄

Steve Cram (GBR)
1500 metres
Born: October 14, 1960, Jarrow, England.
Height: 186cm/6ft 1in.
Weight: 69kg/152lb.
Career Highlights
Olympic Games: *1500* eighth 1980.
World Championships: *1500* gold 1983.
European Championships: *1500* gold 1982.
Commonwealth Games: *1500* gold 1982.
European Cup: *1500* gold 1983, bronze 1981.

From the moment Cram broke the world age group record for a mile and won a late place in England's team for the Edmonton Commonwealth Games, he was destined for the top. But he had to live in the shadow of Coe and Ovett and,

whilst in one way that was a perfect apprenticeship, in another it must have been frustrating, particularly in 1982. He won the European and Commonwealth titles in Athens and Brisbane only because Coe and Ovett were missing, said the cynics.

So last year Cram still had to prove himself which he did when winning the World Championships in entirely convincing style, despite Ovett's tactical aberration. Now Cram is the man to beat, and the Geordie, who was married to fiancée Karen Walters in the winter, is the favourite for the Los Angeles 1500 metres.

There are those who feel that Cram's future lies at 5000 metres, but he is rapidly proving the rightful heir to Coe and Ovett. Although he has never run the 800 metres in a major championship or international race, he has finished top of the world rankings for the distance in both 1982 and 1983.

Joaquim Cruz (BRA)
800 metres
Born: March 12, 1963, Rio de Janeiro, Brazil.
Height: 186cm/6ft 1½in.
Weight: 73kg/161lb.
Career Highlights
World Championships: *800* bronze 1983.
Records
South American: *800* 1981 (1:44.3).

The world junior record holder in 1981 burst into world class when he beat Juantorena in the South American trials to go to the Rome World Cup. He ran naively in Rome, but clearly had talent.

Cruz spent 1982 trying to learn English so that he could go to the University of Oregon in Eugene, where he is now enrolled, and his barnstorming front running made him a hit in 1983.

Maurizio Damilano (ITA)
20 kilometre walk
Born: April 6, 1957, Scarnafigi, Italy.
Height: 182cm/5ft 11½in.
Weight: 71kg/156.5lb.
Career Highlights
Olympic Games: *20k* gold 1980.
World Championships: *20k* seventh 1983.
European Championships: *20k* sixth 1978.
World Student Games: *20k* silver 1983, gold 1981.
Lugano Cup: *20k* sixth 1981, fourth 1977.
Records
Olympic *20k;* 1980 (1:23.36).

Steve Cram, once the bit-player now the centre stage star of British middle distance running after triple triumph in European, Commonwealth and World 1500 metres championships ◄ ◄

The king of the road, Australia's Robert de Castella, firm favourite for the Marathon title after his destruction of Salazar ►

▲
Joaquim Cruz burst into prominence by beating Juantorena

Damilano profited from an error by the 1976 Olympic Champion, Daniel Bautista. The Mexican 'lifted' while in sight of the Lenin Stadium, which left the Soviet Anatoliy Solomin in the lead. But he was pulled out too, and Damilano, who had settled for bronze, came into the stadium to win by over a minute. His twin brother Giorgio, coached like Maurizio by brother Sandro, was eleventh in Moscow.

Robert de Castella (AUS)
Marathon
Born: May 27, 1957, Melbourne, Australia.
Height: 180cm/5ft 11in.
Weight: 65kg/143lb.
Career Highlights
Olympic Games: *marathon* tenth 1980.
World Championships: *marathon* gold 1983.
Commonwealth Games: *marathon* gold 1982.

The best bet for the marathon gold in Los Angeles, de Castella has proved himself to be the hardest competitor in the toughest event.

A biophysicist from Canberra, de Castella has the second fastest time in history, 2h 08:18. Even more important, he wins the big races. He showed remarkable judgement to take the Commonwealth title after Juma Ikangaa had set a suicidal early pace, and was just as cool in winning the first world title.

Rod Dixon and John Walker were the inseparable Flying Kiwis in the Seventies with one crucial difference: Walker got his Olympic gold in Montreal and Dixon is still looking ▶

But the race that really confirmed his position as the world's top man was in Rotterdam before the World Championships. It was a head-to-head between the Australian and Alberto Salazar, the fastest man of all time and winner of three successive New York races. De Castella burned off the Cuban-born American and had more trouble from Carlos Lopes of Portugal.

Coached by Pat Clohessy and married to Gaylene, a former Australian cross-country champion, de Castella caused one hiccup in the smooth organisation of the World Championships. He had to send back his medal because they'd spelt his name wrongly!

Rod Dixon (NZL)
5000/10,000 metres/marathon
Born: July 7, 1950, Auckland, New Zealand.
Height: 187cm/6ft 1½in.
Weight: 71kg/156.5lb.
Career Highlights
Olympic Games: *1500* bronze 1972; *5000* bronze 1976.
New York marathon: first 1983.

Dixon has been concentrating on the lucrative American road-racing circuit since 1977. But after running a 2:11 marathon in 1982 in

Christchurch, he has realized he can yet chase Olympic glory. He followed it with a 2h 09 victory in New York last year and would be one of the favourites for Los Angeles.

However, he knows the burden of being a favourite. He was expected to take the 5000 metres in Montreal, but despite being ideally placed on the shoulder of Lasse Viren he could make no impact.

Rob Druppers (HOL)
800 metres
Born: April 29, 1962, Utrecht, Netherlands.
Height: 187cm/6ft 1½in.
Weight: 80kg/176lb.
Career Highlights
World Championships: *800* silver 1983.
European Championships: *800* fifth 1982.

The Dutch public relations man burst into world class early in 1982, when he ran 1:44.70. He was fifth in the Athens European Championships, which did not indicate his true worth. His silver in Helsinki did, however, as he followed the pace set by Peter Elliott.

Khashief El Hassan (SUD)
400 metres
Born: March 26, 1956, Sudan.
Height: 175cm/5ft 8½ in.
Weight: 68kg/150lb.
Career Highlights
World Cup: *400* seventh 1981, gold 1979.
Record
African *400* 1982 (44.76)

El Hassan was at Oregon State University and beat Bert Cameron to the 1982 national collegiate title. His inconsistency has, however, stopped him being the world figure he should be.

Dutchman Rob Druppers matured rapidly in 1983 to claim a World Championship silver medal ▶ ▶

Peter Elliott (GBR)
800 metres
Born: October 9, 1962,
Rawmarsh, South Yorkshire,
England.
Height: 180cm/5ft 11in.
Weight: 66kg/147lb.
Career Highlights
World Championships: *800* fourth
1983.
European Cup: *800* bronze 1983.

Widely regarded as the heir-apparent to Sebastian Coe, the joiner from South Yorkshire has packed a lot into a short career. In 1982 he won the AAA 800 metres title but failed to get selected for the Commonwealth Games. He went on holiday, stopped training and although he shared in a British quartet's 4 x 800 metres record, had to decline a chance of running in the 1982 European Championships. Ironically he could have run in the Commonwealth Games, because both Coe and Ovett dropped out.

He deservedly won a place in the Helsinki team and finished a gutsy fourth.

Frank Emmelmann the East German sprinter ▼

Frank Emmelmann (GDR)
Sprints
Born: September 15, 1961,
Schneidlingen, East Germany.
Height: 186cm/6ft 1in.
Weight: 76kg/167.5lb.
Career Highlights:
World Championships: *200* fifth
1983.
European Championships: *100*
gold 1982; *200* bronze 1982.
World Cup: *100* bronze 1981; *200*
bronze 1981.
European Cup: *100* gold 1983,
silver 1981; *200* gold 1981.

The only European other than Mennea to threaten Allan Wells in the last few years, Emmelmann can only get better. He disappointed in the World Championship 100 metres but took fifth in the 200 metres, his best event.

Graeme Fell (GBR)
3000 steeplechase
Born: March 19, 1959, Ilford,
England.
Height: 185cm/6ft 0½in.
Weight: 73kg/161 lb.
Career Highlights
World Championships: *3000*
s/chase sixth 1983.
European Championships: *3000*
s/chase tenth 1982.
Commonwealth Games: *3000*
s/chase silver 1982.
European Cup: *3000 s/chase*
silver 1983.

Fell finished as the third Briton in the World Championships, but a few days later created a British record in Berlin. He is now studying at San Diego University.

Hans-Peter Ferner (FRG)
800 metres
Born: June 6, 1956, Neuburg,
Donau, West Germany.
Height: 179cm/5ft 10in.
Weight: 69kg/152lb.
Career Highlights
European Championships: *800*
gold 1982.
World Student Games: *800* bronze
1979.

Hans-Peter Ferner had never even won the German Championships when he took gold in Athens and shocked the athletics world by beating Sebastian Coe. Ferner's own reaction was *'it's bizarre'*. He dropped to seventh in the World Championships, which is a truer reflection of his form.

Greg Foster (USA)
110 metres hurdles
Born: August 4, 1958, Chicago,
USA.
Height: 192cm/6ft 3½in.
Weight: 83kg/184lb.
Career Highlights
World Championships: *110h* gold
1983.
World Cup: *110h* gold 1981.

The second fastest 110 metres hurdler of all time, Foster still lives in the shadow of world record holder Renaldo Nehemiah, who became an American footballer.

But Foster won the World Championships, although he faltered over the last two flights, and will be favourite for Los Angeles.

Michael Franks (USA)
400 metres
Born: September 23, 1963, St
Louis, USA.
Height: 180cm/5ft 11in.
Weight: 68kg/150lb.
Career Highlights
World Championships: *400* silver
1983.

Michael Franks went to Helsinki as the slowest of the four Americans, but thrust his way into world class, running a personal best 45.24 in the semis and a 45.22 in the final.

He was left out of the 4 x 400 metres team in favour of Willie Smith, who fell on the third leg.

Julian Goater (GBR)
5000/10,000 metres
Born: January 12, 1953, England.
Height: 183cm/6ft 0in.
Weight: 66kg/145.5lb.
Career Highlights
World Championships: *5000*
fourteenth 1983.
European Championships: *10,000*
fifth 1982.
Commonwealth Games: *10,000*
bronze 1982.
European Cup: *10,000* silver
1981.
World Student Games: *5000*
bronze 1975, fourth 1973.

Goater, an officer in the RAF, had the reputation as a plodder without a finishing kick, always at the mercy of faster finishing men, until 1981. True he couldn't manufacture a faster sprint, but in that year he finished second in the European Cup 10,000 metres and at the end of the season became the, then, second fastest British 5000 metres runner of all time with 13:15.59.

In 1982 he lowered his 10,000 metres to 27:34.58, which ranked him seventh in the world for the year, and had very respectable performances in the European Championships and Commonwealth Games. He was toying with moving up to the marathon, leaving the RAF and attacking the lucrative American road-racing circuit. But an illness that winter left him short of preparation for 1983 and he had to settle for the 5000 metres in Helsinki. He was the only Briton to make the final.

◄
Hans-Peter Ferner provided the shock of 1982 by beating an ailing Sebastian Coe for the European 800 metres title

Mike Gratton (GBR)

Marathon
Born: November 28, 1954, Canterbury, England.
Height: 179cm/5ft 10½in.
Weight: 65kg/143lb.
Career Highlights
London marathon: first 1983.
Commonwealth Games: *marathon* bronze 1982.

The London marathon was the making of Mike Gratton's career as an athlete. He first caught the public eye in the 1982 race when he was third behind Hugh Jones. He consolidated his position with a solid performance in Brisbane, where aware of his current level he sensibly refused to chase Juma Ikangaa and Robert de Castella.

In 1983 he won the London race. His bearded face adorned the front covers of running magazines for months afterwards and he gave up his job as a school teacher in Canterbury.

He had to drop out of the World Championships marathon because of back trouble. This needed a manipulative operation at the beginning of the year so plans to run a fast time in Japan were scotched and Gratton had to aim to be in top condition in time for the London race.

Agberto Guimares (BRA)

800 metres
Born: August 18, 1957, Brazil.
Height: 175cm/5ft 9in.
Weight: 57kg/125.5lb.
Career Highlights
Olympic Games: *800* fourth 1980.
World Championships: *800* sixth 1983.
World Cup: *800* fifth 1979.
World Student Games: *800* fourth 1977.

Part of Brazil's growing middle distance tradition, Guimares is no longer his country's number one, having been overtaken by Cruz.

Christian Haas (FRG)
100 metres
Born: August 22, 1958,
   Nurnburg, West Germany.
Height: 180cm/5ft 11in.
Weight: 73kg/170lb.
Career Highlights
World Championships: *100* sixth
   1983.
European Cup: *100* fifth 1983,
   sixth 1981.

Haas has never quite delivered the promise he showed, although he did well to finish sixth in the World Championships 100 metres final.
   He holds the European indoor record for 60 metres in 6.55 sec.

Mike Hillardt (AUS)
800/1500 metres
Born: January 22, 1961,
   Indooroopilly, Queensland,
   Australia.
Height: 180cm/5ft 11in.
Weight: 70kg/154lb.
Career Highlights
World Championships: *800*
   semi-final 1983.
Commonwealth Games: *1500* fifth
   1982.
World Cup: *800* fourth 1981.

When the Queensland barman first appeared on the European scene in 1981 at the World Cup in Rome, great things were predicted. Hillardt finished a respectable fourth,

but could not march on from there. He predicted a dust up with Coe and Ovett in Brisbane, but Hillardt could not cope with Cram or the veterans Walker and Boit and slid back to fifth.

Mark Holtom (GBR)
110 metres hurdles
Born: February 6, 1958,
   Stoke-on-Trent, England.
Height: 188cm/6ft 2in.
Weight: 84kg/185lb.
Career Highlights
Commonwealth Games: *110h*
   silver 1982.
European Cup: *110h* eighth 1983,
   gold 1981, fourth 1979.
Record
UK *110h* 1982 (13.43).

Mark Holtom's luck never seems to be in when it comes to the major events. He was coming into form when he made a mess of the Helsinki World Championships semi-finals. Holtom was favourite for the Commonwealth title but was pipped by Canadian Mark McCoy. Still, the run brought him a new British record.

Juma Ikangaa (TAN)
Marathon
Born: July 19, 1957, Tanzania.
Height: 161cm/5ft 3in.
Weight: 53kg/117lb.
Career Highlights
Commonwealth Games: *marathon*
   silver 1982.
African Championships: *marathon*
   gold 1982.

To many people, except those close to Robert de Castella, Juma Ikangaa seemed to have the Commonwealth Games marathon in his pocket. But he was remorselessly overhauled by the Australian. Nevertheless, his time in second place improved the African record to 2h 09:30. He proved this was no fluke in the 1983 Fukuoka Marathon, when he lowered his time to 2h 08:55.

Patriz Ilg (FRG)
3000 Steeplechase
Born: December 5, 1957,
   Aalen-Obera Hungen, West
   Germany.
Height: 172cm/5ft 7½in.
Weight: 63kg/139lb.

West Germany's Christian Haas, still to live up to his early promise ◄◄

Mark Holtom showed he could handle all but the very best when he won the European Cup gold in 1981 in Zagreb ▼

Hugh Jones en route to winning the London Marathon in 1982 and establishing himself as one of the world's elite ▶ ▶

West Germany's Patriz Ilg savours the applause after winning the World steeplechase title ▼

Career Highlights
World Championships: *3000 s/chase* gold 1983.
European Championships: *3000 s/chase* gold 1982; silver 1978.
European Cup: *3000 s/chase* bronze 1981.

Patriz Ilg filled the gap left by the death of 1980 Olympic champion Bronislaw Malinowski, but will need to keep going for a few years yet to match the Pole.

Ben Johnson (CAN)
Sprints
Born: December 30, 1961, Jamaica.
Height: 180cm/5ft 11in.
Weight: 64kg/141lb.
Career Highlights
Commonwealth Games: *100* silver 1982.

Johnson's 1982 form, when he took the Brisbane silver was not matched in 1983 and he was proved an inconsistent runner.

Hugh Jones (GBR)
Marathon
Born: November 1, 1955, London, England.
Height: 180cm/5ft 10¾in.

Weight: 64kg/141lb.
Career Highlights
World Championships: *marathon* eighth 1983.
European Cup: *marathon* fifth 1980.
London marathon: first 1982.

Injuries have dogged Jones' attempt to establish himself as one of the very best in the world, but if he is fully fit he will be one of the main challengers in Los Angeles.

Tall, thin, and with a shock of red hair, Jones has an unorthodox background for one of the world's elite. Before and after he joined Liverpool University he travelled the world, often hitch-hiking. He went to the USA, South America, Iran, Egypt, Libya and India.

Naturally he could not train properly while travelling but once the wanderlust had gone he developed into a fine marathon runner, winning the AAA title in Rugby in 1981, finishing fifth in the European Cup and then third in New York. In 1982 he was second in Tokyo, and then won the London in 2:09.24, his fastest to date. He was pre-selected for the European Championships in Athens, on the classic course, but had to pull out. Operations were needed on both Achilles tendons, but even so Jones managed a comeback by mid-1983, winning a place in the British World Championship team and finishing eighth in 2:11.15 — a superb performance considering his injuries.

Alberto Juantorena (CUB)
400/800 metres
Born: November 11, 1950,
   Santiago, Cuba.
Height: 190cm/6ft 3in.
Weight: 84kg/185lb.
Career Highlights
Olympic Games: *400* fourth 1980,
   gold 1976, *800* gold 1976.
World Cup: *400* gold 1977; *800*
   gold 1977.
World Student Games: *400* gold
   1973; *800* gold 1977.
Records
World *800* 1976 (1:43.50),
   1977 (1:43.44)
Central American *400* 1976
   (44.26).

When Juantorena was carried
screaming in frustration and agony
from the trackside at Helsinki, a
victim of selfmade misfortune, it
seemed the great Cuban's career
was over. Juantorena had tripped
over the kerb when finishing his
heat and broken a bone in his foot
and torn the ligaments. But his
immediate response was to promise that he would be back for the
Los Angeles Olympics and maybe
at 1500 metres.

That seems unlikely, but what is
certain is that the man they call El
Caballo will go down as the star of
the 1976 Olympics. He became
the first man to win the 400/800
metres double, previously thought

impossible because of the incom-
patible nature of the events. But
Juantorena set a new world record
in the 800 metres, and his time of
44.26 in the one-lap race with
none of the advantages of running
at altitude must rank with Lee
Evans' 43.8 in Mexico.

Juantorena won both races
again in the first World Cup in Dusseldorf, although the 400 metres
had to be re-run because he didn't
hear the starter's pistol. A severe
Achilles tendon injury stopped him
defending both Olympic titles in
Moscow, but he attempted the
400 metres and although not fully
fit nearly got a medal.

Mohammed Kedir (ETH)
5000/10,000 metres
Born: September 6, 1953,
   Ethiopia.
Height: 166cm/5ft 5in.
Weight: 45kg/99lb.
Career Highlights
Olympic Games: *10,000* bronze
   1980; *5000* twelfth 1980.
World Championships: *10,000*
   ninth 1983.
World Cup: *10,000 silver 1981.*

The little stick man from Ethiopia
was expected to assume the mantle of Miruts Yifter, but has never
quite made it. He dutifully set up
Yifter's victories in the Moscow

5000 and 10,000 metres, but was
a disappointment in last year's
World Cross Country Championships at Gateshead, when he lost a
shoe, and the World championships. In Helsinki, despite his size,
he was accused of rough tactics by
Britain's Nick Rose.

Alexander Kharlov (URS)
400 metres hurdles
Born: March 18, 1958, USSR.
Height: 192cm/6ft 3½in.
Weight: 80kg/176lb.
Career Highlights
World Championships: *400h*
   bronze 1983.
European Championships: *400h*
   sixth 1982.
European Cup: *400h* silver 1983.
World Student Games: *400h* gold
   1983.

Kharlov's career took a remarkable
upturn last year. Until then, he was
always likely to make the final but
never figured among the medals.
Then he took gold in the World
Student Games in Edmonton, followed it up with a bronze behind
Ed Moses and Harald Schmid in
Helsinki, before trailing Schmid in
the European Cup at Crystal
Palace.

*Alexander Kharlov, gold in
the World Student Games
highlighted dramatic
improvement over 400
metres hurdles* ▼

Emmitt King (USA)
Sprints
Born: March 24, 1959,
   Tuscaloosa, USA.
Height: 178cm/5ft 10in.
Weight: 78kg/173lb.
Career Highlights
World Championships: *100* bronze
   1983.
Records
World 1983 *4 x 100* (37.86).

◄ ◄
*He stands only 5ft 5in but
Ethiopia's Mohammed
Kedir knows how to look
after himself on the track.
Ask Britain's Nick Rose*

King was the third of the great American sprint trio that had absolute dominance in the World Championship 100 metres. Although overshadowed by Carl Lewis and Calvin Smith he was nevertheless a vital part of the quartet that broke the world 4 x 100 metres relay record in Helsinki.

Nikolay Kirov (URS)
800/1500 metres
Born: November 22, 1957,
    Streshin, USSR.
Height: 176cm/5ft 9in.
Weight: 63kg/139lb.
Career Highlights
Olympic Games: *800* bronze 1980.
European Championships: *1500* sixth 1981; *800* eighth 1981.
European Cup: *1500* seventh 1983, silver 1981; *800* fourth 1981.

The Soviet has never been really able to put his scorching finish to good effect, despite his Olympic bronze. Kirov has been unable to keep up with the pace in big races. Typical was the World Championship when, despite a remarkable last 300 metres, he failed to qualify for the final.

Andreas Knebel (GDR)
400 metres
Born: June 21, 1960,
    Sangerhausen, East Germany.
Height: 178cm/5ft 10in.
Weight: 70kg/154lb.
Career Highlights
European Championships: *400;* silver 1982.
World Cup: *400* sixth 1981.
European Cup: *400* silver 1981.

Once one of the East German hopes to match the up-and-coming West German 400 metres runners, he has been overshadowed by Thomas Schonlebe. He missed the World Championships through injury.

Peter Koech (KEN)
5000/10,000 metres
Born: June 1, 1958, Kilibwoni, Kenya.
Height: 178cm/5ft 10in.
Weight: 68kg/150lb.
Career Highlights
Commonwealth Games: *5000* bronze 1982; *10,000* fifteenth 1982.

A student at Washington State, Koech ran 13:09.50 to become the then second fastest man of all time at 5000 metres. He took the Commonwealth bronze at 5000 metres.

Julius Korir (KEN)
3000 steeplechase
Born: April 21, 1960, Nandi, Kenya.

Height: 172cm/5ft 7½in.
Weight: 64kg/141lb.
Career Highlights
World Championships: s/chase seventh 1983.
Commonwealth Games: s/chase gold 1982.

Korir went to Brisbane as only the sixth fastest man in the Commonwealth Games field and won the title by almost 20 metres from England's Graham Fell. He improved his personal best to 8:20.11 in Helsinki.

Emmitt King, the other American sprinter last season behind Smith and Lewis
◄ ◄

Hans-Jorg Kunze (GDR)
5000/10000 metres
Born: December 28, 1959,
    Rostock, East Germany.
Height: 178cm/5ft 10in.
Weight: 62kg/136.5lb.
Career Highlights
World Championships: *10,000* bronze 1983.
European Championships: *5000* ninth 1982.
World Cup: *5000* silver 1981.
European Cup: *5000* fourth 1983, bronze 1981, gold 1979.
Record
European *5000* 1981 (13:10.40).

The blond medical student has never confirmed his promise at 5000 metres despite his, then, European record. His big moment should have been Athens, but he was outshone by team mate Werner Schildhauer.
Nevertheless, his bronze in the Helsinki 10,000 metres showed that maybe the longer distance is his best, and he will be among the favourites in Los Angeles.

Commonwealth bronze medallist Peter Koech of Kenya
◄

Osvaldo Lara (CUB)

Sprints
Born: July 13, 1955, Havana, Cuba.
Height: 170cm/5ft 7in.
Weight: 72kg/158.5lb.
Career Highlights
Olympic Games: *100* fifth 1980; *200* eighth 1980.
World Student Games: *100* bronze 1977.

Lara has been unable to take over from the great Silvio Leonard but remains one of the world's top sprinters. He has been on the track scene since 1977.

Mel Lattany (USA)

100/200 metres
Born: August 10, 1959, Brunswick, Georgia, USA.
Height: 176cm/5ft 9in.
Weight: 73kg/160lb.
Career Highlights
World Cup: *100* fifth 1981; *200* gold 1981.
Record
World *300* 1983 (32.15).

He is one of the world's unluckiest sprinters. Prone to injury, Lattany suffered like the rest of the US athletes from the 1980 boycott and although he won the 200 metres in the Rome World Cup a year later, he missed out on the World Championships because a spike came off his shoe in the semi-finals of the US trials.

Instead he came to Europe and helped by a howling gale in Edinburgh became the first man to run under 10 seconds for the 100 metres in Britain.

Carl Lewis (USA)

100/200 metres, long jump
Born: July 1, 1961, Birmingham, Alabama, USA.
Height: 188cm/6ft 2in.
Weight: 82kg/180lb.
Career Highlights
World Championships: *100 long jump* gold 1983; *4 x 100 relay* gold 1983.
World Cup: *long jump* gold 1981.
Records
World *4 x 100 relay* 1983 (37.86).
National *200* 1983 (19.75).

Although the phenomenally talented Lewis was ranked Track and Field News Athlete of the Year in 1982 (and deservedly so) and top ranked in the 100 and long jump in 1981 and 1982, all he had to show for it in world terms was a

first place in the long jump in the Rome World Cup in 1981.

Otherwise only Americans had truly seen just how great this man is: the best sprinter long jumper since the immortal Jesse Owens. In 1981 he ran 10.00 for the 100, the fastest ever without the assistance of altitude. In that same year he long jumped 8.62, then the longest jump without the assistance of altitude.

In 1982 he again ran 10.00 dead, but this time improved his long jump to a remarkable 8.76 and he was creeping up on Bob Beamon and his altitude assisted 8.90.

But last year was even better. He arrived at the World Championships in Helsinki as the man everyone wanted to see and quickly gave a press conference in the village theatre, where he impressed the world's newsmen.

He was even better on the track, his high fluid action taking him to success in the 100 metres, the long jump and the 4 x 100. He had to skip away from the long jump final to anchor the USA to their world record victory in the relay.

In the season he ran 9.97 at low altitude, a time which outranks Calvin Smith's 9.93 world record, which was achieved in thin air, and long jumped 8.79 at the American championships getting ever nearer Beamon.

He also created an American 200 record of 19.75 that day and achieved one aim. He hoped to wipe out all the altitude assisted marks and that was his first, the record wiping out Tommie Smith's 19.83 from the 1968 Mexico Olympics.

Now Lewis, whose sister Carol is a talented long jumper herself, plans to beat Smith's 100 metre record and Beamon's long jump best ... what better place to do that than the Los Angeles Olympics.

Carl Lewis, finest sprinter/long jumper since the immortal Jesse Owens and in line for a string of golds ◀

Karel Lismont (BEL)
Marathon
Born: March 8, 1949, Belgium.
Height: 168cm/5ft 6in.
Weight: 55kg/121lb.
Career Highlights
Olympic Games: *marathon* ninth 1980, bronze 1976, silver 1972; *10,000* eleventh 1976.
World Championships: *marathon* ninth 1983.
European Championships: *marathon* bronze 1982, 1976, gold 1971; *10,000* eighteenth 1978, eleventh 1974, sixteenth 1971.

Few men can match Lismont's consistency over the years. He will still be a threat in Los Angeles.

Carlos Lopes (POR)
10,000 marathon
Born: February 18, 1947, Lisbon, Portugal.
Height: 166cm/5ft 5½in.
Weight: 54kg/119lb.
Career Highlights
Olympic Games: *10,000* silver 1976.
World Championships: *10,000* sixth 1983.
European Championships: *10,000* fourth 1982.

At an age when most athletes are thinking of retiring or gently earning some money on the American road race circuit, Carlos Lopes, 36 years old, gave his career an astonishing Indian summer.

He had every reason to take it easy. A patchy career had blossomed gloriously when he chased home Lasse Viren to win silver in Montreal and although injuries stopped him from building on this, he was always one of the world's leading men.

In 1982 at the Athens Europeans he finished fourth, but there was no hint of what was to come in 1983, or that after such a marvellous start it would end so badly.

It began with second place in the World Cross Country Championships in Gateshead, it took an unexpected turn with another second place in the Rotterdam marathon in 2:08.39, the fifth fastest time ever. And then it reached familiar territory with a time of 27:23.34 for the 10,000 in Oslo.

Lopes could not make up his mind which event he wanted to race at the World Championships. First it was the marathon and not the 10,000, eventually it was

Boguslaw Maminski carries the great tradition of Polish steeplechasing. Can he emulate the ill-fated Bronislaw Malinowski?
▼

both. But after a disappointing sixth in the 10,000, he did not even start in the marathon.

James Maina (KEN)
800 metres
Born: April 4, 1954, Nandi, Kenya.
Height: 170cm/5ft 7in.
Weight: 64kg/141lb.
Career Highlights
Commonwealth Games: *800* silver 1982.
World Cup: *800* gold 1979.

An erratic runner, Maina was the favourite for the 1978 Commonwealth title only to break from his lane too early and be disqualified.

Boguslaw Maminski (POL)
3000 steeplechase
Born: December 18, 1955, Poland.
Height: 177cm/5ft 9½in.
Weight: 69kg/152lb.
Career Highlights
Olympic Games: *3000 s/chase* seventh 1980.

World Championships: *3000 s/chase* silver 1983.
European Championships: *3000 s/chase* silver.
World Cup: *3000 s/chase* gold 1981.
European Cup: *3000 s/chase* gold 1983, silver 1981.

Maminski was forced to step into the shoes of the late, great Bronislaw Malinowski, the 1980 Olympic champion who died in a car crash in 1982. But despite it being a hard act to follow, he has stoutly defended the memory.

Russia's Victor Markin became the fastest European over one lap when he took the Olympic title in Moscow ▶▶

Jose Marajo (FRA)
800/1500 metres
Born: August 10, 1954, France.
Height: 177cm/5ft 9½in.
Weight: 64kg/141lb.
Career Highlights
Olympic Games: *800;* seventh
  1980; *1500* seventh 1980.
European Championships: *800*
  eighth 1978, bronze 1977;
  1500 sixth 1978.
World Student Games: *800* bronze
  1977.

One of Europe's top middle distance runners, Marajo is always dangerous, even if rarely a winner. He reached both the 800 and 500 metre finals at the Moscow Olympics, a feat equalled by Coe and Ovett.

Sydney Maree (USA)
1500 metres
Born: September 9, 1956,
  Pretoria, South Africa.

▲
Sydney Maree a threat in the 1500 metres

Height: 180cm/5ft 11in.
Weight: 66kg/145.5lb.
Career Highlights
World Cup: *1500* fifth 1981.
Record
World *1500* 1983 (3:31.24).

The South African, whose international career was halted while he waited for American citizenship, remains an enigma. Illness caused him to flop in Helsinki, but he recovered to break Steve Ovett's world 1500 metres record, only to see it taken back.

Maree lives in Philadelphia and attends Villanova College. Now that he is an established member of the USA team, Maree will be one of the favourites for the Olympic 1500 metres.

Victor Markin (URS)
400 metres
Born: February 23, 1957,
  Oktobrsk, Ust Tarskovo, USSR.
Height: 183cm/6ft 0in.
Weight: 73kg/161lb.
Career Highlights
Olympic Games: *400* gold 1980.
European Championships: *400*
  bronze 1982.
World Cup: *400* fifth 1981.
World Student Games: *400* silver
  1983.
Record
European *400* 1980 (44.60).

This medical student was so unknown, even in the USSR, before the Moscow Olympics that he was not included in the Soviet team handbook. But he exploded in the final to become the fastest European of all time.

He also got a controversial gold in the 4 x 400. He missed the heats on 'medical' grounds but

'recovered' to run in the final 24 hours later. Since then he has never lived up to his 1980 form.

Henry Marsh (USA)
3000 steeplechase
Born: March 15, 1954, Boston,
  Massachusets, USA.
Height: 178cm/5ft 10in.
Weight: 72kg/158lb.
Career Highlights
Olympic Games: *3000 s/chase*
  tenth 1976.
World Championships: *3000*
  s/chase eighth 1983.
World Cup: *3000 s/chase* fourth
  1979.
Record
North American *3000 s/chase*
  1980 (8:15.68).

Marsh will be remembered, particularly in Britain, as the man who tossed away a silver medal, possibly a gold, in Helsinki. He tripped over the final barrier, which allowed Maminski of Poland through for the silver and gave Colin Reitz of Britain an unexpected bronze.

Marsh does not have the best of luck at major events. In the 1981 World Cup in Rome, he ran inside a barrier and was disqualified.

Eamonn Martin (GBR)
5000 metres
Born: October 9, 1958, Basildon,
Essex, England.
Height: 181cm/5ft 11in.
Weight: 71kg/156lb.
Career Highlights
World Championships: *5000*
semi-final 1983.

Martin had the difficult task of standing in for world record holder David Moorcroft as British number one in Helsinki, in his first international. Martin, an engineer with the Ford Motor Co., and coached by former cross country star Mel Batty, took 30 seconds off his best when running 13:20.94 in Oslo. But his lack of experience meant he failed to reach the final in Helsinki.

Mark McCoy (CAN)
High hurdles
Born: December 10, 1961,
Georgetown, Guyana.
Height: 170cm/5ft 7in.
Weight: 65kg/143lb.
Career Highlights
World Championships: *110h*
fourth 1983.
Commonwealth Games: *110h* gold
1982.
World Student Games: *110h*
bronze 1983.

McCoy was the surprise of the Brisbane Commonwealth Games, certainly his form was a shock to England's Mark Holton. The West Indian-born Canadian had bettered 14sec, with a time of 13.97 only the year before. But in Brisbane he improved dramatically to 13.37. He showed this was not a fluke when he took fourth place in Helsinki. He also won a silver medal in the 1982 Commonwealth sprint relay.

McCoy now lives in Scarborough, Ontario.

Mike McFarlane (GBR)
Sprints
Born: May 2, 1960, London,
England.
Height: 178cm/5ft 10in.
Weight: 76kg/167.5lb.
Career Highlights
Commonwealth Games: *100* fifth
1978, fifth 1982; *200* gold
1982.

Injuries have stopped the likeable young Londoner from fulfilling his potential. But he managed to stay fit enough in 1982 to provide what is reckoned to be the only dead heat in a major international championship.

Officials couldn't separate McFarlane and Allan Wells at the end of the 200 metres. The athletes were kept waiting for 25 minutes in the tunnel while the photo finish picture was scrutinized and finally both were awarded Commonwealth golds.

McFarlane ran in the World Championships relay but did not manage to do the qualifying standards for the individual events.

Chris McGeorge took a surprise bronze in Brisbane during the Commonwealth Games.
◄

Chris McGeorge (GBR)
800 metres
Born: January 13, 1962, Carlisle,
England.
Height: 180cm/5ft 10¾in.
Weight: 63kg/138.6lb.
Career Highlights
Commonwealth Games: *800*
bronze 1982.

McGeorge was the heir-apparent to Coe and Ovett, consistently beating the other contender Peter Elliott. But Elliott beat McGeorge in the 1982 AAA Championships and now the boot is on the other foot. Ironically, McGeorge was called out as a late replacement for Coe, when the world record holder dropped out of the Brisbane Commonwealth Games team. And suddenly, McGeorge, now living in Loughborough to be near coach George Gandy, found himself the English number one when Garry Cook fell over in the semi-final. To his credit he finished in third place.

Mike McLeod (GBR)
5000/10,000 metres
Born: January 25, 1952,
Newcastle upon Tyne, England.
Height: 180cm/5ft 10¾in.
Weight: 63kg/138.6lb.
Career Highlights
Olympic Games: *10,000* twelfth
1980.
European Championships: *5000*
twelfth 1982; *10,000*
fourteenth 1978.
Commonwealth Games: *10,000*
ninth 1982.

Mike McFarlane achieved the only dead heat on record in a major Games when he tied with Allan Wells in the Commonwealth 200 metres
◄ ◄

McLeod suffered through most of his career by being the second best 10000 metres runner in Britain and the north east. His considerable talents were always overshadowed by Brendan Foster.

Even when McLeod began to get the better of his great rival there was controversy. But when Foster eventually retired McLeod seemed ready to take advantage.

He won the IAAF Golden 10000 metres in 1979 and 1981 but injuries have stopped him capitalizing on these victories. Towards the end of last year he showed signs that he was returning to full fitness and a healthy McLeod will be a danger in Los Angeles.

Fernando Mamede (POR)
10,000 metres
Born: November 1, 1951, Portugal.
Height: 175cm/5ft 9in.
Weight: 59kg/130lb.
Career Highlights
World Championships: *10,000* fourteenth 1983; *5000* fifteenth 1978.
Record
European 1982 (27:22.95).

Mamede, an unsuccessful 800 metres runner, has become one of the great 10,000 metres men outside the major title races.

Pietro Mennea (ITA)
Sprints
Born: June 28, 1952, Barletta, Italy.
Height: 179cm/5ft 10in.
Weight: 68kg/150lb.
Career Highlights
Olympic Games: *200* gold 1980, fourth 1976, bronze 1972.
World Championships: *100* bronze 1983.
European Championships: *200* gold 1974, 1978, sixth 1971; *100* gold 1978, silver 1974.
World Cup: *200* bronze 1977; *100* fourth 1977.
European Cup: *200* gold 1975, silver 1979, 1983; *100* gold 1979, silver 1975, 1979.
World Student Games: *200* gold 1973, 1975, 1979; *100* gold 1975, bronze 1973.
Record
World *200* 1979 (19.72).
European *100* 1979 (10.01).

Mennea rivals Don Quarrie as the most durable sprinter, and if he goes on much longer he will overtake him. Mennea retired after winning the Moscow Olympic title and missed the Rome World Cup and the Athens European Championships. But he decided to make a comeback — cynics connected it with the launch of his own range of sports clothing and shoes — and was quick to take third place in Helsinki.

He remains possibly the greatest of all European sprinters, despite Valeri Borzov's Munich success. Not only does he hold the world record set at altitude for the 200 metres, but his time of 19.96 at sea level is considered to be the best performance ever.

A superb stylist Mennea relies on co-ordination rather than power and the rise of Allan Wells in the late 1970s gave European sprinting fans some great moments. He edged Wells out of a second Olympic gold in the 200 metres by 2/100ths of a second.

Richard Mitchell (AUS)
400 metres
Born: March 22, 1955, Canberra, Australia.
Height: 183cm/6ft 0in.
Weight: 70kg/154lb.
Career Highlights
Olympic Games: *400* silver 1980, sixth 1976.
Commonwealth Games: *400* silver 1982, gold 1978.
Record
Oceanian and Commonwealth *400* (44.84 1980).

Like all Australian athletes, Mitchell has had the difficult task of

Rick Mitchell finished fastest of all in the Moscow 400 metres final but just failed to catch Russian Victor Markin ▼

'peaking' in the off season, but he successfully managed over many years at the top. He lived in England for a time in a bid to make it easier, but returned to Australia.

He ran his best time finishing second to Victor Markin in Moscow. He ran twice for Haringey, but did not make too much of an impact in Great Britain.

◀ ◀
Pietro Mennea, the Ferrari-fast Italian who will once again be duelling with Scotland's Allan Wells

Ed Moses (USA)
400 metres hurdles
Born: August 31, 1955, Dayton,
Ohio, USA.
Height: 186cm/6ft 1¼in.
Weight: 73kg/161lb.
Career Highlights
Olympic Games: *400h* gold 1976.
World Championships: *400h* gold
1983.
World Cup: *400h* gold 1981,
1979, 1977.
Record
World *400h* 1976 (47.63), 1977
(47.45), 1980 (47.13), 1983
(47.02),

*Britain's David Moorcroft
salutes the acclaim after
winning the
Commonwealth Games
5000 metres title in
Brisbane*
◄ ◄

▲
*Ed Moses, simply the
greatest. Unbeaten since
1977 and the hottest
possible favourite for the
400 metres hurdles gold*

Dave Moorcroft (GBR)
5000 metres
Born: April 10, 1953, Coventry,
England.
Height: 180cm/5ft 11in.
Weight: 68kg/150lb.
Career Highlights
Olympic Games *1500* seventh
1976.
European Championships: *5000*
bronze 1982; *1500* bronze
1978.
Commonwealth Games: *5000*
gold 1982; *1500* gold 1978.
European Cup: *5000* gold 1981.
World Student Games: *1500*
fourth 1975.
Record
World *5000* 1982 (13:00.41).

For all the medals on the mantle piece of the Moorcroft family home in Coventry, his shining achievement took place outside the major championships arena. Moorcroft wrote his name permanently into the history of the sport when, on a July evening in 1982 while England's attention was turned towards the World soccer Cup in Spain, he produced a shattering performance. The venue was the famous Bislett stadium in Oslo, home of so many world records,

and the race was the 5000 metres. Moorcroft had no plan to break the world record, like so many set-up races these days. He just set off and, feeling good, kept up an extraordinary pace that slashed six seconds off Henry Rono's world best.

Yet Moorcroft had really only moved up to 5000 metres because he saw little chance of winning gold whilst Ovett and Coe were around. This was surprising because he had more than a degree of success in the 1500 metres.

Now becoming well known as a television personality Moorcroft remains one of the most unspoiled of the sport's superstars. He works with disadvantaged youth in Coventry and also helps run the Peugot/Talbot foundation for young up-and-coming talent. Those medals helped make up for a disappointing Moscow Olympics, when Moorcroft, one of the favourites, went down with what the athletes called Trotsky's Revenge.

After his world record he went to Athens as favourite, but had to settle for third place. An easier field in Brisbane saw him run away with the Commonwealth title.

Moses is unquestionably event for event the greatest athlete the world has ever seen in terms of dominance over his peers. Sadly, the race everybody wanted to see in Montreal was unable to take place, because John Akii-Bua the 1972 Olympic champion was forced out by the boycott.

Of the 20 fastest marks (under 47.90) Moses has run 18. His string of victories in finals stretches to 87, and the last man to beat him was West Germany's Harald Schmid back in August 1977.

Moses came late to athletics and his rivals must wish he'd chosen some other sport. Politics robbed him of the chance of emulating Glenn Davis, the only man to have won two Olympic titles. There will be no-one willing to bet though that Moses, provided he is fit and well, will not win in Los Angeles. He took eighteen months off after 1980 to overcome illness and injury, but returned as if he 'had never been away and went on to break the world record again after Helsinki. Yet that final almost brought disaster. The laces of his left shoe became loose and he finished with them flying around his ankles.

Moses is an outspoken critic of drug takers.

Thomas Munkelt (GDR) took advantage of USA absentees in Moscow to strike gold ◄

Thomas Munkelt (GDR)

High hurdles
Born: August 3, 1952, Zedtlitz, East Germany.
Height: 185cm/6ft 1in.
Weight: 80kg/176lb.
Career Highlights
Olympic Games: *110h* gold 1980, fifth 1976.
World Championships: *110h* fifth 1983.
European Championships: *110h* gold 1982, 1978, fourth 1974.
World Cup: *110h* silver 1979, gold 1977.
European Cup: *110h* gold 1983, 1979, 1977, silver 1975, bronze 1973.
World Student Games: *110h* silver 1979, bronze 1973.

If anybody had reason to be grateful that the Americans were not in Moscow, it was Munkelt. The best in Europe ever since Guy Drut retired, Munkelt would have expected bronze at best if Renaldo Nehemiah and Greg Foster had not missed the Games. But Munkelt's long reign as Europe's leading man ended in 1983 when Arto Brygarre took silver in Helsinki.

Gerard Nijboer (HOL)

Marathon
Born: August 18, 1955, Rotterdam, Netherlands.
Height: 182cm/5ft 11½in.
Weight: 70kg/154lb.
Career Highlights
Olympic Games: *marathon* silver 1980.
World Championships: *marathon* twenty ninth 1983.
European Championships: *marathon* gold 1982.

The gaunt, angular Dutchman with the dodgy knees has a remarkable record considering that doctors told him he might never run again.

Between his second place in Moscow and his first in Athens Nijboer ran no more than 10km at one go. But he led from gun to tape in Athens to complete one of the most remarkable comebacks in the modern history of the sport.

Sunder Nix (USA)

400 metres
Born: December 2, 1960, Chicago, USA.
Height: 186cm/6ft 1in.
Weight: 77kg/170lb.
Career Highlights
World Championships: *400* bronze 1983.
World Student Games: *400* bronze 1983.

American dominance of the 400 metres has slipped lately, but many experts are tipping the young Indiana University student as a future champion.

Nix's 44.68 was the fastest time in the world in 1982 and last year he became American champion.

Suleiman Nyambui (TAN)

5000/10000 metres
Born: February 13, 1953, Tanzania.
Height: 182cm/5ft 11½in.
Weight: 68kg/150lb.
Career Highlights
Olympic Games: *5000* silver 1980.
Commonwealth Games: *5000* fifth 1978, fourth 1974, *10,000* fifth 1978.

Who knows what Nyambui, one of the first Africans to take advantage of an American scholarship, would have achieved had the Africans not boycotted the Montreal Olympics. As it is, he remains one of the great distance runners, failing to win Olympic gold only because of Miruts Yifter.

The 1976 African boycott robbed Suleiman Nyambui of his first chance of Olympic gold. Miruts Yifter stopped him the second time. ▼

Ernest Obeng (GHA)
Sprints
Born: April 8, 1956, Ghana.
Height: 167cm/5ft 5½in.
Weight: 60kg/132lb.
Career Highlights
World Cup: *100* silver 1981, fifth 1979.
World Student Games: *100* bronze 1981.

Obeng, now a student at Loughborough University with Sebastian Coe, thrust himself into the limelight with a World Cup 100 metres silver in 1981 but has never been able to find the same magic since.

Steve Ovett (GBR)
800/1500 metres
Born: October 9, 1955, Brighton, England.
Height: 183cm/6ft 0in.
Weight: 70kg/154lb.
Career Highlights
Olympic Games: *800* gold 1980, fifth 1976; *1500* bronze 1980.
World Championships: *1500* fourth 1983.
European Championships: *800* silver 1978, 1974; *1500* gold 1978.
World Cup: *1500* gold 1981, 1977.
European Cup: *800* gold 1975; *1500* gold 1977.
Records
World *1500* 1983 (3:30.77), 1980 (3:32.09), (3:31.36).
World *mile* 1981 (3:48.40), 1980 (3:48.8).
World *two miles* 1978 (7:13.51).

One of the greatest and most controversial figures in the history of athletics, Ovett's true character has been obscured in a feud with the British press, which only ended a couple of years ago. But

even that could not hide his true ability.

He made a remarkable comeback last year from an injury which would have finished many lesser runners. Training near his home in Hove, he struck his thigh against some church railings. After an operation he tried desperately to find form but a series of related injuries, most notably a hamstring, kept him out of the European Championships and the Commonwealth Games. He recovered for 1983 but was refused his wish to double in the 800 and 1500 metres in Helsinki, having dropped out of the AAA Championship 800 metres with what turned out to be cramp high in his right hamstring. So he ran only the 1500 metres in Helsinki and in his own words *'ran like an idiot'.*

Ovett still wants to double in Los Angeles, but so far has won preselection only for the 1500 metres, the event at which he holds the world record. He lost it briefly to Sydney Maree last season but won it back in a couple of weeks later in Rieti, Italy.

Ovett's career started in controversy when he was refused a place in the 1974 Commonwealth Games team, although he clearly deserved it. His rivalry with Sebastian Coe has been conducted, sadly for athletics fans, mostly off the track. Amazingly these two stars have met only three times on the track, once in the Prague European 800 metres, when Ovett beat Coe but was beaten by Olaf Beyer, and in Moscow. Ovett won round one in the 800 metres, a race gifted to him by Coe's appalling tactics, but lost the 1500 metres. They were due to meet in a special three race series in 1982, but injury stopped that and also prevented them clashing in Athens and Brisbane.

Coe has been directly responsible for some of Ovett's greatest performances. Ovett had declared that he was not interested in chasing world records, only in winning. But Coe's continued successful assaults on the world records stung Ovett into response. Now Ovett has another talent to contend with, Steve Cram. They not only met in Helsinki, but also in the IAC/Coca Cola meeting at Crystal Palace when Ovett engineered the confrontation. But Cram won two memorable races.

Now established as a television star (he commented on Athens and Brisbane track and field), Ovett's career has many years left to thrill us further.

Ernest Obeng, fellow Loughbough colleague of Sebastian Coe and Ghana's leading sprinter ◄ ◄

Steve Ovett, on the rostrum where most of Britain expects to find him this summer ▼

Doug Padilla (USA)
5000 metres
Born: October 4, 1956, San
  Leandro, California, USA.
Height: 175cm/5ft 9in.
Weight: 59kg/130lb.
Career Highlight
World Championships: *5000* fifth
  1983.

The Californian went into the World
Championships as a potential
champion on the strength of a brilliant 13:17.69 in Oslo. But he
found three rounds difficult to
take.
  However, with the experience of
a major championship under his
belt, this stylish runner will expect
to do better in Los Angeles.

Don Paige (USA)
800 metres
Born: October 13, 1956,
  Syracuse, New York, USA.
Height: 183cm/6ft 0in.
Weight: 67kg/149lb.
Career Highlights
US Olympic Trial: *800* first 1980.

Injury has twice had a great affect
on Paige's career. He lost time in
1976 and 1977, then won the
1980 Olympic trial with a time of
1:44.53. He didn't get to Moscow,
but beat Sebastian Coe shortly
after. Later, he was injured again
and only came back late in 1983.
  He was coached by the legendary James 'Jumbo' Elliott at Villanova.

Olaf Prenzler (GDR)
Sprints
Born: August 24, 1958, Kastorf,
  East Germany.
Height: 78cm/5ft 10in.
Weight: 178kg/172lb.
Career Highlights
European Championships: *100*
  sixth 1982; *200* gold 1982,
  silver 1978.
World Cup: *100* fourth 1979.
European Cup: *200* fourth 1979.

Despite his 1978 European silver
Prenzler remained the outsider for
Athens, where he surprised everybody once again with gold in the
200. He won the East German
Championships but wasn't
selected for Helsinki.

Don Quarrie (JAM)
Sprints
Born: February 25, 1951,
  Kingston, Jamaica.
Height: 175cm/5ft 9in.
Weight: 70kg/154lb.
Career Highlights
Olympic Games: *200* gold 1976;
  100 silver 1976.
Commonwealth Games: *200* gold
  1970, 1974; *100* gold 1970,
  1974, 1978.
World Cup: *200* fourth 1981.
Record
World *200* 1971 (19.8).

Don Quarrie's amazing career
could have started even sooner
than the 1970 Commonwealth
Games in Edinburgh, when as a
whippet-thin 19-year-old he took
both sprints. He was selected as a
17-year-old for the Mexico Olympics but was injured in training in
Mexico City. Sadly Quarrie had to
miss out on the 1983 World
Championships when he collided
with an official while warming up
for his semi-final. But even he
would admit that these days he
would not expect to be among the
medals.
  No other sprinter of modern
times has lasted so well or
achieved so much. The residents
of Kingston are so pleased with
him that they have erected a
statue in his honour.

Elliot Quow (USA)
Sprints
Born: March 3, 1962, Brooklyn,
  New York.
Height: 186cm/6ft 1in.
Weight: 78kg/173lb.
Career Highlights
World Championships: *200* silver
  1983.

Quow was the American champion
over 200 metres in 1983 but he
was never likely to unsettle Smith
in Helsinki and despite a typically
strong finish, was beaten by a clear
metre and a half.

▲
*Legendary Jamaican
sprinter Don Quarrie, so
revered in his home town
they have erected a statue
in his honour*

Colin Reitz (GBR)
3000 steeplechase
Born: April 5, 1960, Ilford,
  England.
Height: 185cm/6ft 1in.
Weight: 73kg/161lb.
Career Highlights
World Championships: *3000
  s/chase* bronze 1983.
European Championships: *3000
  s/chase* ninth 1982.
Commonwealth Games: *3000
  s/chase* eighth 1982.
European Cup: *3000 s/chase*
  silver 1983.

Reitz got one of Helsinki's luckiest
medals, one which had him laughing the last 30 metres to the line.
He was in fourth place when Henry
Marsh fell over the final barrier: '*I
wasn't laughing at Marsh, just at
my own good fortune*', Reitz
explained.
  But he lost his British record, set
last year, to team-mate Graeme
Fell shortly after the World Championships.

◄ ◄
*American Don Paige
became one of the few men
to beat Sebastian Coe over
800 metres when he edged
him by inches in Viareggio
in 1980*

James Robinson (USA)
5000/10,000 metres
Born: August 27, 1954. Oakland, California, USA.
Height: 180cm/5ft 11in.
Weight: 67kg/147.5lb.
Career Highlights
World Championships: *800* fifth 1983.
World Cup: *800* silver 1981, 1979.

One of the most durable 800 metres runners, Robinson is becoming best known as a pacemaker for Europe's record attempts. He was still good enough at almost 29 to take fifth place in Helsinki.

Henry Rono (KEN)
5000/10,000 metres/3000 steeplechase
Born: February 12, 1952, Kaprirsang, Nandi Hills, Kenya.
Height: 170cm/5ft 7in.
Weight: 83kg/182lb.
Career Highlights
Commonwealth Games: *5000* gold 1978; *3000 s/chase* gold 1978.
Records
World *5000* 1981 (13.06.20), 1978 (13:08.4); *10,000* 1978 (27:22.5); *3000 s/chase* 1978 (8:05.4) (7:32.1).

Four world records in 1978 established Henry Rono as one of the all-time greats ▼

Alberto Salazar, America's Marathon hope who once drove himself so hard he collapsed and was given the last rites ▶ ▶

African Games golds and four world records.

Kip Rono (KEN)
3000 metres steeplechase
Born: January 4, 1958, Kenya.
Height: 168cm/5ft 6in.
Weight: 54kg/119lb.
Career Highlights
Commonwealth Games: *s/chase* bronze 1978.
World Cup: *s/chase* gold 1979.

The little front-running Kenyan is always game to inject an exciting surge of pace, but he has yet to develop the necessary sprint finish that wins the major Games titles.

Marcus Ryffel (SUI)
5000/10,000 metres
Born: February 5, 1955, Switzerland.
Height: 167cm/5ft 5½in.
Weight: 55kg/121lb.
Career Highlights
Olympic Games: *5000* fifth 1980.
European Championships: *5000* tenth 1982, silver 1978.

A 1978 European second place in Prague has never been followed up by the stylish Swiss. He faded to 12th in the Helsinki World Championships and could be making his swan song in Los Angeles.

Alberto Salazar (USA)
Marathon
Born: August 7, 1958, Havana, Cuba.

Rono's small collection of gold medals does not do justice to his enormous talent. He has never been able to harness his great natural resources properly, over-racing on the American college circuit and, unfortunately, contracting illnesses.

He was kept away from the Montreal and Moscow Olympics by the Kenyan boycotts, but in 1978 had a phenomenal year. He won two Commonwealth golds, two

Height: 181cm/5ft 11in.
Weight: 64kg/141lb.
Career Highlights
World Championships: *10,000* seventeenth 1983.
World Cup: *10,000* bronze 1981.
New York marathon: first 1980, 1981, 1982.
Boston marathon: first 1982.
Records
World *marathon* 1981 (2:08.12).
North American *5000* 1982 (13:11.93); *10,000* 1982 (27:25.61).

By his own standards 1983 was a bad year for Alberto Salazar. Illness forced him down to seventeenth place in the World Championship 10000 metres. Also, he lost his first marathon to his great rival Robert de Castella in Rotterdam earlier in the year. He was disappointed, too, with his placing in the Fukuoka race although this showed he was over the illness and injury.

He did not start marathon running until 1980, when he won New York in 2:09.41. A year later he ran the Big Apple race again and this time did a world's best. He added Boston to his list in 1982, winning in sub-2:09 time and then won New York in his slowest time so far 2:09.29. Yet Salazar was lucky to be running at all. For in the Falmouth seven mile road race in 1978, he collapsed and was given the last rites. Fortunately, he recovered.

Mariano Scartezzini (ITA)

3000 steeplechase
Born: November 7, 1954, Trento, Italy.
Height: 186cm/6ft 1in.
Weight: 96kg/211.2lb.
World Championships: *s/chase* ninth 1983.
European Championships: *s/chase* seventh 1982.
World Cup: *s/chase* silver 1981, bronze 1979.
European Cup: *s/chase* gold 1981, 1979.
World Student Games: *s/chase* bronze 1981, silver 1979, eighth 1975.

This stick-thin Italian has always been at his best in one-off races such as the cup meetings. He has yet to cope with heats and a final, and he is getting on now.

His best time of 8:12.5 (an Italian record) would have got him a silver in Moscow, but he did it a month later, not having competed in the Moscow Olympics. Even then he was only second.

Werner Schildauer (GDR)

5000/10,000 metres
Born: June 5, 1959, Dessau, East Germany.
Height: 181cm/5ft 11in.
Weight: 68kg/150lb.
Career Highlights
Olympic Games: *10,000* seventh 1980.
World Championships: *10,000* silver 1983; *5000* silver 1983.
European Championships: *10,000* silver 1982; *5000* silver 1982.
World Cup: *10,000* gold 1981, sixth 1979.
European Cup: *10,000* gold 1983, 1981, fourth 1979.

The gangling East German electrician seems destined to be a perpetual bridesmaid. In four big races in two years — two at the Athens Europeans, two in Helsinki -- he was beaten into second place. The man who has the Indian sign on him at 10,000 is the Italian Alberto Cova, who sneaks races in the last few strides.

Schildauer will still be one of the favourites in Los Angeles. Although, like all the other East Germans, he rarely shows his form outside the major events, few will bet against him taking a medal.

Harald Schmid (FRG)

400 metres hurdles
Born: September 29, 1957, Hanau, West Germany.
Height: 187cm/6ft 1½in.
Weight: 82kg/181lb.
Career Highlights
World Championships: *400h* silver 1983.
European Championships: *400h* gold 1982, 1978.
World Cup: *400h* silver 1979, bronze 1977.
European Cup: *400h* gold 1983, 1981, 1979.
World Student Games: *400h* gold 1979.
Record
European: *400h* 1982 (47.48).

How Harald Schmid must wish that Ed Moses had found another event. Schmid's European record, set when winning the European title in Athens, puts him far ahead of anyone other than Moses. He has, though, the small satisfaction of being the last man to defeat the great super hero of athletics.

Schmid turned briefly to the 800 metres, perhaps as a way to escape Moses, but although he clocked a highly respectable 1:44.84 in 1979 the muscular German decided to stick with his main event.

Steve Scott (USA)

1500 metres
Born: May 5, 1956, Upland, California, USA.
Height: 185cm/6ft 1in.
Weight: 75kg/165lb.
Career Highlights
World Championships: *1500* silver 1983.
World Cup: *1500* fourth 1979, seventh 1977.
Records
North American *mile* 1982 (3:47.69); *1500* 1981 (3:31.96).

Steve Scott's cheerful but unavailing pursuit of Coe, Ovett, and now Cram, should bring the Los Angeles Olympics to a peak of high excitement. Scott has been US 1500 metres champion every year since 1977, except in 1981 when he was beaten by Sydney Maree. But when facing Coe and Ovett in Europe, the curly-haired Californian was always second best. Even when he set his best time for a mile in 1982, Coe and Ovett were both injured and unable to face him.

He finally caught Coe at Crystal Palace last year in the AAA Championship mile, but it was obvious that the Olympic 1500 metres champion was below his best. Come Helsinki though, and another Briton, the young Cram was ready to take Scott. He smilingly accepted the defeat, but pointed out that Los Angeles is his home town. His improvement is such that no-one can bet against him.

Toshi Seko (JPN)

10,000 metres/marathon
Born: July 15, 1956, Japan.
Height: 169cm/5ft 6½in.
Weight: 64kg/141lb.
Career Highlights
Boston marathon: first 1981.
Tokyo marathon: first 1982.
Records
Marathon 1983, Asian *10,000* 1980 (27:43.44).

The crew-cut Seko, a student of Zen, became the fastest Japanese marathoner of all time when he recorded 2hr 8:38 to win the 1982 Tokyo marathon. He confirmed his world class in 1984 by finishing

Man against Superman . . . West German Harald Schmid who must attempt to beat the unbeatable Ed Moses over 400 metres hurdles ◄ ◄

The Soviets are still searching for someone to match Valery Borzov but Sidorov, despite going through the same conditioning, is not the answer, although he is an excellent relay runner.

Cameron Sharp, maintaining Scotland's great sprinting tradition and the heir apparent to Allan Wells
◀ ◀

first in the Fukioka marathon in 2hr 08:52.

Gidamis Shahanga (TAN)
10,000 metres/marathon
Born: September 4, 1957, Tanzania.
Height: 177cm/5ft 9½in.
Weight: 57kg/125.5lb.
Career Highlights
Olympic Games: *marathon* fifteenth 1980.
World Championships: *10,000* fifth 1983.
Commonwealth Games: *10,000* gold 1982; *marathon* sixth 1982, gold 1978.

Shahanga's victory in the Edmonton Commonwealth Games was achieved, according to him, when he was only 17, but he is generally reckoned to have been 21, still a very young age to win a major marathon title.
   In Brisbane after his 10,000 metres victory he was still insisting he was 21 and stating that contrary to common belief his christian name is spelt Gidamis not Gidimas.

Cameron Sharp (GBR)
Sprints
Born: June 3, 1958, Edinburgh, Scotland.

Height: 182cm/5ft 11½in.
Weight: 77kg/170lb.
Career Highlights
European Championships: *200* silver 1982; *100* fourth 1982.
Commonwealth Games: *100* bronze 1982; *200* bronze 1982.

Cameron Sharp, guided by Britain's National Director of Coaching Frank Dick, emerged from the shadow of Allan Wells, Olympic champion and a fellow Scot, at the Athens European Championships.
   Sharp finished fourth in the 100 metres, his favourite event. But Dick has always believed his protégé was a natural 200 metres runner, and Sharp took the silver in the longer sprint.
   Unfortunately for Sharp, Wells was fit enough to run in the Brisbane Commonwealth Games a month later and he pipped him in both races.

Nickolai Sidorov (URS)
Sprints
Born: November 23, 1956, USSR.
Height: 190cm/6ft 3in.
Weight: 84kg/185lb.
Career Highlights
European Championships: *100* fifth 1982.
World Cup: *100* fourth 1981.

Erwin Skamrahl (FRG)
200/400 metres
Born: March 8, 1958, Oberg, West Germany.
Height: 175cm/5ft 9in.
Weight: 70kg/154lb.
Career Highlights
World Championships: *400* fourth 1983.
European Championships: *200* fourth 1982.
European Cup: *200* bronze 1983, fourth 1981.
Record
European *400* 1983 (44.50).

Skamrahl caused a scare among the ranks of the top 400 metres men when he broke the European record early last year, the first season that he had concentrated on the distance.
   He was always a talented one-lap runner, but preferred the 200 metres. His fourth place in Helsinki shows what a threat he will be to Cameron and the Americans in Los Angeles.

▲
Erwin Skamrahl of West Germany, European 400 metre record holder who will threaten the black domination in Los Angeles

Geoff Smith left Liverpool fire brigade to burn up the roads in America ▶ ▶

Barry Smith (GBR)
5000/10000 metres
Born: April 16, 1953, London, England.
Height: 168cm/5ft 6in.
Weight: 60kg/132lb.
Career Highlight
Olympic Games: *5000* semi-finalist 1980.
IAAF Golden: *5000* first 1981.

The IAAF Golden 5000 metres champion in 1981, Smith seemed set for the big time. But an Achilles injury stopped him making the European or Commonwealth meetings in 1982. Following an operation, he is now back and running well.

Smith moved to the north east and his development as a distance runner came when he joined Gateshead. He is coached by Lindsay Dunn, who also helped Brendan Foster.

Calvin Smith (USA)
Sprints
Born: January 8, 1961, Bolton, Mississippi, USA.
Height: 175cm/5ft 9in.
Weight: 66kg/145lb.
Career Highlights
World Championships: *200* gold 1983; *100* silver 1983.
World Student Games: *100* silver 1981.
Records
World *100* (9.93) *4 x 100* 1983.

The fastest man in the world, Calvin Smith of America ▼

Seeing Smith on the track you would not think he was a world class sprinter. His head rolls and he looks ready to expire. But he is

the fastest man of all time.

There was little in his career to suggest that the quietly spoken boy from the deep south would become one of the all time greats. But before going to Helsinki he took advantage of the high altitude at Colorado Springs to break the world 100m record.

Geoff Smith (GBR)
5000/10,000 metres/marathon
Born: October 24, 1953, Liverpool, England.
Height: 167cm/5ft 6in.
Weight: 63.5kg/140lb.
Career Highlights
New York *marathon* second 1983.

Smith started late as a runner, preferring football until he was 23, but quickly showed his talent. Injuries have stopped him putting together a consistent series of results, but last year he showed he might become one of the great marathon runners. He was second to Rod Dixon in New York, finishing in 2h 09:08 – the fastest-ever time by a British runner.

While he still harbours hopes of making the British Olympic team at 10,000, he could well be selected at the marathon distance. He might have won in New York had he legally cut the corners like Dixon instead of becoming hypnotized by the blue line down the middle of the road. Quick enough to run a mile in 3:55.8 in 1981, Smith had never run beyond the half marathon distance before. A disastrous Moscow Olympics persuaded him to leave the fire brigade in his native Liverpool – '*I might have been working during the Toxteth riots*' – to enrol as a student at Providence College in New England.

Willie Smith (USA)
400 metres
Born: February 28, 1956, Rochester, Pennsylvania, USA.
Height: 173cm/5ft 8in.
Weight: 73kg/161lb.
Career Highlights
US Championships: *400* first 1980, 1979.

Despite a long and successful career, Smith will now always be remembered as the American who fell in the first World Championship 4 x 400 metres final and cost his team the gold.

Smith was the best in the world in 1979 – United States Champion in 1979 and 1980. With 44.73 in 1980 he would certainly have been among the medals in Moscow, but for the boycott.

The tallest distance runner competing, Finland's Martti Vainio used those extra inches to gain a World Championship medal when he hurled himself bodily across the line in Helsinki ▶ ▶

Elliot Tabron (USA)
400 metres
Born: May 23, 1960, Detroit, Michigan, USA.
Height: 180cm/5ft 11in.
Weight: 75kg/165lb.
Career Highlights
World Student Games: *400* fourth 1983.

One of the new breed attempting to restore the US reputation as the world's top 400 metres nation in time for the Los Angeles Olympics. There were doubts about his competitive ability when he finished fifth in the Helsinki World Championships first round. He went through to the second round as a fastest loser — but was eliminated.

Sam Turner, choice of event for tall American ▶

Sam Turner (USA)
Hurdles
Born: June 17, 1957, Los Angeles, California, USA.
Height: 193cm/6ft 4in.
Weight: 88kg/195lb.
Career Highlights
World Championships: *110h* eighth 1983.

Turner has had to choose between high hurdles and the 400 metres hurdles, because he has recorded a time of 49.04 at the longer event, without specializing in it.

He may very well turn to it though after his Helsinki experi-ence in the 110 metres event, when he hit the first hurdle very heavily and finished last. His run up to Helsinki had been blighted by the persistent presence of fel-low American Tonie Campbell, who finished fifth in the American trials and so was not selected for the World Championship team.

Martti Vainio (FIN)
5000/10,000 metres
Born: December 30, 1950, Vehkalahti, Finland.
Height: 192cm/6ft 3in.
Weight: 72kg/158lb.
Career Highlights
Olympic Games: *5000* eleventh 1980; *10,000* thirteenth 1970.
World Championships: *5000* bronze 1983; *10,000* fourth 1983.
European Championships: *10,000* bronze 1982, gold 1978; *5000* eighth 1982, sixth 1978.
World Cup: *10,000,* fifth 1981.
European Cup: *10,000,* fourth 1977.

The tall Finnish salesman burst into the limelight in 1978 at the European Championships, when his long prancing style took him to the 10,000 metres title. But he failed to follow the Lasse Viren tradition in Moscow and was hard put to shine in the first World Championships in his homeland. But after struggling into fourth place in the 10,000 metres, Vainio made a supreme effort in the 5000 metres, throwing himself over the line for a medal.

Craig Virgin (USA)
5000/10000 metres
Born: August 2, 1955, Belleville, Illinois, USA.
Height: 179cm/5ft 10in.
Weight: 140kg/63kg/lb.
Career Highlight
World Cup: silver 1979.

A double winner of the world cross country championship in Paris in 1979, and Rome in 1981, Virgin has suffered bad luck through injury and seen his unofficial title as America's leading distance track star taken over by Alberto Salazar.

Virgin is determined to come back for the Los Angeles Games, having been forced to miss the World Championships. He was picked, but had to drop out. His place was taken by Bill McChes-ney.

Virgin runs his own public rela-tions firm.

Detlef Wagenknecht (GDR)
800 metres
Born: January 3, 1959, Berlin,
    East Germany.
Height: 193cm/6ft 4in.
Weight: 75kg/165lb.
Career Highlights
Olympic Games: *800* sixth 1980.
European Championships: *800*
    sixth, 1982, 1978.
World Cup: *800* bronze 1981.
European Cup: *800* silver 1983.

Peter Coe reckoned Wagenknecht
would be the most dangerous man
in the 1980 Olympic final. It didn't
turn out that way, but Wagenknecht is always dangerous.

John Walker (NZL)
800/1500 metres
Born: January 12, 1952,
    Papukura, New Zealand.
Height: 183cm/6ft 0in.
Weight: 74kg/163lb.
Career Highlights
Olympic Games: *1500* gold 1976.
World IChampionships: *1500* ninth
    1983.
Commonwealth Games: *1500*
    silver 1982, silver 1974; *800*
    fourth 1982, bronze 1974.
World Cup: *1500* silver 1981.
Record
World *mile* 1975 (3:49.4)
World *2000* 1976 (4:51.4).

John Walker's best days are clearly
behind him but he is still one of the
most consistent runners around.
The first man ever to duck under
3:50 for a mile, Walker suffered a
serious Achilles tendon injury in
the late 1970s and has done well
to come back.

He first came to the public
notice when he chased home Filbert Bayi in the 1974 Commonwealth Games 1500 final. Bayi,
front running all the way, hung on
to record a world record 3:32.2.
Walker wanted revenge in Montreal
but was not to get it; Bayi was part
of the African boycott. Walker won
the gold, but was unable to defend
in Moscow because of another
boycott.

Married with two children,
Walker is a familiar figure on the
European circuit. He feels that had
he lived in England, able to nip
backwards and forwards to the top
European races, he would have
been able to do even better. He
tried living in the USA but returned
to New Zealand, living out of a
suitcase in the summer when
competing on the European circuit.

Hartmut Weber (FRG)
400 metres
Born: October 17, 1960, Kamen,
    West Germany.
Height: 186cm/6ft 1in.
Weight: 70kg/154lb.
Career Highlights
World Championships: *400* fifth
    1983.
European Championships: *400*
    gold 1982.
World Cup: *400* fourth 1981.
European Cup: *400* gold, 1983,
    1981.

The bespectacled Weber, champion in Athens in 1982, could well
turn to the 400 hurdles in the
future.

Last year he managed 49.10
which would have made him British
number one. His switch would
coincide with Erwin Skamrahl
breaking the European record and
leading Weber in the World Championship final.

Ronald Weigel (GDR)
50 kilometre walk
Born: August 8, 1958,
    Hildburghausen, East
    Germany.
Height: 176cm/5ft 9in.
Weight: 56kg/123lb.
Career Highlight
World Championships: *50k* gold
    1983.

The young journalist student had a
great story to write about on
August 12 last year when he strode
to victory in the World Championships 50 kilometre walk.

*Hartmut Weber of West
Germany could switch from
the flat 400 to 400 hurdles*
◄

*John Walker is a veteran
now, but the tall blond New
Zealander who held the
mile record and won gold in
Montreal is still a feared
campaigner*
◄ ◄

Allan Wells (GBR)

Sprints
Born: May 3, 1952, Edinburgh, Scotland.
Height: 183cm/6ft 0in.
Weight: 77kg/170lb.
Career Highlights
Olympic Games: *100* gold 1980; *200* silver 1980.
World Championships: *100* fourth 1983; *200* fourth 1983.
European Championships: *100* sixth 1978.
Commonwealth Games: *100* gold 1982, silver 1978; *200* gold 1978, 1982.
World Cup: *100* gold 1981; *200* silver 1981.
European Cup: *100* gold 1981, silver 1983, bronze 1979; *200* gold 1979, 1983, silver 1981.

At the beginning of 1978 Allan Wells was an Edinburgh marine engineer and an average-to-good long jumper. He had fallen in love with that event when raking the long jump pit at the Commonwealth Games held in his native city in 1970.

By the end of the summer of 1978 Wells was on his way to becoming one of the world's leading sprinters, taking gold and silver in the Edmonton Commonwealth Games. At that time he decided he could start better without blocks, but he used them at the Moscow Olympics to once again take gold and silver. Wells will always have to live with the fact that some people think he won the Moscow medals only because the Americans were not taking part. But the last time an American had won the 100 metres gold was Jim Hines in 1968.

Ironically Wells went to Moscow expecting to do better in the 200 metres, just as Sebastian Coe expected to win the 800 metres. Instead Wells won the premier sprint title and Coe the middle distance blue riband, the 1500 metres. On the last day they had breakfast together in the Olympic village and admitted that they were quite pleased with the way things had turned out.

Wells, who belongs to the power school of sprinting, won the IAAF Golden sprints in 1981, holding off the American challenge. But his build up the next year was faltering. He missed the Athens European Championships, preferring to get himself right for the Commonwealth Games in Brisbane. It was a policy which worked well because

the Scot won the 100 metres and then took gold in the 200 metres, although he had the rare experience of dead heating in the final. The officials took 25 minutes to decide that they could not separate Wells and England's Mike McFarlane and gave them both gold medals.

By now Wells had moved, with his wife Margot, from Scotland to be near his new coach John Allan in Guildford. But the relationship between the sprinter and coach did not develop in the way Wells wished and he is now coached by Margot.

He went to Helsinki recovering from an injury, and his fourth places in both events reflected his lack of conditioning. The British selectors picked him to go to Los Angeles without any trial. 'Just what I needed,' he said, 'Now I can concentrate purely on preparing the way I want and not have to race here, there and everywhere.'

Thomas Wessinghage

(FRG)
5000 metres
Born: February 22, 1952, Hagen/Westfalen, West Germany.
Height: 182cm/5ft 11in.
Weight: 70kg/154lb.
Career Highlights
World Championships: *5000* sixth 1983.
European Championships: *5000* gold 1982, fourth 1978, bronze 1974.
World Cup: *1500* silver 1977.

European Cup: *1500* gold 1975, silver 1979, 1977, 1975; *5000* gold 1983.
World Student Games: *1500* gold 1975.

The bi-lingual German doctor seemed to have made a successful move up from 1500 metres to 5000 metres when he beat an out-of-sorts David Moorcroft in the 1982 European final. But Wessinghage, the third fastest man ever at 1500 metres, could not cope with three rounds in Helsinki. He now lives in Los Angeles to prepare for the Olympic Games.

'Flying doctor' Thomas Wessinghage, European 5000 metres champion ◄

The explosive starting power of Allan Wells, pride of Scotland, who defends his 100 metres title in Los Angeles ▼

Cliff Wiley (USA)
400 metres
Born: May 21, 1955, Baltimore, USA.
Height: 173cm/5ft 8in.
Weight: 61kg/134.5lb.
Career Highlights
World Cup: *400* gold 1981.
World Student Games: *400* gold 1981.

Best known as a sprinter until 1981, Wiley turned to one-lap running and went on to win the World Cup in Rome. He had a remarkable year, claiming the American title, winning against the Soviets and also triumphing at the World University Games.

That was in his first year at the University of Kansas School of Law but in 1982 he was only the third-ranked American. And last year he was only sixth in the American Championships, so did not make the World Championship team, but took the Pan American title. Now he has finished his final exams he will be a threat at the Los Angeles Olympics.

Graham Williamson (GBR)
800/1500 metres
Born: June 15, 1960, Glasgow, Scotland.
Height: 183cm/6ft 0in.
Weight: 64kg/141lb.
Career Highlights
Commonwealth Games: *1500* fourth 1982.
European Cup: *1500* bronze 1979.
World Student Games: *800* silver 1983.

Asked to name the unluckiest athlete in the world, most of his fellow middle distance runners would settle for Williamson. First, aged 18, he failed to win a place in Scotland's team for the Edmonton Commonwealth Games. Although he beat the then 17-year-old Steve Cram in the Emsley Carr Mile, Cram was selected by England. Then Williamson beat Cram in the 1980 Olympic trials when Cram fell over. The selectors asked for a run-off in Oslo when Williamson was suffering from flu and in the middle of exams.

A stress fracture of the shin ruined 1981; in the 1982 Europeans he was tripped, and just before the World Championships he was injured. Yet Williamson, now living near coach George Gandy in Loughborough, remains a potent threat for Los Angeles.

Cliff Wiley, one of America's fearsome battery of world class 400 metre men
◄ ◄

Scotland's Graham Williamson qualifies as one of the sports' unluckiest men. Will fortunes change in Los Angeles?
◄

Marian Woronin (POL)
Sprints
Born: August 13, 1956, Grodzisk, Mazowiecki, Poland.
Height: 185cm/6ft 1in.
Weight: 74kg/163lb.
Career Highlights
Olympic Games: *100* seventh 1980; *200* seventh 1980.
European Championships: *100* bronze 1982.
World Cup: *100* silver 1979, fourth 1981, eighth 1977; *200* bronze 1979, fifth 1983.

The Polish railway technician is one of Europe's most durable sprinters, always in the frame, if never a champion, except indoors. He is four times European indoor 60 metres champion.

West Germany's Willi
Wulbeck came good in
Helsinki, winning the 800
metres title in style
◄

Miruts Yifter 'The Shifter'
scored a memorable double
over 5000 and 10000
metres in Moscow He is
expected to tackle the
Marathon in Los Angeles
▼

Willi Wulbeck (FRG)
800 metres
Born: December 18, 1954,
Oberhausen, West Germany.
Height: 186cm/6ft 1in.
Weight: 70kg/154lb.
Career Highlights
Olympic Games: *800* fourth
1976.
World Championships: *800* gold
1983.
European Championships: *800*
eighth 1982, 1974.
World Cup: *800* bronze 1979,
1977.
European Cup: *800* gold 1983,
1977, silver 1981, seventh
1975.

Wulbeck has never really been
given the credit he deserves, being
better known as the man who
short-armed Sebastian Coe across
the track in the 1977 European
Cup final. Yet Wulbeck has been a
leading world performer since
before the Montreal Olympics,
when he finished fourth behind
Alberto Juantorena. He has never
managed to shine at European
level, yet the student who still lives
in Oberhausen, peaked perfectly
in Helsinki. It was his first major
title and ample revenge for the
Athens victory by his compatriot
Hans-Peter Ferner, a man who had
never beaten him before. Wulbeck
nearly retired after that event.

Miruts Yifter (ETH)
5000/10000 metres/marathon
Born: May 15, 1944, Ethiopia.
Height: 172cm/5ft 7½in.
Weight: 53kg/117lb.
Career Highlights
Olympic Games: *5000* gold 1980;
10,000 gold 1980, bronze
1972.
World Cup: *5000* gold 1979,
1977; *10,000* gold 1979,
1977.
Record
Olympic *5000* 1980 (13:21.00).

Who knows if the ageless Ethiopian Airforce officer, father of six,
will be in Los Angeles? It was
suggested he would run the
marathon in the World Championships but he did not show. Nick-
named 'Yifter the Shifter' because
of his fierce kick, the tiny bald-
headed African missed the start of
the 1972 Olympic 5000 and the
1976 Olympics altogether. But he
shone in Moscow and in the 1977
and 1979 World Cup.

Anna Ambrozene (née Kastetskaya) (URS)
400 metres hurdles
Born: August 14, 1955, Tashkent, USSR.
Height: 173cm/5ft 8in.
Weight: 61kg/134.5lb
Career Highlights
World Championships: *400h* silver 1983.
European Championships: *400h* fourth 1982.
World Cup: *400h* bronze 1981.
European Cup: *400h* silver 1983, 1981.
World Student Games: gold 1981.
Record
World *400h* 1983 (54.02).

Ambrozene's world record did not help her in Helsinki when she was beaten by team mate Yekaterina Fesenko, who could manage only seventh place behind her in Athens the year before.

Although her time was the third fastest ever she was disappointed, having run eight times under 55 seconds in 1983.

Evelyn Ashford (USA)
Sprints
Born: April 15, 1957, Shreveport, Louisiana, USA.
Height: 165cm/5ft 5in.
Weight: 52kg/114.5lb.
Career Highlights
Olympic Games: *100* fifth 1976.
World Cup: *100* gold 1979, 1981, fifth 1977: *200* gold 1979, 1981, fourth 1977.
Records
World *100* 1983 (10.79A).
North American *200* 1979 (21.83).

The only woman likely to break the domination of the Eastern European block Ashford suffered bad luck in Helsinki when an old hamstring injury caused her to break down in the middle of the 100 metres final.

With the Americans missing the Moscow Olympics Ashford has had no chance to test herself against Gohr in a major championship. But she won the 100 metres and 200 metres in both the 1979 and 1981 World Cups.

She lowered the world record to 10.79 at altitude before Helsinki. Married to Ray Washington she is coached by former United States Olympian Pat Connolly.

She has an unorthodox heel-flicking style, which she has refused to modify. She popularized the leotard for sprinters.

Angela Bailey (CAN)
Sprints
Born: February 28, 1962, Coventry, England.
Height: 157cm/5ft 2in.
Weight: 54kg/118lb.
Career Highlights
World Championships: *100* fifth 1983; *200* seventh 1983.
Commonwealth Games: *100* fourth 1982
200 eighth 1982.

Britain's loss was Canada's gain. The youngster won a silver medal in the 1978 Commonwealth Games sprint relay at the age of 16 and is improving all the time. She is coached by John Mumford at the University of Ontario.

Joan Benoit (USA)
Marathon
Born: March 16, 1957, Eugene, USA.
Height: 157cm/5ft 2¼in.
Weight: 46kg/101.5lb.
Career Highlight
Boston marathon: first 1983.
Record
World 1983 (2:22.43).

Benoit's remarkable run in last year's Boston Marathon was at first held under suspicion. But the course was remeasured and found to be accurate, so her world best stood. In that run she took nearly three minutes from Alison Roe's time but didn't go to Helsinki because she missed the trial. She

Evelyn Ashford of the USA is the only girl who seems capable of ending the Eastern European sprint domination ▼

Kathy Cook, tall and talented, is Britain's best hope for a women's medal, probably over 400 metres ▶

So elegant off the track, so ruthless on it, America's Mary Decker will be attempting to emulate her World Championships double. ▶ ▶

North American: *1500* 1980 (3:57.12); *3000* 1982 (8:29.71).

Back in 1973 14-year-old Mary Decker, pigtailed with a brace on her teeth, delighted the whole of the USA by beating Soviet Olympic silver medallist Niole Sabaite in the USA v USSR match in Minsk. Until 1983, however, Mary never lived up to that early promise.

Her failure in the years in between had nothing to do with lack of talent. She was susceptible, probably because of a too-heavy training schedule, to injuries. She needed several shin operations and Dick Brown, who took over as her coach in 1981, says: *'From the knees up she is world class, from the knees down we live from day to day.'*

In between injuries she kept breaking world records, but it was not until 1983 that she met the Soviets in a major meeting and when she did her courageous front running was a feature of the championships.

might have run into trouble with the IAAF if she had. For Benoit is a college coach in Boston and could be declared a professional. She preferred to coach her college team when the trials were on.

Kathy Cook (GBR)
Sprints/400 metres
Born: May 3, 1960, Reading. England.
Height: 180cm/5ft 11in.
Weight: 64kg/141lb.
Career Highlights
Olympic Games: *100* sixth 1980; *200* fifth 1980.
World Championships: *200* bronze 1983.
European Championships: *200* silver 1982.
Commonwealth Games: silver 1982, fifth 1978.
World Cup: *100* silver 1981.
European Cup: *100* silver 1981, bronze 1983; *200* silver 1981, bronze 1983, fourth 1979.
World Student Games: *200* gold 1981, silver 1979; *100* silver 1979.

Although she is primarily known as a sprinter Kathy Cook (née Smallwood) will probably aim for the 400 metres in Los Angeles, an event for which she clearly has much potential. She is the British record holder, although she has never really trained for one lap running.

Married to Garry Cook, one of Britain's top 800 metres men, Kathy now lives in Walsall and runs for Wolverhampton and Bilston. She first sprang to prominence in world terms when as a late replacement in the Rome World

Cup she managed second place. She finished 1982 with individual silvers from the European and Commonwealth Games, but 1983 was somewhat disappointing despite her third place in Helsinki.

She had hoped to start a move towards the 400 metres by running that event in the Brisbane Commonwealth Games, but the England selectors refused.

Mary Decker (USA)
1500/3000 metres
Born: August 4, 1958, Flemington, New Jersey, USA.
Height: 168cm/5ft 6in.
Weight: 51kg/112.51lb.
Career Highlights
World Championships: *1500* gold 1983; *3000* gold 1983.
Record
World *mile* 1982 (4:18.08), 1980 (4:21.68).

Mariane Dickerson (USA)
Marathon
Born: November 14, 1960, St Joseph, Illinois, USA.
Height: 170cm/5ft 7in.
Weight: 44kg/98lb.
Career Highlight
World Championships: *marathon* silver 1983.

Before Helsinki Dickerson, who has a BSc in general engineering at the University of Michigan and is now taking a masters degree, had run only one marathon, 2:43 in June 1982. But she was expected to do well in the World Championships.

Gabriella Dorio (ITA)
800/1500 metres
Born: June 27, 1957, Veggiano, Italy.
Height: 168cm/5ft 6in.
Weight: 52kg/114.5lb.
Career Highlights
Olympic Games: *1500* fourth 1980, sixth 1976; *800* eighth 1980.
World Championships: *1500* seventh 1983.
European Championships: *1500* bronze 1982, sixth 1978, ninth 1974.
World Cup: *1500* silver 1981, seventh 1970, fourth 1981.
World Student Games: *1500* gold 1981, fifth 1979; *800* fourth 1981, fourth 1979.

The fastest 1500 metres runner in 'free' Europe – that is what Gabriella Dorio is able to claim, but her solitary title came in the 1981 World Student Games. She is also among the prettiest 1500 metres runners, with long curly hair. Gabriella also won the 1982 European indoor title in Turin, and, not surprisingly, was the most popular victor.

Olga Dvrina (URS)
1500/3000 metres
Born: February 29, 1952, Vyselky, Moscow, USSR.
Height: 170cm/5ft 7in.
Weight: 59kg/130lb.
Career Highlight
European Championships: *1500* silver 1982.

Western experts suspect that Dvrina was kept back last year so that she would be in a position to attack the 3000 metres in Los Angeles. She has been a member of the Soviet senior team for 12 years in both track and cross country, but only came to the fore in 1982.

Ekaterina Fesenko (URS)
400 metres hurdles
Born: March 10, 1956, USSR.
Height: 172cm/5ft 7½in.
Weight: 61kg/134.5lb.
Career Highlights
World Championships: *400h* gold 1983.
European Championships: *400h* seventh 1982.
World Student Games: *400h* gold 1983.

A surprise gold in Helsinki following her World Student Games win made Fesenko the number one last year.
'I didn't think I would win,' she said 'but my performance was technically perfect.'

Ellen Fiedler (GDR)
400 metres hurdles
Born: November 10, 1958, Demmin, East Germany.
Height: 174cm/5ft 8½in.
Weight: 66kg/145.5lb.
Career Highlights
World Championships: *400h* bronze 1983.

World Cup: *400h* gold 1981.
European Cup: *400h* gold, 1983, 1981.

Favourite for the first world title in Helsinki, Ellen Fiedler faded to third against the Soviet challenge.
She was second in the world title in 1980, when the IAAF organized an event as a consolation for the 400 metres hurdles being left out of the Olympics.

Ellen Fiedler of East Germany will be seeking to regain her top ranking in the 400 metres hurdles in Los Angeles ▼

Jane Furniss (GBR)
1500/3000 metres
Born: August 23, 1960, Sheffield, England.
Height: 165cm/5ft 5in.
Weight: 57kg/125.5lb.
Career Highlights
World Championships: *3000* seventh 1983.
European Cup: *3000* bronze 1983.

While most of the attention centred on Wendy Sly in the Helsinki 3000 metres, Jane Furniss's achievement did not go unnoticed. She ran better than ever before to finish seventh and shock several more fancied runners. She followed this up with another storming run in the European Cup final.

◄ ◄
Soviet veteran Olga Dvrina has been an international athlete for 12 years

Liubov Gurina heads Britain's Lorraine Baker and Shireen Bailey during the GB-USSR international in 1983 ▶ ▶

Jacqueline Gareau (CAN)
Marathon
Born: March 10, 1953, Conte Labelle, Canada.
Height: 157cm/5ft 1¾in.
Weight: 45kg/99lb.
Career Highlight
World Championships: *marathon* fifth 1983.
Boston marathon: first 1980.

Jacqueline Gareau specializes in the Boston marathon, having won it in 1980, finishing fifth in 1981 and second in both 1982 and last year. Her time of 2h 29:27 gave her a first sub 2h 30 mark.

She lives in Montreal and is coached by Gilles Lapierre.

Randy Givens (USA)
Sprints
Born: March 27, 1962, Amityville, USA.
Height: 168cm/5ft 6in.
Weight: 56kg/123lb.
Career Highlights
World Student Games: *200* gold 1983; *200* silver 1983.

Marlies Gohr (GDR), first woman to break the 11 seconds barrier for 100 metres ▼

Givens runs for Florida State and finished fourth in the 1983 American Championships. She won a place in the World Championship team because Chandra Cheeseborough was injured.

Marlies Gohr (GDR)
Sprints
Born: March 21, 1958, Gern, East Germany.
Height: 165cm/5ft 5in.
Weight: 55kg/121lb.
Career Highlights
Olympic Games: *100* silver 1980, eighth 1976.
World Championships: *100* gold 1983.
European Championships: *100* gold 1978, 1982; *200* silver 1982.
World Cup: *100* gold 1977, 1979, 1981, 1983; *200* silver 1979.
World Student Games: *100* gold 1979.
Record
World *100* 1977, 1982 (10.88), 1983 (10.81).

The psychology student was the first woman to crack 11 seconds for the 100 metres when at the East German Championships in 1977 she ran 10.88 cutting off 0.13. Since then she has been the world's greatest exponent of the 100 metres with her short pattering stride. Surprisingly she was beaten in the 1980 Olympic final, but she fought back to win the Helsinki title, although Ashford had to drop out.

Florence Griffith (USA)
Sprints
Born: December 21, 1959, Los Angeles, USA.
Height: 166cm/5ft 5in.
Weight: 59kg/130lb.
Career Highlight
World Championships: *200* fourth 1983.

One of the United States' supporting cast to Evelyn Ashford, she was fourth in the 1980 US Olympic trials, and she won the 1982 national collegiate title.

Liubov Gurina (URS)
800 metres
Born: August 6, 1957, USSR.
Height: 166cm/5ft 3in.
Weight: 56kg/123.5lb.
Career Highlights
World Championships: *800* silver 1983.

Gurina smashed her personal best in the Helsinki World Championships with 1:56.11, but still finished well adrift of Czech powerhouse Kratochvilova. '*I'm not pleased,*' said Liubov. '*I wanted to win.*' She may have to get used to disappointment again.

Linda Haglund (SWE)
Sprints
Born: June 15, 1956, Sweden.
Height: 170cm/5ft 7in.
Weight: 58kg/128lb.
Career Highlights
Olympic Games: *100* fourth 1980, ninth 1972.
European Championships: *100* silver 1978; *200* seventh 1978.

Haglund, one of the quickest starters on record, will need to be the subject of a change of heart by the Swedish authorities if she is to run. She was banned for drug-taking, although in her defence it was suggested she had taken 'medication' on expert advice without knowing its contents.

Bettine Jahn (GDR)
100 metres hurdles
Born: August 3, 1958, Karl Marx Stadt, East Germany.
Height: 170cm/5ft 7in.
Weight: 62kg/136lb.
Career Highlights
Olympic Games: *100h* seventh 1980.
World Championships: *100h* gold 1983.
European Championships: *100h* fourth 1982.
European Cup: *100h* gold 1983.

A textile student, Jahn was only fourth in the Athens European Championships, but was the world's best in 1983 with World Championship and European Cup wins.

Her time of 12.36 in Helsinki was the fastest ever, but the wind was + 2.4 mps, just over the legal limit.

Tatyana Kazankina
(USSR)
800/1500/3000 metres
Born: December 17, 1951,
   Petrovsk, USSR.
Height: 160cm/5ft 3in.
Weight: 50kg/110lb.
Career Highlights
Olympics: *1500* gold 1980,
   1976.
World Championships: *3000*
   bronze 1983.
European Championships: *1500*
   fourth 1974.
World Cup: *1500* first 1977.
European Cup: *1500* first 1975;
   1500 first 1977; *3000* first
   1983.
Record
World *800* 1976 (1:54.94);
   1500 1976 (3:56.00), 1980
   (3:55.00), 1980 (3:52.47).

The tiny Soviet girl has successfully combined the twin roles of
athlete and mother as well as anyone. Although she had been in the
national team since 1972 she did
not make any remarkable impact
until Montreal and the 1976 Olympics.

She had finished fourth in the
1974 European Championship
1500 metres and was selected for
this distance at Montreal. She justified her position as favourite by
reducing her personal best to 3:56
and taking a remarkable 5.4 seconds off the world record. It was an
improvement of 9.9 seconds on
her own best in two races!

The confidence of this run
brought her success in the 800
too. In the period leading up to the
Olympics she lowered her two lap
best time from 2:01.7 to 1.56.6
and although she did not want to
double up the selectors insisted.

It was an inspired decision. In
the first of the two finals, the 800,
her pattering sprint took her from
fifth to first in the last 50 metres to
record a world record 1:54.9 and
four days later the same finishing
burst gave her victory in the 1500
in 4:05.5.

Although in 1977 she won the
World and European Cup 1500s
she was not much seen again until
1980 and Moscow, by which time
she had given birth to a baby girl.
The baby was nearly two when her
mother lowered her world 1500
metres record to 3.55, won the
Olympic title and then, 12 days
later in Zurich, took the record
down to 3:52.47, which was faster
than Paavo Nurmi's male world
record 56 years before.

She went back into retirement to
have another baby and emerged

again for the World Championships
in Helsinki in 1983. But this time
Mary Decker, who had been barred
by President Carter from competing at the Moscow Olympics, was
there and the American girl won,
with Kazankina fading to third in
the last strides. She failed to
appear for the 1500 metres, but
ran in the European Cup 3000
metres at Crystal Palace and won.

Margit Klinger (FRG)
800 metres
Born: June 22, 1960, Honebach,
   West Germany.
Height: 165cm/5ft 5in.
Weight: 55kg/121lb.
Career Highlights
World Championships: *800* fourth
   1983.
European Championships: *800*
   bronze 1982.
European Cup: *800* fourth 1981,
   bronze 1983.
Record
National *800* 1982 (1:57.82).

Margit Klinger is threatening to
break the East European dominance at 800 metres, although
she has the formidable Jarmila
Kratochvilova to beat nowadays.
But Margit, being nine years
younger, has time on her side. She
broke through in the Athens European Championships, when her
time of 1:57.82 behind Olga
Mineyeva and Ludmila Veselkova of
the USSR gave her a new West
German record.

She followed this up with fourth
place in the Helsinki World Championships and then third in the
European Cup, each time beaten
by Kratochvilova. But she can
afford to wait.

Kerstin Knabe (GDR)
100 metres hurdles
Born: July 7, 1959, Oschatz, East
   Germany.
Height: 180cm/5ft 11in.
Weight: 70kg/154lb.
Career Highlights
World Championships: *100h* silver
   1983.

Coached by Frank Rudiger, she
competes for Leipzig. A powerful
sprinter and fluent hurdler, Kerstin
is a typical East German product,
who lives in the shadow of team-
mate Bettine Jahn.

Tatyana Kocembova (TCH)
400 metres
Born: May 2, 1962, Prague,

Czechoslovakia.
Height: 168cm/5ft 6in.
Weight: 55kg/121lb.
Career Highlights
World Championships: *400* silver
   1983.
European Championships: *400*
   bronze 1982.
European Cup: *400* gold 1983.

Understudy to the amazing
Kratochvilova, the young Kocem-
bova looks set to follow Jarmila as a
champion. Inspired by her elder
team-mate's exploits she improved
from sixth place in the 1979 European Juniors to third in Athens,
when she was only 20.

But although the Czech relay
team in the World Championships
contained both the winner and
runner up of the individual event
they could not catch the East
Germans.

*Tatyana Kazankina has held
four World Records at 800
and 1500 metres* ▼

7.08 in January 1983. Incredible versatility.

From 1977 to 1982 she was beaten only four times in finals at 200 and 400, the first in the 1977 Olympic Day meet by Monika Hamann over 200, then in September by Irena Szewinska, the Pole she succeeded as 400m record holder, in the World Cup in Dusseldorf.

The third was in the next World Cup over 200 metres by Evelyn Ashford and finally in the third World Cup in Rome, when Jarmila Kratochvilova, of Czechoslovakia, beat her over 400 metres. It was the first time Koch had been beaten at the one lap event in four years, although Kratochvilova did beat her in a heat of the Moscow Olympics.

Koch gained revenge for the last World Cup defeat by taking the European title in Athens, and beating Kratochvilova while setting her last world record.

Injury prevented her preparing for the 400 in the inaugural world championships in Helsinki and she decided to concentrate on the sprints and relays. She collected three golds and a silver, but in the 400 Kratochvilova became the fastest woman of all time – the first to duck under the 48 second barrier.

They met only in the 4 x 400 metres relay and then not directly. Koch was not on her usual anchor leg, being chosen for the third lap. Kratochvilova was on lap four and she nearly brushed Koch aside as the East German stood exhausted at the end of her leg. Next Kratochvilova beat her over 200 in the European Cup at Crystal Palace and now Koch and her coach, Wolfgang Meier, will have to find something special for the 1984 Olympics in Los Angeles.

Whatever happens in the future she has the satisfaction of knowing that she was voted the best female athlete in the world in 1978, 1979 and 1982.

East Germany's incomparable Marita Koch, first woman to go sub 22 secs for 200 metres and sub 49 secs for 400 metres ◀ ◀

Marita Koch (GDR)
100/200/400 metres
Born: February 18, 1957, Wismar, East Germany.
Height: 170cm/5ft 7in.
Weight: 63kg/139lb.
Career Highlights
Olympics: *400* gold 1980; *4 x 400* silver 1980.
World Championships: *200,* gold 1983; *4 x 100, 4 x 400;* gold 1983; *100* silver 1983.
European Championships: *400* gold 1978, 1982; *4 x 400 relay* gold 1978.
World Cup: *400* silver 1979, 1981; *4 x 400 relay* gold 1977, 1979, 1981; *200* silver 1979.
European Cup: *400* first 1979, 1981; *4 x 400 relay;* gold 1979, 1981; *4 x 100* silver 1983; *200* silver 1983.
Record
World *200;* 1978 (22.06), 1979 (22.02), (21.71); *400;* 1978 (49.19), (49.03), (48.94), 1979 (48.89), (48.60); 1982 (48.16); *4 x 100* 1979 (42.10); *4 x 100* 1982 (3:19.04).

This tall, slim, elegant medical student gives the lie to the popular image of East German women athletes as unsmiling automatons. And she is unquestionably the greatest sprinter/400 metres runner of the last half decade. Now based in Rostock, Marita burst into prominence in the 1975 European Junior Championships in Athens, when she won a gold in the relay and a silver in the individual 400. From then on her path to the very top was paved with gold. She became the first woman to break 49 seconds for the 400m and the first to run under 22 seconds for the 200m. She even set a world indoor best at 60m with

Lyudmila Kondratyeva
(USSR)
100/200 metres
Born: April 11, 1958, Shakhty, USSR.
Height: 168cm/5ft 6in.
Weight: 57kg/125lb.
Career Highlights
Olympic Games: *100* gold 1980.
European Championships: *200* gold 1978; *4 x 100 relay* gold 1978; *100* sixth, semi-finalist 1982.

The power of Jarmila Kratochvilova who scored an 'impossible' double at the World Championships ▶

World Cup: *200* bronze 1979; *100* fourth.
European Cup: *200* first 1979; *100* silver 1979.
Record
National *100* (11.06).

The girl who started her athletic career as a high jumper, before turning to the sprints and the long jump, was a shock winner of the Moscow Olympic 100m, when she beat the overwhelming favourite and then world record holder Marlies Gohr of East Germany. Until then Lyudmila had been best known as a 200 metres runner, winning the Prague European title (by beating Gohr) two years previously. But Gohr had beaten her easily in the 100 and the Soviet was ranked well below her in 1980. Going into the Olympics, she clocked a hand timed 10.9 and although this was doubted she proved it was no fluke with an 11.06 time despite a pulled mus-

cle in the last few strides. Her great victory was a contrast in styles, Kondratyeva, small and lithe with long legs; Gohr short and chunky, with quick moving, short legs.

The injury kept her out of the 200 and the sprint relay, and was still bothering her in 1981. She came back in 1982 to run in the Athens European Championships, but only managed to make the semi-final.

Jarmila Kratochvilova
(TCH)
400/800 metres
Born: January 26, 1951, Czechoslovakia.
Height: 170cm/5ft 7in.
Weight: 67kg/148lb.
Career Highlights
Olympic Games: *400* silver 1980.
World Championships: *400, 800* gold 1983; *4 x 400 relay* silver 1983.

European Championships: *400* semi-finals 1978; *400* silver 1982; *4 x 400* silver 1982.
World Cup: *400* first 1981; *4 x 400* silver (with European team) 1981.
European Cup: *200* first 1983; *800* and *400* gold 1983.
Record
World *400* 1983 (47,99); *800* 1983 (1:53.28).
National *100* 1981 (11.09), 1980 (hand timed 11.0); *200* 1981 (21.97).

This amazing Czech reached the top with a burst after a long, undistinguished career. She took up athletics at the age of 12, running cross country against the boys in her small village some 100 kilometres from Prague, but did not make any sort of impression until 1980 and the Moscow Olympics. Since then the unmarried Jarmila, who has a steady boyfriend, has got better and better and is unquestionably the world's most remarkable female athlete.

In Moscow she had to be content with second place in the 400 behind her great rival Marita Koch. Although she beat Koch in the World Cup 400 in Rome in 1981, Koch's mastery continued in 1982 and Jarmila was once again runner up in the 400m, as the East German set new world record figures of 48.16.

It was this mark which remained Kratochvilova's motivating target during the winter's hard work. As well as usual training she maintains her body strength by throwing hay around on her parents' farm. But with Koch having injury problems and opting out of the 400 in the 1983 World Championships, Jarmila had to find another challenge, and she did in the almost 'impossible' 400/800 double.

It was thought to be impossible because there was only half an hour or so between the 400 semi final and the 800 final on the Tuesday. Jarmila had run only three 800 races in her life although she broke the world record in her third.

Amazingly she attempted the double and captured it, breaking the 400 world record in the process, becoming the first woman in history to duck under 48 seconds. She was 32 years old when she managed that and she decided that 1983 would be her year, ending it with another head to head clash with Koch at 200. They met in the European Cup and Jarmila won on the line.

Brigitte Kraus (FRG)
1500/3000 metres
Born: August 12, 1956,
  Bensberg, West Germany.
Height: 180cm/5ft 11in.
Weight: 57kg/125lb.
Career Highlights
Olympic Games: *1500* semi finals
  1976, 1980.
World Championships: *3000* silver
  1983.
European Cup: *3000* fifth 1977;
  1500 sixth 1979; fourth 1981.
Record
National: *1500* 1978 (4:01.54);
  3000 1983 (8.35.11).

Nothing in the career of the tall, friendly, West German suggested she would win a medal in Helsinki. Until then she had been a typical West European also-ran in a series of races dominated by Eastern European thoroughbreds.

The Soviets kept Olga Mineyeva in reserve last season. She will be ready for Los Angeles.
◀

But in 1983 things changed. She switched back to the 3000 and, no doubt inspired by another Westerner, Mary Decker of America, charged after the leaders in the Helsinki 3000. Decker won, of course, but Kraus hung on and eventually passed the great Tatyana Kazankina in the last few strides.

Olga Mineyeva (URS)
800 metres
Born: October 1, 1952, Degtyarsk,
  Sverdlovsk, USSR.
Height: 177cm/5ft 9½in.
Weight: 61kg/134.5lb.

Career Highlights
Olympic Games: *800* silver
  1980.
European Championships: *800*
  gold 1982.

Such is the strength of Soviet middle distance running that they could afford to give both Olizarenko and Mineyeva a fallow year in 1983 ready for an all-out attack in Los Angeles, even though these two were first and second in Moscow!

Mineyeva competed at a lower level last year, although she popped up in Budapest to beat Klinger, among others.

Nadyezhda Olizarenko, facing the duel of her life against Kratochvilova ▶ ▶

Sue Morley (GBR)
400 metres hurdles
Born: January 6, 1960,
   Rotherham, England.
Height: 167cm/5ft 6in.
Weight: 57kg/125.5lb.
Career Highlights
World Championships: *400h*
   seventh 1983.
Commonwealth Games: *400h*
   fourth 1982.
European Cup: *400h* bronze
   1983.

Sue Morley gave up her job with a local police authority because she couldn't get enough time to concentrate on athletics. The move paid off when she not only reached the World Championships final, but also broke Chris Warden's British record. She was the second non-Eastern-bloc athlete home, behind European champion Ann-Louise Skoglund. Her bronze in the European Cup final was a reward for her single-mindedness.

Sue Morley, British record holder over 400 metres hurdles ▼

Rosa Mota (POR)
Marathon
Born: June 29, 1958, Lisbon,
   Portugal.
Height: 157cm/5ft 2in.
Weight: 45kg/99lb.
Career Highlights
World Championships: *marathon*
   fourth 1983.
European Championships:
   marathon gold 1982.

Mota's first marathon was the European Championships in Athens, which she won, and her second brought fourth place in Helsinki. Her third was in Chicago, where she won in 2:31.12. Each marathon gets faster.
   She also won the Sao Paulo round the houses in 1982, 1983 and 1984.

Nadyezhda Olizarenko
(URS)
800/1500 metres

Born: November 28, 1953,
   Bryansk, USSR.
Height: 165cm/5ft 4in.
Weight: 54kg/119lb.
Career Highlights
Olympic Games: *800* gold 1980;
   1500 bronze 1980.
European Championships: *800*
   silver 1978.
World Cup: *800* silver 1979.
Record
World *800* 1980 (1:54.85),
   (1:53.43).

Olizarenko, married to Olympic steeplechaser Sergey Olizarenko, has only one gold medal in her collection, but what a gold medal. In front of her home crowd in the Moscow Olympics she won the 800 metres and obliterated the world and Olympic records.
   She was running the 400 metres in 1970, and it took her a long seven years to reach world class. As well as the silver in the 800 metres in the Prague European Championships, she also won a silver in the 4 x 400 metres relay.
   She ran 1:58 last year, but the Soviets were saving her for Los Angeles and a battle royal with Kratochvilova.

Tall and cool, Merlene Ottey shows her thoroughbred style ▶

Irina Podyalovskaya, held in reserve for Los Angeles ▶▶

in 1978 at the age of 20, but marriage in 1980 deflected her attention from the Olympics and the baby stopped her competing again at top level until last year.

Yekaterina Podkopayeva (URS)
800/1500 metres
Born: June 11, 1952, Moscow, USSR.
Height: 164cm/5ft 4½in.
Weight: 52kg/114.6lb.
Career Highlight
World Championships: *1500* bronze 1983.

One of the USSR's many 800 metres runners who would be British number one if she had been born in the UK. She ran 1:57 in 1980, but was not good enough to win Olympic selection for the Moscow Games.

Merlene Ottey (JAM)
Sprints
Born: May 10, 1960, Kingston, Jamaica.
Height: 175cm/5ft 9in.
Weight: 58kg/128lb.
Career Highlights
Olympic Games: *200* bronze 1980.
World Championships: *100* fourth 1983, silver 1983.
Commonwealth Games: *100* silver 1982: *200* gold 1982.
Record
Central American *100* 1982 (11.03), *200* 1982 (22.17).

Cousin of Milt Ottey, the Canadian high jumper, Merlene is threatening to match the East Europeans in Los Angeles.

She is currently attending the University in Nebraska.

Maria Pinigina (URS)
400 metres
Born: February 9, 1958, Ivanovka, Kirghiz, USSR.
Height: 171cm/5ft 7in.
Weight: 58kg/128lb.
Career Highlights
World Championships: *400* bronze 1983.
European Championships: *400* fourth 1978.
World Cup: *400* silver 1979.
European Cup: *400* silver 1979, 1983.

Maria is still getting back to her best following the birth of a baby in 1981. She burst into prominence

Irina Podyalovskaya (URS)
800/1500 metres
Born: October 19, 1959, Moscow, Russia.
Height: 165cm/5ft 5in.
Weight: 52kg/114.5lb.
Career Highlight
World Student Games: *800* gold 1983.

Podyalovskaya moved down from 5000 metres and was ranked sixth in the USSR over 800 with 1:59.64 in 1982.
   The Russians deliberately left her out of their Helsinki team — they picked only two instead of the maximum three — obviously holding her back so she could concentrate on the Olympics.

▲
Over the hill at 30? Not Maricica Puica of Romania

Ann-Louise Skoglund with her European Championship-winning bouquet ►►

didn't do much at top level until she was twenty-nine. She was the first woman to beat Grete Waitz in a cross country race, but after a successful 1982 she had a bad season in 1983.

Ann-Louise Skoglund
(SWE)
400 metres hurdles
Born: June 28, 1962, Karstad, Sweden.
Height: 175cm/5ft 9in.
Weight: 63kg/132lb.
Career Highlights
World Championships: *400h* sixth 1983.
European Championships: *400h* gold 1982.

The Swedish girl's European title was one of the big shocks of 1982, but although she kept her form last year she was overtaken by five East Europeans in the World Championships.

Maricica Puica (ROM)
1500/3000 metres
Born: July 29, 1950, Bucharest, Romania.
Height: 166cm/5ft 5in.
Weight: 55kg/121lb.
Career Highlights
Olympic Games: *1500* seventh 1980.
European Championships: *1500* fourth 1982, eleventh 1978; *3000* silver 1982, fourth 1978.
World Cup: *3000* silver 1981.
European Cup: *3000* silver 1979, 1977.
World Student Games: *1500* silver 1977.
Records:
World *mile* 1982 (4:17.44).

Maricica Puica is now better known over the country — she

Wendy Sly (GBR)
1500/3000 metres
Born: November 5, 1959, Slough, England.
Height: 163cm/5ft 4in.
Weight: 52kg/114.5lb.
Career Highlights
World Championships: *1500* fifth 1983; *3000* fifth 1983.
Commonwealth Games: *3000* silver 1982.
European Cup: *1500* fourth 1983.
World Student Games: *1500* sixth 1981.

Wendy Sly's emergence in 1983 as a world class distance runner proved a long-held theory, that British girls could match the world's best, if they had regular overseas competition. She had to spend time in the USA to develop into one of the world's top runners.
Married to miler Chris Sly, she won the first IAAF 10000 metres title in December 1983.

Joyce Smith (GBR)
Marathon
Born: October 26, 1937, London,
England.
Height: 169cm/5ft 6½in.
Weight: 54kg/119lb.
Career Highlights
Olympic Games: *1500* semi-finals
1972.
World Championships: *marathon*
ninth 1983.
European Championships: *3000*
bronze 1974; *1500* eighth
1972.
London marathon: first 1981,
1982.

Joyce Smith's story is one of the
most remarkable in athletic history.
At 42, Joyce, with a relatively successful career as a track athlete
behind her, turned to marathon
running.

In 1981, at 43, she won the
London marathon in 2:29.57 the
first time a British woman had
beaten 2:30. The following year
she won London again, and took
14 seconds off her record. No
other British woman has yet run
under 2:30. She missed the European Championships in 1982 —
the first time a women's marathon
had been included in a major
championship. She ran in Helsinki
however, and finished ninth, the
first of the British trio to finish.
Before this late burst of activity
Joyce had been good enough to
win a bronze in the women's 3000
metres in Rome.

Shirley Strong (GBR)
100 metres hurdles
Born: November 18, 1958,
Northwich, England.
Height: 168cm/5ft 6in.
Weight: 53kg/117lb.
Career Highlights
World Championships: *100h* fifth
1983.
Commonwealth Games: *100h* gold
1982, silver 1978.
European Cup: *100h* fifth 1983,
fourth 1981.

First non-Eastern European
finisher in Helsinki, Strong, blonde
and glamorous, broke into world
class in late 1982, when she won a
Commonwealth gold.

A heavy smoker, she received a
large sponsorship late last year
which enabled her to concentrate
totally on her sport.

Angella Taylor (CAN)
Sprints
Born: September 28, 1958,
Kingston, Jamaica.
Height: 162cm/5ft 3½in.
Weight: 61kg/134.5lb.
Career Highlights
World Championships: *100*
seventh 1983.
Commonwealth Games: *100* gold
1982; *200* bronze 1982.
World Cup: *100* fourth 1981, fifth
1979; *200* fourth 1981, fifth
1979.
World Student Games: *100* bronze
1983; *200* fourth 1983.

One of the new breed of Canadian
runners from the West Indies —
Canada is benefiting from the
Caribbean, just like Britain.

Taylor won the Commonwealth
100 metres title but couldn't sustain her form into 1983.

Grete Waitz (NOR)
Marathon
Born: October 11, 1953, Oslo,
Norway.
Height: 172cm/5ft 7in.
Weight: 54kg/119lb.
Career Highlights
World Championships: *marathon*
gold 1983.
European Championships: *1500*
fifth 1978, bronze 1974; *3000*
bronze 1978.
World Cup: *3000* silver 1979, gold
1977.
Records:
World *marathon* 1983 (best
2:25.29).
World *3000* 1976 (8:45.4), 1975
(8:46.6).
New York marathon: first 1978,
1979, 1980, 1982.
London marathon: first 1983.
World Cross Country: gold 1978,
1979, 1980, 1981, 1983.

Grete Waitz at last found a major
championship event which suited
her when they added the women's
marathon to the World Championship programme. For although the
blond Norwegian, coached by her
schoolteacher husband Jack, has
twice held the world 3000 record
she had always been outkicked on
the track.

On the cross country field it has
been a different matter. In six
races from 1978 she won five
world cross country titles. The
crowds in New York loved her,
because she won their marathon
three times, each time improving
the world's best time, until she was
forced to drop out in 1981. That
marked the start of a 'low' in her
career. She developed a stress
fracture in her right foot and this
forced her out of the Athens European Championships, the first
major championship marathon for
women.

She came back to win New York
in 1982 and then in London
equalled the world best, set by
Allison Roe of New Zealand in New
York in 1981. But as she predicted, the time lasted only one
day. Joan Benoit of the USA ran a
new world best in Boston 24 hours
later. Unfortunately Benoit was not
in the Helsinki field, having
refused to take part in the American trial. Amazingly it was the first
time Grete had run a marathon
without being surrounded by a
pack of admiring men.

▲
*Angella Taylor, helping to
put the zip back into
Canada*

◄ ◄
*Britain's fabulous Over 40,
Joyce Smith, housewife,
mum, and Marathon
marvel*

Priscilla Welch (GBR)

Marathon
Born: November 22, 1944,
    Bedfordshire, England.
Height: 165cm/5ft 5in.
Weight: 47.5kg/105lb.
Career Highlights
New York marathon: second 1983.

Priscilla Welch's first marathon was a 3h 26 effort in Stockholm in 1979, the year she took up jogging. Her best was 2h 32:3 in New York when she finished second. The time was the second fastest ever run by a British woman. Only Joyce Smith among her compatriots had run faster.

The ex-Wren's rise is typical of the running boom that swept over from the USA. She has got steadily faster and is now aiming at the Olympics. Her lack of experience is alleviated by regular running sessions with former Commonwealth 1500 metres champion Sheila Carey and advice from John Anderson, coach to Dave Moorcroft.

Diane Williams, boycotted out of Moscow
◄

◄ ◄
Barbel Wockel, aiming for a record fifth gold medal in Los Angeles

Diane Williams (USA)

Sprints
Born: December 14, 1961,
    Chicago, USA.
Height: 162cm/5ft 3½in.
Weight: 55kg/121lb.
Career Highlights
World Championships: *100* bronze
    1983.

A former student of Michigan State, Williams was one of the unlucky Americans who made the Olympic team in 1980 but did not go to Moscow because of President Carter's boycott.

Barbel Wockel (GDR)

Sprints
Born: March 21, 1955, Leipzig,
    East Germany.
Height: 174cm/5ft 8½in.
Weight: 62kg/137.5lb.
Career Highlights
Olympic Games: *200* gold 1976,
    1980; *relay* gold 1976, 1980.
European Championships: *100*
    silver 1982, seventh 1974; *200*
    gold 1982.
World Cup: *200* silver 1977,
    bronze 1982.
European Cup: *200* gold 1981,
    bronze 1977.
Record
Olympic: *200* 1980 (22.03 1980).

One of the great competitors who has never been given proper credit. Between Montreal and Moscow she took time off to have a baby but still won the 200 metres in 1980. She has been overshadowed by Gohr and Koch but the tall, powerful Wockel, while never holding a world record, is the one to back when it matters.

She did not take part in Helsinki because of a virus in July, but is aiming to win a record fifth gold in Los Angeles. No woman has taken more than four golds. Her best chance would seem to be in the 4 x 400 metres relay.

Athletics: Field Events

Field events appeared quite early on in the history of the Ancient Olympic Games, in the *pentathlon*, a five-event contest involving running, long jumping, throwing and wrestling. Jumpers were permitted to use hand-held weights which allowed longer distances to be achieved. It is recorded that Chionis of Sparta, who won gold medals in three successive Olympics, jumped 7.05m (23ft 1½in) in the middle of the seventh century BC. If correct this record remained unbeaten for 2500 years.

Comparisons are invidious, however, for the events contested in ancient times bear faint resemblance to their modern counterparts, and style and accuracy were often more important than the distance achieved. The weights of discus and javelin implements and styles of throwing were also different from today's. Javelins were usually thrown with the aid of a sling fixed to the end of the shaft, while discus throwers threw from a raised dais.

In the first Olympic Games of modern times, at Athens in 1896, there were six field events — four jumps, a shot and a discus competition. The shot and discus were contested from marked out squares of 2.13m (7ft 0in) and 2.50m (8ft 2½in) respectively, rather than the circles now used. The first Olympic champion of the new era was James Connolly of the United States, the winner of the triple jump (then known as the hop, step and jump). He and his team mates won all six field events, a domination continued four years later in Paris. By 1900 the athletics programme had been extended to 24 events and included a tug-of-war. There were ten field contests, the hammer and three standing jumps having been added since Athens. These standing jumps — high, long and triple — were attempted from a standing position without prior movement of the feet, and they gave the Olympics one of its most remarkable champions. Stricken by polio as a child, Ray Ewry (USA) amassed a total of ten individual gold medals over four Games (including those of 1906). No other Olympic competitor has ever equalled this total.

Another American, Irving Baxter, achieved a unique double in Paris. He won both the high jump and pole vault titles, as well as placing in all three standing jumps. The hammer was thrown from a 2.74m (9ft) circle and won by John Flanagan (USA) who began a domination of the event by Irish-born throwers which lasted until 1936. The rather lax entry regulations of the time were illustrated by the winning tug-of-war team which was composed of four men from Sweden and four from Denmark. The French organising committee made some unfortunate decisions including the transfer of a number of finals to Sunday. This effectively barred a number of potential American winners from those events as their colleges, which had sent them to the Games, had strict rules about competition on that day. It almost certainly prevented Myer Prinstein, an athlete of the Jewish faith who attended a strongly Methodist university, from gaining the long jump title. Even stranger, his qualifying jump from the Saturday was allowed to count in the final and he was awarded the silver medal. Third place went to an Irish Catholic representing Great Britain. The winner, Alvin Kraenzlein, was from one of the American universities that allowed their athletes to compete on Sunday. He ended the Games with four individual gold medals, a record never equalled by a track and field athlete at a single Games.

The field events of the 1904 Games at St Louis were an American preserve with only three medals out of a possible 33 going to foreign competitors, including the only gold medallist Etienne Desmarteau, the winner of the new 56lb weight throw. Desmarteau, a Montreal policeman, was thrown off the force for taking unofficial leave in order to compete in St Louis. Needless to say he was immediately reinstated. Sadly, he enjoyed his fame for only a short time as he died from typhoid the following year. A park in his home city was named after him. In the long jump, justice of another kind was finally served when the unfortunate Prinstein won with a new Olympic record jump. As expected, Ray Ewry triumphed in the standing jumps, while in the standing high jump a silver medal was won by fellow American Joseph Stadler. Stadler and his team-mate, hurdler George Poage, were the first black athletes to win Olympic medals.

The so-called Intercalated Games of 1906 were held as a tenth anniversary celebration of the inaugural meeting. There were a number of innovations, not least the introduction of the javelin, in which Sweden took all three medals, a feat achieved previously in a field event only by the United States. The Greek style discus throw was won by Finland's Werner Jaervinen, doyen of one of the great Olympic families. One son,

▲
Bob Garrett of the USA, discus and shot champion of 1896

Ray Ewry of the USA, seven gold medals between 1900 and 1908 ▶

Matti, won the 1932 javelin, another, Akilles, placed second in the 1928 and 1932 decathlon competitions, and yet another, Kalle, competed in 1932 as a shot putter. High jumper Con Leahy and triple jumper Peter O'Connor (then world record holder in the long jump) both won the first ever gold medals by Britons in field events. Since their triumphs British jumpers have won only another three, and no British athlete has ever won an Olympic throwing event.

London, in 1908, was the scene of Ray Ewry's swansong, along with another American of almost equal Olympian stature, Martin Sheridan. In the Games of 1904, 1906 and 1908 Sheridan brought his medals total to five gold, three silver and one bronze won in various throws and standing jump events. There was yet another Irish-American victory in the hammer when John Flanagan won his third consecutive title, a feat equalled by few athletes, and only exceeded by the discus thrower Al Oerter in the 1950s and 1960s.

The outstanding personality of the 1912 Games was the American Indian Jim Thorpe. In addition to his superb decathlon and pentathlon victories (a total of 15 individual events) he also placed fifth in the ordinary high jump, only 2cm ($\frac{3}{4}$in) from a bronze medal, and seventh in the long jump. Over a period of five days he competed in 11 separate field events and six track events. The United States took the lion's share of the medals in the jumps, but they were beginning to be challenged by the Scandinavians in the throws, where the Finns were making their presence felt. The standing jumps were contested for the last time, and added a footnote to Olympic history when Platt and Ben Adams (USA) were the first brothers to win medals in the same event at one Games. Javelin throwing reached a new peak when Eric Lemming (SWE) won his third consecutive title with a new world record of 60.64m (198ft 11in). Two days later his runner-up Julius Saaristo of Finland turned the tables

Brother! Platt Adams collects silver in the 1912
▼ standing broad jump
▼ behind Ben Adams

John Flanagan winner of three consecutive Hammer titles
▼

by winning the two-handed event (in which the best throws, using first the right hand and then the left, are added together) and improved the world mark to 61.00m (200ft 1in).

In the first Games after World War I the fortunes of the previously all-conquering United States were sharply reversed in some of the field events. They lost the long jump title for the first time, to William Pettersson of Sweden. This was not to happen again for 44 years. Ville Porhola (FIN) won the shot title after six consecutive American wins, and Finns took the first four places in the javelin. The 56lb weight throw, contested for the last time in the Olympics, was won by Pat McDonald (USA) who became the oldest ever Olympic track and field gold medallist 26 days after his forty-second birthday.

At the Paris Games of 1924 the United States were finally toppled, albeit temporarily, from their position of supremacy in track and field, when they won 'only' 12 of the 27 events on the programme. However, they won eight field events. The high jump gold medallist, Harold Osborn (USA), whose style of pressing the bar back into the uprights as he cleared it led to a change in the rules, also won the decathlon gaining a unique double. Long jumping at these Games was also notable for the event was won by William DeHart Hubbard (USA) — the first black athlete to win an Olympic gold medal. However, Hubbard's winning distance was well below that achieved the previous day by a team-mate, Robert LeGendre, in the pentathlon long jump. LeGendre, who just failed to make the US team in his main event, set a world record of 7.76m (25ft 5½in) in the long jump on his way to gaining the bronze medal in the five-event contest. Japan's Mikio Oda was sixth in the triple jump a portent of things to come. His country would soon make a significant contribution to Olympic jumping events. Malcolm Nokes, third in the hammer competition, became the last Briton to win an Olympic medal in a throwing event. In fact only shot putter Denis Horgan had ever placed higher, with a silver in 1908.

The decline in the United States' fortunes continued in track and field at Amsterdam in 1928, when they gained a mere eight gold medals, of which five were in the field events. Mikio Oda won Japan's first Olympic gold medal with a leap of 15.21m (49ft 11in) in the triple jump. This height was later commemorated by the height of the Olympic flag pole at the 1964 Games in Tokyo. Other 'new' countries made their mark at Amsterdam. The Irishman Pat O'Callaghan, whose homeland was competing as a separate entity for the first time, won the hammer throw for Ireland, while the silver medallist in the long jump was the Haitian Silvio Cator, who broke the world record 40 days later. Another silver medallist, this time in the shot, rejoiced in the name of Herman Brix (USA). Some years later using the name Bruce Bennett, he starred as Tarzan in the movies, before moving on to more dramatic roles. Yet another silver medallist, Matt McGrath (USA) the 1912 hammer champion, won his third medal and in his forty-sixth year became the oldest field event athlete to gain an Olympic medal.

Perhaps the most significant performances of the 1928 Games were those of the competitors in the first Olympic athletic events for women. Two of the five events were the high jump and discus, and both world records were beaten. The charm and beauty of the Canadian high jump winner, Ethel Catherwood, did much to win over many of those opposed to the participation of women in Olympic track and field.

Though the United States regained some of its prestige in the 1932 Games the Americans lost the high jump title to a young Canadian, Duncan McNaughton, who was, ironically, at college in California. However, his win came only after a four-way jump-off with two Americans and a Filipino. The non-medallist of the four, Cornelius Johnson, had his chance again four years later, and then made no mistake. Japanese jumpers were now greatly feared and understandably so as Chuhei Nambu, then world long jump record-holder and bronze medallist in that event, broke his countryman Oda's Olympic and world mark to win the triple jump title. The Irishman Pat O'Callaghan retained his hammer crown while the javelin went to Matti Jaervinen, then the idol of Finland. In fact his winning distance of 72.71m (238ft 6½in) is said to be the height of the tower of the Helsinki stadium built years after his victory. The United States won all three of the women's field events (the javelin had been added to the schedule), with one of the stars of the Games competing in two of them. She was Mildred 'Babe' Didrikson, regarded as one of the greatest sportswomen ever. She later became one of the all-time best lady golfers. At Los Angeles she won the javelin

Imre Nemeth of Hungary, hammer champion in 1948. His son Miklos won the javelin gold in 1976

and 80 metres hurdles events before attempting a triple in the high jump. A most unusual ruling came in this event. Didrikson and her team mate Jean Shiley both cleared a world record height of 1.65m (5ft 5in), and then tied in a jump-off. The judges then decreed Babe's style of jumping illegal, as her head had cleared the bar first — against the regulation at that time. However, they didn't disqualify her completely, merely placing her second — one of the most bizarre decisions ever made in the Olympics.

The host country, Germany, won two of the first field events of the 1936 Games, the women's javelin and men's shot. The other one, men's high jump, went to one of the so-called 'black auxiliaries' of the US team, Cornelius Johnson. To emphasize his superiority he won the event still wearing his sweat suit, then removed it to set an Olympic record. But the hero of these Games was the immortal Jesse Owens (USA), whose long jump victory came between those in the 100 metres and 200 metres. His Olympic record of 8.06m (26ft 5½in) lasted for 24 years. In the triple jump Naoto Tajima, made it three in a row for Japan while two of his countrymen gave the US pole vaulters a long, grim struggle before having to settle for silver and bronze medals behind Earle Meadows. There was an amazing 11-way tie for sixth place in this competition. One of the greatest upsets occurred in the javelin when shot put bronze medallist Gerhard Stoeck of Germany beat the all-conquering Finns. Several of the competitors in the women's high jump later carved places for themselves in Olympic history. Dorothy Odam (GBR), placed second, was to repeat her silver medal success twelve years later; Fanny Koen (HOL) won a record four gold medals at Wembley in 1948; and Dora Ratjen of the host country, placed fourth, set a world record in the event in 1939 and was later exposed as Herman Ratjen, a man who had lived as a girl for a number of years.

It was unfortunate that the personality of the 1948 Games, now Fanny Blankers-Koen, of Holland, did not compete in any of the field events. As the then world record holder in both high and long jumps she must assuredly have added to her laurels. In her absence the spotlight in the women's field events, now increased to five, fell on Micheline Ostermeyer of France, whose gold medals in shot and discus, and bronze medal in the high jump belied her talent as a concert pianist. Despite the ravages of war and the absence of the Germans four records were set. Comparatively the standard in the men's events was lower than usual and some medals were won with mediocre performances. Nevertheless the gold medals were not won cheaply. Outstanding competitors were discus champion Adolfo Consolini of Italy, whose giant runner-up, countryman Giuseppe Tosi, was a member of the Papal Guard, and hammer champion Imre Nemeth of Hungary, whose son was to emulate him in the 1976 javelin. The Finns regained the javelin title at Wembley by courtesy of Tapio Rautavaara, who became a film star back home. Third place in the pole vault went to Bob Richards (USA) who went on to become the most famous athletic clergyman of all time.

◄
*Hal Connolly, 1956
hammer champion who
married the women's discus
champion, Olga Fikotova of
Czechoslovakia*

▲
*Al Oerter, four times
Olympic discus champion*

At the Helsinki Games of 1952 Olympic field event records crashed. In the men's contests only Owen's long jump mark survived, while in the female competitions only the high jump mark was not shattered. World records were broken: in the women's shot, by Galina Zybina (URS); in the hammer, by Jozsef Csermak (HUN); and in the triple jump, twice by Adhemar Ferreira da Silva of Brazil. The Soviet team, competing for the first time in the Olympic Games, won seven of the available nine medals in the women's throws. By winning the high jump Esther Brand became the first South African woman, and the last athlete from her country, to win an Olympic athletics gold medal. The winner of the male event, Walt Davis (USA), a victim of polio as a boy, became the tallest ever track and field gold medallist, when he cleared a bar set at his own height of 2.04m (6ft 8¼in). The odds-on favourite for the long jump title, George Brown (USA) horrified the fans, and himself, with three no-jumps, and exited from the competition. The women's discus title, won by Nina Romashkova, was the first gold medal in athletics to be won by an athlete representing the Soviet Union, although Tzarist Russia had been represented by medal winning athletes in the early Games. One of the most popular Helsinki winners was Dana Zatopkova of Czecho-slovakia who took the javelin gold medal within an hour of her husband, Emil, winning the 5000 metre event.

Three field event champions from Helsinki repeated their successes at Melbourne in 1956: the 'vaulting vicar' Bob Richards in the pole vault; Brazil's da Silva in the triple jump; and Parry O'Brien (USA) in the shot. World records went in the women's high and long jumps and in the men's javelin (the latter by a remarkable margin of 2.05m (6ft 8¾in). Two outstanding Olympic careers began at Melbourne. That of American Willye White stretched over five women's long jump finals, although she never bettered the silver medal she won in Melbourne. Her team mate Al Oerter won the first of four consecutive discus victories, an unprecedented feat. A fairytale postscript to the Games' field events came a year later when the American hammer champion, Hal Connolly, married the Czech winner of the ladies discus, Olga Fikotova, after they had fallen in love during the XVIth Olympics.

Although the Olympic record was beaten in 12 of the 13 field events at Rome in 1960, only the men's javelin mark surviving, media and crowd attention tended to be directed to the track events. Nevertheless, there was much drama and fine performances on the field. In the women's high jump a British athlete (Thelma Hopkins) won the silver medal for the fifth consecutive time. Bitterly disappointing from a British point of view was the failure of Mary Bignal (later Rand) to reproduce her qualifying round form in the long jump final. She led the qualifiers with 6.33m (20ft 9in), a distance which would have guaranteed the silver medal in that final, but nerves affected her performance and she placed only ninth. In the javelin Dana Zatopkova won the silver to become the oldest woman (37 years 8 months) to win an Olympic track and field medal. The winner of the discus, Nina Ponomaryeva (URS) recaptured the title she had first won in 1952, having come third in Melbourne. She was thus the only woman to regain an Olympic athletics title after losing it. In 1956 she had been accused of stealing a hat from a West End store and this had led to the cancellation of Britain's projected match against the Soviet Union. In the long jump the 24-year-old Olympic record of Jesse Owens was finally broken by Ralph Boston (USA), who had also broken Owens's world mark a month before. In the men's hammer and the women's discus the gold medal sweethearts of four years before, Connolly and Fikotova, now both representing the United States, placed eighth and seventh respectively. In the javelin perseverance finally paid off for Viktor Tsibulenko (USR). He had placed fourth in 1952 and third in 1956 but in Rome he finally hit the jackpot, when Janusz Sidlo of Poland, who had a longer throw in the qualifying round, failed to match it in the final. The huge Tamara Press (URS) went one better than her sister Irina, who had won the hurdles, by taking the gold medal in the shot and adding a silver in the discus.

There was another mass onslaught on the record book at Tokyo in 1964 – the Olympic mark was beaten in all but two of the 13 field events. These included a world best in the women's long jump by Mary Rand (GBR), the 'failure' of the 1960 Games. She was the first British woman to win an Olympic gold medal in an athletics event. Another world mark went in the women's javelin throw when Yelena Gorchakova (URS) broke the record in the qualifying competition. In the final she only just managed to salvage a bronze medal with a throw over 5m less than her new record. Parry O'Brien (USA), competing in his fourth Games, just failed to gain a fourth medal in the shot, although his 19.20m (63ft) put was superior to those that had previously won him two golds and a silver. The long jump victory of Lynn Davies gave Britain its first men's Olympic field events medal since 1924, and also the distinction of being the only country to win both long jumps at the same Games. Some American supporters, no doubt upset by the surprise defeat of defending champion Ralph Boston, suggested that the Welshman had only won because he was more used to the 'British' conditions – wet and windy – that prevailed on the day. Six months later when Davies beat the American again, indoors at Wembley, a British fan, sitting with some Americans, is reported to have put out his hand, looked up at the ceiling and said 'Ah, it's stopped'. Well beaten by Mary Rand in the women's jump, 18-year-old Irena Kirszenstein of Poland nevertheless won a silver medal to add to her two track event medals. Over the next four Olympic Games she would amass three gold, two silver and two bronze medals – a record, for a woman, of seven medals in five different events. At this Games Tamara Press went one better than at Rome by winning both shot and discus, and 'little' sister Irina, though missing out on a hurdles medal, won the new pentathlon competition by a big margin.

In 1968 the altitude of Mexico City was beneficial to field event athletes. It was undoubtedly a major factor behind Bob Beamon's (USA) stupifying leap in the long jump – he broke the world record by an unbelievable margin of 45cm ($17\frac{3}{4}$in) with a leap of 8.90m (29ft $2\frac{1}{2}$in) – a performance considered at the time to be of the twenty-first century. Mary Rand's mark was also beaten, exactly four years to the day after she had set it, by Viorica Viscopoleanu of Romania. Again Olympic records were broken in all but two events. In the triple jump there was one of the greatest ever mass attacks on a world record – it was improved five times by three athletes. Al Oerter became an Olympic immortal by winning his fourth consecutive discus title, while in the women's event Lia Manoliu of Romania, halfway through her thirty-seventh year, became the oldest woman ever to win an Olympic athletics event. By competing at the next Games as well she also became the only athlete, male or female, to compete in six Olympic Games. The high jump was won by Dick Fosbury (USA) whose highly unorthodox style of clearing the bar on his back soon swept the athletics world and revolutionized the event. The pole vault went on for seven hours before Bob Seagren (USA) won on countback, from two Germans, one from the West and the other from the East. The Soviet javelin thrower Janis Lusis was finally able to look his wife, Elvira, in the eye as he matched her gold medal win of 1960.

The United States really had a bad time at Munich in 1972 when they won only a single field event gold medal, in the men's long jump. Their losses included the pole vault title which had been theirs since 1896, apart from a slight hiccup at the Intercalated Games of 1906. However, in their defence, it should be noted that the United States vaulters were upset by a last minute ban on their then unorthodox poles. They also lost in two other American 'parade' events, the shot and discus. But most onlookers were too entranced by the tremendous standard of competition to even notice. The climax of the field event programme was the high jump victory and world record by the darling of the home crowd, Ulrike Meyfarth, at 16 years and 4 months the youngest athlete ever to win an individual Olympic gold medal. This followed other wins by home crowd favourites in the women's long jump, Heide Rosendahl, and men's javelin, in which Klaus Wolfermann beat defending champion Lusis by 2cm (less than an inch).

The African boycott had little effect on the field events at Montreal in 1976, with records broken in eight of them. The highlight was the unexpected world record in the javelin by Hungary's Miklos Nemeth, who added over 4m (13ft) to the Olympic mark. He now had a gold medal to match his father's from 1948. Viktor Saneyev (URS) won a record third consecutive triple jump title and went on to barely lose a fourth in Moscow. American athletes had to be content with only the discus and long jump gold medals. In the latter Arnie Robinson improved two places on his 1972 position to win, while Munich champion Randy Williams dropped one place. Other than Saneyev, only Ruth

In mid-air to history . . . Bob Beamon launches his phenomenal world record long jump of 29ft $2\frac{1}{2}$in in Mexico City's thin air ▲

Fuchs (GDR) in the javelin retained a title from the previous Games. For the first time since 1904 one country (the Soviet Union) won all three medals in the hammer. In the men's shot reigning world record holder Aleksandr Baryshnikov (URS) won the bronze medal using the new spin technique. Although only 5cm (2in) separated the medallists it was still a larger margin (by 1cm or $\frac{1}{4}$in) than that in the 1972 competition. Jacek Wszola of Poland, just five months prior to his twentieth birthday, was the youngest individual track and field champion of 1976 when he won the high jump in very wet conditions.

Many of the world's best field event athletes were absent from Moscow in 1980 because of a boycott by many countries protesting against the Soviet invasion of Afghanistan. Nevertheless, performances were excellent and included three superb world records. In the high jump an unheralded newcomer, Gerd Wessig (GDR) cleared 2.36m (7ft $8\frac{3}{4}$in) on his second attempt, and in the pole vault Wladyslaw Kozakiewicz of Poland also made it, jumping 5.78m (18ft $11\frac{1}{2}$in) on his second try. Unfortunately, the Pole had to endure some barracking from sections of the crowd, a happily rare phenomenon at Olympic gatherings. In retaining his hammer title Yuri Sedykh (URS) regained the world mark with 81.80m (268ft 4in) and again led his countrymen to a clean sweep of the medals. The long jump went to Lutz Dombrowski (GDR) with the second best leap of all time 8.54m (28ft $0\frac{1}{4}$in), while his female counterpart, Tatyana Kolpakova (URS) also became the second best jumper of all time with her 7.06m (23ft 2in). Other than Sedykh only the winner of the women's discus, Evelin Jahl (GDR), retained a title won at Montreal. By winning the women's javelin Maria Colon of Cuba won the first gold medal by a female athlete from the Caribbean.

Patrick Abada (FRA)
Pole vault
Born: March 20, 1954, France.
Height: 189cm/6ft 2½in.
Weight: 80kg/176lb.
Career Highlights
Olympic Games: *pole vault* fourth 1976.
World Championships: *pole vault* sixth 1983.
European Championships: *pole vault* ninth 1978, 1974.
World Student Games: *pole vault* bronze 1979.
World Cup: *pole vault* silver 1979.
European Cup: *pole vault* gold 1983, silver 1979, fourth 1974.

Kevin Atkins, sensation in Helsinki ►►

Patrick Abada of France, number three in the world in 1983 ▼

The veteran Abada made a great comeback after missing 1980/81. He failed to get to Athens but took third place in the French trials in 1983, and finished as top Frenchman in Helsinki.

He was rated number three in the world in 1983.

Ajayi Agbebaku (NGB)
Triple jump
Born: December 6, 1955, Benin, Nigeria.
Height: 185cm/6ft 1in.
Weight: 80kg/176lb.
Career Highlights
World Championships: *triple jump* bronze 1983.
World Cup: *triple jump* eighth 1981, seventh 1979.
World Student Games: *triple jump* gold 1983.

A surprise bronze medallist in the World Championships in 1983, Agbebaku has threatened to make good for several years, since enrolling at El Paso University in Texas.

In 1981 Agbebaku broke the African triple jump record with a leap of 16.88 metres.

Kevin Atkins (USA)
Shot
Born: January 27, 1960, USA.
Height: 196cm/6ft 5in.
Weight: 131kg/288.2lb.
Career Highlight
USA Championship: *shot* gold 1982.

Gennady Avdeyenko (URS)
High jump
Born: November 4, 1963, Odessa, USSR.
Height: 202cm/6ft 7½in.
Weight: 84kg/185lb.
Career Highlight
World Championships: *high jump* gold 1983.

He went to World Championships as Soviet number three, and took advantage of the cold and wet conditions to win. Avdeyenko was only sixth in the Spartakiad in 1983 with a best of 2.25 outdoors.

Avdeyenko is in the army, but wants to go to physical education college. Yet because he has perfect pitch, his teachers wanted him to go to music college.

Bela Bakosi (HUN)
Triple jump
Born: June 18, 1975, Budapest, Hungary.
Height: 180cm/5ft 11in.
Weight: 67kg/147.4lb.
Career Highlights
Olympic Games: triple jump seventh 1980.
World Championships: *triple jump* seventh 1983.
European Championships: *triple jump* bronze 1982, fifteenth 1978.
World Cup: *triple jump;* fifth 1981.
World Student Games: *triple jump* silver 1981, seventh 1979.

Some thought that Bakosi was fortunate to get the 1981 World Cup place in the Rest of Europe team ahead of Britain's Aston Moore. Bakosi could only finish fifth on that occasion, whereas Moore's second place in the European Cup final suggested he might have done better.

Willie Banks (USA)
Triple jump
Born: March 11, 1956, Travis, California, USA.
Height: 190cm/6ft 3in.
Weight: 77kg/170lb.
Career Highlights
World Championships: *triple jump* silver 1983.
Pan American Games: *triple jump* silver 1979.
World Cup: *triple jump* bronze 1981.

Willie Banks has turned one of track and field's more esoteric disciplines into a fun event with his bubbling personality and infec-

Atkins won the American championship at the age of 22 in 1982 and big things were expected of him. But he could not get it together in Helsinki and was a sensational non-qualifier considering he managed 21.61 in 1983. His best in Helsinki was 19.48.

from grace in Moscow, the huge black-jowled East German, still a 'sportstudent' at the age of 28, has ruled world shot-putting since he won a surprise gold in Montreal.

The Willie Banks roadshow attracts attention whenever it sets down. It should be particularly popular in California.
◄ ◄

Sergey Bubka (URS)
Pole vault
Born: December 14, 1963, USSR.
Height: 180cm/5ft 10¾in.
Weight: 68kg/150lb.
Career Highlight
World Championships: *pole vault* gold 1983.

Although Bubka, the world's best junior, went into the World Championships as the Soviet number three behind Volkov and Poliakov, the USSR hierarchy were looking for great things from him.
    He did not disappoint them, and Volkov finished second. Early in 1984 he set a new world indoor record with 5.84 in Los Angeles.

King of the shotputters for eight years... East Germany's Udo Beyer
◄

tious humour. Even though the music-loving Californian finished second in Helsinki, he still gave the winner, Hoffman, all the encouragement he could, making sure the crowd appreciated the Pole's efforts.

Udo Beyer (GDR)
Shot
Born: August 9, 1955, Eisenmittenstadt, East Germany.
Height: 195cm/6ft 4½in.
Weight: 125kg/275.5lb.
Career Highlights
Olympic Games: *shot* bronze 1980, gold 1976.
World Championships: *shot* sixth 1983.
European Championships: *shot* gold 1982, 1978, eighth 1974.
World Cup: *shot* gold 1981, 1979, 1977.
European Cup: *shot* gold 1981, 1979, 1977.
World Student Games: *shot* gold 1979.
Records
World 1983 (22.20), 1978 (22.15).

Apart from an injury-affected World Championship and a slip

▲
*American pole vault record
holder Jeff Buckingham*

*Latest in the line of great
Czech discus throwers,
Imrich Bugar* ▶ ▶

Jeff Buckingham (USA)
Pole vault
Born: June 14, 1960, Gardner,
Kansas, USA.
Height: 170cm/5ft 7in.
Weight: 70kg/155lb.
Career Highlights
World Championships: *pole vault*
thirteenth 1983.
World Student Games: *pole vault*
fifth 1983.
Record
North American *pole vault* 1983
(5.71).

The long-haired Buckingham was
the shock of 1983 with his 5.71
American record but, in bad condition in Helsinki, he failed to make
the expected impact.

Imrich Bugar (TCH)
Discus
Born: April 14, 1955, Streda,
Czechoslovakia.
Height: 190cm/6ft 3in.
Weight: 110kg/242.5lb.
Career Highlights
Olympic Games: *discus* silver
1980.
World Championships: *discus* gold
1983.
European Championships: *discus*
gold 1982, bronze 1978.
World Cup: *discus* bronze 1981.
World Student Games: *discus* fifth
1979.

Czechoslovakia's ability to produce
world class discus throwers continues with Bugar, who takes over
from the great Ludvik Danek —
world record holder back in the
1960s. But Danek·only managed

silver and bronze in the 1964 and
1968 Olympics plus the 1971
European gold. Already, Bugar has
collected World Championship
gold and an Olympic silver. But he
still chases a world record.

Mike Carter (USA)
Shot
Born: October 29, 1960, Dallas,
USA.
Height: 188cm/6ft 2in.
Weight: 125kg/275lb.
Career Highlights
World Student Games: *shot* gold
1983.

Amazingly, Carter failed to qualify
for the American trials final last
year, but this year will be concentrating on athletics at the expense
of American football.

He needed a very heavy plaster
cast on his leg after an accident at
football, but recovered from this
and he won the World Student
Games title.

Mike Conley (USA)
Long/triple jump
Born: October 5, 1962, Chicago,

USA.
Height: 188cm/6ft 2in.
Weight: 78kg/171lb.
Career Highlights
World Championships: *long jump*
bronze 1983; *triple jump*
fourth 1983.
World Student Games: *triple jump*
silver 1983.

Five centimetres stopped Conley
becoming a double medallist in
Helsinki. He won a long jump
bronze, beating Laszlo Szalma on
count back, but was 5cm off
bronze in the triple.

His concentration for 1984 will
be centred on the triple jump.

Keith Connor (GBR)
Triple jump
Born: September 16, 1957,
Anguilla, West Indies.
Height: 186cm/6ft 1¼in.
Weight: 77kg/169lb.
Career Highlights
Olympic Games: *triple jump* fourth
1980.
European Championships: *triple
jump* gold 1982, sixth 1978.
Commonwealth Games: *triple
jump* gold 1982, 1978.

Britain's Keith Connor —
'our most natural athlete,'
says Daley Thompson — will
be seeking to make up for
his bitter World
Championship
disappointment
◄

World Student Games: *triple jump* bronze 1981.
European Cup: *triple jump* fourth 1983, 1977.
Record
European and Commonwealth: *triple jump* 1982 (17.57).

Connor went into the World Championships as favourite, he came out as a non-qualifier. A shattering blow, but one which the West Indian-born triple jumper has managed to put into perspective.

Connor, whose 17.57 in 1982 is the second best jump of all time, has left Southern Methodist University in Dallas, although he returned there to prepare for the Olympics. And if he can regain the form he showed in 1982 he will be favourite. That year he won the NCAA indoor and outdoor titles, the second at high altitude in Provo, Utah. The thin air undoubtedly helped him to his 17.57 at that meeting.

Despite a damaged ankle he won the European title in Athens with 17.29, and then came the competition in the Commonwealth Games between Connor and Ken Lorraway. The Australian had taken Connor's all-comers record earlier in the season but now Connor got his own back, managing 17.72 and 17.81, although both were wind-assisted. It was his second Commonwealth title.

Brad Cooper (BAH)
Discus/shot
Born: June 30, 1957, Bahamas.
Height: 188cm/6ft 2in.
Weight: 132kg/290lb.
Career Highlights
World Championships: *discus* twelfth 1983.
Commonwealth Games: *discus* gold 1982, silver 1978; *shot* fourteenth 1978.

An immense man, Cooper shows the difference in throwing event standards between the Commonwealth, the USA and Eastern bloc. He was a sure-fire favourite for the

discus in Brisbane and won with a Games record of 64.04. But that would have been good enough only for eighth place in Helsinki the following year. As it was, Cooper was way down with 58.70, his only valid attempt.

Luis Delis (CUB)
Discus
Born: December 6, 1957, Havana, Cuba.
Height: 185cm/6ft 1in.
Weight: 105kg/231.5lb.
Career Highlights
Olympic Games: *discus,* bronze 1980.
World Championships: *discus* silver 1983.
World Cup: *discus* silver 1981, bronze 1979.
World Student Games: *discus* gold 1983.
Record
Central American *discus* 1982 (70.58); *shot* 1982 (19.89).

If there was any justice, Delis

would be defending an Olympic title in Los Angeles. Delis's furthest throw at the Moscow Games was good enough to win the gold, but the officials marked it a metre and a half less than from where it landed and the Russian, Viktor Rashchupkin, went on to win the gold. But Delis has been consistently the best in the world since, although he now faces a challenge from Bugar.

Lutz Dombrowski (GDR)
Long jump/triple jump
Born: June 25, 1959, Karl Marx Stadt, East Germany.
Height: 186cm/6ft 1in.
Weight: 87kg/191.5lb.
Career Highlights
Olympic Games: *long jump* gold 1980.
European Championships: *long jump* gold 1982.
World Cup: *long jump* silver 1979; *triple jump* sixth 1981.
European Cup: *long jump* gold 1979; *triple jump* fifth 1981.
Record
European: *long jump* 1980 (8.54).

Dombrowski is a long jumper, who wants to be a triple jumper but is not as good at it. Until 1977 triple jump was his main event, but the risk of injury led his coach to ban him from it in order to concentrate on long jumping – a wise move as it turned out. Dombrowski, also a 10.4 100 metres man, won the 1979 European Cup and finished second to Larry Myricks in the World Cup.

At the Moscow Olympics Dombrowski produced a European record leap of 8.54 which at the time was the second best jump of all time. Only Bob Beamon's 8.90 at the Mexico Olympics had bettered it. Even if the Americans had been there they would have found the powerfully built East German difficult to beat. Since then of course Myricks and Carl Lewis have both gone further.

Dombrowski returned to triple jumping in 1981 – after all when you are an Olympic champion you can make some demands – but without much success.

He was back long jumping at the Athens European Championships and won. He broke his leg in a car accident at the beginning of 1983 and missed the World Championships. He began long jumping again in January 1984 and a 7.93 jump indoors showed he was on his way back.

Back from a car crash . . . East German jumper Lutz Dombrowski ▶ ▶

Jason Grimes (USA)
Long jump
Born: September 10, 1959, Knoxville, USA.
Height: 179cm/5ft 10in.
Weight: 77kg/170lb.
Career Highlights
World Championships: *long jump;* silver 1983.

You have to feel sorry for Grimes. In normal circumstances he would have been a champion. But he is competing at the same time as Carl Lewis. However, he did take the World Championships silver in 1983.

John Herbert (GBR)
Triple jump/long jump
Born: April 20, 1962, London, England.
Height: 188cm/6ft 2in.
Weight: 76kg/167.5lb.
Career Highlights
European Championships: *triple jump* twelfth 1982.
Commonwealth Games: *triple jump* fifth 1982; *long jump* fourth 1982.
European Cup: *long jump* sixth 1983.

Herbert, being groomed as the successor to Keith Connor, spent the early part of last winter in Australia with Connor at the Australian Institute of Sport. He has to develop his enormous potential and this could be his breakthrough season.

Tom Hintnaus (BRA)
Pole vault
Born: February 15, 1958, Sao
    Paulo, Brazil.
Height: 185cm/6ft 0½in.
Weight: 82kg/180.4lb.
Career Highlight
World Championships: *pole vault*
    fifth 1983.

Tom Hintnaus was ranked only fourth in the USA in 1980, but grabbed his chance to win selection for the American team that did not go to the Olympics.

In 1983 though, he opted to compete for his native Brazil and finishèd above all three of the American vaulters in Helsinki.

Zdzislaw Hoffman (POL)
Triple jump
Born: August 27, 1959,
    Swiebodzin, Poland.
Height: 190cm/6ft 2¾in.
Weight: 83kg/182lb.
Career Highlights
World Championships: *triple jump*
    gold 1983.
European Cup: *triple jump* silver
    1983.

Zdzislaw Hoffman was one of several surprise field events winners in Helsinki. Having finished in the army he settled down to an injury-free period of training and was on form when it counted.

Gary Honey (AUS)
Long jump
Born: July 26, 1959,
    Thomastown, Victoria,
    Australia.
Height: 183cm/6ft 0in.
Weight: 74kg/163lb.
Career Highlights
World Championships: *long jump*
    sixth 1983.
Commonwealth Games: *long jump*
    gold 1982.
World Cup: *long jump* silver 1981,
    fifth 1979.

A great competitor, Honey's best may be only 8.13, but in major events he seems to be able to beat rivals who on paper are far ahead. In the Commonwealth Games final he broke the Games record with 8.13, which was also an Australian best.

The PE teacher thus rubbed out an embarrassing anomaly, for Daley Thompson's 8.11 in the 1978 Commonwealth decathlon was superior to the individual record.

Gary Honey, great competitive instinct ▼

Zhu Jian Hua (CHN)
High jump
Born: May 29, 1963, Shanghai,
    China.
Height: 193cm/6ft 4in.
Weight: 68kg/150lb.
Career Highlights
World Championships: *high jump*
    bronze 1983.
World Cup: *high jump* ninth 1981.
Record
World 1983 (2.37).

Is Zhu Jian Hua at the forefront of a Chinese invasion of athletics?

The tall student captured the world record in 1983 yet his dashing confident style was good enough only for third place in Helsinki. But he has a remarkable talent, and will undoubtedly fulfil his potential.

◀ ◀
Zdzislaw Hoffman salutes the Finnish people after his triple jump triumph in Helsinki

Al Joyner (USA)
Triple jump
Born: January 19, 1960, USA.
Height: 185cm/6ft 1in.
Weight: 76kg/168lb.
Career Highlights
World Championships: *triple jump* eighth 1983.
World Student Games: *triple jump* seventh 1983.

Another of the new young breed of triple jumpers, Joyner completes a formidable US trio with Banks and Couley.

Vladimir Kiseleyov (URS)
Shot
Born: January 1, 1957, Myski, USSR.
Height: 188cm/6ft 2in.
Weight: 124kg/272.8lb.
Career Highlights
Olympic Games: *shot* gold 1980.
European Championships: *shot* seventh 1982.

World Student Games: *shot* fourth 1979.
Record
Olympic *shot* 1980 (21.35).

The chunky Kiseleyov startled everybody in Moscow by coming from nowhere to win with a new Olympic record. But in 1982 in Athens he was well down the field, and he didn't make the Helsinki team. So whether he will recover to defend his title in Los Angeles must be open to doubt.

Wladyslaw Kozakiewicz (POL)
Pole vault
Born: December 12, 1953, Solecznilin, Russia.
Height: 187cm/6ft 1½in.
Weight: 83kg/183lb.
Career Highlights
Olympic Games: *pole vault* gold 1980, 1976.
World Championships: *pole vault*

eighth 1983.
European Championships: *pole vault* fourth 1978, silver 1974.
World Cup: *pole vault* silver 1977.
European Cup: *pole vault* bronze 1979, gold 1979, 1975.
World Student Games: *pole vault* gold 1979, 1977.
Record
World *pole vault* 1980 (5.78), (5.72); Olympic 1980 (5.78).

Wladyslaw Kozakiewicz, overcoming gamesmanship in Moscow ▼

There can be few more satisfying moments for a Pole than to win an Olympic gold medal in Moscow with a world record performance, especially when, like Kozakiewicz, you were actually born in the Soviet Union. His win was achieved in the face of much provocation — intense whistling from the Russian crowd and gamesmanship on behalf of the officials.

The victory was a total consolation for the 1976 Olympics when he went to Montreal as Polish number one, but was injured, finished eleventh, and saw team mate Tadeusz Slusarski grab the gold.

◄◄
Vladimir Kiseleyov of the USSR, problems making the grade for Los Angeles

Flat out for gold in Moscow, USSR's javelin champion Danius Kula ► ►

Danius Kula (URS)
Javelin
Born: April 28, 1959, Latvia, USSR.
Height: 189cm/6ft 2½in.
Weight: 94kg/207lb.
Career Highlights
Olympic Games: *javelin* gold 1980.
World Championships: *javelin* bronze 1983.
European Championships: *javelin* fourth 1982.
World Cup: *javelin* gold 1981.
European Cup: *javelin* gold 1981.
World Student Games: *javelin* gold 1983, 1981.

An all-round athlete who has high jumped 2.06 metres, Kula was fortunate to win in Moscow. His third round throw landed, in the opinion of most experts, flat as a pancake. But the officials, who were ludicrously accused of opening the Lenin Stadium doors to create a favourable draught, ruled his throw was valid.

He went on to take three more throws and qualified for the title.

Zdyslaw Kwasny (POL)
Hammer
Born: November 11, 1960, Miedzyckida, Poland.
Height: 193cm/6ft 4in.
Weight: 102kg/224.4lb.
Career Highlights
World Championships: *hammer* bronze 1983.
European Cup: *hammer* silver 1983.

Zdyslaw Kwasny of Poland relegated from silver to bronze by a Soviet protest in Moscow ▼

Kwasny was involved in the first World Championships' most controversial incident — the Soviet protest after he was given the silver medal. The USSR officials noticed on the video tape that when the unknown Pole delivered his best throw he fouled. The jury of appeal agreed with the protest and Olympic champion Yuri Sedykh, from the USSR, moved up from third and Kwasny was left with bronze.

Part of the Polish field events revolution last year Kwasny, will be a danger in Los Angeles to the Soviet dominance of the Olympic hammer.

Dave Laut (USA)
Shot
Born: December 21, 1956, Findlay, Ohio, USA.
Height: 193cm/6ft 4in
Weight: 123kg/270lb.
Career Highlights:
World Championships: *shot* fourth 1983.
World Cup: *shot* fourth 1979, bronze 1981.
Record
National 1982 (22.01) (co holder with Brian Oldfield).

Laut won his first American title in 1979 and then again in 1981 and 1983. Like the rest of the American team he could not go to Moscow, but he partly compensated by reaching more than 70ft in 1981 and creating his American record in 1982. A third place in the Rome World Cup behind Udo Beyer of East Germany and Yevgeni Mironov of the USSR showed his improvement as well, and he went into the 1983 World Championships as one of the favourites.

He was ranked second to Beyer, who had just pulled out a new world record, and when Laut led the qualifying with 21.08 he must have been confident. But on the day he could not get it together and his first round throw of 20.60 was the best he could manage.

He lives in California with his wife, the former Jane Laubacher.

Sergey Litvinov (USSR)
Hammer
Born: January 23, 1958,
　Krasnodar, USSR.
Height: 179cm/5ft 10in.
Weight: 97kg/214lb.
Career Highlights
Olympic Games: *hammer* silver
　1980.
World Championships: *hammer*
　gold 1983.
European Championships:
　hammer bronze 1982.
World Cup: *hammer* gold 1979.
European Cup: *hammer* silver
　1979.
Record
World *hammer* 1980 (81.66),
　1982 (83.98), 1983 (84.14).

Nobody had ever beaten Yuri Sedykh in a major championship until 1983 and leading up to the World Championships it still seemed that the mighty Russian would do it again, even though Litvinov led the rankings with his new world record.

But this time Litvinov triumphed. His first throw was 82.68 and no one could get anywhere near that.

So revenge must have been sweet for Litvinov. He broke his first world record in May of 1980, but saw Sedykh win the Olympics. He broke it for the second time in June of 1982, but later that year, sure enough, Sedykh was on form to take the European title.

Now the Russian soldier will go to Los Angeles as favourite and rightly so. But he won't underestimate Sedykh.

Sergey Litvinov, sweet revenge in Helsinki ▶

Detlef Michel, surprise of the World Championships ▶ ▶

Ken Lorraway (AUS)
Triple/Long jump
Born: February 6, 1956,
　Canberra, Australia.
Height: 5ft 10in.
Weight: 158.5lb.
Career Highlights
Olympic Games: *triple jump* 1980
　eighth.
Commonwealth Games: *triple jump* silver 1982, fourth 1978;
　long jump eighth 1982.
World Cup: sixth 1981.
Record
National and UK All-Comers 1982
　(17.46).

The unlucky Lorraway missed out on the World Championships because of injury, when he would have been the favourite to profit from Keith Connor's inexplicable loss of form.

The injury was all the worse because the likeable Australian bank worker had pushed himself into second place in the 1982 world rankings. His 17.46 at Crystal Palace was second only to Connor's 17.57, achieved at altitude. But Connor managed to beat Lorraway, a confirmed smoker, in the meeting that mattered most to the Australian, the Brisbane Commonwealth Games.

Detlef Michel (GDR)
Javelin
Born: October 13, 1955, Berlin,
　East Germany.
Height: 188cm/6ft 2in.
Weight: 95kg/209.5lb.
Career Highlights
World Championships: *javelin* gold
　1983.
European Championships: *javelin*
　bronze 1982, fourth 1978.
World Cup: *javelin* silver 1981.

European Cup: *javelin* gold 1983,
　1981, fourth 1975.
Record
European 1983 (96.72).

The 28 year-old gas engineer took advantage of the loss of form by the big guns in Helsinki to get a shock gold.

Dietmar Mogenburg (FRG)
High jump
Born: August 15, 1961,
Leverkusen, West Germany.
Height: 201cm/6ft 7in.
Weight: 78kg/172lb.
Career Highlights
World Championships: *high jump* fourth 1983.
European Championship: *high jump* gold 1982.
European Cup: *high jump* bronze 1983, silver 1979.
Record
World *high jump* 1980 (2.35).

The tall architectural student had more reason that most to be angry at the West German boycott of the 1980 Olympics. For then Mogenburg was unquestionably the best high jumper in the world. He kept his form through to Athens, but had to settle for defeat in bad conditions in Helsinki and then again at Crystal Palace in the European Cup final.

Larry Myricks (USA)
Long jump/sprints
Born: March 10, 1956, Jackson, Mississippi, USA.
Height: 186cm/6ft 1in.
Weight: 75kg/165lb.
Career Highlight
World Cup: *long jump* gold 1979.

A talented all-rounder, Myricks would have been favourite to win the Moscow long jump, but the Californian-based American is very unlikely to win gold in Los Angeles, not with Carl Lewis, another sprinter/long jumper around.

Indeed, since 1980 Myricks has returned to the 200 metres, although he was hampered by injury in Helsinki.

Brian Oldfield (USA)
Shot
Born: June 1, 1945, Pasadena, USA.
Height: 196cm/6ft 5in.
Weight: 120kg/264.5lb.
Career Highlight
Olympic Games: *shot* sixth 1972.

Oldfield turned professional in January of 1973, and as a paid athlete shattered the amateur record with 22.86 in 1975. He was reinstated in 1980 as an amateur, and broke the American record with 22.02.

He was fourth in last year's American trials and Oldfield, a member of Athletes in Action, will still be a threat in 1984.

Billy Olson (USA)
Pole vault
Born: July 19, 1958, Abilene, Texas, USA.
Height: 188cm/6ft 2in.
Weight: 73kg/161lb.
Career Highlights
World Cup: *pole vault* bronze 1981.

The bespectacled Texan dominated the 1983 United States indoor season with the world's first 19ft pole vault indoors. But he suffered an injury before the World Championships and could not register a height in difficult conditions.

Mike O'Rourke (NZL)
Javelin
Born: August 25, 1955, Auckland, New Zealand.
Height: 190cm/6ft 2¾in.
Weight: 100kg/220.4lb.
Career Highlights
Commonwealth Games: *javelin;* gold 1982, silver 1978.
World Cup: *javelin;* sixth 1981, 1977; silver 1979.
Record
Commonwealth *javelin* 1982 (89.58).

O'Rourke is unrivalled in his event in the Commonwealth but still falls short of top world class. He makes his living as a carpenter.

Milt Ottey (CAN)

High jump
Born: December 29, 1959,
    Kingston, Jamaica.
Height: 178cm/5ft 10in.
Weight: 66kg/145.5lb.
Career Highlights
World Championships: *high jump*
    ninth 1983.
Commonwealth Games: *high jump*
    gold 1982.
World Cup: *high jump* fifth 1981,
    1979.
World Student Games: *high jump*
    eleventh 1983.
Record
North American and
    Commonwealth *high jump*
    1982 (2.32).

Ottey had a brilliant 1982, winning
the NCAA championships with his
North American record, winning at
the Weltklasse meeting in Zurich,
in West Berlin, in the Eight Nations
meeting in Tokyo, and the
Commonwealth Games.
    He moved to Canada at the age
of ten.

Tyke Peacock (USA)

High jump
Born: February 24, 1961, Urbana,
    Illinois, USA.
Height: 185cm/6ft 1in.
Weight: 79kg/175lb.
Career Highlights
World Championships: *high jump*
    silver 1983.
World Cup: *high jump* gold 1981.

Peacock ranked number one in the
world in 1981, when he won the
World Cup in Rome.
    Shorter than average for a top
high jumper, Peacock took the
pressure of a magnificent Helsinki
competition brilliantly, but had to
settle for second place.
    He now lives in Fresno, Califor-
nia and is looking forward to being
at home for the Olympics.

Tom Petranoff (USA)

Javelin
Born: April 8, 1958, Northridge,
    California, USA.
Height: 185cm/6ft 1in.
Weight: 97kg/215lb.
Career Highlights
World Championships: *javelin*
    silver 1983.
Record
World *javelin* 1983 (99.72).

Petranoff caused the javelin
superstars of Europe to quake in
their shoes when they heard of his
99.72 world record throw, exactly
three metres further than Ferenc
Paragi's world record.
    He didn't look too impressive on
the pre-Helsinki circuit around
Europe, but managed to get it
back together for second place in
the World Championships. Amazingly, he was ranked only twice in
the USA before 1983.

Karl-Heinz Rheim (FRG)

Hammer
Born: March 31, 1951, Konz bei
    Trier, West Germany.
Height: 187cm/6ft 1½in.
Weight: 107kg/236lb.
Career Highlights
Olympic Games: *hammer* fourth
    1976, tenth 1972.
World Championships: *hammer*
seventh 1983.
European Championships:
    hammer bronze 1978.
World Cup: *hammer* silver 1981,
    1979, gold 1977.
European Cup: *hammer* fourth
    1983, silver 1981, gold 1979,
    1977, 1975.
Record
World *hammer* 1978 (80.32),
    1975 (78.50).

Rheim, a lover of classical music,
is rated as the best hammer
thrower never to win an Olympic
medal.
    In 1975 he broke the world
record six times in one competition, the only time this feat has
been achieved.
    He failed in his cherished ambi-
tion to become the first man over
80 metres but he broke the record
again in 1978 and was forced out
of Moscow by the boycott.

*Karl-Heinz Rheim, first
man over 80 metres in the
hammer*
▼

◀
*Stadiums are getting too
small for American Tom
Petranoff who hurled the
javelin almost 100 metres
in 1983*

Yuri Seydykh, the mighty man of the hammer. Is he past his peak?
◄

Edward Sarul (POL)
Shot
Born: November 16, 1958,
    Poland.
Height: 195cm/6ft 5in.
Weight: 105kg/231lb.
Career Highlights
World Championships: *shot* gold
    1983.
European Cup: *shot* gold 1983.

One of the biggest shocks in Helsinki came when Sarul won the gold in the shot. In 1982 he had been ranked 18th in the world. His best of 20.64 did not even put him in the all time top 50.

Yet he beat all the big names and showed his victory was no fluke by winning the European Cup final at Crystal Palace a couple of weeks later.

Yuri Sedykh (URS)
Hammer
Born: June 11, 1955,
    Novo-Cherkassk, USSR.
Height: 191cm/6ft 3in.
Weight: 110kg/242.5lb.
Career Highlights
Olympic Games: *hammer* gold
    1980, 1976.
World Championships: *hammer*
    silver 1983.
European Championships:
    hammer gold 1982, 1978.
World Cup: *hammer* gold 1981,
    fourth 1977.
European Cup: *hammer* gold
    1981, bronze 1977.
World Student Games: *hammer*
    bronze 1979, 1975.
Record
World *hammer* 1980 (81.80),
    (80.64).

Olympic *hammer* 1980 (81.80).

Unquestionably the greatest hammer thrower and competitor of modern times, Sedykh has mastered the art of peaking for the major occasion.

Look at his record in the European and World Cups and World Student Games, and then at the European Championships and, above all, the Olympic Games. In 1980 his compatriot Sergey Litvinov broke the world record before the Moscow Games, but Sedykh triumphed with that most satisfying of achievements, an Olympic gold with a world record performance.

It happened once again before the Athens Europeans, but Litvinov finally got his man in Hel-

Thierry Vigneron, world record holder at the age of 20 ▶ ▶

sinki. Sedykh actually finished third there, but was given silver after the Soviets protested that Kwasny of Poland fouled when producing his best throw.

Coached by 1972 Olympic champion Anatoliy Bondarchuk, Sedykh is a technical innovator in his event, but may be past his best now.

Tadeusz Slusarski (POL)
Pole vault
Born: May 19, 1950, Zary, Poland.
Height: 178cm/5ft 10in.
Weight: 76kg/167.5lb.
Career Highlights
Olympic Games: *pole vault* silver 1980, gold 1976, twelfth 1972.
World Championships: *pole vault* fourth 1983.
European Championships: *pole vault* twelfth 1982, seventh 1974.
European Cup: *pole vault* fifth 1983.
World Student Games: *pole vault* silver 1977.

Slusarski was the Polish number two going into the Montreal Olympics, but an injury to Kozakiewicz elevated him to number one and Slusarski took his chance with both hands.

Dwight Stones, back on the world circuit after a ban for professionalism ▼

He was still going strong at the age of 33 in the World Championships in 1983. His experience helped him overcome the adverse conditions, and he cannot be ruled out in Los Angeles.

Dwight Stones (USA)
High jump
Born: December 6, 1953, Irvine, California, USA.
Height: 195cm/6ft 5in.
Weight: 82kg/182lb.
Career Highlights
Olympic Games: *high jump* bronze 1976.
World Championships: *high jump* bronze 1972, sixth 1983.
World Cup: *high jump* silver 1977.
Records
World *high jump* 1976 (2.32), (2.31), 1973 (2.30).
North American *high jump* (2.33).

Stones returned to the amateur ranks after a period as a professional, but although he regained his place in the United States team he found Europe's young lions too hard to beat.

Winning big titles has been Stones' problem. He was clearly the world's top high jumper in the 1970s but has no gold medal to show for it.

An outspoken opponent of outmoded amateur laws, Stones was just ahead of his time. Still the co-holder of the US record.

Thierry Vigneron (FRA)
Pole vault
Born: March 9, 1960, Paris, France.
Height: 181cm/5ft 11in.
Weight: 71kg/156.5lb.
Career Highlights
Olympic Games: *pole vault* seventh 1980.
World Championships: *pole vault* eighth 1983.
European Championships: *pole vault* fifth 1982.
World Student Games: *pole vault* silver 1983, fourth 1981.
Records
World 1983 (5.83), 1981 (5.80), 1980 (5.75).

Thierry Vigneron may yet go down as a startling performer who cannot win a medal.

Vigneron was only 20 when he first broke the world record and a mere 21 when he became the first man to vault 5.80. In the 1980 Olympics and the European Championships in 1982 he was well down and in the World Championships he struggled into eighth place. Yet in Rome on September 1 1983, he regained his world record, lost four days earlier to Pierre Quinon with 5.83.

Konstantin Volkov (URS)
Pole vault
Born: February 28, 1960, Irkutsk, USSR.
Height: 185cm/6ft 1in.
Weight: 75kg/165lb.
Career Highlights
Olympic Games: *pole vault* silver 1980.
World Championships: *pole vault* silver 1983.
World Cup: *pole vault* gold 1981, bronze 1979.
European Cup: *pole vault* gold 1981, 1979.
World Student Games: *pole vault* gold 1983, 1981, sixth 1979.

Volkov has threatened to win a major title ever since he burst into the limelight in 1979 with a world junior record.

But whilst he has done well in the cup competitions, he has been pipped at both the Olympics and World Championships, and saw compatriot Vladimir Polyakov take the world record in 1981.

Weir, a student at Southern Methodist University in Dallas, has maintained his position as British number one, and helped in the improvement in British hammer throwing.

Also Britain's number one discus thrower, in 1981 he was second in the National Collegiate championships in the US.

Weir is the world record holder for the 35lb weight throw, never having lost in 30 competitions, and should be throwing the hammer five metres further than he does. He is handicapped by technical faults.

Gerd Wessig (GDR)
High jump
Born: July 16, 1959, Lubz, East Germany.
Height: 196cm/6ft 5in.
Weight: 82kg/181lb.
Career Highlight
Olympic Games: *high jump* gold 1980.
Record
World and Olympic *high jump* 1980 (2.36).

All the indications are that Wessig will be in Los Angeles. The only high point of his remarkable career came in Moscow with gold and a world record.

Wessig went into the competition with a personal best of 2.27m outdoors but he added 9cm, and did not seem to be under any pressure.

He jumped 2.26m in 1982 when he also managed 7865 in a

decathlon. He managed more than 8000 in the 10 discipline event last year but did not jump in any of the international meetings.

Jacek Wszola (POL)
High jump
Born: December 30, 1956, Warsaw, Poland.
Height: 196cm/6ft 5in.
Weight: 83kg/182lb.
Career Highlights
Olympic Games: *high jump* silver 1980, gold 1976.
European Championships: *high jump* sixth 1978, fifth 1974.
World Cup: *high jump* silver, 1979, bronze 1977.
European Cup: *high jump* fifth 1983, 1975, silver 1979.
World Student Games: *high jump* thirteenth 1983, fourth 1979, gold 1977.
Record
World *high jump* 1980 (2.35).

When Jacek Wszola was only seventeen he was fifth in the Rome European Championships. Two years later, and still a teenager, he shocked Dwight Stones and won the Olympic title.

He kept at the top of the notoriously erratic world of high jumping to finish with a silver in Moscow. But two years later in Athens his chances of a medal were finished when he was sent home. The Poles had a contract with Adidas, Wszola wore Tiger shoes and refused to change them, so he was pulled out.

British number one in hammer and discus, Robert Weir who trains in America ▼

Robert Weir (GBR)
Hammer/discus
Born: February 4, 1961, Birmingham, England.
Height: 187cm/6ft 1½in.
Weight: 113kg/249lb.
Career Highlights
Commonwealth Games: *hammer* gold 1982; *discus* fifth 1982.
European Cup: *discus* fifth 1983, 1981.
World Student Games: *hammer* silver 1983; *discus* sixth 1983.

Favourite for the high jump gold, East Germany's Gerd Wessig ▶ ▶

Debbie Brill (CAN)

High jump
Born: March 10, 1953, Mission, British Columbia, Canada.
Height: 177cm/5ft 9½in.
Weight: 60kg/132lb.
Career Highlights
Olympic Games: *high jump* eighth 1972.
World Championships: *high jump* sixth 1983.
Commonwealth Games: gold 1982, 1970, silver 1978.
World Cup: *high jump* gold 1979, bronze 1977.
World Student Games: *high jump* silver 1977, seventh 1975.

A twelve-year gap separated Brill's two Commonwealth Games triumphs and proved that even at twenty-nine, and a mother, she can take on the best in the world. She missed the Christchurch Commonwealth Games to have her baby and was still going well in 1983, when she was placed sixth in Helsinki.

Tamara Bykova (URS)

High jump
Born: December 21, 1958, USSR.
Height: 179cm/5ft 10in.
Weight: 65kg/143lb.
Career Highlights
Olympic Games: *high jump* ninth 1980.
World Championships: *high jump* gold 1983.
European Championships: *high jump* silver 1982.
World Cup: *high jump* silver 1981.
European Cup: *high jump* silver 1983.
World Student Games: *high jump* gold 1983, bronze 1981.
Record
World *high jump* 1983 (2.03), (2.04).

Bykova's duels with Ulrike Meyfarth have been one of the highlights of the last three years. The West German beat her in the 1981 World Cup and the Athens European Championships.

Meyfarth also won when they both broke the world record with 2.03 in the Crystal Palace European Cup final. But Bykova won the most important title in Helsinki and after the European final claimed the world record as her own in Pisa on August 25.

A fascinating racial mixture, half Greek/half Russian, the statuesque blonde will be favourite.

Maria Colon (CUB)

Javelin
Born: March 25, 1958, Baracoa, Cuba.
Height: 175cm/5ft 9in.
Weight: 70kg/154lb.
Career Highlights
Olympic Games: *javelin* gold 1980.
World Championships: *javelin* eighth 1983.
World Cup: *javelin* bronze 1979.
Records
Central American *javelin* 1980 (68.40).
Olympic *javelin* 1980 (68.40).

Married to coach Angel Salzedo, Maria won the Moscow Olympic title with her first throw, thus defeating the defending champion Ruth Fuchs and the then world record holder Tatyana Biryulina, and becoming the first Carribean woman to take Olympic gold.

Anisoara Cusmir (ROM)

Long jump
Born: June 28, 1962, Romania.
Height: 171cm/5ft 7in.
Weight: 64kg/141lb.
Career Highlights
World Championships: *long jump*

Half Greek, half Russian and a star in any language, high jumper Tamara Bykova ▶

Bev Kinch . . . outjumping
Mary Rand after 19 years ▼
▶

Romania's Anisoara
Cusmir . . . watch for her
jet-propelled take-off
▼

silver 1983.
European Championships: *long
jump* silver 1982.
World Student Games: *long jump*
gold 1983, silver 1981.
Record
World *long jump* 1983 (7.43).

Helena Fibingerova (TCH)
Shot
Born: July 13, 1949, Vicemerice,
Czechoslovakia.
Height: 179cm/5ft 10½in.
Weight: 96kg/211.5lb.
Career Highlights
Olympic Games: *shot* bronze
1976, seventh 1972.
World Championships: *shot* gold
1983.
European Championships: *shot*
silver 1982, 1978, bronze
1974.
World Cup: *shot* silver 1981,
1979, 1977.
European Cup: *shot* gold 1983.
Record
World *shot* 1977 (22.32), 1976
(21.99).

Fibingerora's exuberant delight in
winning the first world title was not
surprising. Until then, she had
always been the bridesmaid. Her
father died earlier in 1983 and she
said simply: 'I did it for him'.

She has won the European
indoor titles record six times.

Bev Kinch (GBR)
100 metres/long jump

Born: January 14, 1964, Ipswich,
England.
Height: 162.5cm/5ft 4in.
Weight: 61kg/134.5lb.
Career Highlights
World Championships: *long jump*
fifth 1983.
European Cup: *long jump* bronze
1983.
World Student Games: *100* gold
1983; *long jump* fourth 1983.

Bev Kinch became the girl to at
last beat Mary Rand's nineteen-
year-old British long jump record
of 6.76m (22ft 2¼in) at the 1983
World Championships in Helsinki
with a leap of 6.90m (22.7¾in). It
had become the longest standing
record in British books and Bev's
outstanding series of jumps – the
shortest of which was 6.81m (22ft
4¼in) – gained her fifth place and
announced her as a world class
force. Earlier that summer, Bev
Kinch had sprinted away with the
World Student Games 100 metres
title to uphold the opinion of her
coach Doug Wilson, that her true
potential lies on the track.

Bev has moved from her Ipswich
home and joined Hounslow AC to
be nearer to her coach.

Cusmir's astonishing rise to fame
went hand-in-hand with Vali
Ionescu, who won the European
title in Athens. The blonde Romanian with the extravagant run-up
seemed to have the world title in
her pocket when she cleared 7.43
in 1983, adding 23cm to the 7.20
Ionescu set in 1982. But she was
beaten by 18-year-old Heike
Daute.

Heike Daute (GDR)
Long jump
Born: December 16, 1964, Gora,
East Germany.
Height: 180cm/5ft 11in.
Weight: 65kg/143lb.
Career Highlights
World Championships: *long jump*
gold 1983.
European Championships: *long
jump* fourth 1982.
European Cup: *long jump* gold
1983.

Two gold medals last year, at the
age of only eighteen, including a
shock first place in Helsinki,
showed that the student is set for
a great career.

She was Helsinki's youngest
champion, and has been setting
age group records since she was
14 years old.

Carol Lewis (USA)
Long jump
Born: August 8, 1963, Alabama,
USA.
Height: 178cm/5ft 10in.
Weight: 68kg/150lb.
Career Highlight
World Championships: *long jump*
bronze 1983.

The little sister of Carl Lewis, she is
a fine athlete in her own right, as
her performance in Helsinki
showed. Her 7.04, which gave her
third place, was the best by an
American. She won the US title in
1982 and 1983, and was selected
for the US 'Olympic' team in 1980
while still a schoolgirl.
    She is at college in Houston.

*Tiina Lillak, a world
championship with her
very last throw* ▶ ▶

Tiina Lillak (FIN)
Javelin
Born: April 15, 1961, Helsinki,
Finland.
Height: 180cm/5ft 11in.
Weight: 73kg/161lb.
Career Highlights
World Championships: *javelin* gold
1983.
European Championships: *javelin*
fourth 1982.
Record
World *javelin* 1983 (74.76), 1982
(72.40).

Just imagine the pressure on the
attractive Finn. Here she was
competing in Finland's favourite
event in her home town in the
inaugural World Championships.
As yet Finland had not won a gold
medal, and they were not in with

any chance of getting one except
for Tiina. Her face looked down
from every advertisement hoarding
it seemed, yet here she was trailing
the British second string into the
last round. Then Lillak drew back
her arm and threw. The javelin
soared beyond the 70m mark and
the title was hers. The crowd went
wild and Tiina danced around the

track in a premature lap of honour.
    Coached by Kalevi Harkonen,
the father of Finland's top male
thrower Arto Harkonen, Lillak was
Finland's only gold medallist, and
whilst she had the advantage of
competing in her 'own' stadium,
where she knew every trick of the
wind, she deserved her triumph
after a great season.
    Earlier in the year she was
involved in a 'frisson' between Britain and Finland. Britain's top
thrower Tessa Sanderson had
refused to throw for Britain in Finland, so the Finnish Federation
refused to let Lillak throw against

Sanderson in the Tarmac Games
in Edinburgh.

Ulrike Meyfarth (FRG)
High jump
Born: May 4, 1956, Frankfurt,
West Germany.
Height: 188cm/6ft 2in.
Weight: 71kg/156.5lb.
Career Highlights
Olympic Games: *high jump* gold
1972.
World Championships: *high jump*
silver 1983.
European Championships: *high
jump* gold 1982, fifth 1978,
seventh 1974.
World Cup: *high jump* gold 1981
European Cup: *high jump* gold
1983, silver 1981, 1975.
World Student Games: silver
1979.
Records
World *high jump* 1983 (2.03),
1982 (2.02), 1972 (1.92).

Meyfarth was only sixteen when
she became the darling of West
Germany by winning the Olympic
title in Munich. A year later she
took the European junior silver.
But her career never took off as
expected, and it was not until
1981 that she recovered the form
she had shown nine years earlier.
    Last year saw a series of
remarkable duels with Tamara
Bykova. Meyfarth lost the world
title, but beat the Soviet in the
Crystal Palace European Cup
where both jumped 2.03 to break
the world record (Bykova was later
to claim it all her own in Pisa).

*Ulrike Meyfarth of West
Germany breaks the world
high jump record in 1983* ▶

Part of the formidable Greek javelin force, Sofia Sakorafa ▶ ▶

Martina Opitz (GDR)
Discus
Born: December 12, 1960, Leipzig, East Germany.
Height: 178cm/5ft 10in.
Weight: 80kg/176lb.
Career Highlights
World Championships: *discus* gold 1983.
European Cup: *discus* gold 1983.

A sociology student who improved nearly 6m in 1983. She should dominate the event for years to come.

Opitz came from nowhere to finish fourth in the GDR championships and had never competed internationally until Helsinki. It was wondered if she could sustain the win but her Crystal Palace performance showed she could.

Hot favourite for the discus title, East German Martina Opitz

Louise Ritter (USA)
High jump
Born: February 18, 1958, Dallas, Texas, USA.
Height: 178cm/5ft 11in.
Weight: 61kg/134.5lb.
Career Highlights
World Championships: *high jump* bronze 1983.
World Cup: *high jump* fifth 1979, fourth 1977.
World Student Games: *high jump* thirteenth 1977.
Record
North American *high jump* 1983 (2.01).

Holder of the American record, she would have been in the American Olympic team had they gone to Moscow.

She enjoys playing basketball and water skiing and went to Texas Women's University.

Sofia Sakorafa (GRE)
Javelin
Born: April 29, 1957, Athens, Greece.
Height: 175cm/5ft 9in.
Weight: 65kg/143lb.
Career Highlights
European Championships: *javelin* bronze 1982.
World Student Games: *javelin* ninth 1977.
Record
World *javelin* 1982 (74.20).

Sakorafa made a rapid improvement of 11 metres from 63.46 to 74.20 in 1982, but had to give second best to her countrywoman Verouli in Athens, a defeat that shattered the then world record holder.

A shoulder injury kept her out of the World Championships.

Tessa Sanderson (GBR)
Javelin
Born: March 14, 1956, Kingston, Jamaica.
Height: 168cm/5ft 6in.

Weight: 66kg/145.5lb.
Career Highlights
Olympic Games: *javelin* tenth 1976.
World Championships: *javelin* fourth 1983.
European Championships: *javelin* silver 1978.
Commonwealth Games: *javelin* gold 1983, fifth 1974.
World Cup: *javelin* bronze 1977.
European Cup: *javelin* silver 1981, bronze 1979, 1977.

Tenth place in the Montreal Games, a Commonwealth gold followed by a European silver and Sanderson was set to become the first woman to break through the 70m barrier and win Olympic gold in Moscow. But she froze, failed to qualify and placed a big question mark over her ability to compete.

A serious arm and Achilles injury in the winter of 1982 cost her places in the Athens Europeans and Brisbane Commonwealth Games. She returned in time for the World Championships but could only manage fourth.

Sara Simeoni (ITA)
High jump
Born: April 11, 1953, Rivoli, Veronese, Italy.
Height: 178cm/5ft 10in.
Weight: 61kg/134.5lb.
Career Highlights
Olympic Games: *high jump* gold 1980, silver 1976, sixth 1972.
European Championships: *high jump* bronze 1982, gold 1978, bronze 1974, ninth 1971.
World Cup: *high jump* silver 1979, 1977.
European Cup: *high jump* silver 1979.
World Student Games: *high jump* gold 1981, 1977, silver 1975, bronze 1973, 1979.
Records
World *high jump* 1978 (2.00), (2.01)
Olympic *high jump* 1980 (1.97).

Tall, graceful Simeoni damaged a calf muscle in the World Championship qualifying rounds, which kept her out of the medal hunt. But there were already signs that her career was on the wane. She was unable to match Meyfarth and Bykova in Athens.

But she remains one of the most compelling sights in athletics and no-one who watched will forget her performances in Prague and Moscow.

Ilona Slupianek-Briesenick (GDR)
Shot
Born: September 24, 1956, Demmin, East Germany.
Height: 180cm/5ft 11in.
Weight: 90kg/198.5lb.
Career Highlights
Olympic Games: *shot* gold 1980, sixth 1976.
World Championships: *shot* bronze 1983.
European Championships: gold 1982, 1978.
World Cup: gold 1981, 1979, 1977.
European Cup: gold 1981, 1979, 1977.
World Student Games: gold 1979.
Records
World *shot* 1980 (22.45), (22.36).
Olympic *shot* 1980 (22.41).

Slupianek's hand injury undoubtedly cost her the first World Championship gold, but whenever she competes she seems to upset some people. She was suspended, and then reinstated, after being found guilty of taking anabolic steroids. This blots her record as the finest shot putter of modern times.

She is now Mrs Briesenick — her husband is the double European shot champion, 1971 and 1974, who stopped Geoff Capes winning the European gold.

Anna Verouli (GRE)
Javelin
Born: November 13, 1956, Athens, Greece.
Height: 160cm/5ft 4in.
Weight: 65kg/143lb.
Career Highlights
World Championship: *javelin* bronze 1983.
European Championship: *javelin* gold 1982.
World Student Games: *javelin* eleventh 1981.

Verouli sent the Athens crowd into ecstasy when she won the 1982 European title and surprised her Greek team mate Sakorafa. She played a supporting role to Lillak and Whitbread in Helsinki.

Fatima Whitbread (GBR)
Javelin
Born: March 3, 1961, Hackney, London, England.
Height: 165cm/5ft 5in.
Weight: 74kg/163lb.
Career Highlights
World Championships: *javelin* silver 1983.
European Championships: *javelin* eighth 1982.
Commonwealth Games: *javelin* bronze 1982, sixth 1978.
European Cup: *javelin* gold 1983.

Back after a drug-taking ban, Ilona Slupianek of East Germany ▶

Fatima Whitbread, one throw from gold in Helsinki ▶ ▶

A few inches taller, and the young Whitbread would be unbeatable. But despite being too short she has already had quite a career. Until last year she was the up-and-coming number two to Tessa Sanderson. But then her first throw in Helsinki put her into the lead, and it was not until the last throw that Finland's Lillak overtook her.

She is coached by her mother Margaret a former British international.

Decathlon and Heptathlon

The concept of the all-rounder goes back to the ancient Olympic Games when one of the earliest contests was the pentathlon. In this the first event was a jump (usually the long jump performed with the aid of hand held weights). The best contestants then progressed to the javelin, and the top four from that ran a short race. The first three runners then threw the discus, and the best discus throwers finally wrestled each other for the overall title. The winner of this competition could truthfully

Jim Thorpe,
the American-Indian who
dominated the Games of
1912

claim to be the world's greatest athlete, a description which is applied to Olympic decathlon champions today.

The first modern Olympics did not have such an all-round competition, although a number of athletes did attain distinction in a variety of events. It was not until 1904 in St Louis that a ten-event competition was included in the Games. To the chagrin of the American hosts it was won by Irish-born Tom Kiely representing Great Britain. It consisted of 100 yard and 1-mile runs, 120-yard hurdles, 880-yard walk, high jump and long jump, pole vault, shot, hammer and 56lb weight throw, all contested on the same day.

In the 1906 Games at Athens an attempt was made to emulate the Ancient Games and Hjalmar Mellander of Sweden won a five-event pentathlon comprising a standing long jump, Greek style discus, javelin throw, a one stade (192m) run, and a Greco-Roman wrestling bout.

There was no competition for the all-rounder in 1908, but in 1912 the Swedes made up for that omission by having two contests. They were a five-event pentathlon (comprising long jump, javelin, 200 metres, discus and 1500 metres) held on one day, and the ten-event decathlon, which like today, consisted of 100 metres, long jump, shot, high jump, 400 metres, 110 metres hurdles, discus, pole vault, javelin and 1500 metres. This competition was held over a period of three days. Nowadays it is contested over two. The winner of both gold medals at Stockholm was the remarkable American Indian Jim Thorpe. He finished first in four of the pentathlon events, and first in four events in the decathlon. When he was presented with his medals King Gustave of Sweden referred to him as 'the greatest athlete in the world', to which Thorpe is said to have replied, 'Thanks, King'. A few months later a newspaper reporter uncovered the fact that Thorpe had played minor league baseball for money a few years before. Although the amount was very small, and Thorpe certainly had not known that it would affect his Olympic status, his medals were recalled and his name and achievements were removed from Olympic annals for 70 years. In 1982, finally bowing to public pressure, the IOC 'pardoned' the long dead athlete and reinstated him in the records. However, he was, quite ludicrously, only made co-holder of the titles with athletes who had been awarded the gold medals although well beaten by him. Fifth place in that 1912 pentathlon went to Avery Brundage (USA) who was later to become President of the IOC.

In 1920 both pentathlon and decathlon were won by Scandinavians, a Finn and a Norwegian, but the decathlon silver medal went to Brutus Hamilton (USA) and the fourth place to Gosta Holmer (SWE), both later highly respected coaches.

The multi-event contests attracted a lot of interest in 1924, particularly the unique double completed by Harold Osborn (USA) who added the decathlon title, won with a world record score, to the high jump crown he had gained a few days earlier. In the pentathlon Eero Lehtonen retained his Antwerp title for Finland, a feat overshadowed by the outstanding performance of the bronze medallist Robert LeGendre (USA) who shattered the world long jump mark, surpassing the winning effort in the individual long jump event. LeGendre had failed to qualify for individual long jump in the US trials. This was the last time that the men's athletic pentathlon was held at the Olympic Games.

The world record was beaten again in the 1928 decathlon, although with hindsight there was an anomaly. The silver medallist Akilles Jaervinen, one of that famous Olympian family from Finland, placed second on his score using the 1912 points tables then in force. Four years later, at Los Angeles, he was placed second again. If the modern tables had been in use he would have won the gold medal on both occasions. Jim Bausch, the actual 1932 champion, began a run of American successes which was not interrupted until 1964.

New international scoring tables were adopted in 1934, and in Berlin in 1936, Glen Morris established a magnificent world record of 7900 points to win the gold medal by a wide margin. He later signed a movie contract and played Tarzan on the screen. His world mark lasted for 14 years. The man who broke it, Bob Mathias (USA), first appeared on the scene as a precocious 17½-year-old and won the 1948 gold medal, becoming the youngest male individual track and field champion in Olympic history. The scores were well down on the Berlin performances but World War II had not long been over. During the next four years

◄ *Milt Campbell, decathlon champion of 1956*

Mathias beat Morris's record and he arrived at Helsinki firm favourite to retain his title, a unique achievement. This he did in great style setting yet another world mark, using the recently introduced scoring tables. His 912 point margin of victory over the second man was also a record. Two years later he starred in a film about his life, and then entered the political arena and was elected to the US House of Representatives for eight years. Mathias and his team mates, Milt Campbell and Floyd Simmons, won all three medals – the last time, other than in track events, that the United States would achieve a clean sweep in Olympic athletics.

The 1956 decathlon competition was very much a USA versus USSR match with athletes from those countries filling the first four places. The Helsinki runner-up, Milt Campbell won the title from his team-mate Rafer Johnson. Four years later Johnson won the gold medal at Rome but only after one of the closest tussles in Olympic history, with his University of California colleague Chuan-Kwang Yan, representing Taiwan.

At Tokyo in 1964 a pentathlon for women was introduced. It consisted of 80 metres hurdles, shot, high jump, long jump and 200 metres, and was won by the 1960 hurdles champion Irina Press (URS) with her sixth consecutive world record, ahead of 1964 long jump champion Mary Rand (GBR). The decathlon was won by Willi Holdorf of Germany, as the United States failed to gain a medal in the competition for the first time ever.

However, the United States, represented by Bill Toomey, regained the decathlon title in 1968 with a new Olympic record score, and the altitude of Mexico City aided him to a startling 400-metre time of 45.6 at the end of the first day. For the first time in the Games three men exceeded 8000 points. The women's pentathlon was won by Ingrid Becker (FRG) who had already placed sixth in the individual long jump.

In 1972 at Munich the Soviet challenge in the decathlon reached its zenith as Nikolai Avilov broke Toomey's three-year-old world record with 8454 points to win from a team-mate, with the best United States decathlete in fourth place. For many people, however, the women's pentathlon, with 100 metres hurdles replacing the 80 metres event, contained more excitement. Britain's Mary Peters, an erstwhile shot putter who had placed fourth in the 1964 pentathlon, beat the home favourite, Heide Rosendahl, by just 10 points with a superlative, for her, run in the last event the 200 metres. Her total, using the 1971 scoring tables, was a new world record of 4801 points.

By 1976 the United States had a new world record holder in Bruce Jenner, who also won the Olympic title at Montreal by over 200 points, breaking his own record. Soon after the Games he went into advertising and acting and made a considerable fortune. At the end of the pentathlon two girls, Sigrun Siegl and Christine Laser, both from the GDR, had the same number of points, an unusual situation. The title went to Siegl because she had finished ahead of her rival in three of the five disciplines.

Celebrating his eighteenth birthday in eighteenth place at Montreal, was Britain's Daley Thompson, who prior to the Moscow Games had broken Jenner's world record. At the Games Thompson swept all before him finishing first in three events on the first day of competition. In the pentathlon the 200 metres had been replaced by 800 metres. The standard of competition was outstanding with the winner, Nadyezda Tkachenko (URS) producing a new world mark of 5083 points, while all three medallists bettered the previous record.

The pentathlon for women was replaced by the heptathlon in 1981, and this will be contested in the 1984 Games. It consists of 100 metres hurdles, shot, high jump, 200 metres, long jump, javelin and 800 metres.

▲
Rafer Johnson, from silver to gold in 1960

Jurgen Hingsen (FRG)

Decathlon
Born: June 25, 1958, Duisburg, West Germany.
Height: 200cm/6ft 6½in.
Weight: 97kg/220lb.
Career Highlights
World Championships: *decathlon* silver 1983.
European Championships: *decathlon* silver 1982, thirteenth 1978.
European Cup: *decathlon* silver 1982, tenth 1979.
World Student Games: *decathlon* silver 1979.
Record
World *decathlon* 1983 (8779).

Jurgen Hingsen's world record early in 1983 was the perfect spur for Daley Thompson and proved to be the tall West German's undoing. With Thompson going into Helsinki nursing an injury, Hingsen knew his best chance of victory had come. But Thompson proved irresistible. Now based in the States, Jurgen, known as 'Hollywood Hingsen' because of his giant physique and good looks, is the one Daley Thompson has to beat in Los Angeles.

Daley Thompson (GBR)

Decathlon
Born: July 30, 1958, London, England.
Height: 185cm/6ft 1in.
Weight: 86kg/189.5lb.
Career Highlights
Olympic Games: *decathlon* gold 1980, eighteenth 1976.

World Championship: *decathlon* gold 1983.
European Championships: *decathlon* gold 1982, silver 1978.
Commonwealth Games: *decathlon* gold 1982, 1978.
Records
World *decathlon* 1982 (8743), (8704), 1980 (8622).

Francis 'Daley' Thompson, the son of a Nigerian father and Scottish mother, is simply the best all-round athlete the world has ever seen, and that's not just the opinion of Francis Daley Thompson! He now holds all the major titles it is possible for a British athlete to hold, the only thing missing going into 1984 is the World record, taken from him last year by West Germany's Jurgen Hingsen.

Thompson has great natural gifts — he would be an international class sprinter, 400 metres runner or long jumper — but he is also one of nature's competitors, a fact which was never better illustrated than in the World Championships. He went to Helsinki nursing an injury which would have stopped lesser men from taking part. In fact Thompson wasn't sure of competing until the day the two West Germans, Hingsen and Siggi Wentz, refused to speak to him: 'I made up my mind to beat them there and then', he grinned.

Always prickly after victory — he has a running feud with some newspapermen — Thompson was in tears after losing in the Prague Europeans. Aged just 20, he had already won the Commonwealth title in Edmonton a few days before going to Prague. The effort was too much, and Thompson felt unable to settle for silver. He hasn't had to since then.

As befits one of the world's great sportsmen, Thompson has a sheaf of endorsements. He is sponsored by Lucozade, Brut and Adidas, but his involvement with the sports goods company led to a lessening in his popularity with the BBC. Whilst everyone else turned up for the 1982 sportsman of the year show in a suit, Thompson was dressed from head to toe in Adidas, and when he received the award he was so nervous that he let slip an expletive.

Siegfried Wentz (GER)

Decathlon
Born: March 7, 1960, Rothenbach, Bayern, West Germany.
Height: 193cm/6ft 4in.
Weight: 89kg/196lb.
Career Highlights
World Championships: *decathlon* bronze 1983.
European Championships: *decathlon* twentieth 1982.
European Cup: *decathlon* bronze 1983, fourth 1981.

The big medical student, who won the European junior title in 1979, is being tipped as the successor to Daley Thompson. But although he pushed hard in Helsinki he was well behind Thompson and Jurgen Hingsen, his West German teammate.

Defending Olympic champion Daley Thompson of Great Britain ▼

Sabine Everts (FRG)

Heptathlon/long jump
Born: March 4, 1961, Dusseldorf, West Germany.
Height: 169cm/5ft 6½in.
Weight: 55kg/121lb.
Career Highlights
World Championships: *heptathlon* fourth 1983.
European Championships: *heptathlon* bronze 1982; *long jump* sixth 1982.
European Cup: *heptathlon* bronze 1981, sixth 1983; *pentathlon* seventh 1979; *400h* fifth 1983; *long jump* fifth 1983.

This classical music-loving student is the only West European heptathlete who can truly test the wonderful duo the other side of the Iron Curtain, but her small stature handicaps her in events such as the shot.

Ramona Neubert (GDR)

Heptathlon
Born: July 26, 1958, Pirna, East Germany.
Height: 173cm/5ft 8in.
Weight: 64kg/141lb.
Career Highlights
Olympic Games: *pentathlon* fourth 1980.
World Championships: *heptathlon* gold 1983.
European Championships: *heptathlon* gold 1982; *pentathlon* eighth 1978.
European Cup: *pentathlon* bronze 1979; *heptathlon* gold 1981, 1983.
Records
World: *heptathlon;* 1983 (6836), 1982 (6773), 1981 (6716), (6621).

A medical student who is now unchallenged at the heptathlon, winning the world title and breaking the world record in 1983. She has never lost in nine attempts at the event, and four of them were world records.

Glynnis Nunn (AUS)

Heptathlon/100 metres hurdles/long jump
Born: December 18, 1958, Brooklyn Park, South Australia.
Height: 168cm/5ft 6in.
Weight: 58kg/127.6lb.
Career Highlights
World Championships: *heptathlon* seventh 1983; *long jump* semi-finals 1983; *100h* semi-finals 1983.
Commonwealth Games: *heptathlon* gold 1982; *100h*

sixth 1982; *long jump* seventh 1982.

Nunn is a talented athlete who lacks the physique to match her rivals when it comes to the throwing events. Her ability in the hurdles and jumps shows what she could do if she could match them in the shot and javelin.

Glynnis is a student teacher.

Sabine Paetz (GDR)

Heptathlon
Born: October 16, 1957, Dobeln, East Germany.
Height: 174cm/5ft 8½in.
Weight: 72kg/158.5lb.
Career Highlights
World Championships: *heptathlon* silver 1983.
European Championships: *heptathlon* silver 1982.
European Cup: *heptathlon* fourth 1981, 1979.

A sport's student in Leipzig, Sabine Paetz was called Mobius before she married in February 1983. She was a perennial runner-up to Neubert.

Judy Simpson (GBR)

Heptathlon
Born: November 14, 1960, Rugby, England.
Height: 184cm/6ft 0½in.
Weight: 72kg/158.5lb.
Career Highlights
Olympic Games: *pentathlon* thirteenth 1980.
World Championships: *100h* semi-finals 1983.
European Championships: *heptathlon* seventh 1982.
Commonwealth Games:

heptathlon silver 1982; *100h* fifth 1982.
European Cup: *heptathlon* fifth 1983.
World Student Games: *heptathlon* fourth 1981.

A great favourite wherever she competes because of her good looks and long legs, plus an ebullient personality, the former Judy Livermore is threatening to break through to the very top and threaten the East Germans.

She has a very good first half programme but, so far, is let down by the second day. She seemed set to improve dramatically in Helsinki but failed to register a valid javelin throw.

She is also a good enough hurdler to take third place in the British team, and reached the semi finals in the World Championships, and took fifth place in Brisbane.

She married pole vaulter Robin Simpson early in 1984.

▲
Sabine Everts of West Germany struggles to match the Eastern European powerhouses

Queen of the heptathlon, East Germany's Ramona Neubert ▼

Swimming

◄ *Mark Spitz . . . the most successful Olympic swimmer of all time with seven golds and seven world records at Munich, 1972*

Who in 1896, when swimming was included in the first of the modern Olympic Games in Athens, would have envisaged such a dream becoming a reality? Only four swimming competitions took place at those inaugural Games. These included a 100 metre race 'exclusively for sailors of ships anchored in the port of Piraeus'. The other events were 100 metres freestyle, 500 metres and 1200 metres and the first to be honoured with a gold medal was a Hungarian, Alfred Hajos, who won the 100 metres freestyle in 1:22.2 ahead of Gardrez Williams, of the United States, and an Austrian, Otto Herschman, who took the bronze.

Hajos further showed his outstanding prowess by also winning the 1200 metres in 18:22.2, 2½ minutes clear of the Greek runner-up, Jean Andreou.

When relating these times to present day standards it should be noted that all the races were held in the cold sea of the Bay of Zea, near Piraeus. Twenty-eight years after his Olympic 'double', Hajos received another top Olympic award, this time in the architectural category for his design of the internationally famous swimming pool at St Margaret's Island in Budapest.

The Paris Olympics of 1900 saw the swimming again in the open air but in the greater comfort of a pool built in the Seine at Asnieres. A completely changed programme of racing events included a 200 metres obstacle championship and a 60 metres underwater swim. Neither of those competitions has been held since, though they still race the 200 metres freestyle and 200 metres backstroke.

Britain's John Jarvis figured prominently in Paris by taking the gold medals for 1000 metres and 4000 metres, the one and only time races at these distances were included in an Olympic programme. The British, represented by Osburne Club, of Manchester, also won the water polo, held for the first time and a recognised activity in today's Olympics.

The organizing of the 1904 Games in St Louis was left virtually to the Americans. They chose to have the races over distances in yards and in an irregular-shaped pool in the middle of an artificial lake specially prepared for an international exhibition.

The Americans, who had still to win an Olympic swimming title, were convinced they had, in Charles Daniels, a competitor capable of striking gold and he proved them right by winning both the 220 and 440 yards freestyle finals and anchoring their national squad in the 4 x 50 yards relay. He would have had a fourth gold but for the Hungarian Zoltan Halmay beating him to the touch in the 100 yards.

Highboard diving was introduced in these Games and Dr. George Sheldon duly delighted his American compatriots by scoring a decisive points success. And there was further elation in the US camp when the New York AC team trounced the Chicago Club 6-0 to win the water polo final.

A powerful sidestroke featured in the wins of the German Emil Rausch in the 880 yards and one mile events.

In 1908, London built a special Olympic pool, 100 metres long, in the centre of the White City athletics stadium at Shepherds Bush. All the racing was over metric distances. Charles Daniels was there again to meet the challenge of Zoltan Halmay and a desperate duel between the two led to Daniels taking the freestyle sprint title (100 metres) from Halmay in a world record 65.4. Halmay also beat the previous best world time. A highly developed American crawl style gave the American the edge this time.

But Britain were not to be denied their share of the glory. Henry Taylor set new world marks for 400 metres (5:36.8) and 1500 metres (22:48.4), and completed a hat-trick of golds as anchor-man to Britain's winning 4 x 200 metres relay team. Fred Holman also gave the home country a world record-breaking win in the 200 metres breaststroke (3:09.2).

In Stockholm four years later, women's events were included in the Olympic swimming for the first time at 100 metres freestyle, 4 x 100 metres relay and highboard diving. While Fanny Durack, of Australia, became the first woman to win an Olympic swimming gold medal there was no stopping the British quartet outclassing the opposition in the sprint relay.

If one Olympic swimming record is to survive, it must surely be the achievement of the American Mark Spitz at the 1972 Games in Munich. There he won an unprecedented seven gold medals and was involved in the breaking of seven world records.

The previous highest number of gold medals won by a swimmer was the four by another popular American, Don Schollander, in Tokyo in 1964.

While the whole world of sport was acclaiming the mastery of Spitz in Munich, Spitz himself was savouring the satisfaction of vindicating himself following disappointing performances at the Mexico City Games four years earlier. Having already broken world records, he went to Mexico a strong favourite to win at least three individual titles, but returned home with only two golds — both from relays.

His loss of peak form in Mexico City brought him almost as much world-wide publicity as did his successes in Munich. It was the blow of those defeats in Mexico, where his only individual awards were a silver in the 100 metre butterfly and a bronze in the 100 metre freestyle, that made Spitz vow he would make amends next time.

No swimmer trained with greater determination in the four years that followed and his reward in Munich was to stand on the victory rostrum to receive winning awards for the 100 and 200 metres freestyle, the 100 and 200 metre butterfly, the 4 x 100 metres and 4 x 200 metres freestyle relays and the 4 x 100 metres medley.

Though only 22 at the close of those Games, Spitz decided to retire from competition. In his 12 years of racing he had achieved 32 world records, 25 in individual events and seven in relays, and in his book that followed he wrote: *'I have no regrets in quitting. I held the world record in everything I swam in the 1972 Olympics and accomplished what was for me the ultimate dream.'*

Sweden's Arne Borg, edged out by Weissmuller in 1924 ▼ ▼

The two greatest swimmers of their era meet . . . Johnny Weissmuller (USA), left, and Duke Kahanomoku (USA) at the 1924 Paris Games. Both went on to Hollywood careers. ▼

But greater interest was being shown in a powerful Hawaiian member of the American men's team who answered to the name Duke Paoa Kahinu Makoe Huilikohoa Kahanamoku. In the first heat of the 100 metres freestyle he brought the world record down to 62.6, improved it to 62.4 in the semi-final and was only one second slower in winning the final.

Kahanamoku was one of the first to develop the vertical flutter kick with the American crawl. George Hodgson brought Canada to the fore in these Games by winning the 400 metres and 1500 metres freestyle finals in world record times. The notable British champion, John Hatfield, was left to collect the silver in both finals.

World War I prevented the Olympics taking place in 1916, but Kahanamoku was still the dominating sprinter at Antwerp in 1920 and produced an Olympic record, retaining his 100 metres title with 61.4. He also anchored the United States to a world record-breaking 10:04.4 win in the 4 x 200 metres relay.

The strength of American swimming was now beginning to stamp its mark on the Games. In addition to filling the first three places in the 100 metres freestyle, finishing first and second in the 400 metres freestyle and 100 metres backstroke and taking the gold in the 1500 metres, their women's team provided all the medal winners in the 100 metre and 300 metres freestyle events and also set a world record in winning the 4 x 100 metres relay. And to cap their achievements at these Olympics, American girls finished 1-2-3 in the springboard diving with 14-year-old Aileen Riggin receiving the gold.

Though he was now 34, the 1924 Olympics in Paris saw Kahanamoku in the forefront of the swimming action yet again, only to be denied a further gold in the 100 metres freestyle by an 20-year-old team-mate who was to become one of the most famous names in world swimming— Johnny Weissmuller.

Weissmuller and his Illinois club coach, Bill Bachrach, had made a detailed scientific study of the American crawl and devised a faster stroke by concentrating on a deeper leg action and at the same time producing a stronger pull with his arms. The overall effort enabled Weissmuller to ride higher in the water and so reduce resistance to his forward movement. He also introduced a new style, turning his head to breathe independently of his arm action to keep a close watch on opponents on each side of him.

The beautifully proportioned 6ft 3in (1.90m) Weissmuller had Kahanamoku well in his sights as he powered to that first Olympic gold in Paris in 59 seconds, the first time in the history of the Games that the minute had been broken for the 100 metres. Kahanamoku touched home in second place in exactly the same time that had won him the title in Antwerp four years previously.

In all Weissmuller captured three golds at those Games. In the 400 metres freestyle he fought off a tremendous challenge from two of the sports greats, Arne Borg of Sweden, and the Australian Andrew Charlton, and in doing so brought the world record for the event down to 5: 4.2.

The American's third triumph came in the 4 x 200 metres which produced another world record of 9:53.4. Not content with these successes, Weissmuller also helped his country win a bronze medal in the water polo.

Further triumphs in racing and diving left nobody in doubt that the United States were the number one swimming nation and to emphasize this even further the American girls produced two world records and four new Olympic marks, winning 15 of a possible 19 medals.

At the Amsterdam Olympics in 1928 Weissmuller proved himself the supreme sprinter again. This time he reduced the Olympic record to 58.6, retaining the 100 metres title and once more anchored a successful American 4 x 200 metres relay team to an Olympic record 9:36.2.

Following his great achievements as an amateur, which included setting 28 world records ranging from 100 yards to 880 yards, Weissmuller won further fame as Tarzan in films.

Japanese swimming coaches wasted no time in filming Weissmuller's revolutionary racing crawl and the value of this was soon apparent at the Los Angeles Olympics of 1932 when Japan stunned the Americans by taking the 100 metres freestyle gold with Yasuji Miyazaki beating Weissmuller's Olympic record at 58.2 and Tatsugo Kawaishi also providing them with the silver in a tight finish with Albert Schwartz of the United States at 58.6.

While the United States gained satisfaction from 'Buster' Crabbe winning the 400 metres freestyle, the Japanese were still not to be outdone and in addition to taking all the medals in the 100 metres backstroke they also filled the top two placings in the 1500 metres freestyle and 200 metres breaststroke and beat the Americans in a world best time for the 4 x 200 metres relay title.

But there was consolation for the United States team. Their divers won all the medals in both the springboard and highboard for men and women.

Berlin 1936 saw no relaxing in the intensity of the rivalry between the American and Japanese swimmers. The US won the 400 metres freestyle, the 100 metres backstroke and both the dives and Japan the 1500 metres, 200 metres breaststroke and 4 x 200 metres relay. Both countries, however, were thwarted in their endeavours to capture the 100 metres sprint when Hungarian Ferenc Csik surprisingly snatched the title in 57 .6 after two Japanese had reduced the Olympic record for the event to 57 .5 in the heats. A Dutch girl, Hendrika Mastenbroek, called a halt to American domination of the women's Olympic competitions by winning both the 100 metres and 400 metres freestyle and taking her team to victory in the 4 x 100 metres relay as well as racing a close second to her compatriot Dina Senff in the 100 metres backstroke.

But the Americans were back on top for the next Olympics in London in 1948. In the absence of the Japanese following World War II, the United States won all the men's racing and diving events and also took their share of the women's awards.

By the time of the 1952 Helsinki Olympics, international sport was recovering well from the ravages of the war and this was shown by the range of the challenge to the Americans for the swimming honours. Whereas the United States still managed to collect six of the men's eight golds there was a far greater share-out of the place medals. And only by Pat McCormick winning both dives did the United States manage gold from the women's series.

The awarding of the 1956 Olympics to Melbourne inspired a new era for Australian swimming. Determined not to be a disappointment to their own supporters the Aussie coaches developed what was probably their country's greatest all-time team. Jon Henricks won the 100 metres freestyle, Murray Rose the 400 metres and 1500 metres, David Theile the 100 metres backstroke, and the sprint squad the 4 x 200 metres relay. And their successes did not end there. Dawn Fraser, destined to become the greatest of all Australian women swimming stars took the 100 metres freestyle in 62.0, almost four seconds faster than any previous Olympic winner, and Lorna Crapp, who finished second in the race, went on to score another notable triumph for Australia in the 400 metres with Dawn in second place. Both helped in another record-breaking success in the 4 x 100 metres relay.

At the height of all the Aussie excitement, Judy Grinham gave the British team a boost with a thrilling victory by a touch in the 100 metres backstroke from Connie Cone of the United States with Margaret Edwards, also from Britain, a close third.

The 100 metres at the Rome Olympics of 1960 led to a decision that is still talked about. Timekeepers gave America's Lance Larson as the winner, one-tenth of a second faster than John Devitt of Australia. But the judges placed Devitt first and all protests from the Americans were to no avail. The official time for both was given as 55.2, a new Olympic record.

Australia's finest . . . Dawn Fraser, sprint champion in three consecutive Olympics
▼

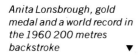

Duncan Goodhew . . .
maintained Britain's
tradition in the Moscow
breaststroke   ▶

Anita Lonsbrough, gold
medal and a world record in
the 1960 200 metres
backstroke   ▼

This was not the only gold the US had to concede to the Australians. Murray Rose successfully defended his 400 metres crown and Jon Konrads, another remarkable Australian 'find', sliced almost 40 seconds off the 1500 metres record with Rose chasing him home for the silver. David Theile also asserted his mastery again in the 100 metre backstroke. Nevertheless, the Americans still managed to grab their share of the golds by winning the 4 x 200 metres relay and a newly introduced 4 x 100 metres medley as well as both the men's diving finals, the 200 metres breaststroke and 200 metres butterfly. Five golds were also won by their girls but they could not stop a determined Yorkshire lass, Anita Lonsbrough, keeping Britain on the gold standard with a world record-breaking win in the 200 metres breaststroke.

While Australia were still a power to be reckoned with in the 1964 Tokyo Games, it was Don Schollander who became the hero of the swimming by anchoring the two successful American relay teams in addition to winning the 100 metres and 400 metres freestyle finals. No swimmer had previously won four golds at an Olympic Games.

Dawn Fraser also made history by winning the women's 100 metres freestyle title for a third successive time, the feat heightened by the fact that she completed the hat-trick by becoming the first woman at the Olympics to swim 100 metres inside the minute — with 59.5. She made 39 world records during her racing career, a feat more remarkable because she suffered from bronchial asthma.

Mexico City in 1968 provided those of us privileged to be present with the pleasure of seeing that greatest of all backstroke champions, Roland Matthes, of the GDR, claim a magnificent record-breaking double, a feat he was to repeat in Munich four years later. It was the effortless-looking rhythmic power of his stroke that won him so much admiration.

His world records have gone but the memory of his superb stroke lingers on. Matthes is now married to Kornelia Ender who in Montreal became the first woman swimmer to win four gold medals at one Olympics. Only Mark Spitz stopped Matthes from becoming the swimming star of Munich.

The world record-breaking swim that won Britain's David Wilkie the gold medal for the 200 metres breaststroke at the 1976 Games in Montreal was thrilling, but the final length in the 1500 metres final was no less memorable. Three swimmers, all inside world record schedule, turned level for the final length and in a desperate finish after such a punishing pace, Brian Goodell, of the United States, finally won from Bobby Hackett, also of the United States, and Australia's Steve Holland, with a world record 15:02.40. Only two seconds separated them at the finish with each beating the previous world best.

Yet in Moscow four years later Vladimir Salnikov swam even faster, winning the gold for the Soviet Union with an incredible 14:58.27.

Can Adrian Moorhouse continue Britain's great breaststroke tradition and add gold to the ones collected by Wilkie and the prematurely bald Duncan Goodhew in the past two Olympics? Goodhew, chrome-domed since falling out of a tree as a child, was one of the most popular champions of 1980.

What times might be achieved by great champions like Salnikov and the successors of Kornelia Ender in the GDR women's team in Los Angeles this summer?

Eastern Europe have also taken a grip of the water polo competition in recent Olympics. Since 1932 only Italy (twice) have broken the domination which has seen Hungary win six times and Russia twice.

The great Johnny Weissmuller collected a bronze as a member of the US team in 1924.

David Ambartsumian
(URS)
Highboard diving
Born: June 24, 1956, Kafan, USSR.
Height: 175cm/5ft 9in.
Weight: 71kg/157lb.
Career Highlights
Olympic Games: *highboard* bronze 1980.
World Cup: *highboard* bronze 1983.
European Championships: *highboard* gold 1981, 1983.
European Cup: *highboard* silver 1983.

For a diver, experience is more important than youth, and Ambartsumian – who will be 28 at the time of the 1984 Games – has steadily improved during his long career.

Alex Baumann (CAN)
200/400 medley
Born: April 21, 1964, Prague, Czechoslovakia.
Height: 188cm/6ft 2in.
Weight: 80kg/176lb.
Career Highlights
Commonwealth Games: *200 medley* gold 1982; *400 medley* gold 1982; *4 x 100 freestyle* bronze 1982.
Record
World and Commonwealth: *200 medley* 1982 (2:02.25)
Commonwealth: *400m medley* 1983 (4:19.80)

Baumann left Czechoslovakia for New Zealand with his family when he was two. Four years later they went to Canada and made their home at Sudbury, Ontario. He proclaims his pride in his country

of adoption by the tiny, delicate maple leaf and his nickname Sasha, tattooed in colour, on his left breast over his heart and has repaid his welcome by becoming one of its greatest sportsmen.

He was named in Canada's 1980 'Olympic team', at 16, but could not take part in Moscow because the Dominion boycotted the last Games. Tenderitis in a shoulder – something suffered by many swimmers undergoing very heavy training – started to trouble him in April 1980. It did not respond quickly to treatment, eventually forcing him out of competition for most of the 1982 season, including the World Championships in Ecuador.

However, he came back for the Commonwealth Games that autumn in Brisbane where he was the only world record-breaker in the pool, winning the 200m medley in 2:02.25. This time was still the world record at the end of 1983.

He is also a high speed short course racer and has broken Canadian records for 200, 400 and 1500 metres freestyle as well as for his speciality medley events. He opened 1984 by setting world best 25m pool times of 1:58.96 and 4:10.67 for 200 and 400 metres medley respectively.

Craig Beardsley (USA)
200 butterfly
Born: December 14, 1960, New York City, USA.
Height: 180cm/5ft 11in.
Weight: 73kg/150lb.
Career Highlights
World Championships: *200 butterfly* bronze 1982.

Pan American Games: *200 butterfly* gold 1979, 1983.
Records
World: former *200 butterfly* 1981 (1:58.01).

A graduate of the University of Florida, Beardsley was named US male 'Swimmer of the Year' by American magazine *'Swimming World'* in 1981 for his world 200m butterfly record. This time had not been bettered in 1982 when the World Championships took place and it was a shock when the American finished only in third place behind West Germany's Michael Gross and Russian veteran Sergey Fesenko. Gross failed, by eight tenths of a second, to break Beardsley's world figures then although he sliced a second off it a year later.

▲
Experience is on the side of Russia's David Ambartsumian

US Swimmer of the Year in 1981, Craig Beardsley
◄

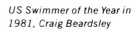

Rick Carey (USA)
100/200 backstroke/400 medley
Born: March 13, 1963, Mt Kisco,
New York, USA.
Height: 180cm/5ft 11in.
Weight: 77kg/170lb.
Career Highlights
World Championships: *200
backstroke* gold 1982; *4 x 100
medley* gold 1982; *100
backstroke* silver 1982.
Pan American Games: *100
backstroke* gold 1983; *200
backstroke* gold 1983; *4 x 100
medley* gold 1983.
Records
World: *100 backstroke* 1983
(55.38); *200 backstroke*
1983 (1:58.93).

◀ *Canada's Victor Davis . . .
bad tempered in Brisbane*

John Naber's 100 and 200m
backstroke times of 55.49 and
1:59.19 were the oldest in the
world record book until Rick Carey,
20, turned out at the US long
course championships in Clovis in
the summer of 1983. But all
records are there to be beaten and,
after seven years, Naber's were
though only by fractions of a second.

Carey twice trimmed the 100m
mark with 55.44 in a heat and
55.38 in the final. He improved
the 200m figures by 0.26 to
1:58.93, also in a heat, to become
the first man under 1:59. A week
later, at the Pan-American Games
in Caracas, he completed his hat
trick of 100m backstroke world
records with 55.19, for a total
improvement over Naber of three
tenths of a second. As long ago as
1979, the then Fox Lane High
schoolboy had been tipped as the
backstroke man of the future. He

proved the forecasters right as he
hopes to do again in Los Angeles
this summer.

For the record book, only Carey
and Naber, who retired after the
1976 Games, have ever broken 2
minutes for 200m and the American pair plus European record holder Dirk Richter of East Germany
are the three backstrokers to have
gone below 56sec for 100m.

Victor Davis (CAN)
100/200 breaststroke
Born: February 10, 1964,
Waterloo, Ontario, Canada.
Height: 185cm/6ft 1in.
Weight: 84kg/185lb.
Career Highlights
World Championships: *200
breaststroke* gold 1982; *100
breaststroke* silver 1982.
Commonwealth Games: *200
breaststroke;* gold 1982; *100
breaststroke* silver 1982.
Record
World: *200 breaststroke* 1982
(2:14.77).

Davis, from Waterloo, Ontario was
only the tenth best in the world for
200m breaststroke and 13th for
100m at the end of 1981. By
August, 1982, in Ecuador, he was
world champion and record holder
for the former and runner-up to
America's world record holder
Steve Lundquist over the shorter
distance.

After a 2.8sec easy victory in
the Commonwealth Games 200m
breaststroke in Brisbane that
October, Davis confidently
expected also to take the 100m.
But he and his coaches had
under-estimated England's Adrian
Moorhouse who went into the lead
after the turn and never let the
tempestuous Canadian get past.

This bad day, the last of the
Games swimming, was made even
worse for Davis when his medley
relay squad were disqualified for a
flying take-over between himself
and butterflyer Dan Thompson. It
was all so needless, for the Cana-
dians had touched 2.5sec ahead
of Australia. It was also the third
time out of five relay events that a
squad from Canada had been disqualified in Brisbane. Despite the
presence of the Queen in the Royal
Box, Davis kicked a chair across
the centre span of the pool and
joined a walk-out of the whole
Canadian swimming team before
the relay medals had been presented. They then damaged the
inside and outside of the brand
new Commonwealth pool.

Little was heard of Davis in
1983. He did not rank in the top
50 in the world for either of his
speciality distances. But he
opened 1984 by setting world best
short course (25m pool) times for
100m (1:00.61) and 200m
(2:09.81) in Winnipeg in January.

◀ ◀

*Rick Carey of the USA,
second man to go sub two
minutes for 200 metres*

Sergey Fesenko (URS)
200 butterfly/400 medley
Born: January 29, 1959, Krivoj
   Rog, Ukraine, USSR.
Height: 188cm/6ft 2in.
Weight: 80kg/164lb.
Career Highlights
Olympic Games: *200 butterfly*
   gold 1980; *400 medley* silver
   1980.
World Championships: *400
   medley;* silver 1978; *200
   butterfly;* silver 1982; *400
   medley* bronze 1982.
European Championships: *400
   medley* gold 1977, *200
   butterfly* silver 1983, bronze
   1981.

*Italy's hope for a first
Olympic title . . . Giovanni
Franceschi* ▶ ▶

The international career of
Fesenko began in 1977 and he has
been a medal winner at every
major event since for his speciality
200m butterfly and/or 400m
medley races. His tally includes
three golds, five silvers and two
bronze.

Some of his battles have been
with Britain's Philip Hubble, whom
he beat into second place at the
Moscow Olympics but finished
behind at the 1981 European
Championships where the Briton
took the silver and the Ukrainian
the bronze.

To see his wife and child in the
Ukraine, he must travel 10 hours
each way by train from Moscow
where he swims. With all his racing
commitments he does not get
home very often. Fesenko, now
25, is likely to be one of the oldest
swimming competitors in Los
Angeles.

Giovanni Franceschi (ITA)
200/400 medley
Born: March 26, 1963, Milan,
   Italy.
Height: 192cm/6ft 3½in.
Weight: 80kg/176lb.
Career Highlights
World Championships: *200
   medley* bronze 1982.
European Championships: *200
   medley* gold 1983; *400 medley*
   gold 1983.

Records
European: *200 medley* 1983
   (2:02.48); *400 medley* 1983
   (4:20.41).

Tall, lanky Franceschi would have
raised the roof — if there had been
a roof — in Rome in 1983 when he
won the European 200 and 400m
medley gold medals in European
record times. His times then made
him the second fastest in the world
last year, behind Canada's Alex
Baumann. Italy has never had a
male or female Olympic swimming
champion. Giovanni is the best
hope the country has had in many
a year.

*Moscow gold medallist
Sergey Fesenko of the
USSR*
▼

▲
Fastest swimmer in the world . . . America's Rowdy Gaines

Butterfly specialist Matt Gribble of the USA
▼

Ambrose 'Rowdy' Gaines
(USA)
100/200 freestyle
Born: February 17, 1959, Winter Haven, Florida, USA.
Height: 183cm/6ft 1in.
Weight: 73kg/160lb.
Career Highlights
World Championships: *200 freestyle* silver 1982, 1978; *4 x 100 freestyle* gold 1982, 1978; *4 x 200 freestyle* gold 1982; *4 x 100 medley* gold 1982; *100 freestyle* silver 1982.
Pan American Games: *200 freestyle* gold 1979, bronze 1983; *4 x 100 freestyle* gold 1983, 1979; *4 x 200 freestyle* gold 1983, 1979; *100 freestyle* gold 1983; *4 x 100 medley relay* gold 1983.
Pan Pacific Games: *100 freestyle* gold 1983; *4 x 100 freestyle* gold 1983; *4 x 200 freestyle* gold 1983; *4 x 100m medley* gold 1983.
Record
World: *100 freestyle* (49.36).

Gaines, the fastest man in the world as holder of the 100m freestyle record, has yet to win an Olympic Games or World Championships individual title.

His Olympic chance in 1980 disappeared when the United States pulled out from Moscow. At the World Championships two years later, he had to bow in the blue riband sprint to East Germany's Joerg Woithe by 0.03sec and in the 200m, for which at that time he was also the world record holder, Rowdy lost the touch by 0.08sec to Michael Gross of West Germany.

He was scathing about his efforts in Ecuador. About the 100m he said: 'I did a dumb thing . . . I was told to go out with Joerg on the first 50 and didn't. It wasn't a case of me not being able to, I just held back figuring I could catch him on the last 50, but I waited too long.'

Although he had broken the world 200m record only 10 days before the championships with 1:48.93, Gaines went out too slowly and had nothing left at the end of the race. He talked of retiring after those two disappointments but thought better about 1983, when he won many golds at the Pan-American and Pan-Pacific Games. He is very much in the swim with his eyes on gold in Los Angeles.

Matt Gribble (USA)
100 butterfly/400 medley
Born: March 28, 1962, Houston, Texas, USA.
Height: 180cm/5ft 11in.
Weight: 68kg/150lb.
Career Highlights
World Championships: *100 butterfly* gold 1982; *4 x 100 medley* gold 1982.
Pan American Games: *100 butterfly* gold 1983; *4 x 100 medley* gold 1983.
Pan Pacific Games: *100 butterfly* gold 1983; *4 x 100 medley* gold 1983.
Record
World: *100 butterfly* 1983 (53.44).

A sprint butterfly expert, Gribble's 1983 world record put him nearly three tenths of a second — half a metre — faster than any other man and 1.5sec ahead of the winning time of Sweden's Par Arvidsson in 1980 when, like all America's stars, he missed the chance of competing in Moscow.

Lethargic and lethal . . .
West Germany's Michael
Gross
◄

Michael Gross (FDR)

200 freestyle/100/200
butterfly/400/800 medley
Born: June 17, 1964, Frankfurt,
Germany.
Height: 201cm/6ft 7in.
Weight: 84kg/189lb.
Career Highlights
World Championships: *200
freestyle* gold 1982; *4 x 200
medley* bronze 1982; *200
butterfly* gold 1982; *100
butterfly* silver 1982; *4 x 100
medley* bronze 1982.
European Championships: *200
butterfly* gold 1981; *4 x 200
freestyle* silver 1981; *4 x 100
medley* bronze 1981; *200
freestyle* gold 1983; *100
butterfly* gold 1983; *4 x 200
freestyle* gold 1983; *4 x 100
medley* silver 1983.
Records
World and European: *200
freestyle* 1983 (1:47.87); *200
butterfly* 1983 (1:57.05).

The strikingly tall Gross is one of
the most remarkable swimmers
the world has seen. His almost
lethargic stroke disguises immense
power, he needs only about two
strokes to cover the same distance
for which his rivals take three.

In winning the European 200m
butterfly title in Rome in 1983 he
cut more than two seconds from
his own continental record and a
second from the world mark of
America's Craig Beardsley in beating Olympic champion Sergey
Fesenko by five metres.

He was equally devastating in
the 200m freestyle which he won
from East Germany's Joerg Woithe
by 4m in a world record 1:47.87
improving his own mark, set two
months earlier, by four tenths. His
anchor leg 'split' of 1:47.21 in the
4 x 200m relay helped West Germany to a world record, four-metre
victory over East Germany and he
also took the 100m butterfly in a
European record of 54.00, a time
bettered by only two men in 1983.

Gross needs a special long bed,
because of his height, and one is
flown to the major events for him.
He is also very much his own man
and will not allow his success and
fame to be made use of – unless it
suits him. It will take a mighty man
to beat him over 200m freestyle or
butterfly in Los Angeles.

Philip Hubble (GBR)

100/200 butterfly/
100/200 freestyle
Born: July 19, 1960,
Beaconsfield, England.
Height: 185cm/6ft 1in.
Weight: 78kg/172lb.
Career Highlights
Olympic Games: *200 butterfly*
silver 1980.
European Championships: *200
butterfly* silver 1981.
Commonwealth Games: *200
butterfly* gold 1982, bronze
1978; *4 x 200 freestyle* silver
1982, bronze 1978; *100
butterfly* silver 1982; *4 x 100
freestyle* silver 1982; *4 x 100
medley* silver 1982.
Record
Commonwealth: former *200
butterfly* 1981 (2:00.21).

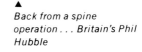

The determined Briton's swimming
ambitions have taken him to the
United States for training and,
currently, to Canada. His medal
achievements, since 1978, have
been remarkable especially on
occasions such as the European
Championships of 1981, when he
said 'I was lucky to get into the
British team.'

Hubble underwent a lower spine
operation in mid-December 1983
yet six weeks later still managed to
reach the final of the Canadian
short course 100m butterfly
championship and, despite loss of
training, only just missed the last
eight for 200m.

▲

*Back from a spine
operation . . . Britain's Phil
Hubble*

Perfection on the boards . . . American diver Greg Louganis ◄

Per Johansson (SWE)
100 freestyle
Born: January 25, 1963, Borlange, Sweden.
Career Highlights
Olympic Games: *100 freestyle* bronze 1980.
World Championships: *100 freestyle* bronze 1982; *4 x 100 freestyle* bronze 1982.
European Championships: *100 freestyle* gold 1983, 1981; *4 x 100 freestyle* silver 1983, 1981; *4 x 100 medley* silver 1981.

A man of remarkable competitive spirit, Johansson has become world and twice European 100m freestyle champion beating men such as Rowdy Gaines of the United States, the world record holder and Joerg Woithe from East Germany, the European number one when he was in no way the favourite.

He is again unlikely to be considered a high medal hope for Los Angeles, except by those who remember his achievements of the past. His rivals would be unwise to forget his fighting history.

Greg Louganis (USA)
Highboard, springboard diving
Born: January 29, 1960, El Cajon, California, USA.
Height: 173cm/5ft 8in.
Weight: 66kg/145lb.
Career Highlights
Olympic Games: *highboard* silver 1976.

World Championships: *springboard* gold 1983; *highboard* gold 1982, 1978.
World Cup: *highboard* gold 1979.

The Torvill and Dean of the diving board, he achieves perfection wherever he competes. In the 1982 World Championship, his reverse one and a half somersault straight springboard dive earned six 10s and one 9.5 from the seven judges. Earlier when he claimed the highboard title he became the first man to score more than 700 points for his 11 dives.

Steve Lundquist (USA)
100/200 breaststroke/
400 medley
Born: February 20, 1961, Atlanta, Georgia, USA.
Height: 188cm/6ft 2in.
Weight: 84kg/185lb.
Career Highlights
World Championships: *100 breaststroke* gold 1982; *4 x 100 medley* gold 1982.
Pan American Games: *100 breaststroke* gold 1983; *200 breaststroke* gold 1983; *4 x 100 medley* gold 1983; *200 medley* bronze 1983.
Record
World: *100 breaststroke* 1983 (1:02.34).

Steve Lundquist, the US Swimmer of the Year in 1982, continued his winning ways by twice breaking the world record for 100m breast-

stroke in a two-week span in August 1983. At the US Championships in Clovis, he cut his old mark by 0.19sec to 1:02.34. Then, at the Pan American Games in Caracas he trimmed it further to 1:02.28. He also broke the long-standing American 200m record set by Olympic silver medallist John Hencken in 1976, improving the mark by almost 2sec to 2:15.38.

Yet another American forced to miss the Moscow Games, Lundquist, with a great deal of experience and success behind him, will be looking to Los Angeles to avenge his disappointments of four years ago.

Steve Lundquist, two world records in a fortnight ▼

Aleksey Markovskiy (URS)

100 freestyle/100 butterfly
Born: May 17, 1957, Kurgun,
   USSR.
Height: 188cm/6ft 2in.
Weight: 83kg/183lb.
World Championships: *4 x 100
   freestyle* silver 1982; *4 x 100
   medley* silver 1982.
European Championships: *100
   butterfly* gold 1981; *4 x 100
   freestyle* gold 1981; *4 x 100
   medley* gold 1981; *4 x 100
   freestyle* gold 1983; *4 x 100
   medley* gold 1983; *100
   butterfly* bronze 1983.

A Soviet Union freestyle and butterfly sprinter who has not only had his own individual success at European Championships but has been a key man in his country's relay teams since 1982, Aleksey and can be expected to fulfil a similar role in 1984.

John Moffet (USA)

100/200 breaststroke
Born: July 27, 1964, Banning,
   California, USA.
Height: 183cm/6ft 0in.
Weight: 78kg/172lb.
Career Highlights
World Championships: *100
   breaststroke* bronze 1982; *200
   breaststroke* bronze 1982.
Pan Pacific Games: *100
   breaststroke* silver 1983.
Pan American Games: *100
   breaststroke* silver 1983.

Moffet was the second fastest 100m breaststroke swimmer in the World in 1983, only eight hundredths of a second behind his world record holder team mate Steve Lundquist who beat him by this margin at the Pan American Games in Caracas.

He will celebrate his 20th birthday on the day before the opening ceremony in Los Angeles where he hopes he can win a present for himself by way of an Olympic swimming medal.

Adrian Moorhouse (GBR)

100/200 breaststroke
Born: May 24, 1964, Bradford,
   England.
Height: 185cm/6ft 1in.
Weight: 83kg/183lb.
Career Highlights
European Championships: *200
   breaststroke* gold 1983, bronze
   1981; *100 breaststroke* silver
   1983.
Commonwealth Games: *100
   breaststroke* gold 1982; *200
   breaststroke* bronze 1982.

Moorhouse, the latest of a long line of outstanding British breaststroke stars, who include Olympic champions David Wilkie (200m in 1976) and Duncan Goodhew (100m in 1980), has an impressive list of successes since he took over their mantles in 1981.

He is one of the fastest men in the world up and down the pool

but, like so many Britons, has thrown away even greater success by weakness in the technical details of the whole race – such as poor starts, turns and even a determined finishing touch. He combined all three errors at the 1983 European Championships yet only lost the 100m title to the USSR's Robertas Zhulpa by five hundredths of a second. With only two of the three mistakes, he could have added this gold to his outstanding victory in the 200m with Olympic champion Zhulpa finishing only in third place.

Moorhouse showed his competitive fire at the 1982 Commonwealth Games in Brisbane where he shocked the complacent Canadian team by defeating their star Victor Davis in the 100m.

The technical details are high on the agenda of his coach, Terry Denison, in Leeds. If Moorhouse can also accept that good starts and turns are important, then he will be Britain's main medal hope in Los Angeles.

*Adrian Moorhouse . . .
Britain's main medal hope*
▼

◄
*John Moffett . . .
celebrating his 20th
birthday in Los Angeles*

Anthony Mosse (NZL)
200 butterfly
Born: October 29, 1964, Hong
   Kong.
Height: 185cm/6ft 1in.
Weight: 79kg/174lb.
Career Highlights
World Student Games: *200
   butterfly* bronze 1983.
Pan-Pacific Games: *200 butterfly*
   silver 1983.
Record
Commonwealth: *200 butterfly*
   1984 (1:59.30).

This quiet, slim New Zealander,
who lived for much of his life in
Hong Kong where his father was
an airline captain, has made great
swimming strides since he took
seventh place in the 200m butterfly at the 1982 Commonwealth
Games. His times improved in
almost every major swim and in
January 1984, at a multi-nation
meeting in Holland, he set a
Commonwealth record with
1:59.30 to join the elite men who
have broken 2 minutes for the
event. This performance was the
sixth fastest of all time.

With his career only just beginning, even greater improvements
can be expected from Mosse during his build up to Los Angeles. A
New Zealand man has never won
an individual Olympic swimming
medal and the only woman to succeed is Jean Stewart, 100m backstroke bronze medallist in Helsinki
in 1952. Can Mosse be the one to
bring his country back into the
Olympic history book?

Borut Petric (YUG)
400/1500 freestyle/400 medley
Born: December 28, 1961, Triglav
   Kranj, Yugoslavia.
Height: 187cm/6ft 1½in.
Weight: 84kg/185lb.
Career Highlights
European Championships: *1500
   freestyle* silver 1981, bronze
   1983, 1977; *400 freestyle*
   gold 1981; silver 1983.
World Championships: 1500
   freestyle silver 1978.
Mediterranean Games: *400
   freestyle* gold 1979; *1500
   freestyle* gold 1979; *400
   medley* gold 1979.

Borut Petric, Yugoslavia's only
world class man swimmer, has the
honour of also being the only man
to beat Soviet Vladimir Salnikov in
a major competition. He did this in
his own country, at the 1981 European Championships in the his-
toric seaside city of Split, where he
took the 400m freestyle crown
from super-star Salnikov by
0.14sec.

His record of success over the
longer races — 400 and 1500m
freestyle and sometimes the
400m medley — is remarkable
remembering that the level of
swimming in Yugoslavia is not generally high. His events need a massive training effort and until his
younger brother Darjan came on
the scene much of his work had to
be done on his own.

He has travelled world-wide as a
swimming ambassador for his
country and he will be trying to do
the same in Los Angeles this
summer.

Darjan Petric (YUG)
400/1500 freestyle
Born: August 24, 1964, Triglav
   Kranj, Yugoslavia.
Height: 181cm/5ft 11in.
Weight: 80kg/176lb.
Career Highlights
World Championships: *1500
   freestyle* bronze 1982.
European Championships: *400
   freestyle* bronze 1981, 1983.

Darjan Petric, nearly three years
younger than his more famous
brother, sprang the surprise of the
1981 European Championships
when he took the bronze in the
400m freestyle behind Borut and
Salnikov.

He has only once beaten Borut
in a major event, this was in the
1982 World Championships in
Ecuador where he finished fourth,
one place ahead of his brother.
Which Petric will be the more successful in Los Angeles remains to
be seen.

*Darjan Petric . . . following
in brother's wake*
▼

◀
*Yugoslav's swimming
ambassador . . . Borut
Petric*

Ricardo Prado (BRA)
200 backstroke/200
butterfly/400 medley
Born: January 3, 1965, Rio de
Janeiro, Brazil.
Height: 173cm/5ft 8in.
Weight: 68kg/150lb.
Career Highlights
World Championships: *400
medley* gold 1982.
Pan American Games: *200
medley* gold 1983; *400 medley*
gold 1983; *200 backstroke*
silver 1983; *200 butterfly* silver
1983.
Record
World: *400 medley* 1982
(4:19.78).

The American-trained Brazilian
made his piece of swimming history in Guayaquil, Ecuador, on
August 2, 1982 when he became
the first from his country and from
South America to win a world
championships – and he did it in
world record time.

It was an immaculate performance by the small, slim man
from Rio de Janeiro, for he beat his
nearest rival Jens-Peter Berndt
from East Germany by 5.5 metres.
About his victory he said: 'The
crowd was great for me, the cheer-
ing really helped. My breaststroke
and freestyle splits were not great
but the important thing was to
win.'

This was somewhat under rating
his performance for he showed
complete command of all four
strokes that make up the medley
event. And he underlined his versatility at the 1983 Pan American
Games by not only winning both
the 200m and 400m medley but
by taking silvers in the 200m
backstroke and butterfly championships as well.

Brazil has won only two Olympic
swimming medals, both bronze by
Tetsuo Okamoto for the 1500m in
1952 and Manuel Dos Santos in
the 100m freestyle in 1960. Young
Prado has a great chance to
improve his country's medal count
in Los Angeles.

*Brazil's first world
champion . . . Ricardo
Prado* ▼

Dirk Richter (GDR)
100 backstroke
Born: September 12, 1964,
Cottbus, East Germany.
Height: 188cm/6ft 2in.
Weight: 80kg/176lb.
Career Highlights
World Championships: *100
backstroke* gold 1982.
European Championships: *100
backstroke* gold 1983.
Record
European: *100 backstroke* 1984
(55.94).

Richter really made his mark at the
1982 World Championships in
beating America's Rick Carey in
the 100m backstroke in a European record of 55.95 to become
the first European under the
minute. That time has only been
bettered by Carey and the former
Olympic and world record holder
John Naber (USA) who retired
eight years ago.

The world backstroke scene was
dominated between 1967 and
1975 by Richter's East German
compatriot Roland Matthes. The
battle between Dirk and Rick in
Los Angeles should be a confrontation not to be missed.

◄ ◄

*First European to go below
a minute in the 100m
backstroke . . .
East Germany's Dirk Richter*

Vladimir Salnikov — (URS)

400/1500 freestyle
Born: May 21, 1960, Leningrad, USSR.
Height: 184cm/6ft 0in.
Weight: 71kg/157lb.
Career Highlights
Olympic Games: *400 freestyle* gold 1980; *1500 freestyle* gold 1980; *4 x 200 freestyle* gold 1980.
World Championships: *400 freestyle* gold 1982, 1978; *1500 freestyle* gold 1978.
European Championships: *400 freestyle* gold 1983, silver 1981; *1500 freestyle* gold 1983, 1981, 1977.
Records
World: *400 freestyle* (3:48.32); *1500 freestyle* (14:54.76); *800 freestyle* (7:53.33).

Salnikov has dominated the distance swimming scene since September 4, 1977 when he won his first big title, the European 1500m freestyle at the age of 17. And in 50 long course races over the distance since, no man has finished ahead of him.

A hero in his own country, a great ambassador for the Soviet Union and one of the most popular of all the world's swimmers, his tally of championships has been majestic. They include nine out a possible 10 major golds — the 1980 Olympic, 1978 and 1982 World and 1983 European 400 and 1500m events as well as the 1981 European crown.

The only man to beat him, in fact, was Borut Petric of Yugoslavia, racing in his own country, who defeated Salnikov in the 1981 European Championships in Split. It is thought Salnikov underesti-mated the effect of the patriot crowd on Petric.

The many world record-breaking achievements of Salnikov, a physical science student from Leningrad, include three historical barrier-breaking swims — the first man under 3:50 for 400m, 8min for 800m and 15min for 1500m. He can also claim to be the first man to set a world record in the brand new pool built for the Los Angeles Olympics on the campus of the Universtiy of Southern California. This he did in July 1983 at the try-out meeting for the Games in what was an obviously planned attack on his own 800m figures.

If there is a 'hot tip' for 1984 gold in swimming, the USSR's Salnikov, World Swimmer of the Year in 1979, 1980, 1981, 1982 and 1983, is top of the list.

Chris Snode (GBR)

Highboard, springboard diving
Born: March 23, 1959, Sutton, England.
Height: 175cm/5ft 9in.
Weight: 70kg/154lb.
Career Highlights
World Cup: *springboard;* gold 1979.
Commonwealth Games: *springboard* gold 1982, 1978; *highboard* gold 1982, 1978.

Snode was 17 and inexperienced when he took part in his first major diving competition at the Olympic Games of 1976 in Montreal. For long he had been coached by Johnny Rasch in London and, indeed, Rasch managed to find the money to go to Canada to see his protégé in action. Sadly,

Accident prone . . . Chris Snode of Britain

Johnny died suddenly in Montreal before the Games.

Chris remembered his coach's words: 'If you want to go to the top you must go to the United States'. So he got himself a scholarship to the University of Florida at Gainesville and that was the start of his real diving career.

Somewhat accident prone, Snode damaged a hand before the Moscow Olympics and picked up a virus there that put him into his main event with a high temperature. Not a man for excuses, it took a long time to discover just how ill he was when he competed in the springboard final and managed to come sixth.

His latest accident — and all divers are subject to bodily damage because of the intricate somersaulting and twisting movements they perform — was in the summer of 1983. He hit the back of his head on the board in Innsbruck and was temporarily knocked out. A similar accident, but this time from the highboard, during the World Student Games in Canada on the same day resulted in a Russian diver being killed.

Within a week, Snode was in Los Angeles, for the Olympic try-out meet. And with no training since the accident he took second place for the three metre springboard behind double Olympic and world champion Greg Luganis. No one really expects the great American star to be beaten from either board this summer but there are many with good chances to take the silvers behind him. From the springboard, in particular, Snode has as good a chance as anyone.

Vladimir Salnikov, hottest of favourites for a swimming gold
◄ ◄

Michael West (CAN)
100/200 backstroke
Born: August 31, 1964,
Kitchener, Canada.
Height: 188cm/6ft 2in.
Weight: 73kg/161lb.
Career Highlights
Pan American Games: *100
backstroke* bronze 1983; *200
backstroke* bronze 1983.
Commonwealth Games: *100
backstroke* gold 1982; *200
backstroke* bronze 1982.
Records
Commonwealth: *100 backstroke*
1983 (56.45); *200 backstroke*
1983 (2:01.83).

West, from Waterloo, Ontario, is
one of Canada's budding new stars
with backstroke his speciality. He
ended 1983 as the fifth fastest for
100m and sixth over 200m but
opened 1984 with a short course
(25m pool) best performance of
1:57.90 for 200m. This latest
effort suggests that 1984 is going
to be a good year for Mike. It
remains to be seen whether he can
beat the established stars to win
Canada's first Olympic men's
backstroke medal.

Joerg Woithe (GDR)
100/200 freestyle
Born: April 11, 1963, Berlin, East
Germany.
Height: 195cm/6ft 5in.
Weight: 80kg/176lb.
Career Highlights
Olympic Games: *100 freestyle*
1980; *4 x 200 freestyle;* silver
1980.
World Championships: *100
freestyle* gold 1982; *200
freestyle* silver 1982.
European Championships: *100
freestyle* silver 1983, 1981;
200 freestyle silver 1983; *4 x
200 freestyle* silver 1983; *4 x
100 medley* bronze 1983,
1981.

Woithe has had some great freestyle victories and some surprising
defeats. For example, he beat
world record holder Rowdy Gaines
of the United States in the World
Championships 100m in Guayaquil in 1982. Yet, he was twice
beaten by Sweden's Per
Johansson over the same distance
at the 1981 and 1983 European
Championships.
   Despite the swing of the pen-
dulum Woithe is one of the greats
of world sprinting and who takes
the medals in Los Angeles will
depend as much on split second
attention to every detail of the race
and nerve as on sheer speed.

Sergey Zabolotnov (URS)
200 backstroke
Born: March 14, 1963, Tashkent,
USSR.
European Championships: *200
backstroke* gold 1983.
World Student Games: *200
backstroke* gold 1983.
Record
European: *200 backstroke* 1984
(2:00.39).

The third fastest man of all time
for 200m backstroke – and in the
Los Angeles context the second
best since John Naber (USA)
retired after his Olympic victories
in 1976 – the man from Tashkent
must be considered a good medal
prospect in Los Angeles. Ahead of
him on the current rankings lists is
Rick Carey (USA) and close behind
his own countryman Vladimir
Shemetov. Carey looks the way out
favourite but the Soviet Union will
have a great fight for the silver.

Robertas Zhulpa (URS)
100/200 breaststroke
Born: March 20, 1960, Vilnius,
USSR.
Height: 193cm/6ft 4in.
Weight: 82kg/181lb.
Career Highlights
Olympic Games: *200 breaststroke*
gold 1981.
World Championships: *200
breaststroke* silver 1982.
European Championships: *100
breaststroke* gold 1983; *200
breaststroke* gold 1981, bronze
1983.

Generally considered to be better
over 200m breaststroke than the
100m, Zhulpa was the surprise
winner of the shorter distance title
at the 1983 European Championships and equally surprisingly
beaten into third place, by Britain's Adrian Moorhouse and Alban
Vermes from Hungary in his Olympic gold medal longer race.

Now a highly experienced competitor, number one in the world
for 200m breaststroke in 1979,
1980 and 1981 and second in
1982 and 1983, the man from Vilnius can never be counted out of
the running when the big competitions come along.

▲
*European 200m
backstroke champion
Sergey Zabolotnov*

*Robertas Zhulpa of the
USSR . . . has the
temperament for the big
competitions*
▼

Aiming for an Olympic hat-trick for the USSR . . . Larisa Belokon ►

The world's tallest woman swimmer . . . Romania's Carmen Bunaciu ► ►

Brita Baldus (GDR)
Springboard diving
Born: June 4, 1965, Leipzig, Germany.
Height: 157cm/5ft 1in.
Weight: 49kg/108lb.
Career Highlights
World Championships: *springboard* gold 1983, fifth 1982.
European Championships: *springboard* gold 1983.

She is one of the many talented East German women divers who will be chasing a medal in Los Angeles this summer.

Larisa Belokon (URS)
100/200 breaststroke
Born: May 18, 1964, Tashkent, USSR.
Height: 174cm/5ft 8½in.
Weight: 65kg/143lb.
Career Highlights
World Championships: *100 breaststroke* winner/consolation final 1982.

European Championships: *200 breaststroke* silver 1981; *100 breaststroke* bronze 1981.
World Student Games: *100 breaststroke* gold 1983; *200 breaststroke* gold 1983.
European Cup: top woman swimmer 1983.

The latest in a long line of outstanding Soviet Union women breaststroke swimmers, Larisa was named the top woman at the 1983 European Cup in Ankara, Turkey. Her target in Los Angeles is to complete a Soviet Olympic hat-trick for the 200m, following Marina Koshevaia (1976) and Larisa Kachushite (1980).

Carmen Bunaciu (ROM)
100/200 backstroke
Born: September 15, 1961, Sibiu, Romania.
Height: 190cm/6ft 3in.
Weight: 79kg/174lb.
Career Highlights
World Championships: *200 backstroke* bronze 1982.
European Championships: *100 backstroke* bronze 1981, 1983.
World Student Games: *100, 200 backstroke* silver 1983.

The tallest of the women swimming stars at 190cm (6ft 3in). Carmen Bunaciu has come close to bringing her country its first pool title but luck has not been with her. She had the best time of the year in July 1981 but she was ill before the European Championships in September and only managed the bronze although her earlier 1:02.19 was not beaten that year.

She began her seventh major racing season by winning the 50m, 100m and 200m backstroke titles in Holland in January and despite the fact it was very early in the season, her 1:02.68 was near to her 1981 summer fastest performance.

Tracy Caulkins (USA)
200/400 medley/
200 butterfly/100 breaststroke
Born: January 11, 1963, Nashville, Tennesse, USA.
Height: 175cm/5ft 9in.
Weight: 59kg/130lb.
Career Highlights
World Championships: *200 butterfly* gold 1978; *200 medley* gold 1978, bronze 1982; *400 medley* gold 1978, bronze 1982; *4 x 100 freestyle* gold 1978; *4 x 100 medley* gold 1978; *100 breaststroke* silver 1978.
Pan American Games: *200 medley* gold 1979, 1983; *400 medley* gold 1979, 1983; *4 x 100 relay* gold 1979, 1983; *100 breaststroke* silver 1979; *400 freestyle* silver 1979; *200 butterfly* silver 1983.

One of the greatest, most versatile

swimmers ever, Tracy has won major medals or American championships for all four individual strokes as well as the combined four-stroke individual medley.

She gained her first national titles in 1977 at 14 and was the youngest ever recipient of the Sullivan Award as the top amateur competitor of the United States, in 1978, the year she won a record five gold medals and a silver at the

Tracy Caulkins, one of swimming's greatest all-rounders ▼

World Championships in West Berlin. She is a former world record holder for 200m butterfly and 200m and 400m medley, at one time held 15 American records and has won more national championships than any other US swimmer, man or woman.

The Tennessee girl was an innovator of what has become known as 'The Caulkins flutter' in breaststroke swimming. This con-

troversial technique, whereby the legs rise above the water during the recovery phase and drop down again for the next outward and driving kick, was quickly imitated by stars such as Anne Ottenbrite of Canada.

In breaststroke, no up and down movements of the legs are permitted. The extended argument about supple Tracy and her followers was whether this kind of flutter (or dolphin) action was merely involuntary and thus possibly legal or if it had a propulsive element, in which case it would be illegal. Although the international federation (FINA) slightly amended its rules to allow 'involuntary' flutters, the legality of this technique has not yet been settled.

In Moscow Tracy Caulkins would have had a magnificent chance of avenging the trouncing of her countrywomen at the Montreal Olympics of 1976 — by East Germany and lone swimmers from the USSR and Australia who took all the individual titles. Unluckily for her, the United States was among the boycott nations in 1980.

The question, four years later and in her 10th competitive season, is whether she can raise her sights again to win in Los Angeles or join the ranks of the greats who never were Olympic champions.

Tiffany Cohen (USA)

400/800 freestyle
Born: June 11, 1966, Culver City, California, USA.
Height: 167cm/5ft 6in.
Weight: 50kg/110¼lb.
Career Highlights
World Championships: *400 freestyle* bronze 1982.
Pan-American Games: *400 freestyle* gold 1983; *800 freestyle* gold 1983.
Pan-Pacific Games: *400 freestyle* gold 1983; *800 freestyle* gold 1983.

A member of the famous Mission Viejo club in California, coached by Mark Schubert, Tiffany used to race distance events in the shadow of her four years older compatriot Kim Linehan, the world 1500m freestyle record holder. But in 1983, she emerged as number one in the world for 400m, two hundredths of a second in front of European champion Astrid Strauss of East Germany — 4:08.05 to 4:08.07 and only half a second behind Strauss in the 800m. A battle between the two of them could be a Los Angeles epic.

June Croft (GBR)
100/200/400/800 freestyle
Born: June 17, 1963, Bryn, Wales.
Height: 175cm/5ft 9in.
Weight: 60kg/132lb.
Career Highlights
Olympic Games: *4 x 100 medley*
    silver 1980.
Commonwealth Games: *100*
    freestyle gold 1982; *200*
    freestyle gold 1982; *4 x 100*
    freestyle gold 1982; *4 x 100*
    medley silver 1982; *400*
    freestyle bronze 1982.
Records
Commonwealth: *100 freestyle*
    1982 (56.60) 200 freestyle
    1982 (1:59.74).

June, who swims for the Wigan (Lancashire) club, has only twice — so far — justified her potential and her pre-event rankings. These were at the Moscow Olympics when she anchored the British medley relay squad to surprise silvers behind East Germany but ahead of the Soviet team and in the 1982 Commonwealth Games where she took three gold medals and became only the fifth woman in the world to break two minutes for 200m freestyle.

Her big disappointments include the 1982 World Championships in Guayaquil, Ecuador. She went into the 200m freestyle as the fastest of the year and favourite but could only manage seventh.

This disaster nearly drove her out of swimming but six months training in California in the winter and spring of 1983 gave her the break from the old routine that she badly needed and experience of the tough US swimming scene.

June, training harder than ever and with a new, longer front crawl arm action, came within three tenths of her Commonwealth record in her first big long course race of 1984 — in Holland in January. She knows she must keep her nerves steady for the summer challenge if she is to close her distinguished career with an individual Olympic medal.

Michelle Ford (AUS)
400/800 freestyle/200 butterfly
Born: July 15, 1962, New South
    Wales, Australia.
Height: 165cm/5ft 5in.
Weight: 62kg/137lb.
Career Highlights
Olympic Games: *800 freestyle*
    gold 1980; *200 butterfly* silver
    1980.
Commonwealth Games: *200*
    butterfly gold 1982, 1978;
    400 freestyle silver 1978; *800*
    freestyle silver 1978; *200*
    medley bronze 1978; *4 x 100*
    medley bronze 1978; *800*
    butterfly silver 1982.

Michelle, who has trained in recent years in the United States, was left out of the Australian team for the 1982 World Championships for no apparent good reason. Yet she has served her country well, winning medals as an outside chance rather than a favourite. One such victory was in the 800m freestyle at the Moscow Olympics where she set a Games record of 8:28.90, nearly four seconds in front of East Germany's Ines Diers.

Ines Geissler (GDR)
100/200 butterfly/400 medley
Born: February 16, 1953,
    Marienberg, East Germany.
Height: 165cm/5ft 5in.
Weight: 58kg/128lb.
Career Highlights
Olympic Games: *200 butterfly*
    gold 1980.
World Championships: *4 x 100*
    medley gold 1982; *200*
    butterfly gold 1982; *100*
    butterfly silver 1982.
European Championships: *4 x 100*
    medley gold 1983, 1981; *100*
    butterfly gold 1983; *200*
    butterfly silver 1983.
Record
European: *200 butterfly* (2:8.50).

Ines, 17 when she won the Olympic 200m butterfly title in Moscow, was the surprise winner of this event at the 1982 World Championships in Guayaquil where she beat Mary Meagher of the United States who, on paper, was nearly three seconds faster.

Afterwards, the East German said: 'I thought it was a false start because the horn sounded as if it bleeped twice. But the others kept going and so did I. I'm not pleased with the time, but it was a tactical race all about winning and not best times.'

The East German's European figures are still 2.5 seconds slower than Meagher's 1981 world mark. The Los Angeles Olympics could show which of the pair is the better competitor.

▲
Surprise world champion, Ines Geissler of East Germany

◄
June Croft . . . disappointments almost drove her out of the sport

Sylvia Gerasch (GDR)

100/200 breaststroke
Born: March 16, 1969, Cottbus,
East Germany.
Height: 168cm/5ft 6in.
Weight: 54kg/119lb.
Career Highlights
European Championships: *100
breaststroke* silver 1983; *200
breaststroke* silver 1983.
European Youth Championships:
100 breaststroke gold 1983;
200 breaststroke gold
1983.

Sylvia's career record is small — so
far — just as her physique is tiny
compared with many of her East
German team-mates. Yet at 14, in
1983, she came within three hundredths of a second of beating the
much taller Ute Geweniger in the
European 200m breaststroke
championship and was also second to her in the 100m. She is a
girl with a big future.

Ute Geweniger (GDR)

100/200 breaststroke/200/400
medley
Born: February 24,
Karl-Marx-Stadt, East
Germany.
Height: 181cm/5ft 11in.
Weight: 67kg/148lb.
Career Highlights
Olympic Games: *100 breaststroke*
gold 1978; *4 x 100 medley*
gold 1980.
World Championships: *100
breaststroke* gold 1982; *4 x
100 medley* gold 1982; *200
breaststroke* silver 1982; *200
medley* silver 1982.
European Championships: *100
breaststroke* gold 1983, 1981;
200 breaststroke gold 1983,
1981; *100 butterfly* gold 1981;
200 medley gold 1983, 1981;
4 x 100 medley gold 1983,
1981; *400 medley* silver 1981.
Records
World and European: six *100
breaststroke* (1:8.51) and one
200 medley (2:11.73). Nine
times under 1:10.0 for *100
breaststroke* and undefeated
since February 2, 1981 (21
consecutive victories).

Ute's nickname at home is 'Bones'
because she is so tall, slim and
loose limbed. She has dominated
the world sprint breaststroke scene
since winning her first major title in
Moscow and is no slow coach in
the 200m breaststroke and medley.

She dominated the European
Championships in Split in 1981,
and her four individual and one
relay gold medals were the most
ever won by a man or woman at a
single championship.

Geweniger was only 16 when she
won her Olympic title in 1980. She
will be 20 in Los Angeles, and
though this is mature by international swimming standards, this
does not suggest that Miss Bones
is past her prime.

Larisa Gorchakova (URS)

100/200 backstroke
Born: July 9, 1964, Volzhoskiy,
USSR.
Height: 174cm/5ft 9in.
Weight: 64kg/141lb.
Career Highlights
European Championships: *200
backstroke;* bronze 1981 and
1983.
World Student Games: *100
backstroke* gold 1983;
200 backstroke; gold
1983.

This most consistent Soviet backstroker ranked ninth and seventh
in the world in 1983. But with
many East Germans ahead of her,
and only two able to take part in
the Olympics, her Games rankings
are sixth and fourth. She will be
just 20 at Los Angeles and should
be at the peak of her ever improving career.

*Tall and talented . . . Ute
Geweniger of East Germany*
▶

Sarah Hardcastle (GBR)
800/800 freestyle
Born: April 9, 1969, Chelmsford,
England.
Height: 178cm/5ft 10in.
Weight: 45kg/99lb.
Career Highlights
European Championships: *800
freestyle* bronze 1983.
European Youth Championships:
800 freestyle gold 1983, silver
1982; *400 freestyle* silver
1983, bronze 1982; *400
medley* silver 1983.
Record
European: Best 14-year-old
performer *400 and 800
freestyle.*

Sarah won a surprise bronze
medal, behind two powerful East
Germans, in the 800m at the
1983 European Championships.
So Britain will be expecting a great
deal – perhaps too much – from
this very tall, slender girl at the Los
Angeles Olympics. She was able to
succeed despite a painful right
knee, which was diagnosed as
'growing pains', quite common in
not fully developed youngsters
between 10 and 14 years.
   For all her mature and 'professional' approach to all she does in
the water, it would be more proper
to look for her Olympic success
four years from now, at the 1988
Games in Seoul. Yet hopes will be
raised because of Sarah's excellent start to the 1984 year. In Holland, in January, she won an international 800m event in a personal
best of 8:38.75. This would have
ranked her number five No.5 in
the world in 1983 under the two
competitors per event Olympic rule
(or seventh overall). And to put this
swim in context, all the other 1983
ranking swims above her were set
at the height of the racing season,
not the beginning.
   Perhaps, Los Angeles is not too
soon for her to think of Olympic
medals in the 800 or even the
400m freestyle.

Irina Laricheva (URS)
100/200/400/800 freestyle
Born: July 22, 1963, Novosibirsk,
USSR.
Height: 178cm/5ft 10in.
Weight: 62kg/137lb.
Career Highlights
European Championships: *400
freestyle* bronze 1983.
World Student Games: *100
freestyle* gold 1983; *200
freestyle* gold 1983; *400
freestyle* gold 1983; *800
freestyle* gold 1983.

The USSR's outstanding distance
swimmer will be 21 just in time for
the 1984 Games. On the Olympic
entry basis of two per event, she
ranked sixth for 400m and 800m
freestyle in 1983 with times three
and six seconds faster than in
1982. Similar improvements this
year could edge her towards a
medal chance.

Laurie Lehner (USA)
100 butterfly
Born: October 11, 1957, Merrill,
Wisconsin, USA.
Height: 183cm/6ft 0in.
Weight: 62kg/137lb.
Career Highlights
Pan American Games: *100
butterfly* gold 1983; *4 x 100
medley* gold 1983.
Pan-Pacific Games: *100 butterfly*
gold 1983; *4 x 100 medley*
gold 1983.
Record
World: *100 butterfly* 1983
(59.54).

The 26-year-old, younger sister of
Wendy Boglioli who won the bronze
medal in the 100m butterfly and
gold in the 4 x 100m freestyle relay
at the 1976 Montreal Olympics,

Laurie was a late developer in
swimming terms. She was only
14th in the world for her sister's
speciality event in 1980 and did
not rank in the top 50 in 1981.
   Laurie just missed selection of
the US team for the 1982 World
Championships despite having the
sixth best time in the world.
Unluckily for her, two Americans –
Mary T. Meagher and Melanie
Buddemeyer, respectively the gold
and silver medallists – were ahead
of her. Last year she was the only
woman to break the minute for
100m butterfly.

Kim Linehan (USA)
400/800 freestyle
Born: December 11, 1962,
Bronxville, New York, USA.
Height: 167cm/5ft 6in.
Weight: 54kg/120lb.
Career Highlights
World Championships: *800
freestyle* gold 1982, bronze
1978; *400 freestyle* bronze
1978.
Record
World: *1500 freestyle* 1979
(6:04.49).

Kim is another of the unlucky US

*Kim Lineham still waiting
for an Olympic opportunity.*
▼

She floats like a butterfly . . . America's Mary T. Meagher ▶

Weight: 42kg/105lb.
Career Highlights
World Cup: highboard silver 1983.
European Championships:
   highboard gold 1983.

A highboard specialist whose successes include second place in the FINA World Cup in 1983 as well as a 55 points victory over Bianka Meyer of East Germany in the European Championship last year.

Mary T. Meagher (USA)
100/200 butterfly
Born: October 27, 1964,
   Louisville, Kentucky, USA.
Height: 170cm/5ft 7in.
Weight: 58kg/127lb.
Career Highlights
World Championships: 100
   butterfly gold 1982; 200
   butterfly silver 1982; 4 x 100
   silver 1982.
Pan-American Games: 200
   butterfly gold 1979, 1983.
Pan-Pacific Games: 200 butterfly
   gold 1983.
Records
World: 100 butterfly 1981
   (57.93), 200 butterfly 1981
   (2:05.96).

Mary T. Meagher (pronounced Maha), the fastest butterflyer the world has ever seen, has had only one real set-back in her career. This was in the 200m event at the 1982 World Championships in Guayaquil, Ecuador, where she lost by the large margin of 1.1sec to East Germany's Olympic champion Ines Geissler.

Of that race, the charming Mary T. said: 'Well, I guess losing will be good for me in the end. I kept waiting for Ines to slow down, but she never did. This experience will just make me work that much harder.'

At the end of 1983, her world records, both set in 1981, of 57.93 for 100m and 2:05.96 for 200m were respectively 1.5sec and 2sec better than any other woman ever. When they were established the records were 2.5sec and 3.5sec faster than a woman before.

The Kentucky girl, then 15, was on the US Olympic team that could not go to Moscow. Instead, she swam in the US Championships in California in the days immediately following the Games and won both butterfly titles, in 59.41 and a world record 2:06.37. The Olympic gold medal times of East Germany's Caren Metschuck and Miss Geissler were only 1:00.42 and 2:10.44.

Olympic team who did not go to Moscow. She could have won the 400 and 800 freestyle there, for she finished 1980 as the fastest woman for both events, one second faster than the Games gold medallists Ines Diers (East Germany) and Michelle Ford (Australia).

She dropped out of serious swimming in 1983 but was back, training in Canada, at the end of last year with her eyes on winning those golds she was not able to try for four years ago.

Alla Lobankina (URS)
Highboard diving
Born: December 23, 1967, Penza, USSR.
Height: 155cm/5ft 0in.

Birgit Meineke (GDR)

100/200 freestyle
Born: July 4, 1964, Berlin, East
Germany.
Height: 180cm/5ft 11in.
Weight: 69kg/152lb.
Career Highlights
World Championships: *4 x 100
freestyle* gold 1982, silver
1978; *100 freestyle* gold
1982; *4 x 100 medley* gold
1982; *200 freestyle* silver
1982.
European Championships: *4 x 100
freestyle* gold 1983, 1981; *100
freestyle* gold 1983, silver
1981; *200 freestyle* gold 1983,
silver 1981; *4 x 200 freestyle*
gold 1983; *4 x 100 medley*
gold 1983.

East Germany's top freestyle
sprinter since the retirement of
double Olympic champion Barbara
Krause, Birgit Meineke has swum
100m under 56sec eight times —
her 55.18 in winning the 1983
European title being the best.

She is her country's main hope
to complete a hat-trick in this blue
riband event for women, following
in the steps of Kornelia Ender
(1976) and Miss Krause (1980).
And, of course, she is the key
swimmer of her squad for the
freestyle and medley relays and a
good prospect for the 200m freestyle, being the number one in the
world in 1983.

Hiroko Nagasaki (JPN)

100/200 breaststroke
Born: July 27, 1968, Akita, Japan.
Height: 166cm/5ft 5in.
Weight: 57kg/126lb.
Career Highlights
Los Angeles Pre-Olympic meeting:
100 breaststroke gold 1983;
200 breaststroke gold 1983.
Pan-Pacific Games: *100
breaststroke* gold 1983; *200
breaststroke* gold 1983.

Hiroko missed a bronze medal in
the 200m breaststroke at the
1982 World Championships by
just 0.13sec. But she was the surprise success in Los Angeles at the
pre-Olympic meeting in July 1983.
Not only did she win both her speciality events but for the longer distance she improved her year old
time by more than three seconds
to 2:29.91. This proved to be fastest of the year and the fourth best
of all time. She went home to
Tokyo to win the Pan-Pacific titles
for 100m and 200m breaststroke.

Only two Japanese women have
ever been Olympic swimming
champions. They are Hideko
Maehata in the 200m breaststroke
in 1936 — her Olympic record in a
heat 48 years ago was 3:01.9 —
and Mayumi Aoki for the 100m
butterfly in 1972. With these
exceptions, Japan has not had a
serious Olympic challenger among
its women swimmers . . . until now.

Megan Neyer (USA)

Springboard diving
Born: June 11, 1962, Ashland,
Kentucky, USA.
Height: 157cm/5ft 1in.
Weight: 52kg/115lb.
Career Highlights
World Championships:
springboard gold 1983.
World Cup: *springboard* silver
1981.

Megan, a member of the Mission
Viejo club in California and trained
by Ron O'Brien, whose pupils
include double world champion
Greg Louganis, has steadily
climbed the diving tree to her world
springboard title in Ecuador in
1983.

She won both the US Olympic
springboard and highboard trials in
1980, held despite the fact her
country had decided not to compete in the Games four years ago.
Los Angeles could be her chance
to make up for her Moscow disappointment.

▲
*Fastest breaststroker of the
year in 1983 . . . Japan's
Hiroko Nagasaki*

◄
*East Germany's latest
freestyle powerhouse . . .
Birgit Meineke*

First woman under a
minute for 100m
backstroke... East
German's Kristin Otto ▶ ▶

Kathleen Nord (GDR)

200/400 medley
Born: December 26, 1965,
Magdeburg, East Germany.
Height: 175cm/5ft 9in.
Weight: 60kg/132lb.
Career Highlights
World Championships: *400
medley* silver 1982.
European Championships: *400
medley* gold 1983; *200 medley*
silver 1983.

Kathleen's greatest claim to fame
– so far – is that she became the
first woman in five years to beat
her mighty East German team
mate Petra Schneider over 400m
medley. She did this, by four
tenths of a second, at the 1983
European Championships in Rome
where she also took the silver for
200m medley.

Like most great medley swimmers, she is a world class performer on the four strokes that
make up this most difficult of
events. Her times include 1:01.25
and 2:10.90 for butterfly, 1:13.54
and 2:37.66 for breaststroke and
2:02.16 for 200m freestyle.

▲
*Dogged by
disqualifications...
Canada's Anne Ottenbrite*

Anne Ottenbrite (CAN)

100/200 breaststroke
Born: December 5, 1966, Whitby,
Ontario, Canada.
Height: 175cm/5ft 9in.
Weight: 59kg/130lb.
Career Highlights
World Championships: *100
breaststroke* silver (tied) 1982;
200 breaststroke bronze 1982.
Commonwealth Games: *200
breaststroke* gold 1982; *100
breaststroke* silver 1982.
Pan American Games: *100*

breaststroke gold 1983, *4 x
100 medley* silver 1983.
Records
Commonwealth: 100 breaststroke
1983 (1:10.63),
(1:10.63); *200 breaststroke*
1983 (2:30.55).

Anne was not ranked in the world's
top 25 in 1981 but had a meteoric
rise the following year to win two
medals at each of the World
Championships and Common-
wealth Games in 1982. She was
ranked No. 3 in the world for both
distances in 1983.

She is an exponent of 'the
Caulkins flutter' kick in breaststroke (see Tracy Caulkins) but the
judges have not always passed her
style as within the rules. She was
twice disqualified last year, in
Leeds, where Britain met Canada
and the Soviet Union in a triangu-
lar match. And she was disqualified again, at the Pan-American
Games, in the 200m breaststroke,
although she survived to win the
100m title.

Kristin Otto (GDR)

100 freestyle/100 backstroke/
400 medley
Born: February 7, 1965, Leipzig,
East Germany.
Height: 174cm/5ft 8½in.
Weight: 53kg/117lb.
Career Highlights
World Championships: *100
backstroke* gold 1982; *4 x 100
freestyle,* gold 1982; *4 x 100
medley* gold 1982.
European Championships: *4 x
200 freestyle* gold (world
record) 1983; *100 freestyle*
silver 1983.

Kristin is another East German
woman with a multiplicity of talents who has won major events for
freestyle, backstroke and medley.
She also goes down in the swimming history books as the first
woman to go under the minute for
100m backstroke – and even
though this was in a 25m pool,
with the advantage of two extra
turns, it was a barrier breaking performance.

◄
From backstroke to butterfly . . . East Germany's versatile Cornelia Polit

Cornelia Polit (GDR)
100/200 breaststroke/
200 butterfly
Born: February 18, 1963,
Teutschenthal,
East Germany.
Height: 178cm/5ft 10in.
Weight: 68kg/150lb.
Career Highlights
Olympic Games: *200 backstroke* silver 1980.
European Championships: *200 backstroke* gold 1981; *100 backstroke* silver 1981; *200 butterfly* gold 1983.
European Youth Championships: *100 backstroke* gold 1978; *200 backstroke* gold 1978; *200 butterfly* bronze 1978.

Cornelia was a leading world backstroker with butterfly her second stroke, but from 1982 concentrated on the latter style because East Germany had found many new backstroke stars but not so many butterfly stars.

In winning the 200m butterfly title at the 1983 European Championships, she inflicted a rare defeat on her team-mate Ines Geissler, the Olympic and world gold medallist. Her time in Rome was a continental record and put her at the head of the world rankings last year. Only Mary T. Meagher has swum faster.

Petra Schneider (GDR)
400 freestyle/200/400 medley
Born: January 11, 1963,

Karl-Marx-Stadt, East
Germany.
Height: 173cm/5ft 8in.
Weight: 64kg/141lb.
Career Highlights
Olympic Games: *400 medley* gold 1980; *400 freestyle* silver 1980.
World Championships: *200 medley* gold 1982, bronze 1978; *400 medley* gold 1982; *400 freestyle* silver 1982.
European Championships: *400 medley* gold 1981; *200 medley* silver 1981; *400 medley* silver 1983.
Records
World and European: *400 medley* 1982 (4:36.10), *200 medley* (2:13.00).

Petra, the world's Swimmer of the Year in 1980 and 1982, had 25 consecutive victories for 400m medley from August 23, 1978 to August 22, 1983. Then, in Rome, she had to accept defeat from her East German team-mate Kathleen Nord in the European Championships.

Although Schneider had to settle for the silver, she still held on to the world record she established in Ecuador in 1982 for Nord only clocked 4:39.95, 3.75sec slower than Petra's best.

The two East Germans are the only women to have broken 4:40 for the distance and their clash in Los Angeles, where Schneider could be making her final major swimming appearance, is some-

thing to be anticipated with relish. When Petra does quit, she will retire with a history of success seldom bettered.

Cornelia Sirch (GDR)
200 backstroke
Born: 23 October 1966, Erfurt, East Germany.
Height: 178cm/5ft 10in.
Weight: 68kg/150lb.
Career Highlights
World Championships: *200 backstroke* gold 1982.
European Championships: *200 backstroke* gold 1983; *4 x 200 freestyle* gold 1983; *100 backstroke* silver 1983.
Records
World: *200 backstroke* (2:9.91 1982); *4 x 100 freestyle* (1983).

Cornelia was only 15 in 1982 when she won the world 200m backstroke title in a world record 2:09.91, five seconds ahead of Georgina Parkes of Australia. After the race, she said: *'I am very young and hope to improve'* a rather charming remark and oh so true!

In fact, she is the only woman to have broken 2:10 for the distance and no one has yet come within 1.8sec of that time. She did not race quite up to that level in 1983, but still headed the world ranking list one second faster than her nearest rival and team mate Birthe Weigang.

Anke Sonnenbrodt (GDR)
400/800 freestyle
Born: November 23, 1966,
   Woldeck, East Germany.
Height: 177cm/5ft 10in.
Weight: 65kg/143lb.
Career Highlights
European Championships: *400
   freestyle* silver 1983; *800
   freestyle* silver 1983.
European Youth Championships:
   400 freestyle bronze 1980;
   800 freestyle; bronze 1980.
Record
European: former *800 freestyle*
   1983 (8:31.07).

◀ *The girl from Hollywood . . .
America's Jill Sterkel*

One of East Germany's new distance freestyle swimmers, Anke must be a Los Angeles medal prospect after her silver medals, behind team-mate Astrid Strauss, in Rome in 1983.

Jill Sterkel (USA)
100/200 freestyle
Born: May 27, 1961, Hollywood,
   California, USA.
Height: 180cm/5ft 11in.
Weight: 77kg/170lb.
Career Highlights
Olympic Games: *4 x 100 freestyle*
   gold 1976.
World Championships: *100
   freestyle* bronze 1982; *4 x 100
   freestyle* gold 1978, silver
   1982; *4 x 100 medley* silver
   1982.
Pan American Games: *4 x 100
   freestyle* gold 1979, 1975; *100
   freestyle* silver 1979, 1975;
   100 butterfly gold 1979; *4 x
   100 medley* gold 1979.
World Student Games: *100
   freestyle* gold 1981; *200
   freestyle* gold 1981; *4 x 100
   freestyle* gold 1981; *100
   butterfly* gold 1981; *4 x 100
   medley* gold 1981.

A tower of strength in the American team – physically as well as competitively – Jill was good enough to be chosen for her national team at the age of 14 and won Pan American Games gold and silver medals.

Probably her most exciting moment was in the final event on the last day of the swimming at the Montreal Olympics in 1976 when the United States, with her help, at last won a woman's title, the 4 x 100m freestyle. Until that moment, the formerly mighty American girls had not taken a single gold.

Even in 1983, after a nine year international career, Jill was still good enough to take the bronze for

100m freestyle in the US championships. Now she is trying to be the first American woman swimmer to be on three Olympic squads. If she succeeds, this will go down in United States sports history but not, unfortunately, in the Olympic record book because her squad were not allowed to go to the Moscow Games.

Astrid Strauss (GDR)
200/400/800 freestyle
Born: December 24, 1968, Berlin,
   East Germany.
Height: 180cm/5ft 11in.
Weight: 65kg/133lb.
Career Highlights

European Championships *400
   freestyle* gold 1983; *800
   freestyle* gold 1983; *4 x 200
   freestyle* gold 1983; *200
   freestyle* silver 1983.
Record
European: *400 freestyle*
   (4:08.07).

This powerful 15-year-old, a newcomer to the East German team in 1983, is one of the world's top distance freestylers. Last year she headed the 800m world rankings, was only two hundredths of a second behind Tiffany Cohen in the 400m listing and third for 200m. She must be a good candidate for Olympic medals in Los Angeles for her speciality events.

◀
*East German newcomer
Astrid Strauss*

Conny Van Bentum (HOL)
100/200 freestyle
Born: August 12, 1965,
   Barneveld, Netherlands.
Height: 180cm/5ft 11in.
Weight: 68kg/139lb.
Career Highlights
Olympic Games: *4 x 100 freestyle*
   bronze 1980.
World Championships: *4 x 100*
   freestyle bronze 1982.
European Championships: *100*
   freestyle bronze 1981; *200*
   freestyle bronze 1981; *4 x 100*
   freestyle silver 1983, bronze
   1981; *4 x 100 medley* silver
   1983; *4 x 200 medley* bronze
   1983.

Temporarily put in the shade by Annemarie Verstappen's 200m victory in the 1982 World Championships Conny is emerging as the more consistent of these two tall and speedy Dutch women. In Olympic terms (of two per event per nation), she was the number three in the world for 100 and 200m freestyle last year but her key role in Los Angeles could be to help Holland to medals in the two relays.

Annemarie Verstappen
(HOL)
100/200 freestyle/400 medley
Born: October 3, 1965,
   Rosmalen, Netherlands.
Height: 180cm/5ft 11in.
Weight: 65kg/143lb.
Career Highlights
World Championships: *200*
   freestyle gold 1982; *100*
   freestyle silver 1982; *4 x 100*
   freestyle bronze 1982.
European Championships: *4 x 100*
   freestyle silver 1983; *4 x 100*
   medley silver 1983; *4 x 200*
   freestyle bronze 1983.

Annemarie was the surprise winner of the 200m freestyle title at the 1982 World Championships when she beat the favourite Birgit Meineke by more than one second.

Also a world class backstroke, butterfly and medley swimmer, she ranked in the top 10 for all these events plus the shorter freestyle distances in 1981. In 1982 she was top of the 200m list and second for 100m and fifth for the latter event in 1983.

Because of her versatility, it is difficult to forecast which races she will contest in Los Angeles. Whatever the choice, she must be in line for an Olympic medal to add to her collection.

Sue Walsh (USA)
100/200 backstroke/400 medley
Born: February 19, 1962, Buffalo,
   New York, USA.
Height: 175cm/5ft 9in.
Weight: 59kg/130lb.
Career Highlights
World Championships: *100*
   backstroke bronze 1982; *4 x*
   100 medley silver 1982.
Pan American Games: *100*
   backstroke gold 1983; *4 x 100*
   medley gold 1983; *backstroke*
   silver 1983.
Pan-Pacific Games: *100*
   backstroke gold 1983; *200*
   backstroke gold 1983; *4 x 100*
   medley gold 1983.

Another of the US 'veterans' working hard to be picked for the Los Angeles Games, She is now in her ninth major competitive season and on her 1983 form holds the bronze medal position in the world ranking lists. But the Americans are experts at raising their performance levels for the really big occasions – and what could be bigger than their very own Olympics this year?

Cynthia 'Sippy' Woodhead
(USA)
200/400/800 freestyle/400 medley
Born: February 7, 1964, Riverside,
   California, USA.
Height: 165cm/5ft 5in.
Weight: 54kg/119lb.
Career Highlights
World Championships: *200*
   freestyle gold 1978; *4 x 100*
   freestyle gold 1978; *4 x 100*
   medley gold 1978; *400*
   freestyle silver 1978; *800*
   freestyle silver 1978.
Pan American Games: *100*
   freestyle gold 1979; *200*
   freestyle gold 1983, 1979;
   400 freestyle gold 1979, silver
   1983; *4 x 100 medley* gold
   1979; *4 x 100 freestyle* gold
   1983.
Pan-Pacific Games: *200 freestyle*
   gold 1983; *4 x 100 freestyle*
   gold 1983.
FINA World Cup: *100 freestyle*
   gold 1979; *200 freestyle* gold
   1979; *400 freestyle* gold
   1979; *4 x 100 freestyle* gold
   1979.
Record
World: *200 freestyle* 1979
   (1:58.23).

Sippy Woodhead is another of the brilliant young American swimmers whose careers and inspiration were destroyed when the US boycotted

▲
*Making up for Moscow
disappointment . . . Cynthia
Woodhead of America*

the Moscow Olympics in 1980.

Just the year before, at 15, she had gained four gold medals at the first and only FINA World Swimming Cup in Tokyo where she set a world record for 200m freestyle of 1:58.23 which at the end of 1983 had not been beaten.

In the days immediately following the Moscow Olympics, she won the US 100 and 200m freestyle titles and was second over 400m and 800m.

Still in the world's all-time best performance lists, standing from first to fith over the wide range of her swimming talent, she is a 'veteran' (at 20) hoping to assuage her 1980 disappointments with success in Los Angeles.

Wendy Wyland (USA)
Highboard diving
Born: November 25, 1964,
   Jackson, Michigan, USA.
Height: 157cm/5ft 2in.
Weight: 50kg/110lb.
Career Highlights
World Championships: *highboard;*
   gold 1983.
Pan American Games: *highboard*
   gold 1983; *springboard* silver
   1983.

Another Ron O'Brien diving pupil, Wendy, along with Greg Louganis and Megan Neyer helped to give this world renowned coach a clean sweep of the World Championship diving titles in Guayaquil, Ecuador, in 1982. Like the others, she will have the advantage in Los Angeles of virtually diving 'at home' for she trains with the Californian club Mission Viejo on the doorstep of the Olympic venue.

Gymnastics

The girls who made the world sit up and notice gymnastics . . . Olga Korbut, (left) and her Soviet team-mate Lyudmilla Tourescheva (right)

If one person can claim to have caused a sporting revolution in modern times it was the elegant, elfin Olga Korbut. The 17-year-old Soviet girl's fresh and cheeky approach to gymnastics made the world stop and look — in awe and delight. The performances she gave at the Munich Olympics in 1972 were breathtaking, they were new. The thunderous applause she received had never been heard in a gymnastics hall before. And in her wake came a new breed of gymnastics followers and a generation of young girls inspired to go out and emulate her magical athleticism.

Until the sixties, gymnastics was a sport only for the aficionado. It gained little coverage in newspapers and even less on television. The 1964 Tokyo Games changed all that. In the hope of broadcasting several Japanese successes to the world, the television coverage concentrated on the gymnastics competition at great length. The producers were rewarded with their Japanese successes in the men's events, and all eyes fell on the outstanding female competitor — not Japanese — Vera Caslavska of Czechoslovakia.

The cameras captured the beauty and grace of the young Czech girl, about whom the gymnastics world had been raving. Suddenly, there she was, for all to see. But no one knew anything about her, and not much

more about the sport. So, from that day, gymnastics became an integral part of the media's portfolio.

Gymnastics was first practised by the Chinese and Greeks over 2500 years ago, and formed an important part of the Ancient Olympic Games in 700 BC. The great Greek philosopher Aristotle wrote: *'Gymnastics is not just an art, it is also a science, an anthropological science with a social purpose.'* After the abolition of the Ancient Olympics in 393 AD little was heard of gymnastics. Perhaps one could liken the skills of artists like Matilda Makejoy, to modern-day floor exercises. Matilda was one of the dancers who used to travel with minstrels, performing before royalty — in her case Edward I — and she would perform a floor exercise to the accompaniment of the minstrels' music.

At the end of the eighteenth century, Swede Per Ling and German Johan Ludwig Jahn developed techniques that were the foundations of modern gymnastics. Ling concentrated on the rhythmic aspect of the sport, lending his techniques to physical education studies the world over, while Jahn, the founder of the world's first 'gym club', developed gymnastic apparatus, and the skills that were necessary to use it. Germany formed the world's first National Gymnastics Association — the International Federation being founded in Liège, Belgium in 1881.

Gymnastics was introduced to England in 1820 by Phokion Heinrich Clias — an American living in Switzerland. Its popularity spread and in 1860 the Army, recognizing the need for physical fitness after the Crimean War, established the Army Gymnastic Staff. This was the forerunner of the Army Physical Training Corps as it is known today — the corps being one reason for the Army's success in international competition.

The British Gymnastics Association was formed in 1888, and in 1896, the year of the first modern Olympics, the inaugural British Championships were held at the Northampton Corn Exchange.

Gymnastics was included in the 1896 Olympics, the events being staged in the middle of the athletics track. Germany dominated those first Games — as they did in the early part of the twentieth century — with Karl Schumann the first Olympic champion. Schumann won three gymnastic gold medals in 1896 as well as a gold in the wrestling — the first man to win golds in two different sports. It was in the gymnastics that Greece won its first gold medal of the modern games when Ioannis Mitropoulos won the rings title — a victory which brought an emotional response from the home crowd at the medal ceremony.

The Germans and then the Scandinavians were the early pacemakers in world gymnastics. Then came the Americans, who had their

The Swedish gymnastics team on the beam during the 1912 Stockholm Games

share of success between the two wars. After World War II, Eastern European Countries began to figure strongly, and one of their first leading gymnasts was Helena Rokaczy of Poland, women's overall champion at the inaugural World Championships in Basle in 1950.

The Soviets re-entered the Olympics in 1952 after an absence of 40 years and immediately showed what a force they were going to be in gymnastics by taking five of the eight men's titles, and four of the six ladies' titles. Viktor Chukarin and Maria Gorokhovskaya won the men's and women's overall titles. The Soviets improved their medal haul at the 1956 Melbourne Games winning six men's titles and five women's.

The 1956 Games introduced two giants of the sport — muscular Boris Shaklin and the lithesome Larissa Latynina. Both hailed from Kiev, both were city councillors in their home town, and both reigned supreme in their sport for the remainder of that decade. Shaklin won 10 world and Olympic titles, while Latynina won 12 world and Olympic golds, and a total of 31 medals in the two championships. Her 18 Olympic medals is a record for either sex in any sport in the history of the modern Olympics. The majority of Latynina's titles were won after she had given birth to her daughter. Amazingly also, she had a great love of borscht soup and dumplings, but still managed to maintain her figure. Appointed Soviet team coach for the 1972 Olympics, she will be with the team in Los Angeles in the same capacity.

The Soviet domination was threatened in the 1960s with the emergence of Japan. The USSR lost their men's team title to Japan in Rome in 1960 and did not regain it until 1980. Some of the outstanding gymnasts who played a part in the USSR's 'dethronement' were: Yukio Endo, overall individual champion in 1964: Sawao Kato, overall champion in 1968 and 1972: Akinori Nakayama, winner of four individual gold medals: and Mitsuo Tsukahara, horizontal bar double gold medallist, after whom the Tsukahara movement is named.

However, the Soviets have now restored themselves to their former position as leading men's nation, thanks to their successes on home soil at Moscow in 1980, and have a record 161 Olympic medals to their credit — 61 of them gold.

Larissa Latynina . . . a record 18 Olympic medals for the USSR

Soviet women lost their queen when Latynina was replaced by the Czechoslovakian Vera Caslavska. Winner of a record seven gold medals at the 1964 and 1968 Olympics, Vera was also overall individual world champion three times.

The 1968 Olympics were certainly memorable for Caslavska. First she went into hiding before the Games, as she had publically opposed the Soviet invasion of her country. Then, at the Games themselves she performed her amazing 'Mexican Hat Dance' routine in the floor exercise. The tickets for the final day of the women's gymnastics programme were like gold — everyone wanted to see Caslavska. The competition over, she went to Mexico City's Roman Catholic cathedral and married fellow Czech athlete Josef Odlozil, 1964 Olympic 1500 metre silver medallist. And on returning home, she gave one of the four gold medals she had won to each of Czechoslovakia's four leaders — Messrs Dubcek, Svoboda, Cernik and Smrkorsky.

Women's gymnastics continued to produce further worthy and talented champions. Next in line was the attractive Lyudmilla Tourescheva, later to marry Soviet sprinter Valeriy Borzov. Lyudmilla was without doubt the most skilful of all the gymnasts at the 1972 Olympics, but the 'star' as far as the audience was concerned, was Olga Korbut.

The success of Korbut put the accent on youth — and in Montreal four years later Nadia Comaneci of Romania, at 14 years 313 days, became the youngest ever Olympic gymnastics gold medallist. In winning her titles, she became the first person in Olympic history to register the perfect score of 10.00. The scoreboard was not geared for such a score and had to display a 1.00 instead. Anticipating more 'perfection', 18,000 people turned up for the final day's events — they were rewarded with Nadia at her best. In all, she was awarded seven maximums at the Games.

The 1980 Olympics produced their own star — and this time it was the men who took the limelight with Soviet Alexsandr Ditiatin winning a medal in each of the eight classes of competition. The success ranks him alongside his predecessor Nikolai Andrianov as one of the two greatest Russian — if not world — male gymnasts of all time. Andrianov won 28 medals in world and Olympic championships.

In men's gymnastics, six gymnasts compete for a team prize. There is also an overall individual title. The gymnasts then contest individual titles on each piece of apparatus; pommel horse, floor competition, rings, vault, parallel bars and horizontal bar. Like the men, the women contest a team and an overall competition, but their individual pieces of apparatus are different: vault, asymmetrical bars, beam, and floor exercise.

In the team competition, each competitor performs a compulsory and an optional exercise on each piece of apparatus. They are marked out of 10 for each exercise, and the team with the greatest aggregate score is the winner. The leading 36 individuals from the team competition then qualify for the overall *individual* competition and perform a further optional exercise on each piece of apparatus, receiving additional marks out of 10. This further score is added to their *average* score brought forward from their previous two exercises — the best scores deciding the winner.

From there, the top six gymnasts on each piece of apparatus in the team competition, take part in a separate competition on each piece. This is a further optional exercise, and the score is added to the average of the scores obtained in the first two exercises in the team competition.

There are four judges in international competitions and the highest and lowest scores are ignored. It is important that the judges should be of the highest integrity but the Romanian squad cast doubt on the judges during the overall individual women's competition at the 1980 Moscow Olympics. Nadia Comaneci, needing a 9.90 to win, by her own admission performed badly on the beam, but in view of the marking that had gone before, expected a 9.90 or 9.95. However, the judges marks were 9.80, 9.85, 9.90 and 10.00 — so her final marks were 9.875. The argument that ensued lasted for 27 minutes and in full view of the television cameras. Finally it was announced that the result stood, and Comaneci had to settle for a silver medal.

The Los Angeles Olympics will see rhythmic gymnastics as an Olympic sport for the first time, and who knows, there may be another Olga Korbut or Nadia Comaneci waiting to be revealed in this new event.

Vlademir Artemov, one of the USSR's rising young stars ▼▼

Artur Akopian, dangerous manoeuvres on the high bar ▼

Artur Akopian (URS)

Born: September 28, 1961,
    Erevan, USSR.
Height: 170cm/5ft 7in.
Weight: 60kg/132lb.
Career Highlights
World Championships: *overall*
    bronze 1983; *vault* gold 1983.

A consistent performer, Artur Akopian is at his best on the high bar, and was the first gymnast ever to perform the 'Tkatcher' immediately followed by a 'Gienger' — an extremely complicated, and dangerous sequence of movements.

Artur made his international debut in 1979, and was a member of the Soviet team that won the gold medal at that year's World Championships.

He was in the Soviet squad prior to the 1980 Olympics but never made the team. He finished third in the 1983 World Championships in Budapest and will be hoping for a place in the Olympic team this time.

Vlademir Artemov (URS)

Born: 1962, Moscow, USSR.
Height: 168cm/5ft 6in.
Weight: 63kg/139lb.
Career Highlights
World Championships: *parallel
    bars;* joint gold 1983.

One of the many rising young male Soviet gymnasts, Vlademir Artemov made his senior debut in 1983, and crowned the year by taking the gold medal in the parallel bars at the World Championships in Budapest.

The previous year, he made his international debut in the World Student Games, and later went on to finish second in the European Junior Championships behind Belozertchev.

121

Dimitri Belozertchev (URS)

Born: December 22, 1966, USSR.
Height: 168cm/5ft 6in.
Weight: 66kg/146lb.
Career Highlights
World Championships: *overall* gold 1983: *rings* gold 1983: *high bar* gold 1983: *pommel horse* gold 1983.
European Championships: *overall* gold 1983.

Dimitri Belozertchev will be the man the rest of the field will have to beat at the Los Angeles Olympics.

He certainly goes to the Olympics as the 'in form' competitor, having won both the European and world titles in 1983 — four individual golds and one silver coming in the latter, including three perfect scores of 10. He is the youngest person to have won either title.

He first hit the headlines in 1982 when he won the individual title at the European Junior Championships, at which he also won five of the six gold medals in the individual apparatus competition. He was given special permission — as he was under age — to compete in the Senior Soviet Championships, in which he finished fifth overall.

His 1983 successes were completed by his winning of the Spartakiad.

Dimitri Belozertchev, youngest winner of the world title ▼

Bart Conner (USA)

Born: March 28, 1958, Chicago, USA.
Height: 165cm/5ft 5in.
Weight: 53kg/117lb.
Career Highlights:
World Championships: *parallel bars* gold 1979; *team* bronze 1979.

Bart Conner was a member of the United States team during the late 1970s, when he and Kurt Thomas made the US one of the leading nations in men's gymnastics.

Bart himself claimed one World Championship gold, on the parallel bars in 1979, and in that same year had his best individual overall performance, finishing fifth.

Tong Fei (CHN)

Born: 1961, China.
Height: 165cm/5ft 5in.
Weight: 60kg/132lb.
Career Highlights
World Championships: *team* gold 1983; *floor exercise* gold 1983; *parallel bars* joint bronze 1983.

Tong Fei has been the inspiration behind China's success at international level over the past couple of years, and this was highlighted by his performances at the 1983 World Championships.

He helped his country to win the team title but was so fatigued by the team competition that he slumped from second in the individual all round competition at the start of the final session to 35th overall. However, he was rewarded with an individual gold in the floor exercise.

The potential of Tong Fei was seen at the 1981 World Championships, when, a virtual unknown, he finished fourth overall. The following year, he was runner up in the World Cup competition.

Mitch Gaylord (USA)

Born: 1961, Los Angeles, United States.
Height: 175cm/5ft 8½in.
Weight: 69kg/150lb.
Career Highlights
World Championships: *overall* eighth 1983.

Mitch Gaylord was the highest placed American at the 1983 World Championships in Budapest (eighth). He must be considered a possible outsider for a medal in Los Angeles — he will be performing on home ground. Mitch made his international debut in 1980.

The inspiration of China — 23-year-old Tong Fei ▶

Gyorgy Guczoghy (HUN)
Born: March 3, 1962, Budapest, Hungary.
Height: 170cm/5ft 7in.
Weight: 66kg/146lb.
Career Highlights
European Championships: *overall* bronze 1983.

Gyorgy Guczoghy has succeeded Zoltan Magyar as leading Hungarian male gymnast, and his successes in 1983 — third in the European Championships and fifth in the World Championships — make him a medal prospect for the Los Angeles Olympics.

He was first recognized in 1979, when he shared the pommel horse title at the European Championships with the great Ditiatin. The pommel horse is by far his best routine, and he followed up his 1979 success by taking the outright European title on that piece of apparatus at the 1981 European Championships, and the bronze at that year's World Championships.

Koji Gushiken (JPN)
Born: December 11, 1956, Japan.
Height: 165cm/5ft 5in.
Weight: 53kg/117lb.
Career Highlights
World Championships: *pommel horse* bronze 1979; *parallel bars* joint gold 1981; *floor* bronze 1981; *overall* bronze 1981; *rings* joint gold 1983; *overall* silver 1983.

The 1984 Olympics will be the first contested by versatile Japanese gymnast Koji Gushiken, and his all-round ability must make him the best of the contenders to challenge reigning World Champion Belozertchev for the supreme title in Los Angeles.

An outstanding competitor, his performances over the past four years, have helped re-establish Japanese gymnastics on the world map.

Yuri Korolev (URS)
Born: 1962, Vladimir, USSR.
Height: 167cm/5ft 6in.
Weight: 65kg/143lb.
Career Highlights
World Championships: *overall* gold 1981.
European Championships: *overall* silver 1981; *overall* silver 1983.

Yuri Korolev first gained international honours after the Moscow Olympics, and will be looking forward to competing in Los Angeles this summer.

He was one of the most active members of the Soviet team in 1983, taking part in a competition every month, and lead the team to victory over the United States in April.

Runner up in the European Championships in 1981 (and again in 1983) the highlight of his career was when he won the world title in Moscow in 1981.

Korolev hails from the same town as one of the USSR's greatest ever male gymnasts, Nikolai Andrianov.

Bogdan Makuts (URS)
Born: April 4, 1960, Lvov, USSR.
Height: 169cm/5ft 1in.
Weight: 65kg/143lb.
Career Highlights
World Championships: *overall* silver 1981.
European Championships: *overall* silver 1979; *parallel bars* gold 1979; *vault* gold 1979; *overall* bronze 1981; *parallel bars* gold 1981; *vault* gold 1981.

A member of the Soviet team since 1979, Bogdan Makuts has been one of their most consistent performers.

His high level of consistency started when he won six gold medals and one silver at the 1979 World Student Games. That same year he won the parallel bars and vault titles at the European Championships — retaining both titles at the 1981 Championships.

A member of the Armed Forces in Lvov, he will be hoping for a better performance in Los Angeles than he gave in Moscow, when his only medal was the gold he won as a member of the Soviet team.

Yuri Korolev, world ▲
champion in 1981

*Koji Gushiken, Japan's
young all-round master*
◄ ◄

High bar specialist
Alexandr Pogorelov of the
USSR ▶

Alexandr Pogorelov (URS)
Born: November 1, 1961, Moscow,
USSR.
Height: 171cm/5ft 7in.
Weight: 66kg/146lb.
Career Highlights
World Championships: high bar
bronze 1983.

Alexandr Pogorelov joined the
senior ranks in 1981, and was third
in the 1982 World Student Games
in Canada.

Eight years at the top ...
Alexandr Tkatchov ▼

He finished sixth overall in the
1983 European Championships,
and obtained the bronze medal on
the high bar at the 1983 World
Championships in Budapest.

Pavel Sut (URS)
Born: August 10, 1961, Minsk,
USSR.
Height: 170cm/5ft 6in.
Weight: 63kg/139lb.
Career Highlights
World Championships: team gold
1981.

A member of the national side
since 1981, Pavel Sut made a
good start to his international
career, by helping the Soviet team
to retain their title at the 1981
World Championships.

Now married to former world
champion, Natalia Shaposhnikova,
they live in Minsk, where she
teaches gymnastics.

Alexandr Tkatchov (URS)
Born: November 4, 1957,
Semilouki, USSR.
Height: 172cm/5ft 7in.
Weight: 67kg/148lb.
Career Highlights
Olympic Games: parallel bars
gold 1980; rings silver
1980.
World Championships: high bar
gold 1981.
European Championships: floor
exercise gold 1977;
high bar gold 1979;
overall gold 1981;
high bar gold 1981.

Married to former international
gymnast Lydia Gorbik, Alexandr
Tkatchov is one of the most
experienced members of the current Soviet squad, having made his
international debut in 1976.

His 19 medals in Olympic, world
and European competitions since
1977, make him one of the most
successful members of the squad.

Experience of Tkatchov's kind is
a must to any team, and for that
reason he could be in the Soviet
team competing at Los Angeles.

Phillipe Vatuone (FRA)
Born: August 13, 1962, Sète,
France.
Height: 170cm/5ft 7in.
Weight: 62kg/137lb.
Career Highlights
World Championships: high bar
silver 1983.

The leading Western European
male gymnast at present, Phillipe
Vatuone of France caused a surprise at the 1983 World Championships by taking the silver medal
— jointly with the USSR's Pogorelov
— in the high bar competition.

Phillipe's success in Budapest
gave France their first individual
World Championship medallist
since 1950, when Raymond Dot
won the bronze on the parallel bars
in the days before the Eastern
European domination of the sport.
Perhaps, Phillipe could be France's
first Olympic gold medallist since
1924.

Lavina Agache (ROM)

Born: February 11, 1966, Caiute, Romania.
Height: 148cm/4ft 10in.
Weight: 38kg/84lb.
Career Highlights
World Championships: *vault* joint silver 1983; *asymmetric bars* joint silver 1983; *beam* bronze 1983.
European Championships: *overall* silver 1983.

Lavina Agache first gained international recognition at the 1981 World Championships in Moscow, when finishing fifth in the vault

The successor to Nadia Comaneci? Lavina Agache of Romania ▶

A real crowd pleaser . . . the USSR's Elana Davydova ▼

competition.

She was hailed as Romania's possible successor to the great Nadia Comaneci, and the following year that claim was partly justified, when she finished third in the overall competition in the World Cup, behind Soviets, Bicherova and Yurchenko.

Her most successful season by far has been 1983. Runner up in the European Championship, she won three individual medals at the World Championships in Budapest. These successes must put her in confident mood for the Los Angeles Olympics, at which she will be the most likely gymnast to topple the Soviet girls.

Olga Bicherova (URS)

Born: October, 1966, Moscow, USSR.
Height: 148cm/4ft 10in.
Weight: 37kg/82lb.
Career Highlights
World Championships: *overall* gold 1981.
European Championships: *overall* gold 1983.

Olga Bicherova goes to the Los Angeles Olympics as the leading female gymnast in the world: she is reigning European Champion and joint World Cup holder.

She has proved to be a consistent performer over the past couple of years, and has a tre-mendous ability to overcome any nerves that she may have before major competition. She is a great favourite with spectators.

Erika Csanyi (HUN)

Born: May 22, 1965, Budapest, Hungary.
Height: 159cm/ 5ft 2in.
Weight: 50kg/110lb.
Career Highlights
Olympic Games: *floor exercise* seventh 1980.

Erika Csanyi of Hungary was strongly tipped as one of the favourites to break the Soviet domination in world gymnastics, when she went to Fort Worth for the 1979 World Championships, but she broke a leg in training.

She first came to prominence at the 1978 European Junior Championships, finishing eighth overall. She is the daughter of Hungary's most famous male gymnast of the 1960s.

She finished eighteenth overall in the 1983 World Championships, and will be competing in her second Olympics in Los Angeles. While recent form does not indicate she will be among the medallists, she does have the experience, which — if matched with a bit of luck — could make her one of the outsiders to watch in Los Angeles.

Elana Davydova (URS)

Born: August 7, 1961, Voronezh, USSR.
Height: 156cm/5ft 1in.
Weight: 47kg/104lb.
Career Highlights
Olympic Games: *overall* gold 1980; *beam* silver 1980.
World Championships: *overall* bronze 1981.

A member of the Soviet senior squad since 1975, it was surprising that Elana Davydova had not won a medal in a major championship at the time of the 1980 Moscow Olympics. However, it was *not* surprising that she won the overall individual title at those Games.

A great favourite with the audience, she has always had the ability to take honours, and that ability was turned into gold when it counted — in the Olympic final.

Currently the most experienced member of the Soviet ladies' team, Davydova has a struggle to get into the team. However, she is determined to fight her way back so that she can defend her title in Los Angeles.

▲
*Poetry in motion rhythmic
gymnast Irina Gabashvili*

Tatiana Frolova (URS)
Born: April 26, 1966, Minsk,
   USSR.
Height: 148cm/4ft 10in.
Weight: 48kg/106lb.
Career Highlights
World Championships: *team* gold
   1983.

An outstanding junior gymnast
since she was 12, Tatiana Frolova
was on the verge of the senior
Soviet squad for 18 months,
before being selected for the
USSR versus United States match
in April 1983.
   She was a member of the Soviet
team who won the gold at the
World Championships in 1983 in
Budapest.

Irina Gabashvili (URS)
Born: May 13, 1968, Volgograd,
   USSR.
Height: 153cm/5ft 0in.
Weight: 42kg/93lb.
Career Highlights:
World Rhythmic Championships:
   overall bronze 1979; *ball
   exercise* gold 1979.

One of the USSR's hopes for a title
in the newly introduced rhythmic
programme for the 1984 Olympics, Irina Gabashvili performs an
amazing ball exercise routine to
'Ave Maria' and if she uses this
routine in Los Angeles, she will
have the audience enthralled.

Maxi Gnauck (GDR)
Born: October 10, 1964, East
   Germany.
Height: 156cm/5ft 1in.
Weight: 43kg/95lb.
Career Highlights
Olympic Games: *overall* joint
   silver 1980; *floor exercise*
   bronze 1980; *asymmetric bars*
   gold 1980.
World Championships: *overall*
   silver 1979.
European Championships: *overall*
   gold 1981.

One of the most successful non-
Soviet gymnasts in recent times,
Maxi Gnauck will be competing in
her second Olympics in 1984, hoping to add to her collection of three
individual and one team medal
acquired at Moscow in 1980.
   Maxi first came to prominence
in 1979, when she finished second
overall in that year's World Championships in Dallas. The year after
her Olympic successes, she won
the European title as well as taking
gold in three of the four individual
events — with a silver in the fourth.
Also in 1981, at the World Championships, she won gold on three of
the four pieces of apparatus, but
this time she did not win a medal
in the overall competition.
   Seventh overall in the 1983
World Championships, she won
the asymmetric bars title — her
best event — and will be hoping to
retain this title in Los Angeles.

Natalia Ilienko (URS)
Born: March 26, 1967, Alma-Ata,
   USSR.
Height: 156cm/5ft 1in.
Weight: 46kg/101lb.
Career Highlights
World Championships: *floor
   exercises* gold 1981.

The most graceful of the current
Soviet gymnasts, Natalia Ilienko is
best performing the floor exercise,
at which she won the gold medal in
the 1981 World Championships.
   Since that World Championship
success, she has been concentrating on improving her performances in the other exercises in
readiness for Los Angeles.

*The grace and charm of
Natalia Ilienko* ▶

Dalia Kutkaite (URS)

Born: 1965, Vinius, USSR.
Height: 158cm/5ft 2in.
Weight: 44kg/97lb.
Career Highlights
European Rhythmic
    Championships: *overall* gold
    1982; *clubs* gold 1982;
    ribbons gold 1982.

Currently the number one rhythmic gymnast in the Soviet Union, Dalia Kutkaite won three gold medals at the 1982 European Championships, including the overall individual title.

1983 was an even better year — she retained her national title, and won the Spartakiad.

Olga Mosteponova (URS)

Born: January 3, 1968, USSR.
Height: 149cm/4ft 10in.
Weight: 38kg/84lb.
Career Highlights
World Championships: *overall*
    silver 1983; *beam* gold 1983.

Overall bronze medallist in the 1982 European Junior Championships, Olga Mosteponova was reserve for the Soviet team at the senior European Championships in 1983, and not long after her fifteenth birthday, she made the senior squad for the first time.

Her selection was fully justified, for having taken the silver medal in the Soviet Championships, she was runner up in the World Championships, and took the gold on the beam, and the silver medal in the floor exercise.

Svetlana Murzunenko

(URS)
Born: July 7, 1968, Minsk, USSR.
Height: 150cm/4ft 11in.
Weight: 46kg/101lb.
Career Highlights
USSR Junior Championships:
    overall gold 1982.

Svetlana Murzunenko will be only 16 years old at the time of the Los Angeles Olympics.

An outstanding junior prospect, she performs brilliant routines on both the bars and beam.

Tatiana Shishova (URS)

Born: October 17, 1966,
    Leningrad, USSR.
Height: 156cm/5ft 1in.
Weight: 43kg/95lb.
Career Highlights
USSR Junior Championships:
    overall gold 1982.

Tatiana Shishova became a member of the senior Soviet rhythmic gymnastics squad in 1983, having won the national junior title the previous year.

Her best chance of a medal at the 1984 Olympics will come in her favourite discipline, the ribbon exercise.

Ekaterina Szabo (ROM)

Born: January 22, 1966, Zag,
    Romania.
Height: 143cm/4ft 8in.
Weight: 35kg/80lb.
Career Highlights
World Championships: *overall*
    bronze 1983; *floor exercise* gold
    1983; *asymmetric bars* joint
    silver 1983; *vault* joint
    silver 1983.
European Championships: *overall*
    joint bronze 1983.

The 1982 European Junior Champion, Ekaterina Szabo shot to fame in more senior company in 1983, proving herself to be yet another one of Romania's outstanding gymnasts.

Third in both the European and World championships, she will spearhead the Romanian attack on the Soviets at the Los Angeles Olympics. With Szabo and her team-mate Agache, the Romanians will be a real challenge to their Soviet counterparts.

Natalia Yurchenko (URS)

Born: January 26, 1965, Siberia,
    USSR.
Height: 160cm/5ft 2in.
Weight: 48kg/106lb.
Career Highlights
World Championships: *overall* gold
    1983.

Taller than the average modern Soviet gymnast, Natalia Yurchenko is not handicapped by this, as was seen in her performance at the 1983 World Championships when she took the overall individual title. It was double gold for Natalia who was a member of the Soviet winning team. Strangely though, she failed to win a medal of any colour in the individual apparatus competition.

Hailing from Siberia, it was felt she would not get the experience neccessary to make her a top class gymnast if she remained there, and she moved when she was 10, to the Rostov on Don Club — the home of two other famous Soviet gymnasts, Tourescheva and

Former European Junior Champion Ekaterina Szabo
◄

Vaulting to immortality, Natalia Yurchenko of the USSR
▼

Shaposhnikova.

She first came to prominence in 1982 when she was joint winner for the World Cup title with Bicherova, and in 1983 she won the Spartakiad, as well as that world title. Natalia is one of an elite band of gymnasts who have had a movement named after them — the 'Yurchenko Vault'.

Boxing

Boxing figured in the ancient Olympic Games, and has been a vital feature of the 16 modern Olympiads. It has produced a host of fascinating champions but not all of them have moved on to professional glory.

Four future world heavyweight champions have struck gold, but the greatest Olympian of them all at the weight has never turned pro to cash in on his titles. Teofilo Stevenson of Cuba was launched at Munich in 1972. He caused a sensation, and took the gold. He won again in Montreal, and completed his hat-trick in Moscow four years ago. He is the only man to win three golds at the same weight and epitomises Cuba's influence on modern-day amateur boxing.

When Olympic boxing began in St Louis in 1904, the United States swept the board, winning all seven weights contested. And despite their absence from Moscow in 1980 the Americans are still way ahead in the gold medal table. They have 33 with the USSR second on 12. However, the Soviets are making ground: they did not take a single gold until Melbourne in 1956 when they collected three.

Britain and Cuba share third place with 11 medals each. The British total includes five won in London in 1908 when there were contests at only five weights. The Cubans have won all theirs at the last three Games.

Lazlo Papp of Hungary in London 1948 on the way to the first of his three consecutive Olympic titles

Of the gold medallists who went on to become heavyweight champion of the world, only two took their Olympic honours at that weight — Joe Frazier in Tokyo in 1964 and George Foreman in Mexico four years later. Floyd Patterson's Olympic gold came at middleweight in 1952, in Helsinki, and Muhammad Ali's in Rome in 1960 at light heavyweight — in those days he was known as Cassius Marcellus Clay.

One world heavyweight title-holder with bitter Olympic memories is the big-hitting Swede Ingemar Johansson. He met American Ed Sanders in the Helsinki final and was disqualified for 'not giving of his best'. He has now been given his silver medal, but it took him 30 years of campaigning.

Another Olympic heavyweight champion fought for the world professional title in his very first paid contest. That was American Pete Rademacher who struck gold in Melbourne and was then stopped by Patterson in six rounds the following year with the world's richest prize at stake.

The only other champion to take three gold medals was the fabulous Hungarian Laszlo Papp; at middleweight in 1948 and at light middleweight in 1952 and 1956. Russia's Boris Lagutin was twice a light middleweight winner and in the early days Britain's Harry Mallin took the middleweight gold twice in succession.

The United States and Britain are the only nations ever to make a clean sweep of the boxing medals. When the Games resumed after World War I, at Antwerp in 1920, there was a five-way split of the gold medals. The Americans won three, one going to future world flyweight champion Frankie Genaro, and Britain two through heavyweight Ronald Rawson and the remarkable Mallin. The others went to Canada, France and South Africa.

Mallin won again in Paris four years later and once more Britain took two titles with Harry Mitchell winning at light heavyweight. This time the American flyweight was Fidel La Barba. He won the gold and went on to earn the world pro title.

At Amsterdam in 1928 it was the Italians who made their mark with three titles. The Argentine won two, Holland, Hungary and New Zealand one each.

The Games went back to the United States in 1932 but at Los Angeles the Americans could not dominate as they had in St. Louis. They took two titles, so did South Africa and The Argentine and the other two went to Canada and Hungary.

Berlin 1936 brought Germany's first-ever Olympic boxing success, and two gold medals, for Herbert Runge at heavyweight and Willie Kaiser at flyweight. Two Frenchmen won titles, but there were no American champions, and none from Britain either.

When the turmoil of World War II was over and the Olympic movement regrouped, 206 competitors from 39 countries came to the Empire Pool at Wembley in 1948. There were 30 bantamweights and 30 featherweights. These Games marked the start of Eastern European power in Olympic boxing, but there were no titles for the Russians. The Czechs took one gold and Hungary two, and at middleweight their hero was Laszlo Papp.

In the final he outpointed the one British survivor, Johnny Wright who won four times to reach the final. Then Wright had to settle for silver as he lost on points to the Hungarian maestro.

The Americans dominated the 1952 Games in Helsinki. They won five gold medals and this time there were two extra weights with the creation of the light middleweight and light welterweight divisions. Papp seized the chance to box at his natural weight, around 11 stones, and became the first light middleweight champion.

In all 251 hopefuls chased the ten titles and they came from 43 nations. Britain did not fare well and flyweight Dai Dower from Wales, later to challenge for the world title, was handed a debatable quarter-final decision against Bulakov of the USSR.

Floyd Patterson stamped his class on the middleweight section with four wins, only one of them on points. In the final he took just 74 seconds to knock out the Romanian Tita.

If the Melbourne Games marked the USSR's first gold medals, they also marked a remarkable British revival. A team of seven produced five medals, two gold, a silver and two bronze. The gold double was achieved by Terry Spinks, a baby-faced Cockney flyweight, and Dick McTaggart, a brush-topped RAF Corporal from Dundee who performed southpaw miracles at lightweight.

Spinks, then only 18, boxed far above any previous form. Shortly before the Games he met the Soviet Vladimir Stolnikov in Moscow and lost clearly, but when they met in the Games quarter-finals Spinks turned the tables brilliantly. Spinks missed out on a first round bye and won five times to take his gold. In the final he met the rugged Micrea Dobrescue and used a pop-and-hop-it technique to outwit a slugger with a square stance.

McTaggart reached his peak in Melbourne and in the final faced a big puncher in the German Harry Kurschat. To everyone's surprise it was the Scot who landed the heavy blows early on and the German took two counts in the first round. He came swinging back, but McTaggart used his boxing brain to keep scoring. He took the title, and the Val Barker Trophy as the supreme stylist at the Games.

Italy took two golds at Rome in 1960 to delight the partisan home crowds, and one of their champions was the great Nino Benvenuti, later to win the world middleweight crown.

Yet all the rest paled against the arrival on the world scene of young Cassius Clay from Louisville, Kentucky. He competed at light heavyweight – the hottest division at these Games – and came through to beat the ironman Pole Zbigniew Pietrzykowski in the final on a 5-0 vote. Even so early in a career that was to bring him fame as Muhammad Ali,

Already the greatest . . . the amateur Cassius clay receives his light heavyweight gold in 1960

the young American was very much the showman and a talented performer with it. The late George Whiting of the Evening Standard summed it up. He wrote: *'You might fault Clay for flashiness but there was no doubting his ability when the need arose.'*

So to Tokyo 1964 and problems for the boxing section. There were rows, rifts and recriminations and it all started even before the action got going. Still, there were 269 entries and the most impressive was the compact Soviet Boris Lagutin as he collected the light middleweight gold, a feat he was to repeat in Mexico four years later.

Joe Frazier, then not quite the Smokin' Joe he was to become as world champion, struggled in the final trying to tag the huge German Hans Huber. He failed to connect cleanly in an untidy contest, but still took the title.

In Mexico City, in 1968, 340 boxers of assorted shapes, sizes and abilities turned up to contest the ten weights. There were 300 bouts and more split decisions than split eyebrows. One majority vote brought Britain their first middleweight gold since Harry Mallin with the agile southpaw Chris Finnegan taking a 3-2 decision over Aleksey Kiselyov of the USSR. Finnegan, later to win British and European titles as a pro and challenge Bob Foster at Wembley for the world light heavyweight title, was magnificent in the final as he put extra beef into his right jab to score steadily. The Soviet's ox-like strength was obvious but it was Finnegan who took the final round to earn the gold, the last British boxer to manage this feat.

▲
Britain's Alan Minter, bronze medallist in Munich and later the world middleweight champion

◄
George Foreman, future world heavyweight champion, took the title in that category in the 1968 Olympics

final. Cuba had nine men in the semi-finals, and finished with three golds. They were the first medals of any kind for Cuba since a fencer won one in 1904.

Britain sent a strong team and had five in the quarter-finals. Sadly this led to only three bronze medals, for light middleweight Alan Minter, later world middleweight champion as a pro, Ralph Evans at light flyweight and Liverpool's George Turpin at bantam.

The Montreal entry in 1976 would have broken the record yet again at 370, but for 90 Africans pulling out at the last minute in one of those unhappy demonstrations that have affected the last few Games.

The Americans staged a revival just across their own borders. They took five golds, a silver and a bronze to equal their haul at Helsinki 24 years before. Ray, later Sugar Ray, Leonard won at light welterweight, showing much of the skill that took him on to the world welterweight title and a multi-million dollar fortune. Britain's Pat Cowdell took a bronze at bantam, and flyweight Charlie Magri figured in one of the upsets.

The future world champion seemed home and dry with a minute to go against Canada's Ian Clyde. Then a right-hander sent Magri down. He rose at four, seemed ready when the mandatory eight-count ended but was stopped by the Bulgarian referee.

The baby of the British party was 17-year-old welterweight Colin Jones from Gorseinon. He went out in the second series, but last year twice fought for the world welterweight title.

So, finally, to Moscow with the Americans absent and the Soviets optimistic. Instead it was Cuba who dominated. They sent 11 men and collected ten medals — six gold, two silver, two bronze.

It was a record-breaking performance and the 29-year-old Stevenson broke a record of his own. He became the first man ever to win three medals at the same weight.

Britain sent a nine-man team, well prepared and with plenty of ability. Again they put five through to the last eight and were unlucky to earn only one medal in the end — a bronze for Liverpool light welterweight Tony Willis.

At lightweight Britain's John Stracey became a mere record-book statistic after losing on points in the second series to the eventual champion, Ronnie Harris from the United States. But that same young Cockney went on to become world welterweight champion as John H. Stracey — and he went to Mexico to stop Jose Napoles to do it.

The Soviets stole the honours with three golds in Mexico and the home nation took two. So did the United States with the massive George Foreman powering to the heavyweight title.

At Munich in 1972 a record 357 boxers turned up and Papp was back as well — not to box but to train the Hungarian team.

When the lithe Cuban Stevenson started his chase for the heavyweight gold he came with warm recommendations from the experts who had already seen him in action. Ali's long-time mentor Angelo Dundee was among them, and Angelo is still surprised that the great Cuban has never cashed in on his talent.

From the moment Stevenson dismantled Duane Bobick from the States in the third round of their quarter-final he was the favourite. He stopped West German Peter Hussing in the semi-finals and then received a walk-over to the gold because Romania's Ion Alexe suffered a fractured thumb in winning his place in the

Valeri Abodzhian (URS)
Super heavyweight
(91kg+/201lb+)
Born: January 23, 1958, USSR.
Height: 193cm/6ft 4in.
Weight: 99kg/216lb.
Career Highlights
World Cup: gold 1981. 'Absolute
  Champion of the USSR'; 1982.

A former basketball player Abodzhian, born of Armenian parents, took up boxing late, at the age of 20. He rose fast, and was unquestionably topping the world in the immediate aftermath of the Moscow Olympics, but has been hit by a series of injuries since.

He impressed in the 1982 World Championships where his 4-1 points loss in the quarter-finals appeared highly debatable. He won golds in four prestigious multi-nationals tournaments in the same year though he was convincingly beaten in Tampere, Finland by the Italian Damiani.

Valeri is an orthodox, well-schooled battler with a heavy right. He is fast on his feet for such a big man. Unfortunately, he is strictly a one-punch merchant, and cannot string them together.

Yuri Alexandrov (URS)
Bantamweight (54kg/119lb)
Born: October 13, 1963,
  Nevinnomyssk, USSR.
Height: 163cm/5ft 4in.
Weight: 55kg/120lb.
Career Highlights
World Championships: gold 1982.
World Cup: bronze 1983.
European Championships:
  best boxer gold, 1983.
USSR senior champion 1983,
  1982; junior champion 1981,
  1979.

The hard-punching, orthodox Alexandrov has always been trained by mentor and coach Anatoli Dementyev, at the Trud Nevinnomyssk club. He first wore the Soviet vest as a junior flyweight taking a silver in the 1981 Comecon Juniors — also known as the Friendship Tournament for the Young — at Gera in East Germany.

An astute, intelligent pocket battleship, Alexandrov is studying to become a sports' instructor at Stavropol Paedagogic Institute. He broke into the big time in 1982 when he won the Soviet senior title and World Championship. The Soviet selectors were delighted to have solved their long-standing problem in the flyweight category, but Alexandrov was to disappoint

them. By 1983, he could no longer truly make the weight limit.

On the Soviet's United States tour and in the World Championship Challenges, officials turned a blind eye to the fact that he was still over the limit by 0.5-1kg — this despite the rigorous pre-bout exercises. So when bantam encumbent Miroshnichenko was both KO'd and caught shoplifting on the same United States tour, young Yuri was allowed to move up.

His defeat by the Italian, Maurizio Stecca, in the semis of the World Cup, confirmed the suspicion that Alexandrov may lack the necessary artillery for the heavier weight, however.

Gyula Alvics (HUN)
Heavyweight (91kg/201lb)
Born: January 12, 1960, Pecs,
  Hungary.
Height: 188cm/6ft 2in.
Weight: 92kg/203lb.
Career Highlights
European Championships: silver
  1983.
Hungarian champion: 1980,
  1981, 1983.

A strong, orthodox puncher with a modest, retiring personality, Alvics has been maturing into world prominence, and is now a threat to any of the division's top men.

Alvics KO'd the two top Cuban heavyweights in 1983, in the East European multi-national Championships and has vanquished all in Europe save for the Ukranian Alexander Jagubkin.

He was picked to represent Europe's all-star team in the Rome World Cup, but was unjustly eliminated on a 3-2 split vote against the local Angelo Musone in the first series.

A seasoned campaigner who has participated in the World Championships and two Europeans to date, Alvics is expected to get into the medals in the Olympics. But he lacks 'killer instinct' and tends to run out of ideas.

In 1983, he changed clubs. He moved from the provincial capital of western Hungary, Pecs, where he had too much popularity and inadequate training facilities, and joined the Honved — the military's club — in Budapest, to be coached by the Badari/Enekes duo. The change has improved his performance enormously.

Gyula is a qualified maintenance engineering technician by trade. He has never been stopped, and is not prone to injury.

Tyrell Biggs (USA)
Super heavyweight (91kg+/201lb)
Born: December 22, 1960,
  Virginia, USA.
Height: 196cm/6ft 5in.
Weight: 100kg/218lb.
Career Highlights
World Championships: gold 1982.
World Championship Challenge
  Matches: winner 1983.
Pan American: bronze 1983,
  (Spring) ABFs Games; gold
  1981, 1982.
Sports Festivals: silver 1981,
  1982.

Broad-shouldered 'Tyrone' Biggs is not the bruiser he looks, but a fast, fleet-footed stylist. He is a relatively light puncher and tends to win contests by the skin of his teeth. He was a budding basket ball star until he took up boxing and joined coach George Benton — a one-time middleweight professional contender — at the Smokin' Joe Frazier Club. This change of direction was at the behest of his father, who had himself been a noted US Army pugilist. Biggs was a natural and within three years was United States champion and number 4 in the world.

By the 1982 Munich World Championships, he had met — and conquered — the vast majority of the top men at the weight, and his victory there was spectacular and convincing, especially over the local Hussing and the Italian Damiani. His sweet style earned chants of 'Ali, Ali' from the German crowd, although one of his wins — against the Soviet Abodzhian was dubious.

He fractured his right hand in the United States national Sports Festival of 1982. Then in the Pan American Championships he crumbled under the hammering fists of the Cuban, Teofilo Stevenson, who KO'd him in the second and damaged his rib-cage.

A graduate of Hampton State College in Virginia, Biggs became a male nurse for a spell. He is now under the wing of music millionaire and aspiring pro promoter Shelley Finkel.

Ibrahim Bilali (KEN)
Flyweight (51kg/112lb)
Born: August 28, 1964, Nairobi,
  Kenya.
Height: 170cm/5ft 7in.
Weight: 51kg/112lb.
Career Highlights
Commonwealth Games: gold
  1982.
African Championships: gold

1983.
East and Central African
    Championships: gold 1982.
Kenyan *light-fly* champion 1981,
    1982; *fly* champion 1983.

'Surf' Bilali was not quite 8 when he took up boxing at the Muthurwa 'Dallas' Social Hall in Nairobi. He learnt the rudiments of the noble art with the help of clubmate Stephen Muchoki, the pride of Kenya who became amateur world champion and a top professional contender. His ring debut did not come until 1979, when – boxing in the colours of the Kenya Railways Club – he lost to Joram 'Hercules' Apudo in the junior championships.

In 1980, Bilali joined the Tusker Breweries club. He lost only one bout during the season, at the hands of John 'Poison' Kamau. By 1981, he had his first senior title in the bag and 1982 was a wonderful year – he got a gold in the 8th Kings Cup in Bangkok, outpointing the highly-regarded Korean Kim Kwang Sun in the final; made it into the quarter-finals of the World Championships; won the Kenyan title again; and collected golds in the East and Central African Games and in the Commonwealth Games.

Surf was named Kenya's Sportsman of the Year for 1982, and looked a great prospect for an Olympic gold in Los Angeles – Africa's first. He was fast, fleet-footed with a sweet, floating style and quick hands, a ring wizard with poise and a big punch, if needed. But all this was at light fly. When Surf moved up into the fly-weights in 1983 things went awry. He won the African title, but got KO'd in the World Cup by Korea's Yong Mo Hoe and was beaten in the Kings Cup by his erstwhile victim Kim Kwang Sun.

Talk in Nairobi suggests that the high school drop-out may drop down to light fly for the Olympics.

Mark Breland (USA)
Welterweight (67kg/147lb)
Born: May 11, 1963, Brooklyn, USA.
Height: 189cm/6ft 2½in.
Weight: 70-72kg/155-158lb.
Career Highlights
World Championships: best boxer gold 1982.
World Championship Challenge Matches: winner 1983.
US Sports Festival: gold 1981; USA/ABF gold 1982, 1983; Golden Gloves champion of

New York an unprecedented five times.

The world's top amateur welterweight in the past two years, this tall, gangling black KO-king with the dynamite right and sweet, effortless style has lost only two contests in his life, both on disputed verdicts. One of these blots on an impeccable record which spans 120-plus bouts, occurred in the juniors. The other was in the 1981 national ABFs against the unsung Darryl Anthony. Mark has beaten all his international opponents.

'Beanstalk' Breland began boxing nine years ago at Brooklyn's Bedford-Stuyvesant club. He still trains under top black coach George Washington, shunning the Olympic Training Camp at Colorado Springs. Counselled – and provided with 'walk-about money' – by Madison Avenue music millionaire Shelley Finkel, he is the darling of the media and is poised to replace Sugar Ray Leonard as pro idol after the Games.

In his big test at the third World Championships at Munich, Mark came through with flying colours. He outclassed the Soviet Serik Konakbaev, one of the top stylists at any weight, putting him down for the first time in his career.

Breland received rave reviews for his part in a major film, *Lords of Discipline,* in which he played a black teenager who integrates into an all-white military academy in the heady days of Martin Luther King in the early 1960s.

A graduate of Brooklyn's Eastern District High School, Mark Breland is soft-spoken, polite, articulate – not a typical product of Brooklyn's rough-and-tough Bedford-Stuyvesant district. His main problem is making the weight.

Luciano Bruno (ITA)
Welterweight (67kg/147lb)
Born: May 3, 1963, Italy.
Height: 172cm/5ft 8in.
Weight: 67kg/147lb.
Career Highlights
World Cup: gold 1983.
European Championships: silver 1983.
European Juniors: silver 1982.
CISM (world military) Championships: silver 1982.
Italian senior champion 1982, 1983; junior champion 1981.

A versatile, orthodox hard-man, who can switch pace and tactics

effortlessly, Bruno is one of the brightest of Italy's new wave of stars. His record is impeccable, and he has a chance of a medal in the Olympics.

A professional soldier, who boxes for the Italian military's SMEF club, he will probably cross over into the paid ranks after the Olympics and should go a long way as a professional.

Yong Beum Chung (KOR)
Welterweight (67kg/147lb)
Born: May 5, 1963, Seoul, South Korea.
Height: 170cm/5ft 7in.
Weight: 67kg/147lb.
Career Highlights
World Championship Challenge Matches: loser 1983.
Asian Championships: gold 1982, 1983.
Korean champion 1982.

PT student, up-and-coming Korean battler Chung is gaining increasing world prominence. He started late and only came into his own in 1982, after boxing for three years.

In the 1982 World Championships, he was a first-series victim on points to the fleet-footed, light-punching Norwegian half-cast, Kristen Reagan, mainly due to his lack of experience. He has improved out of all recognition since. A controversial choice for the Tokyo round of the World Championships Challenges, he boxed effectively against the superb American, Mark Breland, but lost on points.

Bernardo Comas (CUB)
Middleweight (75kg/165lb)
Born: November 14, 1963, Cuba.
Height: 183cm/6ft 0in.
Weight: 77kg/169lb.
Career Highlights
World Championships: gold 1982.
World Championship Challenge Matches: winner 1983.
Pan American Games: gold 1983.
Comecon Juniors: *best boxer* gold 1981.
Cuban champion 1983; runner-up 1982.

Comas was recognized as a budding star in the junior ranks, but the transition into the seniors was difficult. Selection encumbent Jose Gomez, his elder by four years and the king of the world's middles since 1978, had a simple view of his succession – any potential challenge was nipped in the bud at the first opportunity. Comas managed to survive Gomez's onslaught in the final of the 1982 Cordova Cardin tournament in Havana, though he absorbed counts and slumped to a unanimous loss. So, when the flamboyant Gomez persistently missed training camp, preferring the bright lights of the capital, young Bernardo was assigned to represent Cuba in the 1982 World Championships. The youngster had a few wobbly moments, but emerged from the test with flying colours. He KOed the Finn, Tarmo Uusivirta with a thunderous left hook.

Gomez, outraged, could not wait to get his hands on the usurper, and when they met in the 1982 Cuban Championships, he pulled his roughest tactics out of the bag and broke Comas' rib-cage. But he had his come-uppance in 1983 when Comas KO'd the fading star in the Cuban final.

Comas is not the force Gomez once was and lost to American Virgil Hill in the North American Championships, which deprived him of World Cup participation. But he will, nonetheless, start as a favourite for the middleweight gold in Los Angeles.

Noe Cruciano (ITA)
Middleweight (75kg/165lb)
Born: January 26, 1963, Toscana, Italy.
Height: 181cm/5ft 11in.
Weight: 77kg/169lb.
Career Highlights
World Cup: silver 1983.
European Junior Championships: silver 1982.

A young policeman who fights from a southpaw stance, Noe first came to the notice of the international boxing fraternity when he courageously out-punched the more experienced East German Maik Koudele on his home turf, in the semi-finals of the European Juniors in Schwerin. In the final of the same competition he held his ground against England's red-hot Errol Christie (now a rising pro) — though he lost on points — and caused England's best since Randolph Turpin some problems.

His progress to the final of the World Cup in Rome, beating Virgil Hill of the US on the way, was an even greater feat, demonstrating just how much the youngster had improved in a year.

Equipped with a sturdy chin, Noe Cruciani is a cool customer who responds well to pressure and appears to be heading for the top. It remains to be seen whether the Los Angeles Games will prove too soon for him.

Francesco Damiani (ITA)
Super heavyweight
(91kg+/201lb+)
Born: October 4, 1958, Italy.
Height: 198cm/6ft 6in.
Weight: 98kg/214lb.
Career Highlights
Olympic Games: quarter-finalist 1980.
World Championships: silver 1982.
World Cup: gold 1983.
European Championships: gold 1981, 1983.

From a rural district near Bologna, Damiani's hammering fists first drew world attention when he came close to eclipsing the Soviet Pjotr Zayev in the quarter-finals of the Moscow Olympics. The 3-2 verdict in Zayev's favour, was partly because he was fighting on his home turf.

By the 1981 European Championships the Damiani wagon was rolling. His huge rights forced the massive Soviet, Yakovlev, into ungainly escapes in the final. The Italian's great moment came at Munich in 1982, when he humiliated Cuban ace Stevenson in the World Championships. He lost to Biggs of the United States in the final (though he still disputes the validity of the verdict), and almost signed up with pro manager Branchini.

For a while there were rumours of $250,000 offers for Damiani's pro services, and then of the Italian Boxing Federation gazumping them to keep the big peasant boy fighting for the flag. Whatever the truth may have been, Damiani stayed in the amateurs, won a sackful of gold medals and is now the favourite for the Olympic title.

Francesco takes a great shot, and has a lethal right, but he is heavy on his feet and needs manoeuvring to get into postion. He just loves negative East Europeans who want to counter, but is at odds against fleet-footed types like Biggs.

DeWitt also gave him trouble on a 1983 Canada versus Italy bill, though Damiani got the nod. Whatever happens in Los Angeles, the Italian will go pro immediately afterwards, and could well be the long-awaited 'Big White Hope' who will unify the pro world titles.

Willie DeWitt (CAN)
Heavyweight (91kg/201lb)
Born: June 13, 1960, Three Hills, Alberta, Canada.
Height: 188cm/6ft 2in.
Weight: 94kg/207lb.
Career Highlights
World Championship Challenge Matches: winner 1983.
Commonwealth Games: gold 1982.
North American Championships: gold 1982, 1983.
Canadian champion: 1981, 1982, 1983.

A football star plagued by injuries, Willie got interested in boxing while working out on the punch-bag in a health club and took it up in 1978. By the following year, he had landed light-heavy silver in the Canadian Championships.

He has not been particularly lucky in big-trophy events. In the 1981 World Cup in Montreal, he was eliminated in his first outing by the Soviet, Jagubkin in a desperately close bout. He lost by a similar 3-2 margin to the local Peter Hussing in the quarter-finals of the Munich World Championships. In the 1983 World Cup in Rome he stopped Korea's number two, Park, but was injured, and eliminated, in the process.

His rousing North American title wins, including the KO'ing of Cubans in the finals, and his slightly dubious, ascension to the world title in Reno last year, when he was judged winner over Jagubkin, firmly established him as a name to watch.

A lumberjack type with rippling muscles a crouching orthodox stance and a booming right, DeWitt is Jagubkin's only credible opponent in the heavy category. If he can catch up with him, he will undoubtedly take him apart.

Willie DeWitt of Canada . . . his heavy punching could upset them all ▼

Roderick Douglas (GBR)
Light middleweight (71kg/156lb)
Born: October 26, 1964, London, England.
Height: 174cm/5ft 8½in.
Weight: 72.5kg/158lb.
Career Highlights
Commonwealth Federation: champion 1983.
ABA: champion 1983.

Keith Ferdinand of Great Britain . . . disciplined now and determined to be the best ▶

A black Cockney, born in Bow of West Indian parents, Rod joined the St Georges club in 1979, learned the ropes quickly at the hands of coach Peter Morgan and by 1980 was on his way to a junior ABA title.

1982 was his first senior year and in 1983 he won the ABA title. Next he won the Commonwealth Federation gold in Belfast, easily beating the highly-touted Sam Storey on his home ground. He defeated East and West German stars Ralf Hunger and Manfred Zielonka in successive two-nations tournaments.

The last two results catapulted him into Olympic medal reckoning and set the international fraternity a-buzz with his name. Triple GDR champ Hunger, whom Douglas knocked out in the second, was European silver medallist and World Cup bronze medallist in 1983, on both occasions narrowly losing to the eventual winner, Valeri Laptyev of the USSR. Zielonka won a World Championships

bronze and was voted best West German boxer in 1982.

A scrappy, awkward southpaw with plenty of aggression and natural talent, Douglas is the best British Boxer at present, and the only Briton with a clear Olympic medal chance despite his inexperience at top level.

Rod is a draughtsman by trade, but his life is centred on boxing. Dedicated in the gymn, he is very observant and listens to advice. After the Games, he will undoubtedly make a fine professional.

Floyd Favors (USA)
Bantamweight (54kg/119lb)
Born: December 3, 1963, Maryland, USA.
Height: 165cm/5ft 5in.
Weight: 55kg/120lb.
Career Highlights
World Championships: gold 1982.
World Championship Challenge Matches: winner 1983.
Pan American Games: bronze 1982.
USA/ABFs: (Spring) silver 1983.
Sports Festival: gold 1982.

Floyd lives in Capitol Heights, Maryland and boxes for the Eastern Branch Knack Team club where he is trained by coach William Dunlap. He won in the World Championships in Munich and then defended last year beating Kimiaki Takami of Japan in Tokyo.

His domestic record is patchy, with a string of points losses to foes ranging from Israel Acosta to Robert Shannon, Conrad Sanchez, Meldryck Taylor, Lupe Gutierrez and Herbie Bivalacqua. He has since beaten two of his conquerors, Gutierrez and Bivalacqua.

Favors is tough with plenty of flair, versatility and tactical sense. Orthodox, with a big right, he can dish it out and take it. He has been plagued by hand injuries over the past year.

Keith Ferdinand (GBR)
Super heavyweight (91kg+/201lb+)
Born: February 11, 1963, Kingston, Jamaica.
Height: 194.5cm/6ft 4½in.
Weight: 101kg/220lb.
Career Highlights
Commonwealth Federation Championships: gold 1983.
ABA: champion 1983, runner-up 1982.

Huge, massively-muscled 'Ferdie', whose West Indian family lives in Coventry, joined the Royal Navy at 16 and was pushing leather within a year, learning the ropes under Navy coaches Tony Oxley and Alan Dolman. He was a fantastic physical specimen but lacked discipline. Ferdie is a sharp, intelligent fellow, and a hard man in the gym, but he did not get to the gym often

enough, and did not put his mind to his boxing. He was having fun, and everything else came second.

Despite this lack of application, by his 12th bout, he was the Navy and Combined Services champion, facing the vastly more experienced Adrian Elliott in the 1982 ABA final at Wembley, and losing on a majority. A year later he got the coveted ABA title, to carry the White Ensign into the England selection as its regular member. But Ferdie's thinking has changed – he wants to win and be best in the world. The turnabout dates back to 1982 when he was eliminated from the European Juniors, and was convincingly beaten on a Britain-United States bill by the unsung Kimmuel Odum. Suddenly, Ferdinand's international career took off. He chalked up a series of increasingly impressive wins, and when he bumped into two world-rated opponents, he had no reason to be ashamed of the outcome.

His loss to the seasoned Warren Thompson Jr, in Reno, looked unlucky, and his trouncing of the East German beanpole, Ulli Kaden, who won a silver in the 1983 Europeans and is rated fourth in the world, was a feat noted worldwide.

Carlos Garcia Rodriguez

(CUB)
Light welterweight (63.5kg/139lb)
Born: October 27, 1964, Camaguey, Cuba.
Height: 173.5cm/5ft 8½in.
Weight: 67kg/147lb.
Career Highlights
World Championships: gold 1982.
World Championship Challenge Matches: gold 1983.
Central American and Caribbean Championships: gold 1981.
Cuban champion 1982.

Only 16 and a lightweight, Carlos won the Central American title and went to the Comecon Juniors at the Panndorf Hall in Gera, East Germany in 1981. The hosts wanted their star, lightweight Siegfried Mehnert, to take the gold and the best boxer nomination, but were tired of pitting him against the big-hitting, diamond-hard Garcia, who was – oddly – found to be over the limit at first weigh-in, and was not given another chance. The Cubans withdrew from future Comecon Juniors claiming privately that the weigh-in was rigged.

At 17 the youngster completely wrecked the invincible Soviet Vasily Shishov and took the World Championships gold in a most emphatic fashion. He also won golds in every East European multi-nations in which he was entered during the year, and proved the fiercest, most dependable Cuban star of all in 1982.

But 1983 was a different kettle of fish. The dynamic southpaw with the big left hook ran out of gas, and had to pull out all the stops to eke out the narrowest of points wins in the World Championship Challenges at Reno against a peak-form Jerry Page of the United States. He was packed off for a rest and the tall, stylish, but less powerful, Candelario Duvergel took his place at the North American Championships and the World Cup, earning golds in both.

The Cubans have not managed to come up with a viable, topflight welter since 1980, when the all-conquering Andres Aldama was retired on health grounds, so Garcia or Duvergel will fill the welter spot at the Olympics. The final choice will be made close to the Games' start, but Garcia appears to have the inside track for the coveted light-welter berth.

Stefan Gertel (FRG)

Bantamweight (54kg/119lb)
Born: May 12, 1960, Worms, Germany.
Height: 163cm/5ft 4in.
Weight: 54kg/119lb.
Career Highlights
European Championships: bronze 1981.
CISM (world military) Championships: silver 1981.
German champion: 1978-81, 1983.

A compact, pro-styled, orthodox pressure fighter who soaks up punishment in an attempt to make up for his short reach and get to his foe, Gertel has been hovering on the brink of big-time medal contention for years, and may finally fulfil his potential in LA. After the Olympics, he is certain to join the Sauerland/Weller pro circus.

Landscape gardener Stefan – a former soldier – is the best of the fighting Gertels of Worms. A gym fanatic who is always superbly fit, he is likely to do very well in the pros.

Paul Gonzales (USA)

Light flyweight (48kg/106lb)
Born: April 18, 1964, Pecos, Texas, USA.
Height: 174cm/5ft 8½in.
Weight: 50kg/110lb.
Career Highlights
Pan American Games: silver 1983.
USA/ABFs and National Golden Gloves: *fly* gold 1983, silver 1981.
PAL: *tourney* gold 1982.

Gonzales lives in Los Angeles, California, and attends Loyola Marymount University where he is reading architecture. Serious-minded and well-mannered, he comes from a middle-class background and got into boxing ten years ago against the wishes of his parents. He trains under coach Al Stankie at Hollenbeck Boxing Club.

Very tall for – and fairly comfortable at – lightweight, he has an unmatchable reach. He is a straightforward, orthodox box-fighter who can exert tremendous pressure but does not know how to take a step backwards.

Having lost twice to the highly-rated Jesse Benavides (now a bantam) at fly in the finals of major US national tournaments in 1981, his first senior year, he slimmed down to lightfly and hit the headlines. In his very first international, on the US v. USSR bill in March 1983 in Syracuse, New York, Paul shocked the visitors by thrashing the reigning Soviet Olympic champion, Shamil Sabyrov.

Despite his failings – predictability, lack of footwork and relative inexperience at top level – Gonzales will be hard to deny the gold at the Los Angeles Olympics. He will be the only local from the City of Angels in the United States squad, and the sole Latin, which guarantees him great support.

Bernard Gray (USA)

Featherweight (57kg/125lb)
Born: May 27, 1963, Boynton Beach, Florida, USA.
Height: 178cm/5ft 10in.
Weight: 58kg/127lb.
Career Highlights
World Championships: bronze 1982.
World Championship Challenge Matches: points loser (2-3 to Horta, Cuba) 1983.
Pan American Games: bronze 1983.
USA/ABF Championships: runner-up Spring, winner (Winter) 1982.
US Ohio State Fair: gold 1981.

Gray is the second of five fighting brothers who are coached by their father and not attached to any club. Southpaw Bernard, who is in his ninth year of competition, is the best of them but elder brother Clifford — an orthodox lightweight — is also an experienced international with two USA/ABF titles. He lives in his native Boynton Beach, where he attends Palmer High School, but — having joined the Operation Gold programme in 1983 — spends half his time training at the Olympic Camp in Colorado Springs at high altitude.

An intelligent young black, with plenty of self-confidence, Bernard has an uncanny knack for goading opponents into making mistakes, and is one of a handful of US boxers to boast peerless footwork and versatility. More of a defensive stylist, he can be lethal with his left.

Angel Herrera (CUB)
Lightweight (60kg/132lb)
Born: August 2, 1952, Guantanamo, Cuba.
Height: 170cm/5ft 7in.
Weight: 64kg/140.5lb.
Career Highlights
Olympic Games: *light* gold 1980; *feather* gold 1976.
World Championships: *feather* gold 1978; *light* gold 1982.
World Cup: *light* gold 1981.
World Championship Challenge Matches: loser (0-5 to Whitaker of the US) 1983.
Pan American Games: gold 1979, 1981; silver 1983.

Angel Herrera of Cuba . . . seeking an Olympic hat-trick ▼

Father-of-four Herrera, 31, hails from a fisherman's family of 11 children in Guantanamo. From the age of 13, his whole life has centred on boxing, which has provided him with an apartment and middle-class trappings in Havana. But he still takes the kids back to Guantanamo for a spot of fishing.

A predator in the ring, who knows all the tricks and fights like the veteran pro he is, gym fanatic Angel was already 23 and a battle-hardened ring soldier when he attracted the attention of national coaching supremo Alcides Sagarra-Garon.

The taciturn Herrera merited his prominence through his fierce, unquestioning loyalty to his coach, and although his slide over the past 18 months is inescapable, his Olympic nomination has never been in doubt. He will go to Los Angeles to try for a third Olympic gold, and thereby match the record of Hungary's Papp and compatriot Stevenson. He will then become Sagarra-Garon's right-hand man as junior national coach and a lieutenant in Cuba's 50-strong full-time coaching establishment.

That coveted third gold will probably evade him for he is no longer the force he once was. But the redoubtable Angel has surprised before; he dismantled the favoured Soviet Demyanenko in the 1980 Moscow Games. The Cubans think that he may do the same against Whitaker of the United States, his conqueror on four occasions.

Virgil Hill (USA)
Middleweight (75kg/165lb)
Born: January 18, 1964, Missouri, USA.
Height: 183cm/6ft 0in.
Weight: 75kg/165lb.
Career Highlights
World Cup: bronze 1983.
North American Championships: gold 1983.
USA/ABFs Championships: silver 1982.

Virgil lives in Williston, North Dakota where he attends college to study business administration. An outdoor all-sporting type, he plays football and basketball, wrestles in his spare time, and does a lot of fishing and hunting.

His mother was the first female licensed boxing judge in North Dakota, and his father was an ex-boxer. So, Virgil took up the noble art eleven years ago with the encouragement of both parents, and was trained by Bob Hill for five years. He now competes in the colours of the Good Sam Club and is coached by Bruce Wiegley.

Despite his relatively modest senior experience, Virgil has exploded on the international scene, showing tremendous flair and the ability to rise to big occasions. In his first international outing in East Germany he completely out-boxed two highly decorated veterans and stunned the United States touring team's officials. In the 1983 North Americans at Houston, Texas, his finals points victim was the Cuban world champion Bernardo Comas, who could not get near him.

Hill is always superbly fit, has a dynamic, all-go style and tends to cover more canvas in a bout than a pro in a 15-rounder. Taciturn, even timid outside the ring, he thrives under pressure and is an awkward, self-styled southpaw who is very difficult to find and sets a hot pace, frustrating opponents.

Yong Mo Hoe (KOR)
Flyweight (51kg/112lb)
Born: April 21, 1963, Korea.
Height: 169cm/5ft 6½in.
Weight: 51kg/112lb.
Career Highlights
World Championships: bronze 1982.
World Cup: silver 1981, 1983.
Asian Championships: gold 1982, 1983.

A tall, orthodox pressure fighter with a big right, who campaigned as a light-flyweight until 1983, Hoe is a wonderfully co-ordinated pupil of the burgeoning Korean school of boxing, which could dominate the world by the 1988 Seoul Olympics.

Hoe was blatantly robbed in the semi-finals of the Munich World Championships against the Bulgarian Mustafov. His loss, also by a 4-1 margin, in the World Cup final to Cuba's Reyes was also controversial. In LA, where judging standards will be much stricter, he may make up for the disappointments.

Adolfo Horta (CUB)
Featherweight (57kg/125lb)
Born: March 10, 1957, Camaguey, Cuba.
Height: 168cm/5ft 6in.
Weight: 61kg/133lb.
Career Highlights
Olympic Games: silver 1980.
World Championships: gold 1982, *bantam* gold 1978.
World Cup: gold 1981.
World Championship Challenge Matches: winner 1983.
Pan American Games: gold 1983, 1981.

Horta hit the international big-time as a bantam at 19, and instantly proved another virtually unbeatable product of the Sagarra-Garon school, cutting a broad swathe among the stars of the East, vanquishing the best of Americans and winning a gold at 21 at the second World Championships in Belgrade.

Although his final win over the local star, Fazija Sacirovic, was debatable, Horta dispelled all doubts about himself with his spectacular march to the final, especially his relaxed handling in the semis of the very strong, robot-like East German Stefan Forster. Unlike other leading Cubans, he proved more reliant on versatile ringcraft and defensive ability.

A period of relative uncertainty ensued in 1979/80, when he could no longer make bantam. Horta moved up to lightweight for a brief spell, jumping two categories, and suffered a series of losses. But by the 1980 Olympics he was the best featherweight in Cuba and it was the shock of the Moscow finals when he lost to East German Rudi Fink.

Since then, however, Adolfo has been the most consistent of the Cubans, ruling the world of featherweights with a firm hand. Undoubtedly he would have made a great professional.

Intelligent, witty, Horta is a popular figure in the social whirl of Havana and is apparently on the lazy side in the gym. But he invariably gets himself into great shape for the contests that count, and is a lethal southpaw who is universally favoured for the Olympic gold in LA.

Sandor Hranek (HUN)

Light middleweight (71kg/156lb)
Born: January 20, 1961,
  Salgotarjan, Hungary.
Height: 183cm/6ft 0in.
Weight: 70kg/154lb.
Career Highlights
Hungarian champion: 1983,
  1981.

A vastly underrated pugilist, Hranek has been a member of the European elite for the past three years, reaching the quarter-finals of the 1982 World Championships and 1983 Europeans, only to lose there on split votes, and winning several medals in Europe's most prestigious multi-national boxing tournaments.

From the Salgotarjan coal mining town's burgeoning gypsy community, he moved last year to the famed Honved club in Budapest to train under one-time dual Eurochamp Tibor Badari. 'Sanyi' Hranek is a polished, slick, big-hitting ring operator with a whole string of KO victories to his name. His only problem is – 'bottle'. He tends to pale when bumping into big-name opposition.

Considered a real prospect since his junior days, Hranek is clearly heading for the big-time in the amateurs, and could well come good in LA.

John Hyland (GBR)

Bantamweight (54kg/119lb)
Born: June 20, 1962, Liverpool,
  England.
Height: 174cm/5ft 8½in.
Weight: 54kg/118lb.
Career Highlights
Commonwealth Federations: gold
  1983.
ABA champion bantamweight
  1983.
Schools Junior ABA champion
  1978, 1977.

Hyland began boxing at the age of 10 at the St Ambrose club in Speke. A big-hitting southpaw with flair, he was a highly promising junior, but had a hard transition into the senior ranks in the tough North Western Counties ABA, where he had to battle in the shadow of the likes of Keith Wallace and Ray Gilbody. His tremendous scrap with Wallace, who won by the narrowest of margins in the West Lancs finals of the 1981 ABAs, is still remembered. It had 4,000 on their feet at Liverpool Stadium.

His controversial points loss to Scot Joe Kelly in the flyweight final of the 1982 ABAs resulted in Hyland being sidestepped for nomination to the Commonwealth Games in Brisbane, and subsequently led to the retirement of coach Georgie Treble, who had been handling him from the inception of his ring career.

But, where some may have given up, Hyland battled on. He moved up to bantam, got married on his 22nd birthday to Margie, daughter of one-time England international Tommy Bache, won the 1983 ABA title and is now looking to crown his long amateur service with a medal at the Olympics.

A butcher by trade, he works just a few doors away from his home in Speke, where he has always lived. He trains with single-minded dedication, and is admirably disciplined.

Alexander Jagubkin (URS)

Heavyweight (91kg/201lb)
Born: April 25, 1961, Donezk,
  USSR.
Height: 191cm/6ft 3½in.
Weight: 93-97kg/206-211lb.
Career Highlights
World Championships: gold 1982.
World Cup: gold 1983, silver 1981.
European Championships: gold
  1983, 1981.
World Championship Challenge
  Matches: points loser (2-3, to
  DeWitt, Canada) 1983.
World Juniors: bronze 1979.
'Absolute Champion of the USSR',
  1980.

An athletic type who could have reached the top in several sports, 'Sasha' is a good middle-distance runner and gymnast. He is no big-punching brawler, but a hard-to-catch defensive stylist with peerless footwork and very fast hands. He has lost only two bouts in the past three years, both on points, to Carl Williams of the US in the 1981 Montreal World Cup and to the Canadian DeWitt in Reno, Nevada, last year. Williams (a rising pro now) has gone from the amateur scene and the decision against DeWitt was controversial.

Arguably the best-ever Soviet heavyweight, Sasha has been boxing since 1975 at the Avantgarde Donezk club under coach Anatoli Kotov, but owes a lot to USSR national coach Artjem Lavrov, who confirmed his all-dancing, in-and-out style.

John Hyland of Great Britain . . . hard-hitting southpaw bantamweight
▼

A student of civil aviation, the witty, personable Jagubkin is single. A Ukranian by origin, he has a huge following in his native Donezk, but — being highly intelligent — shuns hangers-on and cheap popularity.

If he has a failing in the ring, it is that he tends to be over-cautious and becomes negative under pressure.

Kieran Joyce (IRE)
Welterweight (67kgs/147lbs)
Born: October 9, 1964, Cork, Ireland.
Height: 173cm/5ft 8in.
Weight: 69kg/151lbs.
Career Highlights
European Championships: bronze 1983.
Irish senior champion 1983; junior champion 1982; youth champion 1979/80.

A walk-in type battler who can punch, Kieran has been coming along with giant strides since his debut in the international arena, at the 1982 European Junior Championships in Schwerin, East Germany.

There he was narrowly beaten by a local, the eventual champion Torsten Schmitz. But he has grown in stature, can block and defend now, and his showing in the European Championships at Sofia established him in the eyes of the international fraternity as a dangerous opponent for anyone.

Joyce is strongly pro-styled, and is clearly headed for a paid career in the wake of the Olympics, where he may get into the medal stakes.

Dong Kil Kim (KOR)
Light welterweight (63.5kg/139lb)
Born: May 19, 1963, Kwangjoo, Korea.
Height: 168cm/5ft 6in.
Weight: 64kg/140lb.
Career Highlights
World Championships: silver 1982.
World Cup: bronze 1981.
Asian Championships: silver 1981, golds 1982, 1983.

A consistent, stylish, orthodox battler with fine middle-distance skills and rock-hard uppercuts, Kim has been king of the Asian scene in his category for the past 2½ years. He is a potent force at world level and is poised for a lucrative professional career after the L.A. Games.

He has only lost five of over 170 bouts, all on points, including narrow defeats by Canada's Rick Anderson (now a professional) in the 1981 World Cup semis and Cuba's Carlos Garcia Rodriguez in the final of the World Championships.

Short for the weight, Kim can take all that is thrown at him — wearing down the opposition with his high punch-rate. A student of physical culture in his native Kwangjoo, he spends roughly one-third of a year at the National Training Centre in Seoul City, where he is the favourite of national coach Jyung Chun Park.

Klaus-Dieter Kirchstein
(GDR)
Bantamweight: (54kg/119lb)
Born: August 14, 1960, East Berlin, East Germany.
Height: 165cm/5ft 5in.
Weight: 58kg/128lb.
Career Highlights:
World Championships: bronze 1982.
European Championships: bronze 1983.
GDR champion 1982, runner-up 1979-81.

Kirchstein was one of the four choices of one-time GDR national coach Peter Thomas for the Moscow Olympics in 1980 which were two years ahead when the straw-blond Kirchstein was still a flyweight. He is now a seasoned, compact, chunky southpaw with aggression but he is awkward and lacks flair and versatility.

Kirchstein never made it to Moscow. Thomas and his coaching assistant, Martin Neef — who has been training Klaus-Dieter at the SC Dinamo Berlin club since he was 12 — were removed from the national helm for trying to introduce an advance selection system.

But Kirchstein was recalled to the national selection in 1982, and is now its star. He still bears the scars of his years in the wilderness, and of the style-honing experiments of Thomas and Neef. He is a manufactured boxer who lacks ideas — he always makes it to the best 8 or 4 in big-trophy competitions, but no further.

For him, it's Los Angeles or else. If he does not make it into the medals, the Olympics is likely to signal the close of his international career.

Serik Konakbaev (URS)
Welterweight (67kg/147lb)
Born: October 25, 1959, Alma Alta, USSR.
Height: 183cm/6ft 0in.
Weight: 67kg/147lb.
Career Highlights
Olympic Games: silver 1980.
World Championships: silver 1982.
World Cup: gold 1981, 1979.
European Championships: gold 1981, 1979.

Making his big-time international debut at the 1979 Cologne European Championships, Konakbaev did well on his way to the final, totally eclipsing such long-serving stalwarts as Karoly Hainal of Romania and Karl-Heinz Kruger of the GDR. He dazzled with his fantastic footwork and speed, and looked unbeatable.

But it was a different story in the final. The taller Italian, Patrizio Oliva, completely dominated him although the verdict went to the Soviet causing ringside pandemonium. Oliva beat Konakbaev again, in the Olympics. The foremost proponent of the Russian 'dancing school', a southpaw with the sweetest style, he can baffle 99% of opponents and soars when on top. But when he meets his match, he goes to pieces. Mark Breland of the United States, only the second man to prove too much for him, came quite close to KO'ing 'Superb Serik'. Konakbaev has been kept away from the top Cubans and could come unstuck against one or two of them.

In 1983, the Soviets experimented with replacing Konakbaev with the sturdier, but more pedestrian Pjotr Galkin, but this did not work out. So architectural student Konakbaev, who boxes for the Spartak Alma Ata club and is on the payroll of state security, is back in the welter weight Soviet selection. Only an Olympic gold will prolong his international career.

Soviet Serik Konakbaev ... can fall to pieces under pressure ▼

Valeri Laptyev (URS)

Light middleweight: (71kg/156lb)
Born: 1961, Cherboksary, USSR.
Height: 181cm/5ft 11in.
Weight: 77kg/169lb.
Career Highlights
World Cup: gold 1983.
European Championships: gold
 1983.
European Juniors: gold 1980.

A sports instructor who boxes for Dynamo Cherboksary, he first appeared in the international limelight by winning a gold at the 1980 European Junior Championships in Rimini, Italy as a middleweight.

Not much was heard for some time afterwards, until he was suddenly taken out of mothballs last year and advanced into the Soviet selection, because the encumbent light middleweight Aleksander Koshkin — Olympic silver medallist and world champion — unexpectedly lost three bouts in succession on the Soviet's United States tour.

So Valeri, who did relatively little between 1980 and 1983 apart from winning two classy multinational tournaments — the 1981 TSC Berlin Contest in East Germany and the 1982 Tammer competitons in Tampere, Finland — at middleweight, got dusted off, slimmed down and thrown in at the deep end, with remarkable success.

He won golds in both the European Championships and the World Cup in a division which had seen an exodus of its top talents to the pros and the succumbing to injury of its king in the 1980-82 era, Cuba's Armando Martinez.

The practice is fairly characteristic of Soviet selection tactics. They always keep a couple of potentially promising youngsters on the shelf in categories fronted by a world-level star, so that a quick replacement causes no problem. It is also indicative of the strength and depth of Soviet boxing, that such products often go straight to the top, as happened to Valeri Laptyev.

But soutnpaw Valeri, who appeared to have immensely powerful shoulders and torso even for a middleweight in Rimini, while lacking a telling punch, is rumoured to have weight problems, and has yet to prove his prowess, 1983 results notwithstanding. He will start as favourite for the gold in LA, but may be shocked if the depleted category spawns some meaningful new talent.

Petar Lessov (BUL)

Flyweight (51kg/112lb)
Born: December 12, 1960,
 Sekirovo, Bulgaria.
Height: 175cm/5ft 9in.
Weight: 53.5kg/120lb.
Career Highlights
Olympic Games: gold 1980.
World Cup: bronze 1983, silver
 1981.
European Championships: gold
 1983, 1981.

The Lessovs hail from Sekirovo a suburb of Rakowski City. Petar followed cousin Yordan to the local club in 1975, where coach Lulen Gadzev immediately saw the boys' potential. Sekirovo boxing club is a feeder to Lokomotiv Plovdiv so Petar was first transferred there and finally to top Bulgarian clubside CSKA Sofia, which is run by the military. In the hands of CSKA coach Vassil Kostov, Petar Lessov progressed fast, developing into an evasive, accurate — if somewhat frail — ring technician.

A devout Catholic in politically austere Bulgaria, Petar was sidestepped for selection, but in the end his shining talent got him to the Moscow Olympics, where he made it into the final and won in controversial circumstances.

One of the world's foremost stylists Petar is all at sea against fierce Cubans in particular, and heavy punchers in general. Omar Santiesteban demolished him on three occasions including the final of the 1981 World Cup in Montreal. He was beaten by another Cuban, Pedro Reyes, in the semis of the 1983 World Cup.

Lessov's Moscow Olympic and Varna European Championship golds were both attributable to a Bulgarian, 'Prof' Emil Jetchev who dominated the referees'/judges' commission of AIBA, amateur boxing's world body. In Moscow, the Soviet Miroshnichenko, way ahead on points, was injured in the second round, the bout was stopped and Lessov was declared winner. In Varna, Lessov was injured in the first round. The points were tallied and the Hungarian Varadi was declared 3-2 winner, but the jury overturned the verdict, giving the gold to Lessov.

Petar Lessov has a nominal job with the military, but — because of his Catholic background — is not a commissioned officer like other CSKA boxers. After the Olympics, where he may earn a lesser medal, he is likely to return to Sekirovo and take over the coaching of the local club there.

◄
One of boxing's greatest stylists . . . Petar Lessov of Bulgaria

Armando Martinez (CUB)

Light middleweight (71kg/156lb)
Born: August 29, 1961, Ciego de
 Avila, Cuba.
Height: 173cm/5ft 8in.
Weight: 75kg/165lb.
Career Highlights
Olympic Games: gold 1980.
World Championships: silver
 1982.
World Cup: silver 1981.
Cuban champion 1982.

One of the Cubans' two Moscow Olympics winners, Armando had four mighty battles in 1980-82 with the division's other two kingpins, Aleksander Koshkin of the USSR and Canada's Shawn O'Sullivan. These left him drained and prone to diverse ailments, so that the Cubans gave him a year to recuperate for the Olympics.

Under-dog Martinez first beat Koshkin in the 1980 Olympic final

Cuba's Armando Martinez . . . given a year off to prepare for the Olympics
▼

to emerge a clear winner, and then did much the same in the final of the World Championships, but this time the East European judging mafia stepped in, awarding a ludicrous victory to the Russian.

With Irish-Canadian Shawn, the Cuban fared less well. O'Sullivan went into the lion's den in 1981 and beat Martinez in the Cordova Cardin multi-national Championships in Havana. History repeated itself in the 1981 World Cup final some nine months later, when the Canadian was crowned.

Though he will be only 23 in Los Angeles, Martinez has had an unusually arduous early career of over 300 bouts, of which he has lost less than 20. Whether he can be re-motivated remains to be seen.

Steve McCrory (USA)
Flyweight (51kg/112lb)
Born: April 13, 1964, Detroit, Michigan, USA.
Height: 165cm/5ft 5in.
Weight: 52kg/114lb.
Career Highlights
World Championships Challenge Matches: winner 1983.
Pan American Games: bronze 1983.
North American Championships: gold 1982.
USA/ABF championships: gold 1982, 1983, ABF bronze 1981, Sports Festival; silver 1982.

The brother of professional welterweight world champion Milton, and a stalwart of the Kronk gym since age 8, Steve has always been considered the more talented, and tipped for future pro stardom since his teens. Training under coach Francis Purify, he is the apple of the eye of Kronk supremo Emmanuel Steward and, with his more positive personality, tends to dominate Milt, who is his elder by three years.

Even so Steve has had a hard time on the murderously strong US domestic front, losing to Jesse Benavides three times and to Jose Rosario and Todd Hickman. All have now moved to other categories, so Steve found himself top man again.

Steve, a graduate from Detroit's Pershing High School in 1982, is a very fast, orthodox box-fighter with an immense amount of experience for his age, but his style already contains many pro elements which may prove a hindrance in the Olympics.

Ismail Mustafov (BUL)
Light flyweight (48kg/106lb)
Born: July 1960, Varna, Bulgaria.
Height: 175.5cm/5ft 9in.
Weight: 52-55kg/114-120lb.
Career Highlights
Olympic Games: bronze 1980.
World Championships: gold 1982.
World Cup: gold 1981, bronze 1983.
World Championship Challenge Matches: loser (on a 2-3 vote to Cuba's Sainz) 1983.
European Championships: *best boxer* gold 1981, gold 1983.
Bulgarian junior champion 1979; senior champion 1980-83.

A football player for five years, Mustafov took to boxing at the late age of 17 under coach Kiril Matzulov at the Tcherno More club in Varna, and rose fast on account of his physical advantages at the weight, fine footwork and speed.

1981 was his peak year, and he did not lose a single bout between the summer of 1980 and March, 1983, though the decision in his favour in the 1982 World Championships final over South Korea's Young Mo Hoe was highly controversial. Another curious incident occurred in the final of the 1981 Bulgarian championships, where Blagoev got a 3-2 split vote over him, but the decision was subsequently reversed.

Variously described by Bulgarian officialdom as a 'student' and as an 'employee', without any detail being made available as to the seat of learning or the employer, Mustafov is in fact a full-time boxer, who has a car and draws a salary equivalent to that of a managing director. He is also the toast of Varna, with his father and brother as the leaders of his fan club.

Last year marked the beginning of his slide from the top, with two clear defeats at the hands of relative newcomers and increasing weight problems. His evasive style and powder-puff punching auger badly for Los Angeles, but a boxer

with his experience and record cannot be written off.

Serik Nurkazov (URS)
Featherweight (57kg/125lb)
Born: October 4, 1959, Khazakstan, USSR.
Height: 178cm/5ft 10in.
Weight: 62kg/136lb.
Career Highlights
World Cup: silver 1983.
European Championships: gold 1983, bronze 1981.

From 1976 to 1980, the featherweight place in the selection belonged to the outstanding Soviet ring personality of the 1970s, the Russian Viktor Rybakov. When he moved up to lightweight in the wake of his Olympic debacle in Moscow, there was a race for his place between outgoing national coach Alex Kiselyov's discovery, Samson Chatcharyan and the new coach Artyem Lavrov's ward, Serik Nurkazov.

Nurkazov was nominated to represent the USSR at the Tampere European Championships in 1981. Despite fleet-footed efficiency and clean, superior boxing he was robbed of a deserved victory against the East German Richard Nowakowski (now retired) in the semi-finals. The Russo-Armenian Chatcharyan (or Khachatrian) went to the second World Cup in Montreal, made it into the finals in style but lost to the Cuban ace, Adolfo Horta.

Given the Russian obsession with selecting boxers who 'can stand up to the Cubans' (a legacy of the Moscow Games, where the Cubans took six golds against the host USSR's one), Nurkazov was one up. He had not yet been tested against Horta and in a box-off in Tallin beat Chatcharyan on points. So he went to the World Championships, but was controversially stopped on injury against Bernard Gray of the United States in the quarter-finals. Since then, Nurkazov has been beaten in the World Cup final by Cuban number two Jesus Sollet.

So the PT instructor, who boxes in the colours of Kasagenda Work Reserves is now the featherweight encumbent — but this is a short-term solution. His style has been completely revamped. Gone is the sweet, fluent dancing style — Nurkazov grabs, holds, butts and uses every illegal move and punch in the book to make up for his lack of punching power and confirm his position at the top.

Unbeaten for almost three years, Ismail Mustafov (left) of Bulgaria is now in decline ▶

Shawn O'Sullivan (CAN)
Light middleweight (71kg/156lb)
Born: May 9, 1962, Toronto, Ontario, Canada.
Height: 177cm/5ft 10in.
Weight: 71kg/156lb.
Career Highlights
World Cup: gold, best boxer 1981.
World Championships Challenge Matches: winner 1983.
Commonwealth Games: gold 1982.
North American Championships: gold 1983.

Shawn O'Sullivan's power punching makes him favourite to win the light middleweight gold for Canada
▼

The 1981 World Cup gold won by Shawn O'Sullivan in Montreal's Maurice Richard Arena was Canada's first big Championship gold in 49 years. It was at the 1932 Los Angeles Games that Horace 'Lefty' Gwynne won the bantamweight title, and O'Sullivan looks poised to complete the second leg of this record sequence by getting the first Olympic gold in 52 years, too, and again in LA. Orthodox, and short for the weight, the Toronto University PE undergraduate dishes out punishing hooks and uppercuts at a fearsome rate and soaks up punishment. No one has managed to stand up to him in the past three years. He has beaten Soviets Oleg Kolyadin and Aleksander Koshkin and Cuba's Armando Martinez.

O'Sullivan got into boxing in the footsteps of his father, Michael, who was an amateur in Ireland. He boxes for the Cabbagetown club under coach Peter Wiley, who is likely to accompany him into the professional ranks after the Games.

Jerry Page (USA)
Light welterweight (63.5kg/139lb)
Born: January 15, 1961, Columbus, Ohio, USA.
Height: 174cm/5ft 8½in.
Weight: 63.5kg/139lb.
Career Highlights
World Championship Challenge Matches: loser 1983.
Pan American Games: silver 1983.
USA/ABFs: (Spring) silver 1982, Ohio State Fair gold 1981, Sports Festival gold 1982, National Golden Gloves bronze 1981.

A quick-thinking, serious-minded fighter who is heading for a corporate career eventually Jerry graduated from Linden McKinley High School in 1979. He has been attending Ohio State University in his native Columbus, where he trains under coach Edward Williams at the Sawyer Parks and Recreation Club.

Page started boxing early, at the age of 9, but only came to national prominence in 1980, as a senior. In 1983, at the USA-USSR two-nations contest in Vegas, he meted out a terrible drubbing to the famous Vassily Shishov, and at the World Championship Challenges in Reno he came desperately close to outpointing world champion Carlos Garcia of Cuba, but faded in the final round and was adjudged a 3-2 loser.

An orthodox battler who can both take and give a punch, Jerry can beat anyone on his day, but his attention span is on the short side, and he tends to run out of ideas. He is a brother-in-law of ex-pro world lightweight champion Hilmer Kenty, and will undoubtedly have a go in the paid ranks when the Games are over.

Pedro van Raamsdonk (HOL)
Middleweight (75kg/165lb)
Born: October 2, 1960, Hengelo, Netherlands.
Height: 188cm/6ft 2in.
Weight: 77kg/169lb.
Career Highlights
World Championships: bronze 1982.
European Championships: silver 1981.
Dutch champion: 1983, 1982, 1980, 1979.

His country's best-ever amateur boxer at any weight, Raamsdonk is a national celebrity who is assured of a highly lucrative professional career in the wake of the Los Angeles Olympics, where he has every chance of getting into the medals.

The ward of Ruud van der Linden, who is a journalist/photographer with Amsterdam's De Telegraaf daily newspaper as well as coach/president of the champion Albert Cuyp club, Pedro works in PR and is a highly articulate, high school graduate with a fluent command of English, German and French.

He is also something of a thorn in the side of the Dutch Amateur Boxing Federation. His 2-3 months trips to the United States, where he won a couple of Californian Golden Gloves titles, and his sudden binges are always front page news in Amsterdam.

Raamsdonk has a respectable record, having lost less than 10 of over 120 contests. The only blemish is a defeat suffered at the hands of West German bad-boy Dieter Weinand. His big-trophy victims include Britain's Jimmy Price (now a rising professional), and Silaghi, the Romanian turned West German. In the 1983 Europeans, he was robbed in the elimination round by Bulgarian local lightweight Angelov. Pedro has an orthodox stance, a potent right, and tends to pile up points by jabbing and hooking on the retreat, making use of his height and reach.

Pablo Romero (CUB)
Light heavyweight (81kg/178lb)
Born: January 15, 1962, Pinar del Rio, Cuba.
Height: 186cm/6ft 1in.
Weight: 88kg/192lb.
Career Highlights
World Championships: gold 1982.
World Championship Challenge Matches: winner 1983.
Pan American Games: gold 1983.
North American Championships: silver 1983.
Cuban champion: 1982.

After the retirement of Cuban light-heavy ace Sixto Soria, a battle ensued for the place in the selection. Romero emerged winner over 1980 Olympic representative Ricardo Rochas and 1981 World Cup representative Julio Quintana. His ring habits were cleaner than the others when, in the run-up to the World Championships, East European officialdom, piqued by Cuban supremacy, was declaring war on pro-styled Cuban roughness.

In Munich, Romero proved himself, winning gold though with difficulty. He has collected several medals since, but has yet to become a confirmed member of the Cuban selection.

There are two reasons for the cautious assessment of Romero's prowess. One was his defeat at the hands of Ricky Womack of the United States, as a result of which he had to miss the World Cup, and the other a KO defeat by Quintana in the 1983 Cuban Championships. Romero avenged the defeats, beating Womack in Tokyo and Quintana in Havana, both on points. But Cuban coach Sagarra-Garon does not like unreliability or lack of nerve, one of Romero's failings.

A tall, orthodox stylist without much of a punch, Romero now heads the world and is considered favourite for the Olympic title. But he has a long way to go to gain recognition at home in Cuba.

Louis Sanchez-Castillo (ECU)

Heavyweight (91kg/201lb)
Born: January 12, 1959, Guayaquil, Ecuador.
Height: 175cm/5ft 9in.
Weight: 94kg/208lb.
Career Highlights
World Cup: bronze 1981.
South American Championships: gold 1983, 1982.
Ecuadorian champion: 1983, 1981.

A shortish, beefy heavyweight of the Michael Dokes type, Sanchez-Castillo has participated in surprisingly few bouts, apparently because of a lack of suitable domestic opposition. Most of his engagements have been big Championship tussles.

In the 1980 Olympics, he was eliminated in the first series by eventual bronze-winner Jurgen Fanghanel of the GDR, on points. He eventually avenged this defeat. In the 1982 World Championships, he lost in the second series to the Polish Grzegorz Skrzecz, and in the 1981 World Cup semi-finals the USSR's Jagubkin outpointed him.

A skilful, tactical boxer, who is evasive but lacks a punch, Sanchez-Castillo is no real KO threat. This shortcoming has plagued his career.

Vasily Shishov (URS)

Light welterweight (63.5kg/139lb)

Born: May 26, 1961, Kuybishev, USSR.
Height: 183cm/6ft 0in.
Weight: 69kg/152lb.
Career Highlights
World Cup: bronze 1983, gold 1981.
European Championships: gold 1983, 1981.
World Juniors: silver 1979.
European Juniors: gold 1980.

A 'student' who boxes for CSKA (army sports club) Kuybishev, Shishov is a slimmed down light-middleweight with some unmatchable physical advantages two weights down and consummate boxing skills. He has fantastic footwork, and the ability to get out of tight corners, a high punch-rate, a good tactical brain and southpaw awkwardness. But his punches lack the expected power.

He proved unbeatable for three years in 1979-82 and remains unbeatable on the lowly European scene. However, in the 1982 World Championships in Munich, the dynamic, big-punching Cuban, Carlos Garcia humiliated him and he has not been the same since.

Shishov has been beaten by Jerry Page of the United States in Las Vegas and by Candelario Duvergel of Cuba in the semi-finals of the 1983 World Cup. Best at home and in Europe he is ineffective against the Americans.

Shishov is also having some problems making the 63.5kg weight limit. He is showing the strain, and complains about pressure to keep him in the light-welterweights.

A quiet, sporting type Vasily is a collector of tourist memorabilia from his extensive travels. He has never been known to say a harsh word outside the ring, or throw an illegal punch inside it.

Valentin Silaghi (FRG)

Light-heavyweight (81kg/178lb)
Born: April 21, 1957, Brasso, Romania.
Height: 178cm/5ft 10in.
Weight: 83kg/183lb.
Career Highlights
Olympic Games: bronze 1980.
European Championships: silver 1979, bronze 1981.
Romanian champion: 1981, 1980, 1978.

Having lost a close verdict to eventual winner Bernado Comas of Cuba in the 1982 World Championships in Munich, Romanian veteran Valentin Silaghi, a Hun-garian born as Szilagyi Vencel in Transylvania, absconded from the Romanian squad. With half a dozen other East Europeans he asked for political asylum in West Germany, took up German citizenship and is now to represent his adopted country in the Olympics.

Top among the 60-odd expatriates living and boxing in West Germany in the Bundesliga, Silaghi has proved unbeatable for two years.

He is a rough and tough ring veteran who knows every trick in the book, which is how he managed to beat Britain's Mark Kaylor by a narrow 3-2 margin in the quarter-finals of the Moscow Olympics. Silaghi is an orthodox puncher who can dish out and soak up, a lot of punishment and never gives up.

Pawel Skrzecz (POL)

Light heavyweight (81kg/178lb)
Born: August 25, 1957, Warsaw, Poland.
Height: 173cm/5ft 8in.
Weight: 84kg/183lb.
Career Highlights
Olympic Games: silver 1980.
World Championships: silver 1982.
World Cup: bronze 1983.
European Championships: silver 1983, bronze 1979.

He started boxing at 16, under coach Wienczyslaw Kosinow at

Pawel Skrzecz of Poland (left) . . . late indiscretions cost him the gold in Moscow
▼

Gwardia Warsaw club, together with twin brother Grzegorz. The two joined in answer to an ad placed by the club in the *Express Wieczorny* daily paper and stayed with the sport despite the strong protests of their mother.

Upon entry into the senior ranks, both made it into the international arena, but the quicker-thinking Pawel always stayed ahead and has been the top Pole in the past four years, though invariably falling just short of big tournament golds.

He is a seasoned, highly experienced star, very much in the old Polish tradition. A stand-up type who is ready to mix it at all times with his big right, Pawel's problem is lack of consistency. His performances tend to fluctuate, and he takes unnecessary risks even when a win is in the bag.

The clearest example of this was the 1980 Olympic final. With just 30 seconds to go, and Pawel Skrzecz streets ahead of the Yugoslav Tadija Kacar, he suddenly waded in, trying for a stoppage win. Instead, Pawel got tagged twice, and – as on so many other occasions – ended up second-best.

Having left school at 17, Pawel has been filling nominal jobs with the police, whose club Gwardia is. He is married, and has a two-year old son, Sebastian. After the LA Games, he is planning to move to West Germany for a spell and to box for hard currency in the 'paid amateur' ranks, but may also consider going professional.

Maurizio Stecca (ITA)

Bantamweight (54kg/119lb)
Born: March 9, 1963, Italy.
Height: 173cm/5ft 8in.
Weight: 54kg/118lb.
Career Highlights
World Cup: gold 1983.
European Juniors: *best boxer* gold 1982.
CISM (world military) Championships: *best boxer* gold 1982.
Mediterranean Games: gold 1982.
Italian senior champion: 1982, 1983; youth and junior champion 1978-81.

Two brothers collected golds on the same bill in 1979 in Rimini. The 16-year-old Maurizio Stecca won the bantam junior title and featherweight. Loris, his senior by three years, got the national title a weight up. They were little known then. But today Loris is a leading

professional and Maurizio, the more talented of the two, heads the world's amateur bantams.

Soldier Maurizio – an orthodox stylist with excellent footwork and a rousing attacking style – has been collecting medals for the past two years, whether in the colours of Italy or his – and the military's – club, SMEF.

The only big-trophy event in which he did not go all the way was the European Championships of 1983 in Sofia. There he was adjudged loser to the moderate East German Kirchstein on a 3-2 margin, and the EABA jury refused to overturn the disputed verdict.

Teofilo Stevenson (CUB)

Super heavyweight:
91kg+/201lb+
Born: March 29, 1952, Camaguey, Cuba.
Height: 193cm/6ft 4in.
Weight: 101kg/220lb.
Career Highlights
Olympic Games: gold 1980, 1976, 1972.
World Championships: gold 1978, 1974.
Pan American Games: 3 golds
Central American and Caribbean Championships: 3 golds, 9 Cuban titles.

The Muhammad Ali of the amateurs, Stevenson ruled the world with an iron hand in his peak years, from 1972-78. He has just been ticking over since, having to be forced out of the comfortable life at his three luxury villas by personal calls from Fidel Castro.

But, though he has been written off many times, the increasingly statue-like idol has always managed to summon enough courage to make his detractors eat their words. He has had many close calls, and even losses, in minor events he could not avoid. But he has always delivered in the big ones.

The Moscow Games saw a drastically changed Teofilo. Gone were the rousing rallies and crunching KO wins. The veteran campaigner turned cautious, sneaking marginal victories in boring, eventless bouts. Yet, still, he took the gold, raising his Olympic tally to three – equal to the record of Hungary's Laszlo Papp.

Now he is called upon to better that record and collect a fourth gold. The portents for this are less than auspicious. His defeat at the hands of Damiani in the 1982 World Championships was conclu-

sive, and the great man has lost other one-sided bouts since, including a bad beating in the 1983 North American Championships by US number two Craig Payne.

On the credit side, however, Stevenson demolished world champion Biggs of the US, and he is adamant that he will prepare for LA like never before and get his fourth gold.

King of the amateurs . . . Cuba's great heavyweight Teofilo Stevenson
▼

Frank Tate (USA)

Light middleweight (71kg/156lb)
Born: August 27, 1964, Detroit, USA.
Height: 181cm/5ft 11in.
Weight: 72kg/157/8lb.
Career Highlights
North American Championships: silver 1983.
USA/ABF champion 1983, (Winter) runner-up 1982; Ohio State Fair, gold 1982; National Golden Gloves, bronze 1982.

Another from the Francis Purify stable who is heading for a promising professional career, Frank started boxing eight years ago and gained national prominence on the home front in 1982. He is an orthodox stand-up fighter with an educated jab, who can turn on the power when it is called for.

He graduated from Kettering High School in 1983, has no further academic ambitions or otherwise and lives in the Kronk area, biding his time until after the Olympics, where he is universally expected to get into the medals.

His domestic arch-rival, the more erratic Dennis Milton, received all the foreign trips until 1983. But then Tate drubbed Soviet world champion and Olympic runner-up Aleksander Koshkin in Las Vegas and eclipsed Milton in the ABF finals to take the top spot.

Christophe Tiozzo (FRA)
Light middleweight (71kg/156lb)
Born: June 1, 1963, St Denis, France.
Height: 181cm/5ft 11in.
Weight: 71kg/156lb.
Career Highlights
French champion: 1983, 1982.

A crisp, classic counter-puncher in the best French tradition, Tiozzo — still a junior — ended the long unbeaten home run of Patrick Magnetto, France's best, in 1981, and a great future was forecast. However, young Tiozzo has proved one of the unluckiest boxers, losing five times on highly controversial or unjust verdicts in prestigious tournaments.

The worst occasions were in the 1982 European Junior Championships in Schwerin, where he was deprived of well-deserved victory in the quarter-finals against the USSR's eventual winner, Bolat Shararov, and in the 1983 Senior European Championships in Varna, where the East German Ralf Hunger was given a totally unjust decision, also by a 3-2 margin.

Janos Varadi (HUN)
Flyweight (51kg/112lb)
Born: February 28, 1961, Nyiregyhaza, Hungary.
Height: 162.5cm/5ft 4in.
Weight: 52kg/114lb.
Career Highlights
Olympic Games: bronze 1980.
World Cup: quarter-finalist 1983.
European Championships: silver 1983.
European Juniors: gold 1980.
Hungarian champion: 1983, 1981, 1980.

Varadi began boxing and playing football competitively at 14, and carried on with both sports for three years. Training under an unsung coach, Jozsef Szanto, at the very small, obscure Nyiregyhazi Vasutas club in the eastern part of Hungary which has little fistic tradition, he attracted instant domestic attention when winning two junior titles in succession in spectacular style and at 18 he exploded into the big-time.

A year's military service in 1981/82, subsequent weight problems and disagreements with his coach relegated him to the ranks of the also-rans, but by last year he battled his way to the top, only to be robbed of a deserved European gold against a Bulgarian in Bulgaria.

Janos is a studious, serious-minded type, who got his 'matura' (GCE equivalent) in 1979, followed it up with a diploma from a polytechnic and now works as an engineering draughtsman. He is an avid reader of books of all kinds, has his own bachelor flat (one of the sinecures of earning medals) and karate and classical music are his hobbies.

A gym fanatic, he is now coached by one-time Olympic and European medal-winner Andras Botos. He has a big right and is a stylish, dynamic box-fighter, but lacks the knack of dominating opponents and dictating bouts.

Manuel Vilchez (VEN)
Bantamweight (54kg/119lb)
Born: October 21, 1961, Caracas, Venezuela.
Height: 170cm/5ft 7in.
Weight: 56kg/121lb.
Career Highlights
Pan American Games: gold 1983.

The big-punching, orthodox Venezuelan has little to recommend him in the way of results, but this is mainly because he has not received his fair share of big championship outings. In reality he has a towering talent, which could pay dividends in Los Angeles.

In the 1982 World Championships, Vilchez made it into the quarter-finals, where he gave plenty of trouble to the Ukranian Viktor Miroshnichenko, the eventual runner-up and Olympic silver-medallist.

Since then, he has come along a lot, as evidenced by a string of rousing victories and best boxer awards in Eastern European and South American tournaments. He was side-stepped for selection for the World Cup in favour of compatriot Jesus Pool, who moved up from fly, and many considered this an injustice.

Pernell Whitaker (USA)
Lightweight (60kg/132lb)
Born: January 2, 1964, Norfolk, Virginia, USA.
Height: 165cm/5ft 5in.
Weight: 63kg/140lb.
Career Highlights
World Championships: silver 1982.
World Championship Challenge Matches: winner 1983.
Pan American Games: gold 1983.
USA/ABFs (Spring) gold 1982; Sports Festival gold 1980.

He completed Washington High School in 1982 and now attends Norfolk State University. He is on the United States Operation Gold programme, training part of the time at Colorado Springs under the eye of United States national coach Pat Nappi. He began boxing at the PAC Club in Norfolk 11 years ago, and PAC's coach, Clyde Taylor, has remained his mentor.

Short for the weight, and always moving at a measured pace, Pernell 'Pete' Whitaker trades on his big right, studied awkwardness of style and an ability to outwit opponents. Pete demonstrated this when he first lost conclusively to Cuban all-time great Angel Herrera in the 1982 World Championships final and then vanquished him four times in succession — and by increasingly wider points margins.

A fun-loving negro 'Pete' is less than a compulsive trainer, but becomes dedicated when the occasion demands. He takes a good shot and is a born ring general, who can assess the flow of bouts shrewdly and is highly versatile, ready to switch pace and approach any time. He dictates bouts, imposing his style and will on opponents.

Tony Wilson (GBR)
Light heavyweight (81kg/178lb)
Born: April 25, 1961, Wolverhampton, England.
Height: 181cm/5ft 11in.
Weight: 81kg/178lb.
Career Highlights:
ABA champion 1983.
Junior ABAs: silver 1977.
NABCs: gold 1978.

Hailing from a Jamaican family, with relatives all over the West

merely a dozen times and more than aware of a wasted amateur career, which could have spawned such rich dividends.

Ricky Womack (USA)
Light heavyweight (81kg/178lb)
Born: June 10, 1961, Jackson, Tennessee, USA.
Height: 181cm/5ft 11in.
Weight: 87kg/186lb.
Career Highlights
World Cup: silver 1983
World Championship Challenge Matches: loser 1983.
North American Championships: gold 1983.
USA/ABF champion 1983; (Winter) 1982.

Womack started boxing at 15 after seeing the Montreal Games on TV. He graduated from Higland Park High School, spent time as a cook, and then joined Detroit's famed Kronk gym, where he trains under coach Francis Purify.

Rough and tough in or out of the ring, ambitious Womack considers his amateur career and the Olympics a part of his build-up to a lucrative pro stardom.

Campaigning as a heavyweight to start with, he went down to light-heavy in 1981. He was selected for the United States team the next year, and beat the fancied East German Andreas Schroth, before reverting to heavy again and taking a gold in the USA/ABF Championships in Indianapolis.

The darling of the black United States boxing establishment, he stole the limelight in 1983, with his KO victory over Vitaly Kachanowsky on the US-USSR bill in Las Vegas. The Soviet had to be assisted back to his corner two minutes after the knockdown. Womack's powerful hook also dismantled world champion Pablo Romero of Cuba in the final of the North American Championships in Houston and demolished domestic rivals Sherman Griffin and Bennie Heard in the 1983 ABFs.

But Ricky thrives on involvement too much, paying little heed to the strategy department. Thus by holding, evading and relying on negative tactics, both Kachanowsky and Romero avenged defeat at his hands by narrow points wins in the final of the World Cup and in the Tokyo round of the World Championship Challenges respectively. His Olympic result will depend on how much he learned in the process.

Tony Wilson of Great Britain . . . so talented but still a novice ▲

Indies and the US, Tony is one of the most popular sons of his native Wolverhampton, where he works as an assistant YMCA supervisor and boxes for Wolverhampton ABC.

He has a broad spectrum of sporting and other interests ranging from football, cricket, basketball to music and literature. He took up boxing at 15, following in the footsteps of his father (who did a bit of bare-knuckle stuff in Jamaica) and elder brother Neville (a successful pro), at the encouragement of his maths teacher, one-time England representative John Wilbury.

Perhaps surprisingly, his father strongly opposed the involvement of his intelligent, multi-faceted son, but changed his tune when Tony gained national prominence and made it into successive under-19 and senior England selections.

By 1981, Wilson was ready for the highest level of international exposure, as evidenced by his narrow points defeat against US star Bennie Heard that year. But the ABA shunned participation in World Championships, World Cups and Europeans, and he did not get the opportunities, as a result of which his shining talent regressed.

A turned-around southpaw with a lethal left hook and uppercut, Tony is thus going to LA, in his 24th year, an international novice, having worn the England vest

Judo, weightlifting and wrestling

Judo

The martial art of judo was introduced by Jigoro Kano of Japan in 1882. It was based on precepts of a Chinese priest Chin Genpin who brought Kempo to Japan in 1659.

Kano took the sport to British soil in 1889, and one of his colleagues, Yamashita, introduced Judo to America in 1902 — one of his pupils being President Theodore Roosevelt.

The popularity of the sport spread slowly at first, but in 1918, its popularity in Britain led to the formation of the Budokwai club. Kano died at sea in 1938, returning from an international conference, at which he had hoped to get Judo recognised as an Olympic sport. That dream was to be realised 26 years later.

Fittingly, the Tokyo Olympics of 1964 were chosen for its inauguration. Four titles were at stake and Japan won three. But giant Dutchman Anton Geesink, who had beaten three Japanese on his way to the 1961 world crown, again stepped in to dent national pride, by winning the 'Open' category. The weight divisions were revised in 1967 to give six classes from lightweight (63kg) to the open class, and these were revised yet again in 1979 to give the present eight categories ranging from the 'up to 60kg class' to the 'open class'.

Judo was omitted from the 1968 Olympics, but re-introduced for 1972 when another Dutchman stole the limelight. Wim Ruska won the 93kg and Open classes, to become the first — and only — man to have won two Olympic judo titles. Bakhaavaa Buidaa of Mongolia had his silver medal taken away for failing a dope test — the first judo competitor to lose a medal for that reason in any international competition.

The 1972 Games proved to be traumatic for the Japanese. *Only* winning three of the six titles, they promptly sacked all their trainers and coaches, and put Isao Okani (former Olympic champion) in charge of the team. His new approach resulted in them winning all six titles at the following year's world championships.

Japan are still dominant in world judo, but the gap is narrowing between them and the rest of Europe, particularly the USSR who have now overtaken them as the top country as far as Olympic medals are concerned. Japan still holds on to the record for the most golds.

Weightlifting

The current form of weightlifting originated in Europe, but the ancient Egyptians are known to have had stone lifting competitions, the Pyramids being an everlasting monument to them.

The first championships open to the world in their present form took place on March 28, 1891 at the Cafe Monico, Piccadilly, London. That first title was won by Englishman Lawrence Levy.

At the 1896 Olympics there were no weight categories, and only two gold medals were contested, one for the double handed lift, and one for the single handed lift. Englishman Launceston Elliot won the latter, Britain's one and only Olympic weightlifting champion.

The Olympic competition now covers ten weight categories, ranging from flyweight (52kg) to super heavyweight (over 110kg). There used to be three types of lift in Olympic competition — the press, the snatch and the jerk. But only the last two are used in current Olympic competition. The press was discontinued after the 1972 Games.

Before World War II, the French, Germans and Italians were the most successful lifters. In post war years, however, the Soviets, with almost 500,000 registered lifters have emerged as the world's leading country — reflected by their haul of 33 Olympic golds to the 15 of their closest rivals, the United States.

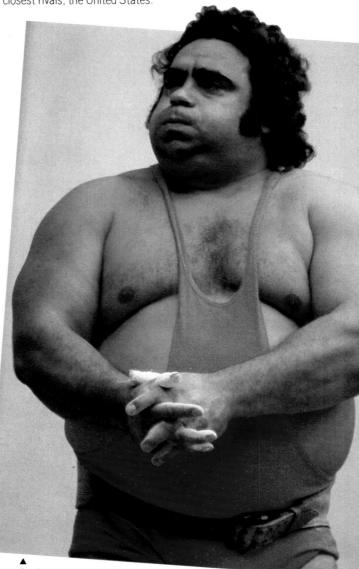

▲
Soviet superman Vasiley Alexeev who broke 80 world records

◄ Wim Ruska, only man to have won two judo golds

America's John Davis, winner of the Olympic heavyweight gold in 1948 and 1952. He also won a record eight world titles. ▶ ▶

One of the greatest weightlifters of all time was the Soviet super heavyweight Vasiley Alexeev. Not only did he win two Olympic titles, he broke 80 world records — more than anyone in *any* sport. Add to this his ten world titles, and nine European titles, and the tag of 'world's strongest man' can hardly be disputed. At one time, he was the most decorated man in the USSR, but it was sad to see him jeered out of the arena by his home crowd at the 1980 Moscow Games when he failed to gain a medal. Such was Alexeev's dedication to the sport that for breakfast he used to eat a 36 egg omelette, and for lunch six steaks, washed down by 20 pints of beer.

The most successful lifter in Olympic history has been American Norbert Schemansky, winner of four medals between 1948 and 1964 in the middle heavyweight and heavyweight classes followed closely by fellow countryman John Davis.

The 1968 Olympics were special for the Miyake brothers from Japan. Both featherweights, Yoshinobu won the gold and Yoshijuki the bronze. Romanian Dragomir Ciroslin will want to forget the 1976 Olympics, for he had the dubious distinction of being the first person in Olympic weightlifting history to be disqualified following a positive dope test. It was doubly unfortunate for his country as he was Romania's only representative in the competition.

Silver medallist in the light heavyweight class at the 1948 London Olympics, Harold Sakata of the United States eventually found 'gold' in the 1960s. He played the part of 'Oddjob' in the film *Goldfinger*.

Wrestling

The sport of wrestling goes back 5000 years, and some of the holds used today date to the ancient civilizations in China, Egypt and Greece.

The first recorded rules for competitive wrestling were drawn up around 900 BC, by Theseus, son of the King of Athens; some of his rules still apply in the Greco-Roman code these days. Wrestling was first seen in the Ancient Olympic Games of circa 704 BC. The most successful fighter of the time was Milo of Croton, who won five Olympic titles. When training, he used to carry a calf around a field on his back!.

Horse racing has always been regarded as 'the sport of kings' but in the sixteenth century, a wrestling contest between Britain and France was watched by King Henry VIII and King Francis I of France. The British fighters overwhelmed the French, and, fed up with Henry's boasting, Francis leapt upon Henry and they commenced their own unscheduled bout. The result— no contest.

There are many different codes of wrestling. The Sumo style is found in Japan, the Yagli style in Turkey, the Sambo in the USSR, the Glima in Iceland, and in Britain the two most famous styles are the Cumberland and Cornish. However, at international level, the only two disciplines contested are Freestyle and the Greco-Roman style — the main difference being that the use of the legs as a means of attack is not allowed in Greco-Roman.

Wrestling developed internationally during the nineteenth century, and in the United States, world heavyweight boxing champion, John L. Sullivan played a large part in its development.

The sport was included in the inaugural Modern Olympics of 1896, but only Greco-Roman. Freestyle was introduced in 1904, and in 1908 both styles were seen at the same Games for the first time. At the Los Angeles Olympics of 1984, each code will contest 10 gold medals, in weights from light flyweight to super heavyweight.

Despite being an Olympic sport since 1896, the International Amateur Wrestling Federation was not formed until 1921. An Englishman, Percy Longhurst was its first Secretary.

In the period between the wars, the United States and Scandinavia dominated the sport. But after the 1939 war, wrestling grew in popularity at a tremendous rate and one of the emergent countries to show early dominance was Turkey.

At the 1948 London Olympics, Turkey won 11 medals — six gold. But, due to an administrative error, entry forms for some of their competitors for the 1952 Helsinki Olympics arrived late, and consequently several of their best fighters stayed at home.

One of the outstanding personalities in the 1950s and early 1960s was Hungarian Imre Polyak who won four Olympic medals (one gold, three silver) between 1952 and 1964 in the Greco-Roman featherweight division — a record haul by an Olympic wrestler. During that period, Britain claimed their only post war wrestling medal when Ken Richmond took the bronze in the freestyle heavyweight class at the 1952 Olympics.

The 1960s saw the emergence of Russian Alexandr Medved, who dominated freestyle heavyweight wrestling, winning three successive Olympic titles in 1964, 1968 and 1972 in the light heavyweight, heavyweight and super heavyweight classes. In addition, Medved won a record ten world titles. Another European to receive world acclaim was Hungarian Greco-Roman exponent, Istvan 'Pici' Kozma, winner of the heavyweight class in the 1964 and 1968 Olympics. But the most invincible of all was Japan's Osamu Watanabe. When he took the freestyle featherweight division at the 1964 Olympics, his victory over the Bulgarian Ivanov was his 186th *consecutive* win (it was also Ivanov's second successive defeat in an Olympic final).

Those 1964 Olympics hold a special place for Metropolitan policeman Dennis McNamara, for in beating Japan's Saitou, he became the first Briton to defeat a Japanese in international competition. The Emperor was not amused.

The 1970's saw the emergence of countries like India and Pakistan — already successful in the Commonwealth Games — as challengers to the leading European Nations. Russia still dominate in Olympic competition with a total of 103 medals. But the United States lead the freestyle events with 74 medals and had they contested the Greco-Roman competition, would no doubt have exceeded the Soviet Union's total.

Greco-Roman wrestling appeared at the first Modern Olympics in 1896 ▼

Britain's Olympic wrestling team in training at the 1908 Games ▼

Neil Adams (GBR)
Judo: 71kg/156lb, 78kg/172lb
Born: September 27, 1958,
   Croydon, England.
Height: 177cm/5ft 9½in.
Weight: 71kg/156lb.
Career Highlights
   Olympic Games: *71kg* silver,
      1980.
   World Championships: *78kg* gold,
      1981, silver 1983; *71kg* bronze
      1979.
   European Championships: *71kg*
      gold 1979.

One of Britain's greatest ever competitors, fair haired Neil has been British 78kg champion every year since 1980, and was the 71kg champion in 1977 and 1979. In the World Championships he won the bronze medal in 1979, and in 1981 was world 78kg champion — losing the title on a disputed split decision in the 1983 final to Japan's Hikage. 1979 saw Neil win his first European Championship gold, and the following year he followed up his British Open success with a silver in the 71kg class at the Moscow Olympics. He won his sixth British Open title in seven years in 1983.

Sergei Arakelov (URS)
Weightlifting: 100kg/220½lb
Born: July 18, 1957, Krasnodar,
   USSR.
Height: 176cm/5ft 9½in.
Weight: 99kg/217lb.
Career Highlights
World Championships: *100kg* gold
   1979, silver 1978.

A member of the Soviet team since 1977 he won his first National title in 1978. That same year he took the silver medal in the World Championships (100kg) and returned the following year to take the gold. He did not compete at the 1980 Olympics, although he was in the squad. He is coached by his team mate, Yurik Sarkisyan.

Eugeny Artyukhin (URS)
Wrestling: Greco-Roman: over
   100kg/220½lb
Born: April 17, 1949, Sheryaevka,
   USSR.
Height: 189cm/6ft 2in.
Weight: 109kg/237lb.
Career Highlights
World Championships: *100kg* gold
   1983.

A serviceman in the Soviet armed forces in Moscow, Artyukhin made his international debut in 1973,

winning his first national title five years later.

The reigning world champion at 100kg+, he will be hoping to emulate the other great Soviet super heavyweight of recent times — Alexsandr Kolchinsky — by taking the Olympic title in Los Angeles.

Brian Aspen (GBR)
Wrestling: freestyle 57kg/126lb
Born: April 6, 1959, Bolton,
   England.
Height: 163cm/5ft 4in.
Weight: 57kg/126lb.
Career Highlights
Commonwealth Games: *57kg* gold
   1982; *62kg* bronze 1978.

When Brian Aspen won the Commonwealth Games bantamweight title at Brisbane in 1982, he not only became England's only wrestling medallist of the Games, but he became his country's first wrestling gold medallist since 1962, and only their third ever Commonwealth champion.

The current British champion in the 57kg class, he will be heading the British challenge for Olympic honours in Los Angeles — his second Olympics.

He first gained recognition when winning the world schoolboy championship in 1974, when only 15.

Anatoly Beloglasov (URS)
Wrestling: freestyle 52kg/115lb,
   57/126lb
Born: September 16, 1956,
   Kaliningrad, USSR.
Height: 158cm/5ft 2½in.
Weight: 52kg/115lb.
Career Highlights
Olympic Games: *52kg* gold 1980.
World Championships: *57kg* gold
   1982, gold 1978; *48kg* gold
   1977.

One of the famous Beloglasov twins, Anatoly and brother Sergei must be two of the most successful of the Soviet freestyle wrestlers of recent times.

Anatoly, a serviceman, and Merited Master of Sport, has been wearing the international jersey of the USSR since 1977 — the year of his first world title. In 1980 he won the Olympic 52kg class — brother Sergei taking the 57kg class.

The 1982 world champion at 57kg, he stepped down a division to contest the 52kg class at the Kiev World Championships of 1983, but could only manage a bronze medal — whilst Sergei was taking gold.

◄ *Neil Adams on his way to another British judo title*

▲ *Olympic freestyle wrestling champion Anatoly Beloglasov*

Sergei Beloglasov (URS)
Wrestling: freestyle 57kg/126lb
Born: September 16, 1956,
   Kaliningrad, USSR.
Height: 154cm/5ft 0½in.
Weight: 57kg/126lb.
Career Highlights
Olympic Games: *57kg* gold 1980.
World Championships: *57kg* gold
   1983; *62kg* gold 1982.

Twin brother of Anatoly, Sergei
Beloglasov can, by virtue of the
fact that he retained a world title in
1983, claim to be the better of the
two brothers in the 1980s.
   Anatoly, with his two world title
wins in the late 1970s had the
edge at that time, but Sergei goes
to the Los Angeles Olympics with
marginally the better chance.
   The reigning Olympic champion
at 57kg, he stepped up to the
heavier 62kg class after the 1980
Games, winning the world title in
1982, but reverted back to the
57kg class, at which he won a
further world title in 1983, and it is
in this division that he will be seen
in Los Angeles.
   A member of the Soviet team
since 1977, he won his first
National title in 1979, and finished
second in the World Championships that year.

Blagoi Blagoev (BUL)
Weightlifting: 82kg/182lb,
   90kg/198lb
Born: December 19, 1956,
   Preslav, Bulgaria.
Height: 165cm/5ft 5in.
Weight: 86kg/189lb.
Career Highlights
World Championships: *90kg* gold
   1981, 1982.
Olympic Games: *82.5kg* silver
   1980.
European Championships: *82.5kg*
   silver 1976.

A soldier in the Bulgarian Army,
Blagoev began lifting in 1972, and
hit the headlines in 1976. First he
finished second in the European
Championships at the age of 19
years three months and then went
on to finish second in the Montreal
Olympics, 82.5kg division, but
was subsequently disqualified.
Four years later he finished second
again in the Olympics, also in the
82.5kg division – this time he was
allowed to keep his medal.
   He was world champion in the
heavier 90kg class in 1981 and
1982 and he set the snatch and
overall world record in this division
at Varna in 1983 with lifts of
195.5kg (431lb) and 420kg
(920¼lb) respectively.

Baijdegar Bold (MGL)
Wrestling: freestyle 68kg/150lb
Born: August 25, 1960, Ulan
   Bator, Mongolia
Height: 170cm/5ft 7in.
Weight: 68kg/150lb.
Career Highlights
World Championships: *68kg;* silver
   1983.

Mongolian, Baijdegar Bold participated in his first Olympics in Moscow in 1980, when he took part in
the 68kg Greco-Roman competition.
   He has, however, switched to
the freestyle code of wrestling, and
this is illustrated by the fact that
he won the silver medal in the
1983 World Championships in
Kiev.

Newton Burrowes (GBR)
Weightlifting: 75kg/165lb,
   82.5kg/182lb
Born: June 5, 1955, Bristol,
   England.
Height: 168cm/5ft 6in.
Weight: 75kg/165lb.
Career Highlights
Commonwealth Games: *82.5kg*
   gold 1982, *75kg*
   silver 1978.

A fitter by trade, Newton first
came to prominence in 1978 when
he took the silver medal in the
Commonwealth Games. Two years
later he won his first British title,
and in the same year went to his
first Olympics, when he finished
eighth overall in the 75kg class,
with a total lift of 302.5kg
(667lb). He won 1982 Commonwealth Games gold medal in the
82.5kg class.

*The other half of USSR's
amazing twins . . . Sergei
Beloglasov*
▼

▲
*Bulgaria's mighty soldier
Blagoi Blagoev*

◀ *Kamil Fatkullin in the red vest of USSR . . . will silver at last turn to gold?*

Raul Cascaret (CUB)
Wrestling: freestyle 68kg/150lb
Born: June 20, 1962, Cuba.
Height: 165cm/5ft 5in.
Weight: 66kg/144lb.
Career Highlights
World Championships: *68kg;* silver 1982.
Pan American Games: *68kg;* gold 1983.

The lightweight Raul Cascaret may be the only wrestling Olympic champion from the western hemisphere in Los Angeles in 1984, despite the fact that he could only manage fifth place in the 1983 World Championships.

The 1984 Games will be his second. He has showed his potential by winning the silver medal in the 1982 World Championships in Edmonton.

Jan Falandys (POL)
Wrestling, freestyle 48kg/106lb
Born: June 18, 1956, Ryeszow, Poland.
Height: 156cm/5ft 1½in.
Weight: 48kg/106lb.
Career Highlights
World Championships: *48kg* bronze 1983, 1979.

An auto mechanic, Jan Falandys won his first Polish title in 1977, and two years later won a bronze medal in the World Championships in the 48kg category.

He represented Poland in the Moscow Olympics, and hopes to come away from the Los Angeles Games with at least a bronze medal to match the one he won at the pre-Olympic World Championships in 1983.

Kamil Fatkullin (URS)
Wrestling: Greco-Roman 57kg/126lb
Born: July 1, 1957, Stalin Village, Tashkent, USSR.
Height: 163cm/5ft 4in.
Weight: 57kg/126lb.
Career Highlights
World Championships: *57kg* silver 1983, *52kg* silver 1979, 1977.

One of wrestling's 'bridesmaids' Kamil Fatkullin has been runner-up in the World Championships on three occasions – 1977, 1979 and 1983.

Despite his lack of successes, he has been one of the USSR's most consistent Greco-Roman fighters since making his international debut in 1977 (the year of his first national title) and was a gold medallist at the 1979 Spartakiad.

Mircea Fratica (ROM)
Judo: 78kg/172lb
Born: July 14, 1957, Bucharest, Romania.
Height: 175cm/5ft 9in.
Weight: 78kg/172lb.
Career Highlights
Olympic Games: *78kg;* bronze.
World Championships: *78kg;* bronze.

▲ *Italy's Enzio Gamba on the Moscow gold medal rostrum with Britain's Neil Adams as runner up*

Mircea took the bronze medal in the 78kg class at the 1980 Moscow Olympics – he was beaten in the semi-final by winner Khabarelli of the USSR. In the 1983 World Championships, he shared the bronze medal with Khabarelli, having been beaten in the semi-final by Britain's Neil Adams.

Enzio Gamba (ITA)
Judo: 71kg/156lb
Born: December 2, 1958, Milan, Italy.
Height: 175cm/5ft 9in.
Weight: 71kg/156lb.
Career Highlights
Olympic Games: *71kg* gold 1980.
World Championships: *71kg* silver 1983.

Gamba was gold medallist in the 71kg (156lb) class at the 1980 Moscow Olympics – beating Neil Adams in the final. His best placing in the world championship was in 1983 when he finished runner up to Japan's Nakanichi.

Nobutoshi Hikage (JAP)
Judo
Born: 1956, Japan.
Height: 176cm/5ft 9½in.
Weight: 78kg/172lb.
Career Highlights
World Championships: *78kg* first 1983.

The Japanese 71kg champion in 1982 and 1983, Nobutoshi Hikage won his first world title in 1983, when he beat Britain's Neil Adams in a disputed final in the 78kg class.
However, whilst the outcome of the contest with Adams was in dispute, in terms of pure skill, he was the better of the two fighters, and on merit deserved his first world title.

Karolj Kasap (YUG)
Wrestling: Greco-Roman 74kg/163lb.
Born: August 5, 1954, Yugoslavia.
Height: 173cm/5ft 8in.
Weight: 74kg/163lb.
Career Highlights
World Championships: *74kg* bronze 1983, silver 1982.

Yugoslavia has a good record in Olympic Greco-Roman wrestling competition since the last war, and welterweight Karolj Kasap will be hoping to maintain that tradition in Los Angeles this summer.

Recent form suggests that he will be a medal contender, though maybe not for gold. He was third in the 74kg class at the 1983 World Championships, having gained a silver medal in the same class the year before.

Shota Khabarelli (URS)
Judo: 78kg/172lb, open class
Born: December 26, 1958, Dzlevisdzhvari, USSR.
Height: 178cm/5ft 10in.
Weight: 78kg/172lb.
Career Highlights
Olympic Games: *78kg* gold 1980.
World Championships: *78kg* bronze 1983.

A member of the Soviet armed forces in Tbilisi, Shota studied PE at the Georgian State Institute, and from there he became an International Class Master of Sport.
He made his international debut in 1979 in the European Championships, where he won the silver medal in the individual competition, and was a member of the gold medal winning Soviet team. The following year, he became the first 78kg Olympic champion. He has still to win a world title. In 1983 he won the bronze medal, losing in the semi-final to eventual winner, Nobutoshi Hikage of Japan.

Viacheslav Klokov (URS)
Weightlifting
Born: 1959, Moscow, USSR.
Weight: 112kg/247lb.
Career Highlights
World Championships: *110kg* gold 1983; *110kg* silver 1981, 1982.

Klokov won his first world title at 110kg/242.5lb (heavyweight) in 1983 having been second in 1981 and 1982. He broke the world record jerk three times in 1983 with 243kg/535½lb, 245kg/540lb and 247½kg/ 545½lb. He also broke the world record total twice with 437½kg/ 964½lb and 440kg/ 970lb.

Robert Kostenberger (AUT)
Judo: 71kg/156lb, over 95kg/210lb.
Born: January 15, 1957, Vienna, Austria.
Height: 185cm/6ft 1in.
Weight: 95kg/210lb.
Career Highlights
European Championships: *over 95kg* gold 1982.

Kostenberger will be hoping to do better in his second Olympics in 1984. He was eliminated in the second round in Moscow in 1980 by Dietmar Lorenz of East Germany, the open class gold medallist. Robert's recent form has seen him win the over 95kg category at the 1982 European Championships.

World champion Viacheslav Klovkov of USSR ▶

Joachim Kunz (GDR)

Weightlifting: 67.5kg/150lb
Born: February 9, 1959, Lempzig,
    East Germany.
Height: 163cm/5ft 4¼in.
Weight: 71kg/156lb.
Career Highlights
Olympic Games: *67.5kg* silver
    1980.
World Championships: *67.5kg* gold
    1981, 1983.

Kunz was silver medallist in the 67.5kg division at the Moscow Olympics — his first Games. The following year he went on to win the world title in that division, setting the world record in the jerk, and overall in the division with a lift of 196kg (432lb) in the jerk, and an overall lift of 345kg (760½lb). He must be a potential medallist in Los Angeles.

Stefan Leletko (POL)

Weightlifting: 52kg/115lb
Born: September 2, 1953, Odra
    Opole, Poland.
Height: 148cm/4ft 10¼in.
Weight: 55kg/120lb.
Career Highlights
World Championships: *52kg* gold
    1978, 1982.

A metal worker, Leletko won his first Polish title in 1975, when he took the 52kg national championship.
    That earned him a trip to the Montreal Olympics when he finished sixth, and by 1978 he was world champion. His next Olympic appearance, however, was something of a disaster. After finishing second in the jerk, he was let down by his snatch, and could finish only fifth overall.
    Compensation came in 1982 with the world title again, and the jerk world record of 143.5kg (316¼lb) at Ljubljana in Yugoslavia.

Andreas Letz (GDR)

Weightlifting: 56kg/124lb
Born: June 5, 1962, East Berlin,
    East Germany.
Height: 158cm/5ft 2½in.
Weight: 59.5kg/130lb.
Career Highlights
Olympic Games: *56kg* fourth
    1980.

Letz's first Olympic appearance was in 1980 when he finished fourth in the 56kg class. He set a world record at Varna, Bulgaria, in 1983 in the 56kg class jerk, when he lifted 169.5kg (353¾lb).

Noel Loban (GBR)

Wrestling: freestyle
    100kg/220½lb
Born: 1960, London, England.
Height: 185cm/6ft 1in.
Weight: 90kg/198lb.
Career Highlights
British Championships: *100kg*
    gold 1983.

The reigning British heavyweight champion, Noel Loban will be competing in his first Olympics in 1984.
    Because of the airline pilots' dispute following the Korean jumbo disaster in 1983, the British team were not represented at the World Championships in Kiev, but shortly after those championships, a meeting was organized in Sweden. The opposition was strong. At that meeting, Loban beat the reigning 90kg world champion, Petr Naniev of the Soviet Union — a boost to his confidence which will improve medal chances in Los Angeles.

Lennart Lundell (SWE)

Wrestling: Greco-Roman
    82kg/181lb
Born: December 13, 1953,
    Lidkoping, Sweden.
Height: 170cm/5ft 7in.
Weight: 81kg/167lb.
Career Highlights
World Championships: *82kg*
    bronze 1983.

Lennart Lundell first appeared at the Olympics in 1976, when he lasted three rounds in the 68kg class in the freestyle event.
    One of the few fighters to successfully make the switch to the Greco-Roman code, 1983 has been a good pre-Olympic year for him — he took the bronze medal in the World Championships in Kiev.

Gheorge Maftei (ROM)

Weightlifting: 56kg/124lb
Born: April 1, 1955, Romania.
Height: 159cm/5ft 2¾in.
Weight: 56kg/122lb.
Career Highlights
Olympic Games: *56kg;* seventh
    1980.

A potential medallist in the 56kg class in Los Angeles, despite the fact that he only finished seventh at Moscow in 1980.

Oksen Mirzoyan (URS)

Weightlifting
Born: 1961, USSR.
Weight: 56kg/123.5lb.
Career Highlights
World Championships:
56kg gold 1983, silver 1982.

Mirzoyan won his first world title at 56kg (bantamweight) with a world record total of 292.5kg/644¾lb in 1983 having placed second the previous year.
    His record has since been beaten by Suleimanov of Bulgaria with 295kg/650¼lb. Mirzoyan holds the world snatch record at 131kg/288¾lb.

*Oksen Mirzoyan . . . world
snatch record holder* ▼

Hidetosti Nakanichi (JAP)
Judo
Born: 1958, Japan.
Height: 170cm/5ft 7in.
Weight: 71kg/157lb.
Career Highlights
World Championships: *71kg* first
1983.

Hailed as the Japanese find of 1983, he won his first world title by beating Italian Enzio Gamba in the final of the 71kg class.

Uwe Neupert (GDR)
Wrestling: freestyle 90kg/198lb
Born: August 5, 1957, East
Germany.
Height: 186cm/6ft 1½in.
Weight: 90kg/198lb.

Career Highlights
Olympic Games: *90kg* silver 1980.
World Championships: *90kg*
gold 1982,
gold 1978.

Uwe Neupert has been on the international scene for nearly ten years and is one of the most experienced light heavyweight freestyle wrestlers in the world today.

A runner up in the 1977 World Championships, he went on to win the 90kg title the following year, and in 1979 was again silver medallist.

A silver medal followed in the 1980 Olympics, and a further world title in 1982. The 1983 championships at Kiev saw him win the bronze medal.

Daniel Nunez (CUB)
Weightlifting: 60kg/132lb
Born: September 12, 1958,
Havana, Cuba.
Height: 159cm/5ft 2¾in.
Weight: 56kg/122lb.
Career Highlights
Olympic Games: *56kg*
gold 1980.
World Championships: *56kg* gold
1978.

The little Cuban first gained world weightlifting recognition when he took the 1978 World Championship 56kg title, and at Moscow two years later he became Olympic champion, with a world record lift. In 1982 he moved to the heavier 60kg class, and in Copenhagen that year set the world snatch record with a lift of 137.5kg (303lb).

Jarmo Overmark (FIN)
Wrestling: Greco-Roman
82kg/181lb
Born: May 26, 1955, Finland.
Height: 183cm/6ft 0in.
Weight: 82kg/169lb.
Career Highlights
World Championships: *82kg;*
bronze 1983.

Jarmo Overmark will be competing in his second Olympics in 1984, having made his bow at Moscow four years earlier. Third in the 82kg class at the 1983 World Championships, he showed considerable improvement from the previous year when he finished sixth.

If he continues that rate of improvement he should be a title contender in Los Angeles.

Angelo Parisi (FRA)
Judo: over 95kg/210lb
Born: January 3, 1953, Italy.
Height: 185cm/6ft 1in.
Weight: 108kg/235lb.
Career Highlights
Olympic Games: *over 95kg* gold
1980; *open* silver 1980, bronze
1972.

Angelo won a bronze medal for Great Britain in the open class at the 1972 Olympics, but then became a member of the French team – his marriage entitled him to make the switch. He won the gold medal for France in the over 95kg class in Moscow in 1980 – beating Britain's Paul Radburn in the semi-final. He also won the silver medal in the open class in Moscow.

Angelo Parisi (left) on the way to his Moscow gold ▶

Strongest man in the world? USSR's super heavyweight Anatoli Pisarenko ▶

Alexsandr Pervyi (URS)
Weightlifting: 75kg/165lb,
82.5kg/182lb
Born: October 28, 1960,
   Belozyorskoye, USSR.
Height: 167cm/5ft 5¾in.
Weight: 74kg/162lb.
Career Highlights
Olympic Games: *75kg;* silver,
   1980.

Hailing from the Donetsk area of Russia, Pervyi is a serviceman in the armed forces, and a Second Class Master of Sport. A member of the Russian team since 1979, he won his first major title that year – the USSR Cup (752kg category). A silver medallist at the

Moscow Olympics, again in the 75kg class, he now lifts at the heavier 82.5kg class, and set the world jerk record in 1982, when he lifted 223.5kg (492.5lb) at Frunze in Russia.

Anatoli Pisarenko (URS)
Weightlifting
Born: January 10, 1958, Kiev,
   USSR.
Height: 188cm/6ft 2in.
Weight: 122kg/262lb.
Career Highlights
World Championships: *super
   heavyweight* gold 1981, 1982,
   1983.

Pisarenko started lifting at the age

of 15, and at the end of his first year, had lifted a total of 170kg. Small for a super heavyweight, he is a real athlete and transformed his sport.

He came to prominence in 1978 when he finished second in the European Junior Championships and third in the World Junior Championships.

He went on to win the first of his three successive super heavyweight senior world titles in 1981.

Surprisingly, he has only once been the super heavyweight champion of the Soviet Union – in 1982. He is a lieutenant in the Soviet Army, and a Student of Sport.

Anatoli, who eats 10 ounces of black caviar a day, was once a multi-world record holder, but his snatch record of 206kg was beaten by 24-year-old Alexander Gunyashev (USSR) with 207.5kg in December 1983.

Paul Radburn (GBR)
Judo: over 95kg/210lb
Born: May 23, 1955, Wanstead,
   London, England.
Height: 193cm/6ft 4in.
Weight: 100kg/218lb.
Career Highlights
Olympic Games: *over 95kg;*
   bronze 1980.
European Championship: *95kg*
   bronze 1977, 1979.

A motor fitter, Paul's first representative honours came in 1975 when he won a bronze medal in the European Junior Championships. He reappeared in 1979 to win the 95kg title at the British Open, and in 1980 won the over 95kg title.

That year saw him take part in his first Olympic Games. Losing to Angelo Parisi in the semifinal, he ended up with a bronze medal.

In 1983 he returned to the 95kg class. Paul is coached at present by the former Olympic medallist, Dave Starbrook.

Hartmut Reich (GDR)
Wrestling: freestyle 52kg/115lb
Born: July 5, 1956, East Germany.
Height: 156cm/5ft 1½in.
Weight: 52kg/114lb.
Career Highlights
World Championships: *52kg*
   bronze 1983,
   gold 1982,
   bronze 1979, 1977,
   silver 1978.

After a series of near misses in the world championships, Hartmut Reich finally won the 52kg class at his sixth attempt in 1982.

A consistent performer, he has a real chance of taking one of the medals in Los Angeles, thus making amends for the 1980 Moscow Games when he came away empty-handed.

More than 21 stone and over 7ft tall . . . Poland's Adam Sandurski ▶ ▶

Janko Rusev (BUL)

Weightlifting: 67.5kg/148.8lb
Born: January 12, 1958, Sofia, Bulgaria.
Height: 166cm/5ft 5½in.
Weight: 74kg/163lb.
Career Highlights
Olympics: *67.5kg* gold 1980.
World Championships: *60kg* silver 1977; *67.5kg* gold 1978, 1979; silver 1983; *75kg* gold 1981, 1981.

Rusev is the 'different Bulgarian', who reached the top relatively late at 20/21 and has stayed there with remarkable consistency, piling one spectacular result on top of another. He is one of the all-time greats of the sport.

His ebullient personality already showed in his very first big-trophy event, the 1977 World European Championships in Stuttgart, where – to have a chance of winning – he upped the world record weight in the jerk by 5kg, got it up but could not hold it. This meant the silver in the 60kg class, but the world of lifters took note of the Bulgarian's gutsy attitude. He came to be universally considered a big-time competitor.

This prediction came true in 1978, when Janko moved up to

Janko Rusev . . . at the top for five years ▼

67.5kg to rule the world for four long years at the weight without a single defeat, and it was the arrival on the scene of compatriot Varbanov which made Rusev migrate to the 75kg category for 1982. He still won all, but in 1983, back at 67.5kg, lost to the East Germany's Joachim Kunz in the World & European Championships by 2.5kg.

Rusev's epic battle against fellow-Bulgarian Mincho Pasov, when they broke the jerk world mark every time they stepped up before Rusev's greater resilience told, will probably remain the high point of the sport for years to come.

Stefan Rusu (ROM)

Wrestling: Greco-Roman 68kg/150lb, 74kg/163lb
Born: February 2, 1956, Bucharest, Romania.
Height: 169cm/5ft 6½in.
Weight: 73kg/160lb.
Career Highlights
Olympic Games: *68kg* gold 1980, silver 1976.
World Championships: *74kg* gold 1982.

Stefan Rusu of Romania will be appearing in his third successive Olympics in 1984. He won silver in his first Games of 1976 and, four years later, gold in the 68kg class. He would, no doubt, like to collect a medal at his third successive Games.

Fifth in his first World Championship in 1977, he improved the following year to take the silver medal, and in 1982 won gold in the heavier, 74kg class. However, 1983 saw him out of the medals in the World Championships at Kiev, finishing fourth, but even so, he must still be feared by his opponents in Los Angeles.

Hitoshi Saito (JAP)

Judo
Born: 1960, Tokyo, Japan.
Height: 189cm/6ft 2½in.
Weight: 140kg/308lb.
Career Highlights
World Championships: *open class* first 1983.

A great rival of team mate Yamashita in the heavyweight class, Hitoshi Saito lifted the open class world title at the thirteenth World Championships in Moscow in 1983, defeating Czech Kocman in the final, whilst Yamashita concentrated on – and won – the heavyweight class.

Adam Sandurski (POL)

Wrestling: freestyle over 100kg/220½kg
Born: February 9, 1953, Ryeszow, Poland
Height: 214cm/7ft 0¼in.
Weight: 135kg/305lb.
Career Highlights
Olympic Games: *100kg+* bronze 1980.
World Championships: *100kg+* silver 1983, 1982.

Hailing from the same town as Poland's other great wrestler, Jan Falandys, Adam Sandurski can be regarded as a 'Giant' in the freestyle wrestling world – he weighs over 21 stone, and towers over seven feet.

An electrician by trade, he first competed internationally at the 1977 World Championships, and the following year he won his first national title. Third in the super heavyweight class at his first Olympics in 1980, he is confident of turning that into gold in Los Angeles.

Marek Seweryn (POL)

Weightlifting: 60kg/132lb
Born: October 17, 1957, Szopienice, Poland.
Height: 160cm/5ft 3in.
Weight: 60kg/131lb.
Career Highlights
Olympic Games: *60kg* bronze 1980.
World Championships: *60kg* gold 1979; *56kg* silver 1978.

Marek's first major title was in 1978 when he won the 56kg division at the European Championships. That same year he won the silver in the World Championships. His first world title came in 1979 when he won the heavier 60kg class, and in his first Olympics in 1980, he won the bronze medal, again in the 60kg class. Marek is a driver by trade.

Tapio Sipila (FIN)
Wrestling: Greco-Roman
68kg/150lb
Born: November 26, 1958,
Finland.
Height: 177cm/5ft 9¾in.
Weight: 68kg/148lb.
Career Highlights
World Championships: *68kg* gold
1983.

Finland's Tapio Sipila has made steady progress since his Olympic debut in 1980 and this culminated in his winning the world title in the 68kg division in 1983.

Tapio must represent Finland's best chance of maintaining their high level of success in Olympic Greco-Roman wrestling, in which they are the second best nation behind the Soviets.

Nikolai Soludukhin (URS)
Judo
Born: January 3, 1955,
Paserkovo, USSR.
Height: 164cm/5ft 4½in.
Weight: 64kg/141lb.
Career Highlights
Olympic Games: *65kg* gold 1980.
World Championships: *65kg* gold,
1983, 1979.

A Merited Master of Sport, Soludukhin has been a member of the Soviet team since 1975, the year of his first national title. He won the world 65kg title in 1979 – lost it in 1981 – and regained it in 1983. He will be in Los Angeles to defend the title he won in Moscow in 1980.

Yurik Sarkisyan (URS)
Weight lifting: 56kg/124lb
60kg/132lb
Born: August 14, 1961, Samagar,
USSR.
Height: 152cm/4ft 11¾in.
Weight: 55kg/120lb.
Career Highlights
Olympic Games: *56kg* silver 1980.
World Championships: *60kg* gold
1982, 1983.

A student at the Armenian State Institute, Sarkisyan is an International Class Master of Sport. A member of the Soviet squad since 1979, he was runner up to Cuba's Nunez in the 1980 Olympic 56kg competition, but set a world junior record lift of 270kg (595lb) in doing so. He won his first world title (60kg) in 1982.

Naim Suleimanov (BUL)
Weightlifting: 56kg/123½lb
Born: November 23, 1967 Pticsar,
Bulgaria.
Weight: 56kg/122lb.
Career Highlights
World Championships: *56kg*
silver 1983.
World Juniors: *52kg*
gold 1982.

Suleimanov started lifting in 1978 and at 14 he shocked the world by winning gold in the World Juniors at Sao Paulo with a 250kg total, which put him second on the senior world list in the 52kg category of groan-and-grunt men. He moved up to the 56kg class in 1983, when he bumped up the world record to the 285kg total in Allenstown, at the fourth Record Makers Tournament in the United States, but lost to Mirzoyan of the USSR (292.5kg) in the World Championships by 2.5kg.

The precocious student lives and goes to school in Kardzhili Arda, and is trained by national coach Ivan Abadjieff.

Naim represents the 'new frontier' of the Bulgarian school which – locked in a no-quarters-given combat with the Soviet Union for world domination – sculpts athletes for dynamic strength with relatively narrow shoulders and big backsides.

In order to keep ahead of the USSR in a race they can't possibly keep going for very long, the Bulgarians are pushing their youngsters to the very limit early on, and they have very short careers as a result. It is a case of the soldiers getting younger and younger as Napoleon runs out of human material, and Naim Suleimanov is the very epitomy of the syndrome.

Andrej Supron (POL)
Wrestling: Greco-Roman
68kg/150lb
Born: October 22, 1952,
Katowice, Poland.
Height: 170cm/5ft 7in.
Weight: 73kg/160lb.
Career Highlights
Olympic Games: *68kg* silver 1980.
World Championships: *68kg* gold
1979.

Only one Pole has won an Olympic Greco-Roman wrestling gold medal – Kazimierz Lipien in 1976 – but Andrej Supron, Poland's leading wrestler at present, must stand a chance of becoming their second at the 1984 Games, when he contests the 74kg class.

Second in the 1983 and 1982 World Championships, the miner from Katowice certainly has the ability to outfight the Soviet and Romanian challengers for the title.

He first competed internationally at the 1971 World Championships – finishing sixth. The following year he took part in his first Olympics. Over ten national titles to his credit, his first European title came in 1975, and four years later he won his first World title – both coming in the 68kg class.

USSR's Nikolai Soludkhin throws Nedkov of Bulgaria during the Moscow Olympics ◄◄

Leonid Taranenko (URS)
Weightlifting: 110kg/243lb
Born: June 13, 1956, Malorita,
    Russia.
Height: 179cm/5ft 10½in.
Weight: 108kg/236lb.
Career Highlights
Olympic Games: *110kg* gold
    1980.
World Championships: *110kg*
    bronze 1979.

Taranenko was a student at the
Byelorussian Institute of Agricul-
ture Mechanization, and is also a
Master of Sport — International
Class.
    He has been a member of
the Soviet lifting team since 1979,
when he won his first national title.
In that year he also won the Spartakiad (110kg class) and was third
in the World Championships. 1980
saw him take the European title,
and the Olympic title — the latter
with a world record lift of 422.5kg
(931¼lb). In 1983 he broke the
snatch and jerk world records, to
add to his overall world record of
435kg (959lb) set in Moscow in
1982.

Nemo Terzilski (BUL)
Weightlifting
Born: 1964, Bulgaria.
Weight: 52kg/114.6lb.
Career Highlights
World Junior Championships:
    52kg gold 1982, 1983.

Terzilski was world junior champion in 1982 and 1983 at 52kg
(flyweight). He holds the world
snatch record in this class with
115½kg/254¼lb, the jerk record at
150kg/330½lb and the total record
at 260kg/573lb.

Stefan Topurov (BUL)
Weightlifting
Born: 1964, Sofia, Bulgaria.
Weight: 60kg/132.3lb.
Career Highlights
World Championships: *60kg* silver
    1983.
World Junior Championships:
    60kg gold 1982.

Topurov became the first man to
take the jerk to treble his bodyweight 180kg/396¾lb at 59.85kg/
132lb at the 1983 World Championships, but still placed only second. He lost to Yurik Sarkisian
(URS) on heavier bodyweight after
both men had equal totals of
312.5kg/688¾lb. He was junior
world champion in 1982 with
280kg/617¼lb.

Alexei Tyurin (URS)
Judo: open
Born: January 30, 1955, Elets
    City, USSR.
Height: 188cm/6ft 2in.
Weight: 130kg/285lb.
Career Highlights
USSR Championship: *Open* gold
    1978.

A member of the armed forces in
Moscow, Tyurin made his international debut in 1978, and is an
International Class Master of
Sport.
    His first major title was in
1978 when he won the open class
at the Russian Championships. He
was in the 1980 Soviet Olympic
squad but did not participate in the
Games.

Detlef Ultsch (GDR)
Judo: 86kg/185lb
Born: November 7, 1955, Leipzig,
    East Germany.
Height: 176cm/5ft 9in.
Weight: 86kg/188lb.
Career Highlights
World Championships: *86kg* gold
    1983, 1979.

Detlef won the 1979 World
Championship in the 86kg class,
lost it in 1981, but regained it in
1983, beating Frenchman Fabien
Canu in the final. In the 1980
Olympic Games he reached the
last eight.

Yurik Vardanyan (URS)
Weightlifting: 75kg/165lb,
    82.5kg/182lb; 82.5kg/182lb
Born: June 13, 1956, Leninakan,
    USSR.
Height: 170cm/5ft 7in.
Weight: 82kg/180lb.
Career Highlights
Olympic Games: *82.5kg;* gold
    1980.
World Championships: *75kg* gold,
    1978, 1977; *82.5kg* gold
    1981, 1979.

A PE teacher at the Armenian
State Institute, Vardanyan is a Merited Master of Sport, and has been
a member of the Soviet team since
1975. He won his first national
title (75kg) in 1977, and in 1977,
1978, 1979 and 1981 he won
world titles. He won the gold medal
in the 82.5kg class at the 1980
Moscow Olympics with a world
record lift of 400kg (881¾lb) and
was the only man at the Olympic Games to win with a world
record lift in *both* the snatch and
the jerk.

Robert van de Walle (BEL)
Judo: 95kg/210lb
Born: May 20, 1954, Brussels,
    Belgium.
Height: 189cm/6ft 2½in.
Weight: 94kg/208lb.
Career Highlights
Olympic Games: *95kg* gold 1980.
World Championships: *95kg* silver
    1979, 1981, bronze, 1983.

Robert van de Walle was noticed in
Britain when he won the British
Open (95kg) in 1977 — retaining
his title the following year, and
winning it again in 1983. A gold
medallist in the 95kg class at the
1980 Olympics, he beat Khubuluri
in the final. Robert rates the
toughest opponent he has fought
in recent years as Britain's Paul
Radburn.

Alexander Varbanov (BUL)
Weightlifting
Born: 1964, Bulgaria.
Weight: 74kg/163.2lb.
Career Highlights
World Championships: *75kg* gold
    1983.

Varbanov won the 75kg (middleweight) world title at his first
appearance in a major championship with a world record total of
370kg/815½lb. His 210kg/
462¾lb jerk was also a world
record. He could be Bulgaria's first
choice in this category for Los
Angeles and may be partnered by
former world champion Janko
Rusev.

▲
*Reigning Olympic
champion Robert van de
Walle of Belgium*

Yasuhiro Yamashita (JAP)
Judo: 95kg/210lb, open
Born: June 1, 1957, Kyshu, Japan.
Height: 187cm/6ft 1½in.
Weight: 130kg/280lb.
Career Highlights
World Championships: *over 95kg* gold 1983, 1981, 1979, *open* gold 1981.

Over 95kg world champion in 1979, 1981 and 1983, he was also the open class world champion in 1981. Yamashita has not lost a fight since 1977.

Yuri Zakharevich (URS)
Weightlifting: 100kg/220½lb
Born: August 18, 1963, Kiev, USSR.
Height: 180m/5ft 10in.
Weight: 112kg/246.9lb.
Career Highlights
Olympic Games: *90kg* silver 1980.
World Championships: *90kg* silver 1981; *110kg* silver 1982.
World Juniors: *90kg* silver 1980, gold 1981; *110kg* gold 1982.

Yuri started lifting unusually early for a Soviet weightlifter, at 10 years old, when only 136cm tall, and his first international results came in 1980. That year, he was second in both the World Juniors and subsequently the Olympics with identical 372kg totals, although he had achieved 385kg earlier, when the rules may have been less rigorously observed.

The dichotomy between big-trophy and record attempt results has been a feature of Zakharevich's career. In 1981, still competing at 90kg, he got his year's best of 405kg early, but won the World Juniors with only 377.5kg and was second to the Bulgarian Blagoev in the World Championships with 397.5kg. At 100kg, he raised his total to 425kg.

Up in the 110kg category, 1982 was to be Yuri's big year. He broke 13 world records, got his total up to 430kg, won the World Juniors with a modest 405kg and slumped to an unexpected, marginal defeat in the senior World Championships by 2.5kg to compatriot Szoc.

Yuri Zakharevich has been an untypical Soviet competitor. The USSR have a lot of potential world-class lifters in all categories and do not have to push their 16-17-year-olds. They build for static — rather than dynamic — strength, so the wear-and-tear on their stars is gradual and they have

long careers: most are still around at 25, and even 28.

But Zakharevich has always followed the 'Bulgarian school', and while he re-wrote the record list single-handed in the 90-110kg categories, his excesses affected him last year. Competing in the 100kg category, in 1983 he jerked 200kg at home, beating even the super-heavy record. But tragedy struck when he had the weight raised in the jerk by an incredible 15kg in the Danubia Cup, from 182.5 to 197.5kg. He almost managed the weight at first attempt, but on the second his elbow went and he was carried to hospital unconscious.

Zacharevich appears poised for a final assault on the heights this

Olympic year, but the consensus is that it will be his last year of top-level competition — all the inner reserves have been mercilessly squeezed out of have-a-go Yuri. He is a sacrificial lamb in the battle with the Bulgarians for world supremacy.

Asen Zlatev (BUL)
Weightlifting
Born: 1960, Bulgaria.
Weight: 82kg/180.8lb.
Career Highlights
Olympic Games: *72kg* gold 1980.
World Championships: *82.5kg* gold 1982, silver 1981, 1983.

Zlatev is a former snatch world record holder at light heavyweight with 180kg/396¾lb.

Another Bulgarian iron man . . . Asen Zlatev
▼

Archery, fencing, modern pentathlon and shooting

Archery

Archery, one of the oldest of all sports contested today, dates back to the twelfth century BC. An important weapon for thousands of years, the bow and arrow began to be used for recreation as well under England's Henry VIII.

The first British archery championships were held at York in August 1844 and the scoring system adopted at those championships is similar to the system still used. With the formation of the world governing body in 1931 – FITA – the first world championships were held the same year in Warsaw.

Archery was first included in the Olympic programme in 1900, and continued until 1920 (with the exception of 1912). Many of the events were different in those early days and targets such as live pigeons were used. Today each competitor shoots 72 arrows at the 9in diameter bull from each of four distances. In the case of the male competitors, the distances are 30, 50, 70 and 90 metres, and for women, 30, 50, 60 and 70 metres. Both team and individual events are contested.

Belgium has won most Olympic golds, thanks to their successes at the turn of the century, but since archery's re-introduction into the Olympic programme in 1972, the United States have dominated both the men's and women's events.

The most successful Olympic archer was Belgian Hubert Van Innis, who won nine medals between 1900 and 1920, six of them gold. One of the most successful archers in the 'inter Olympics' era was another Belgian, Oscar Kessels, who took part in no less than 21 world championships.

A competitor at the 1908 London Olympics was Charlotte Dod of Great Britain. Silver medallist in the women's event (her brother won the gold in the men's event), she was better known as 'Lottie' Dod; five times Wimbledon Lawn Tennis champion (and still the youngest champion at the age of 15 years 285 days), British ladies' golf champion, and British hockey international – surely one of the greatest ever all rounders.

Archery ancient and modern . . . (bottom) the men warm up at Stamford Bridge in 1908; (below) a latter day Maid marion ▼

Franco Riccardi of Italy scores a hit on his way to the 1936 Olympic epée title ▶

160

Fencing

The sword dates back to the bronze age and the first recorded fencing match took place in about 1190 BC. Fencing lost its appeal as a competitive sport towards the end of the eighteenth century – bare knuckle fighting replacing it in popularity. However, fencing revived in popularity in the mid-nineteenth century and towards the end of the century became a branch of the British Gymnastics Association. Its first rules were drawn up in 1896 – the year it appeared at the Olympic Games. Foil and sabre titles were at stake, the epee was included at the next Olympic celebration in 1900. Since then, all three have been contested at each Olympics (except for 1908 when the foil was omitted) and the most successful nations have been France and Hungary with 30 gold medals each.

Like the other combat sports – archery and shooting – women take part in the Olympics, but only in the foil, for which they have individual and team competitions.

Fencing's first world championships were held in 1936, and from then to the mid-1950s were dominated by French and Italian fencers,

the most successful fencer of all time being Christian d'Oriola of France who won four individual world titles and two Olympic titles between 1947 and 1956.

Age is no restriction in fencing and the likes of Britain's Bill Hoskyns, America's Janice Lee York-Romary and Aladar Gerevitch of Hungary all competed in six Olympics. In fact, Gerevitch was a member of the Hungarian team which won the team sabre gold medal in *every* Games between 1932 and 1960.

Fencing is a sport that breeds family successes. Edoardo Mangiarotti of Italy holds the record for winning the most Olympic medals – 13 between 1936 and 1960. One of his brothers, Dario, won three medals, and another brother, Aldo, won four to make a family collection of 20 made up of 10 golds, eight silvers and two bronze.

Another fencing family were the Gerevitch's of Hungary. Aladar won seven golds, one silver and two bronze, his wife Erna won a bronze, son Pal won two bronze medals and, for good measure, father-in-law Albert Bogen won a silver medal.

Dane Ivan Osiier won a silver medal in 1912 and his wife Ellen won a gold in 1924. Not so amazing perhaps, except that Ivan took part in the 1908 London Olympics, and the 1948 Games, also in London.

Modern Pentathlon

The five events of the modern pentathlon have been likened to the skills needed in medieval times to evade one's pursuers: riding, fencing, shooting, swimming, and running.

In the ancient Olympics, the pentathlon was regarded as the *victor ludorum* of the games. The five events in those days consisted of the discus, the javelin, running, jumping and wrestling. In today's modern pentathlon the riding is over an 800 metre course with 15 obstacles, the fencing competition is with the epée, the shooting is with pistols from a distance of 25 metres, the swimming is freestyle over 300 metres and the running is a gruelling 4000 metres cross country run.

The Olympic competition is open to teams of three and individuals. Most teams rely heavily on armed forces personnel to make up their numbers. The present scoring system, which was devised in 1956, allows 1000 points per discipline, with bonuses.

The modern pentathlon first appeared in the Olympic programme in 1912, and the fifth placed man in the individual competition that year was George Patton, 'old blood and guts' General George Patton himself.

The sport had a slow start internationally, but following the formation of the world body in 1948, and the first world championship the following year, it grew in popularity. The Eastern bloc countries — the USSR, Czechoslovakia and Hungary — are now dominant, succeeding the Swedes, who have provided nine individual Olympic winners.

The most successful individual was Hungary's Andras Balczo, winner of six world titles between 1963 and 1969. He also holds the record for the most Olympic medals, eight, and most golds, three. However, two Swedes have their own places in Olympic history: Willie Grut — currently the Secretary General of the World Modern Pentathlon Association — who won three of the five disciplines in the 1948 Games, and Lars Hall who is the only man to have won two individual titles.

Britain will never forget the eventful 1976 Montreal Olympics. First the USSR's Boris Onishenko was disqualified for cheating in the fencing section against Sergeant Jim Fox, and then they had an agonizing wait at the end of the cross country to see if Fox, Danny Nightingale and Adrian Parker had lifted the gold for Britain. Indeed they had — by 108 points from the Czechs.

▲ Britain's gold medal trio of 1976 — (from left) Adrian Parker, Jim Fox and Danny Nightingale

Jim Fox . . . forced to ▲ denounce Russia's Boris Onishenko as a fencing cheat

Shooting pre First World War — the 1908 Olympics ▶

Shooting

The 1984 Olympics sees women competitors taking part in their own events for the first time, with the introduction of the air rifle, small bore rifle and pistol shooting events. This comes 16 years after women first competed, on level terms, with their male counterparts and eight years after America's Margaret Murdock became the first female medallist in an Olympic shooting event with a silver in the small bore rifle.

Shooting has had more categories in the Olympic programme than any other sport. In addition to the 11 events that will be contested in 1984, there have been 14 other disciplines, now discontinued.

The most demanding of all categories is the pistol shooting. The competitor, standing free of any support, has to hit a small ball (50mm diameter, just under 2 inches) from 50 metres (54 yards 2 feet). Competitions for pistol shooting date back to the late eighteenth century when pistols succeeded swords as the principal duelling weapon, and the first official World Pistol Shooting Championships were held in Paris in 1900. In those early days, the Swiss dominated the event, but recent years have seen the Soviets and East Germans take over.

Rifle shooting, the oldest of the events, dates back to the fifteenth century, when the first shooting match is recorded at Zurich in 1472. The British Rifle Association was formed under royal patronage in 1860, and looking for a site to hold its Imperial Prize meeting, they picked Wimbledon Common. Queen Victoria fired the first shot. They moved to their present world famous home at Bisley in 1888.

Shooting, in one form or another, has been contested at every modern Olympic Games with the exception of 1928. One of the outstanding competitors has been Italian, Ennio Mattarelli, the first man to win Olympic, world and European titles. The distinction of winning the most Olympic medals, though, belongs to American Carl Osburn, who won 11 between 1912 and 1924.

Two outstanding Olympic record holders are both shooting competitors. Oscar Swahn of Sweden has the distinction of being the oldest Olympic champion, winning gold 107 days short of his 65th birthday. And at the 1920 Games, aged 72 years 280 days, he became the oldest ever Olympic medallist (bronze). He would have taken part in 1924, but for ill health.

The only person to have won gold medals in both sporting and artistic events at the Olympics was Walter Winans of the United States. He won the Running Deer shooting gold medal in 1908 and a gold medal for sculpture at the 1912 Games.

Shooting can lay claim to one of the Games' most obscure disqualifications. Paul Cerutti of Monaco failed a drug test at the 1976 Olympics and was disqualified from next to last position.

Alister 'Jock' Allan (GBR)

Shooting
Born: January 28, 1944,
    Abingdon, England.
Height: 165cm/5ft 5in.
Weight: 60kg/132lb.
Career highlights
World Championships: *prone rifle*
    gold 1978.
European Championships: *prone*
    and three position gold 1981.
Commonwealth Games: *prone rifle*
    gold 1978; *individual small*
    bore gold 1982.

A sports' supervisor, 'Jock' Allan, although born in England, represents Scotland at the Commonwealth Games, winning individual titles in both 1978 and 1982.

Allan appeared in his first Olympics in Montreal in 1976, and two years later, won the prone rifle title at the World Championships, equalling the world record, which he broke again in 1981 when scoring a maximum 600.

Alexandr Asanov (URS)

Shooting
Born: August 16, 1953; Kyzl-Tooz,
    USSR.
Height: 170cm/5ft 7in.
Weight: 72kg/159lb.
Career highlights
European Championships: *trap*
    gold 1977; *trap* gold 1979.

Asanov has been a member of the Soviet team for 10 years, but he did not win his first major international title until taking the individual trap title at the 1977 European Championships – he was also a member of the winning Soviet team at those Championships.

He first competed in the Olympics on home soil in 1980, but without success. This was surprising, as he went to the Games one of the favourites for the trap event, having won the silver medal in the World Championships in 1979.

1983 saw him win silver in the European Championships, and he will be hoping for a better result than 1980, when he arrives in Los Angeles.

Borislav Batikov (BUL)

Modern pentathlon
Born: May 25, 1959, Bulgaria.
Height: 176cm/5ft 9½in.
Weight: 69kg/154lb.
Career Highlights
World Championship: *modern*
    pentathlon 1983.

Batikov figured prominently in the

▲
Britain's Mark Blenkarne, so close to a medal in Moscow

jumping in the opening round of the 1983 World Championships. Improvements in his other disciplines could put him up amongst the medallists in Los Angeles. He was a member of the Bulgarian team at the 1980 Olympics.

Goran Bjerendal (SWE)

Archery
Born: October 21, 1951, Molndal,
    Sweden.
Height: 182cm/5ft 11in.
Weight: 85kg/187lb.
Career Highlights
Olympic Games: twelfth 1980.

Watchmaker Goran Bjerendal is worth noting as an outsider in Los Angeles.

He finished fifth in the 1983 World Championships, but was lying fourth after the opening two rounds. He could not consolidate that position, but considering the excellent company he was in, it could only have served as good experience for the future.

Mark Blenkarne (GBR)

Archery
Born: October 7, 1957, Bristol,
    England.
Height: 183cm/6ft 0in.

Weight: 70kg/154lb.
Career Highlights
Olympic Games: *double FITA*
    fourth 1980.
Commonwealth Games: gold 1982.

Mark missed a medal by three points at his first Olympics in 1980, but received some consolation by becoming the first men's Commonwealth Games archery champion two years later.

Britain's most consistent archer in recent years, he won the first of his six British titles in 1976, and in 1980, he set a British record for a FITA double round, with a score of 2494.

Elmar Borrmann (FRG)

Fencing
Born: West Germany.
Height: 175cm/5ft 9in.
Weight: 68kg/149lb.
Career Highlights
World Championships: *epée* gold
    1983; bronze 1981.
World Cup: *epée* gold 1983.

Borrmann, a Mercedes Benz salesman in West Germany, is reigning World Champion in the epée. A supreme stylist he must be the favourite for a gold medal in Los Angeles.

Frederico Cervi (ITA)
Fencing
Born: July 9, 1961, Brescia, Italy.
Height: 170cm/5ft 7in.
Weight: 64kg/141lb.
Career Highlights
World Championships: *foil* bronze 1982.

Adaptable at both the foil and epée, Frederico Cervi first came to international prominence at the 1979 World Championships when he came sixth in the individual foil competition, and was a member of the Italian team that won the silver medal — he was only 18 at the time.

The following year he won the world junior foil title, and was a member of the Italian team that took part in the Olympics — Frederico finishing 21st in the individual foil competition.

Malcolm Cooper (GBR)
Shooting
Born: December 20, 1947, Hayling Island, England.
Height: 172cm/5ft 8in.
Weight: 74kg/163lb.

Career Highlights
World Championships: *small bore (standing)* gold 1978.
Commonwealth Games: *small bore (prone)* gold 1982; *small bore team (three position)* gold 1982.

Following his successes in the 1982 Commonwealth Games — he won two gold medals, two silvers, and a bronze — Malcolm goes to his third Olympic Games as one of Britain's best hopes of a shooting medal.

His first Olympic appearance was in 1972. Two years later he made his Commonwealth Games debut.

Vassil Etropolski (BUL)
Fencing
Born: March 18, 1959, Bulgaria.
Height: 182cm/5ft 11in.
Weight: 78kg/172lb.
Career Highlights
World Championships: *sabre* gold 1983.

Twins, Vassil Etropolski and his brother Khristo finished fourth and

fifth respectively in the individual sabre tournament at the 1980 Olympic Games.

The reigning world sabre champion, Vassil will be going to Los Angeles in 1984 looking for his first Olympic medal.

Paul Four (FRA)
Modern pentathlon
Born: February 13, 1956, France.
Height: 175cm/5ft 9in.
Weight: 68kg/149lb.
Career Highlights
World Championships: *modern pentathlon* fourth 1983.

Paul showed his true capabilities at the 1983 World Championships in West Germany where he finished fourth overall. He led for most of the competition, but was let down on the cross country running event.

Fencing is one of his stronger disciplines. He was a member of the French team that took the team bronze medal. He took part in the 1980 Moscow Olympics, and has a real chance of a medal in Los Angeles.

◄
1983 World Champion Elmar Borrmann

Twins Vassil (left) and Khristo Etropolski
▼

Steve Hallard (GBR)
Archery
Born: February 22, 1965, Rugby,
England.
Height: 188cm/6ft 2in.
Weight: 86kg/189.5lb.
Career Highlights
British Championships: gold
1983.

Steve will be only 19 when the 1984 Olympics take place, but already he has shown that he is the likely successor to Mark Blenkarne as Britain's top male archer.

An engineer by trade, his first British title came in 1983, and in the World Championships that year he was the highest placed Briton, in a creditable twentieth place.

In August 1981, when only 16, he set the British record for a FITA single round, with a score of 1265.

Bernhard Hochwald (GDR)
Shooting
Born: June 22, 1957, East
Germany.
Height: 181cm/5ft 11in.
Weight: 76kg/168lb.
Career Highlights
European Championships: *skeet*
gold 1983.

Hochwald will be appearing at his second Olympics – the first was in Moscow in 1980. He starts one of the favourites for the skeet gold, having won that title at the 1983 European Championships in Bucharest.

Milan Kadlec (TCH)
Modern pentathlon
Born: December 3, 1958,
Czechoslovakia.
Height: 178cm/5ft 10in.
Weight: 74kg/162lb.
Career Highlights
Olympic Games: *modern
pentathlon* sixth 1980.
World Championships: *modern
pentathlon* seventh 1983.

Kadlec was in contention after the early rounds of the 1983 World Championships, having done well in the riding and fencing events. He took part in the Moscow Games of 1980, so Los Angeles will be his second Games.

Jin Ho Kim (KOR)
Archery
Born: South Korea.
Career Highlights
World Championships: gold 1979,
1983.

World individual champion, and member of the South Korean gold medal winning team in 1979, Jin Ho Kim regained the same titles in 1983, having lost them to the Russians two year's earlier.

In winning back her title in 1983 she broke four World Championship records in so doing. The 1984 Olympics will be her first, as she did not compete in 1980.

Erno Kolczonay (HUN)
Fencing
Born: May 15, 1953, Budapest,
Hungary.
*Height: 175cm/*5ft 9in.
Weight: 65kg/143lb.
Career Highlights
Olympic Games: *epée* second
1980.
World Championships: *epée*
second 1979; *epée* third 1982.

A member of the famous Honved Club, Erno Kolczonay started his sporting life as a swimmer, then a modern pentathlete, before deciding upon fencing as his speciality – and what a good decision that was.

Erno has now succeeded the other great Hungarian fencer – Gyozo Kulcsar – as his country's top fencer, and will no doubt be hoping to emulate Kulcsar, who won individual medals at three successive Olympics. Erno already has a medal, a silver in the epée in 1980, and he hopes to add to this total at the 1984 Games.

His first major international competition was at the 1974 World Championships in Grenoble when he won a team bronze medal, and four years later in Hamburg he won his first world title, again in the team competition.

Erno was disappointed to be eliminated in the quarter-finals of the 1983 World Championships, but is determined to gain his second individual Olympic medal in 1984.

Vicor Krovopuskov (URS)
Fencing
Born: 1948, USSR.
Height: 178cm/5ft 10in.
Weight: 78kg/172lb.
Career Highlights
Olympic Games: *sabre* gold 1980,
1976.
World Championships: *sabre* gold
1980, 1976.
World Championships: *sabre* gold
1982, 1978.

One of the greatest fencers of all time, he is easily capable of retain-

ing the individual sabre title. In 1966 he won the World Junior Championships and has stayed at the top of the sport ever since. Apart from his Olympic successes, he has twice been World Champion.

Though not regarded as a stylist, the stockily built Soviet is a master tactician, drawing mistakes from his opponent.

Kyosti Laasonen (FIN)
Archery
Born: September 27, 1945,
Finland.
Height: 173cm/5ft 8in.
Weight: 65kg/142lb.
Career Highlights
Olympic Games: bronze 1972.
World Championships: gold 1981.

Bronze medallist in the first post-war Olympic archery competition in 1972, Kyosti Laasonen will be hoping to end a barren spell in international competition at the Los Angeles Olympics.

He had a bad Olympics in 1980, only finishing seventh, but made up for this the following year by taking the world title. However, since then, successes have been scarce.

Pavel Lednev (URS)
Modern pentathlon
Born: March 25, 1943, Gorky City,
Russia.
Height: 184cm/6ft 0½in.
Weight: 82kg/180lb.

*Angelo Mazzoni raises his
arms after reaching the
semi-finals of the 1983
world epée championships*
▼

◄

Rick McKinney . . . facing a Los Angeles showdown with Darrell Pace

Career Highlights
Olympic Games: *modern pentathlon* bronze team silver 1968, bronze, team gold 1972, silver 1976: bronze, team gold 1980.

A Merited Master of Sport, Lednev is a higher education teacher. He has been a member of the Russian modern pentathlon team since 1964, and won his first Russian title in 1968. He has won the world individual title on four occasions – 1973, 1974, 1975 and 1978. In Olympic competition, he first competed in 1968, and has taken part in every Games since. He won his first medals at those 1968 Games – an individual bronze and a team silver. In 1972 he won a team gold and another individual bronze, and in 1976 he won a silver medal in the individual competition. On home soil in 1980 he won another team gold, and a third individual bronze. Although he did not take part in the 1983 World Championships, he will no doubt be attempting to win his eighth Olympic medal in 1984.

Angelo Mazzoni (ITA)
Fencing
Born: April 3, 1961, Milan, Italy.
Height: 180cm/5ft 11in.
Weight: 75kg/159lb.
Career Highlights
World Championships: *epée* semi-finalist 1983.

Fifth in the 1979 World Junior Epée Championships, Angelo Mazzoni won his first Italian title the following year at the age of 19, and was duly selected for the Moscow Olympics.

Although he finished 29th in the Moscow Games, the experience did him nothing but good, and his narrow defeat in the semi-final of the 1983 World Championships will be sending him off to Los Angeles for the 1984 Olympics in a confident mood.

Rick McKinney (USA)
Archery
Born: October 12, 1953, Decatur, Indiana, United States.
Height: 1.68m/5ft 6in.
Weight: 55kg/120lb.
Career Highlights
World Championships: gold 1977, 1983.

The rivalry between Rick McKinney and his team-mate, Darrell Pace, has been a significant feature of world archery over the past seven or eight years. The pair have always vied for the position of leading United States archer. Currently, McKinney can claim that title, having beaten Pace on a tie-break to win the 1983 World Championship – his second title.

The world was robbed of their confrontation at Moscow in 1980, but their meeting in Los Angeles is eagerly awaited.

Alexandr Melentyev (URS)
Shooting
Born: June 27, 1954, Penza, USSR.
Height: 180cm/5ft 11in.
Weight: 72kg/168lb.
Career Highlights
Olympic Games: *free pistol* first 1980.

Melentyev made his international debut in 1979 while a student at the Kirghiz State University for physical athletes. The following year he was a member of the Soviet team in the Olympic Games, and came away with the gold medal in the free pistol competition. The previous year he had been successful in the Soviet national Championships and Spartakiad.

Alexandr took the silver medal in the air pistol event at the 1983 World Championships in Innsbruck.

Paivi Meriluoto (FIN)
Archery
Born: December 12, 1952, Finland.
Height: 171cm/5ft 7½in.
Weight: 61kg/133lb.
Career Highlights
Olympic Games: *double FITA* bronze 1980.

The reigning world record holder at 50 metres, with 331 points out of a maximum of 360, Paivi

Meriluoto has not had a great deal of international success since winning her bronze medal at the 1980 Olympics, but will, no doubt, be hoping to bring herself out of the doldrums in Los Angeles and thus maintain Finland's good record at the Olympic Games.

Laszlo Orban (HUN)
Shooting
Born: July 23, 1960, Budapest, Hungary.
Height: 180cm/5ft 11in.
Weight: 78kg/172lb.
Career Highlights
European Championships: *rapid fire pistol* third 1983.

A member of the famous Budapest Honved Club, Orban has been part of the national team since 1975, when he was just 15. He won his first national title in 1979 – aged 19 – and that same year took the silver medal in the European Junior Championship.

A clerk by profession, he is tipped to be one of the greatest Hungarian shooters of all time, and is certainly a medal prospect for the Olympics.

Darrell Pace (USA)
Archery
Born: October 23, 1956, Cincinatti, Ohio, United States.
Height: 180cm/5ft 11in.
Weight: 68kg/178lb.
Career Highlights
Olympic Games: *double FITA* gold 1976.
World Championships: gold 1979, 1975.

The FITA world record holder for both single and double rounds, Darrell Pace narrowly failed to win his third world title in 1983 – losing to fellow American, and arch rival, Rick McKinney, on a tie-break. However, revenge was taken, as Pace beat McKinney into second place in the 1983 Pan American Games.

Darrell won his first world title in 1975, and in gaining his second in 1979, he became the first man to win the title twice. On that occasion, as on many others, he was involved in a close confrontation with McKinney, the title being won with the last three arrows of a 288 arrow competition.

Richard Phelps (GBR)
Modern pentathlon
Born: April 19, 1961, Gloucester, England.
Height: 180cm/5ft 11in.
Weight: 63kg/139lb.
Career Highlights
World Junior Championship: *modern pentathlon* silver 1980.
British Championship: *modern pentathlon* first 1983, 1982, 1981, 1979.

Richard is a 'waste reclamation engineer' – (scrap dealer!) by profession, and after a successful junior modern pentathlon career has emerged as Britain's best hope for a medal in Los Angeles. He won a silver medal in the World Junior Championships in 1980, and a bronze in 1982 – his last year as a junior. In 1983 he made the switch to senior competition with success, finishing overall sixth in the World Championships. He went into the last day in third position, but then had a disastrous pistol shooting competition, in which he failed to register a bull – his four 9s and two 8s not being good enough. The reigning British Champion, he first won the title in 1979, and has now won it three years in succession, 1981, 1982 and 1983.

Tomi Poikolainen (FIN)
Archery
Born: December 27, 1961, Finland.
Height: 176cm/5ft 9½ in.
Weight: 74kg/163lb.
Career Highlights
Olympic Games: *double FITA* gold 1980.

The reigning Olympic champion, Tomi won the title by beating his nearest rival, the Soviet Isachenko, by just three points.

In all fairness, Poikolainen's victory was helped by the absence of the Americans in 1980, but he did show that he was able to compete with them, when he held on to second place after the 90-metre and 70-metre rounds of the 1983 World Championships, but then he fell away.

However, he has the ability, and may be worth looking at as the best European challenger to the Americans Pace and McKinney in Los Angeles.

John Primrose (CAN)
Shooting
Born: 1942, Canada.
Height: 175cm/5ft 9in.
Weight: 70kg/154lb.
Career Highlights
World Championships: *moving target;* first 1983.
Commonwealth Games: *clay pigeon* first 1974, 1978.

Canadian John Primrose has been shooting since he was 16, and has been competing internationally since 1962, when he appeared in the World Championships in Cairo.

He made his Olympic debut in 1970, and the Los Angeles Games will be his third Olympics.

His best performance was sixth in the clay pigeon event on home soil in 1976.

John goes to Los Angeles as the reigning world moving target champion.

The man to test the Americans . . . Finland's Tomi Poikolainen ▼ ▼

Five times a world champion . . . USSR's Alexandr Romankov ▼

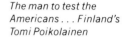

Janusz Pyciak-Peciak
(POL)
Modern pentathlon
Born: February 9, 1949, Poland.
Height: 172cm/5ft 8in.
Weight: 67kg/147lb.
Career Highlights
Olympic Games: *modern
    pentathlon;* gold 1976.
World Championships: *modern
    pentathlon* gold 1977, 1981,
    team gold 1977, 1978, 1981.

Janusz Pyciak-Peciak will be hoping to emulate his 1976 Montreal Olympic feat, by taking the individual title in Los Angeles in 1984. The 1980 Olympics saw him out of the medals completely, and even though he missed the 1983 World Championships, he will no doubt be in the running in Los Angeles. Individual world champion in 1977 and 1981, he was also a member of the gold medal winning Polish team at the 1977, 1978 and 1981 Championships.

Svante Rasmuson (SWE)
Modern pentathlon
Born: November 18, 1955,
    Uppsala, Sweden.
Height: 184cm/6ft 0½in.
Weight: 72kg/169lb.
Career Highlights
World Championships: *modern
    pentathlon;* fifth, 1983.

A medical practitioner, Svante will be competing in his third Olympics in 1984. His first Games in 1976 saw him take part as a member of the Swedish swimming team, and he did well to reach the semi-finals of the 100 metres freestyle. His next Games were in 1980 when he was in the modern pentathlon team. He finished fifth overall in the 1983 World Championships, but was lying second after three disciplines. Needless to say, his strongest discipline is the swimming, and it is worth noting that he has won a Swedish national swimming title.

Alexandr Romankov (URS)
Fencing
Born: December 7, 1953,
    Korsakov, USSR.
Height: 178cm/5ft 10in.
Weight: 70kg/154lb.
Career Highlights
Olympic Games: *foil* silver 1976,
    bronze 1980; *team foil* silver
    1980.
World Championships: *foil* gold
    1974, 1977, 1979, 1982,
    1983.

In 1983, Alexandr Romankov established himself as one of the greatest fencers of all time when he won a record fifth world title, yet surprisingly, he has still to win an Olympic gold medal.

A Merited Master of Sport he won his first national title in 1974 and celebrated by winning that year's world title.

Officially recognised as the world's number one fencer for the first time in 1976, he would surely swap any of his accolades and world titles for that missing Olympic gold – a situation which may be rectified at the Long Beach Convention Centre in 1984.

Ragnar Skanaker (SWE)
Shooting
Born: June 8, 1934, Stora Skedvi,
    Sweden.
Height: 184cm/6ft.
Weight: 78kg/172lb.
Career Highlights
Olympic Games: *free pistol* gold
    1972.
World Championships: *standard
    pistol* gold 1978; *air pistol* gold
    1983.

When Ragnar Skanaker lines up at the Los Angeles Games, he will be one of the oldest competitors there, having just celebrated his 50th birthday, but he will give younger opponents tough opposition in the free pistol competition.

Olympic free pistol champion in 1972, Ragnar won the first of his world titles in 1978, and his latest was at Innsbruck in 1983 when he took the gold in the individual air pistol event. He was also a member of the Swedish team that took the silver medal.

Skanaker has over 20 national titles to his credit and is also world record holder for the standard pistol event, with a score of 583 out of a maximum 600.

Anatoli Starostin (URS)
Modern pentathlon
Born: January 1960, Dushanbe,
    USSR.
Height: 176cm/5ft 9in.
Weight: 68kg/149lbs.
Career Highlights
Olympic Games: *modern
    pentathlon* gold 1980.
World Championships: *modern
    pentathlon* silver 1982; gold
    1983.

A Master of Sport – international class, Starostin is a qualified teacher. He first became a

member of the Soviet team in 1979, and 12 months later he was individual Olympic champion, as well as being a member of the Soviet team that took the gold medal. He was runner up in the individual competition at the 1982 World Championships, going one better in 1983 by winning the title – he was a member of the gold medal winning team in both years. With these credentials, and recent form, he must go to Los Angeles as favourite to win the gold medal.

Tamas Szombathelyi (HUN)
Modern pentathlon
Born: May 1, 1953, Budapest,
    Hungary.
Height: 177cm/5ft 9½in.
Weight: 67kg/147lb.
Career Highlights
World Junior Championships:
    modern pentathlon silver
    1972.
Olympic Games: *modern
    pentathlon* silver 1980.
World Championships: *modern
    pentathlon* silver 1983.

A sports instructor, Tamas started as a swimmer but then switched to the modern pentathlon. A member of the successful Hungarian team at the World Junior Championships in 1971 and 1972, he was also silver medallist in 1972. He won his first national title in 1978, and in his only Olympics to date (1980) he was a silver medallist in both the individual and team event. Soviet Starostin beat him into second place in the individual, as he did in the 1983 World Championships.

Valdas Turla (URS)
Shooting
Born: January 22, 1953, Birzhai,
    USSR.
Height: 176cm/5ft 9in.
Weight: 75kg/159lb.
Career Highlights:
World Records: *air pistol* (590 out
    of 600) 1982; *standard pistol*
    (583 out of 600 – equalled
    record) 1982.

A member of the armed forces, Valdas Turla has been in the Soviet shooting team since 1976 when he won silver and bronze medals in that year's Soviet Championships.

He competed in his first Olympics in Moscow, and currently holds two pistol shooting world records, but major international honours have eluded him. Turla is a Master of Sport.

Natalya Butuzova (URS)
Archery
Born: February 17, 1954, Kagan, USSR.
Height: 165cm/5ft 5in.
Weight: 50kg/110lb.
Career Highlights
Olympic Games: *double FITA* silver 1980.
World Championships: gold 1981.

An office worker in Tashkent, Natalya gained recognition as a top class archer in 1979, when she won both the Spartakiad, and her first national title. The following year she won the silver medal at the Moscow Olympics, and in 1981 she was World Champion.

She did not defend her world title in Los Angeles in 1983 because of the Korean jumbo jet dispute, but will be making the trip in 1984.

Nailya Gilyazova (URS)
Fencing
Born: January 2, 1953, Kazan, USSR.
Height: 161cm/5ft 3in.
Weight: 56kg/126lb.
Career Highlights
Olympic Games: *team foil* gold 1976; *team foil* gold 1980.
World Championship: *foil* gold 1983.

Nailya Gilyazova made her international fencing debut in 1974, and that same year won the individual bronze medal in the foil competition at the World Championships, as well as being a member of the gold medal winning Soviet team — her first of eight world titles, most of them in team events.

The 1976 Montreal Olympics saw her win her first Olympic title — again as a member of the successful foil team, and it was surprising that her first individual national title did not come until 1979. In 1982 she was the individual foil world champion.

Nailya is an International Class Merited Master of Sport in the Soviet Union.

Linda Martin (GBR)
Fencing
Born: June 6, 1954, Deal, Kent, England.
Height: 175cm/5ft 9in.
Weight: 67kg/147lb.
Career Highlights
World Championships: *foil* equal fifth 1982.
European Championships: *foil* bronze 1983.

Britain's main hope for an Olympic fencing title in Los Angeles rest with Linda Martin. Since reaching the final of the 1982 World Championships, Linda has continued to improve.

A bank employee living and training in London, Linda possesses all the attributes of a top class competitor. She combines physical speed and exemplary technique with the innate sense of timing which distinguishes the great champions. In her past, only her nerves have let her down at the critical moments, but a bronze medal at the European Championships indicates that Linda is finding her peak in Olympic year.

Mandy Niklaus (GDR)
Fencing
Born: March 1, 1956, East Germany.
Height: 174cm/5ft 8in.
Weight: 65kg/143lb.
Career Highlights
World Championships: *foil* third 1982.

A member of the strong East German team, Mandy Niklaus will be competing at her second Olympics in 1984, having finished joint ninth in the individual foil at her first Games in Moscow in 1980.

Dorina Vaccaroni (ITA)
Fencing
Born: September 24, 1963, Lido di Venezia, Italy.
Height: 170cm/5ft 6in.
Weight: 47kg/104lb.
Career Highlights
World Championships: *foil* silver 1982, gold 1983.

Italy has twice before produced the women's Olympic fencing champion, and 1984 looks like being the third occasion, as Dorina Vaccaroni goes to Los Angeles fresh from her 1983 World Championship success as the woman to beat.

She first came into the limelight in Italian fencing in 1979 — finishing third in the Mediterranean Games, second in the Junior World Championships, and then sixth in the World Championships.

Only 16 at the time, she was selected for the Moscow Olympics, and did not disgrace herself, finishing sixth overall in the individual competition. Her records since have made her the world's number one — and favourite for that Olympic title.

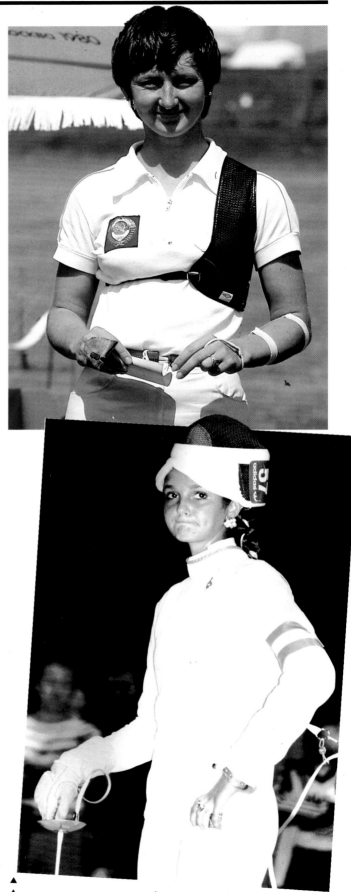

▲
Russia's Natalya Butuzova . . . eyes on a medal

▲
Deadlier than the male . . . Italy's fencing femme fatale Dorina Vaccaroni

Canoeing, rowing and yachting

Canoeing

The oldest type of boat in the world, the canoe, is often associated with Red Indians and Eskimoes. Today's boat took its present form in Canada, and for this reason, the racing canoe is referred to as the 'Canadian'.

As a sport, canoeing was developed by English barrister, John McGregor who on July 26, 1866 founded the Canoe Club which held its inaugural meeting at the Star and Garter Public House in Richmond. The club became the Royal Canoe Club in 1873.

A great pastime as well as a sport, it spread throughout Europe after World War I, particularly in Germany and Scandinavia. The popularity led to the formation of the International Canoeing Association – based in Munich – in 1924, and, having been a demonstration event at that year's Olympics, was granted full status at the 1936 Berlin Games. Competition then was for men only, but women gained their own events at the next Olympic celebration in London in 1948.

International canoeing events are held over a standard 1000 metre course, and are contested by either the canoe or the kayak. The boats are identified by the prefix 'C' or 'K', after which appears a number, indicating how many men or women are in the respective craft ranging from one to four. The latest addition at the Olympics is the womens K4, being seen for the first time in 1984. Like its rowing counterpart, canoeing employs the repêchage system. The French word 'repechage' translated means 'fishing again'.

The main difference between the canoe and the kayak is that the competitor *kneels* in the canoe, and has a paddle with one blade, whereas the kayak competitor *sits* in his craft and has a blade at each end of his paddle.

The leading canoeist of all time was Sweden's Gerd Fredriksson, winner of six Olympic titles between 1948 and 1960. He is closely followed by Soviet Vladimir Parfenovich, who won a record 12 world titles between 1979 and 1983.

The sport is now completely dominated by Eastern European countries, particularly the USSR. Indeed, one has to go back to 1952, when American Frank Havens won gold, to find the last non-European Olympic champion in a canoeing event.

Rowing

'Rowing is a sport the French reserve for their convicts, and the Romans for their slaves.' These words were uttered by Englishman, Lord Mancroft. But how wrong he was, for it was the English who introduced rowing into the sporting calendar.

Strictly an amateur sport, rowing was popular in Britain in the eighteenth century. Irish comedian, Thomas Doggett, lends his name to the oldest sporting prize still contested — he presented his famous badge, orange livery with silver known as the 'Doggett Coat and Badge', to the winner of a sculling contest held on the Thames in 1715.

It was at the end of the eighteenth century that the sport really developed in Britain, and in 1818, the oldest club in England, Leander, was formed. The inaugural Varsity Boat Race was held in 1829, and two years later, the first world professional sculling championships were held in Britain – as were all championships up to 1876. The world champions became national heroes in one of the most popular sports of the period.

The inauguration of the world championships — which consisted mainly of British competitors – led to the popularity of the sport spreading throughout Europe, and in 1892 the International Rowing Federation was formed.

The sport is in two categories: rowing and sculling. In rowing the competitor has one oar, in sculling he has two. International events are run over a 2000-metre course for men, and a 1000-metre course for women, both with six lanes. One feature of rowing — like canoeing — is the repechage system, which allows losers of first round heats to race against each other for a second chance of qualifying. This, the sport feels, gives a better chance of the ultimate winner being the best competitor.

The sport was first included in the Olympic programme in 1900, and women have had their own programme since 1976. At the Los Angeles Games, eight men's titles will be at stake and the women will contest six. The European countries currently dominate the sport, with the East

Germans holding a virtual monopoly in both men's and women's events.

However, because of their successes before World War II, the United States remain the top nation in terms of Olympic medallists. One of their most famous Olympic champions was John Kelly, father of filmstar Grace Kelly, later to become Princess Grace of Monaco. He captured three sculling titles – and his son, John junior, won a bronze in the 1956 single sculls.

Another famous father and son combination was Julius and Jack Beresford of Britain. Julius was a silver medalist at the 1912 Games and son Jack went on to become the only man to win five Olympic medals – three of them gold – at consecutive Olympics.

Delight at winning an Olympic gold can be shown in many ways. But Vyacheslav Ivanov of the USSR – the only man to win three individual gold medals – regretted his exhuberance on receiving his first gold at Melbourne in 1956. He threw it into the air, missed it on the way down and watched as it disappeared into Lake Wendouree. An extensive search by frogmen failed to find the medal – but the International Olympic Committee eventually provided another.

Rodney Pattisson claimed a gold for Britain in the Flying Dutchman at the 1968 Games

Yachting

There will be added interest in yachting in Los Angeles with the introduction of boardsailing for the first time. Boardsailing is one of the newest events, being pioneered as a sport in 1968 in California. It is widely referred to as 'Windsurfing', but this is technically a trade name.

Charles II has a claim to the title 'father of British yachting'. In 1662 he was involved in the first recorded yacht race, for a £100 stake, against the Duke of York. The contest was run on the Thames between Greenwich and Gravesend with his Royal Highness the winner.

In 1720, the Water Club of the Harbour of Cork was formed – the forerunner of the Royal Cork Yacht Club, which is the oldest yacht club in the world. Once the pastime of the rich, the sport mushroomed with the introduction of cheap lightweight dinghies in the late 1960s.

Yachting was scheduled for inclusion in the first Olympic Games of 1896, but bad weather forced it to be abandoned. In the Paris Games of 1900, events were held on the River Seine and at Le Havre. Over the years, many classes have either been withdrawn from the Olympics, or changed their names. However, the current classes with the first year they appeared in the Olympics are as follows: Finn (1952); Flying Dutchman (1960); International 470 (1976); Soling (1972); Star (1932); Tornado (1976).

In each class, seven races are run over a prescribed course. The fastest time receives 0 points, the runner up 3 points and so on. The lowest six scores count, and at the end, the yacht with the fewest points is the winner. When British pair Rodney Pattisson and Iain McDonald Smith won the Flying Dutchman gold at the 1968 Olympics they had scored only *three* points, the lowest total ever.

Yachting has been one of Britain's most successful Olympic sports. They top the medal table with 29 and, with Norway, are joint leading gold medal winners with 14.

It has had its fair share of Royal competitors since the days of Charles II: Crown Prince Olav of Norway won a gold medal in the 6 metre class at the 1928 Olympics, and Prince Constantine of Greece won gold in the Dragon class at the 1960 Games.

The outstanding Olympic competitor has been Denmark's Paul Elvstrom, winner of the gold in the Finn Class (formerly Firefly) at four consecutive Games from 1948 to 1960. Norway's Magnus Konow holds the longevity record, taking part in both the 1908 and 1948 London Olympics – a span of 40 years.

Jorn Borowski (GDR)

Yachting
Born: January 15, 1959, Rostock,
    East Germany.
Height: 177cm/5ft 9in.
Weight: 72kg/159lb.
Career Highlights
World Championships: *470 class*
    gold 1982.

Jorn Borowski started yachting at the age of nine, and by 14 he had won his first senior national title — the 420 class which he won in the 1973 East German Championships. He will be competing in the 470 class in Los Angeles. In 1982 he won the world title in this category with team-mate Swensson.

Boris Budnikov (URS)

Yachting
Born: February 16, 1942, Balakov,
    USSR.
Height: 170cm/5ft 7in.
Weight: 77kg/170lb.
Career Highlights
Olympic Games: *Soling class* silver
    1980.
World Championships: *Soling
    class* silver 1983.

Boris Budnikov must be the USSR's best chance of a gold medal in the yachting events at the Los Angeles Olympics. Runner up in the Soling class in the 1983 World Championships in Holland, he will go to the 1984 Olympics hoping to improve upon the silver medal he won at the Moscow Games in 1980.
    Boris, who is a radio technician in the armed forces in Moscow, began yachting when he was only 10. He made his international debut in 1961, and won his first national title six years later. He competed in the 1976 Olympics, finishing fourth in the Soling class.

Ian Gordon Ferguson (NZL)

Canoeing
Born: June 20, 1952, New
    Zealand.
Height: 179cm/5ft 10in.
Weight: 83kg/183lb.
Career Highlights
World Championships: *K1, 500
    metres* silver 1983.

Runner up in the K1, 500 metres event at the 1983 World Championships, New Zealander Ian Ferguson will be competing in his second Olympics in 1984. He ranks as one of the best of the non European canoeists in the single craft classes.

Robbie Haines (USA)

Yachting
Born: USA.
Height: 179cm/5ft 10in.
Weight: 77kg/170lb.
Career Highlights
World Championships: *Soling
    class* gold 1979: *Soling class*
    gold 1983.

The United States have a good record in the Soling class at the Olympics. They won the gold medal when the event was first staged in 1972, and a silver the following year.
    The United States did not compete in the Moscow Games of 1980, but they must be confident of regaining the title on home ground in Los Angeles, and will be resting their hopes on helmsman Robbie Haines, the reigning Soling World Champion.

Rudiger Helm (GDR)

Canoeing
Born: October 6, 1956,
    Neubrandenburg, East
    Germany.
Height: 188cm/6ft 2in.
Weight: 90kg/198lb.
Career Highlights
Olympic Games: *K1 1000 metres*
    gold 1976; *K1 500 metres*
    bronze 1976; *K4 1000 metres*
    bronze 1976; *K1 1000 metres*
    gold 1980; *K2 500 metres*
    bronze 1980.

Helm is probably the greatest single-craft canoeist over 1000 metres in the world today. If he wins the 1000 metres kayak singles title at Los Angeles he will be following in the footsteps of the great Gert Fredriksson — who came first in three *successive* games. He goes to Los Angeles as the reigning World Champion in the event and on current form, he should retain his title.
    Rudiger started competitive canoeing when he was 12½ years old, and won his first major title, the K4 title at the 1970 Spartakiad, when only 14. Two years later, he won the kayak singles, pairs and fours in the 1000-metre events at the Spartakiad. In 1978 he won his first world titles — the K1 1000 metres, K4 1000 metres, and K2 500 metres. He has won over 20 national titles.

Lasse Hjortnaes (DEN)

Yachting
Born: October 15, 1960,
    Copenhagen, Denmark.

Height: 192cm/6ft 4in.
Weight: 87kg/192lb.
Career Highlights
World Championships: *Finn class*
    gold 1979.
European Championships: *Finn
    class* gold 1977.

When only 17, Dane Lasse Hjortnaes won the European Finn title in Holland in 1977, and two years later — in Australia — he lifted the world title.
    A member of the KGL Dansk Yacht Club, he competed in his first Olympics in 1980, but disappointed his followers by only finishing 13th. However, he is now more experienced and is confident that his next appearance will show a marked improvement and, hopefully, produce a medal.

Peter Michael Kolbe (GDR)

Rowing
Born: East Germany.
Career Highlights
World Championships: *single
    sculls* gold 1983, gold 1981,
    gold 1978, gold 1975.

The most successful sculler of the past decade, Peter Michael Kolbe will be going to Los Angeles as favourite to win the Olympics title he so narrowly failed to win in Montreal in 1976, when he took the silver medal. The 1984 Games will only be his second Olympics, as he missed the 1980 Games.

Vladek Lacina (TCH)

Rowing
Born: June 25, 1949 Czechoslovakia.
Height: 191cm/6ft 0¾in.
Weight: 89kg/195lb.
Career Highlights
Olympic Games: *single sculls*
    fourth 1980.
World Championship: *single sculls*
    silver 1983.

A finalist in the 1983 World Championship, Vladek will be hoping to improve on his 1980 Olympic position, and take a medal in Los Angeles, but before doing so, knows he will have to overcome Kolbe of East Germany — his conqueror in the World Championships.

Mark Neeleman (HOL)

Yachting
Born: April 16, 1959, Reeuwijk,
    Holland.
Height: 184cm/6ft 0in.

Weight: 84kg/185lb.
Career Highlights
World Championships: *Finn class*
bronze 1979.

A member of the BZV Gouda Yachting Club, Mark Neeleman of Holland will be one of the outsiders in the Finn class at the Los Angeles Olympics. He has gained a lot of experience since his bronze medal in the 1979 World Championships, and is capable of springing a surprise at the Long Beach yachting centre.

He finished a creditable eighth at his first Olympics in Moscow in 1980.

Vladimir Parfenovich (URS)

Canoeing
Born: December 2, 1958, Minsk,
USSR.
Height: 191cm/6ft 3in.
Weight: 91kg/200lb.
Career Highlights
Olympic Games: *K1 500 metres*
gold 1980; *K2 500 metres*
gold 1980; *K2 100 metres* gold
1980.

A Merited Master of Sport in the Soviet Union, Vladimir Parfenovich is the only canoeist to have won three gold medals at *one* Olympics — the 1980 Moscow Games.

He started canoeing in 1973, and the following year made his international debut with the Soviet team.

His first National title came in the K1 500 metres event in 1977, and two years later he won both the K1 and K2 500 metre titles at the World Championships. He has maintained his high level of consistency in World Championships — in the 1983 Championships he won the K1 500 metres title yet again, and took the silver medal in the K2 500 metres event.

Wolf Aberhard Richter

(GDR)
Yachting
Born: June 5, 1953, Berlin, East
Germany.
Height: 172cm/5ft 8in.
Weight: 70kg/154lb.
Career Highlights
Spartakiad: *420 class* gold 1970.

Wolf Richter started sailing at the age of 11, and in 1970, when only 17, he won the 420 class title at the Spartakiad. From then on, his career progressed slowly. He had to wait another nine years before he won his first national title — in the

Soling class.

He went to the 1980 Moscow Olympics as part of the strong East German team but he could only finish eighth in the Star class, with team-mate Olaf Engelhardt.

Whilst his list of championship wins is not impressive, Wolf has the experience needed in the sport, and as yachting is one of those sports where a surprise winner can always come from the 'pack', Wolf must be considered as a medal possibility in Los Angeles.

Antonio Santella (ITA)

Yachting
Born: August 24, 1957, Carrara,
Italy.
Height: 173cm/5ft 8in.
Weight: 79kg/174lb.
Career Highlights
Olympic Games: team reserve
1980.

A medical practitioner, Antonio Santella will be competing in his first Olympics in 1984, when he takes part in the 470 class.

Santella, who is a member of the Carrara Nautical Club, was a reserve for the Italian team that went to Moscow for the 1980 Games, although he never actually competed.

Jochen Schuemann (GDR)

Yachting
Born: June 8, 1954, Berlin, East
Germany.
Height: 188cm/6ft 1in.
Weight: 88kg/194lb.
Career Highlights
Olympic Games: *Finn class* gold
1976.
European Championships: *Finn
class* gold 1983.

Like many of the East German team, Jochen Schuemann started yachting at an early age — he was only 12. He won his first national title in 1973, when he was just 19.

He was the European junior Finn champion in 1974 and retained the title the following year.

These victories made him an automatic choice for the Montreal Olympics, and his selection was fully justified when he became the first East German to win the Finn class Olympic title.

He was not as successful in the 1980 Games where he only managed to finish fifth. However, he won the European title in 1983 and this will have boosted his confidence for the Long Beach Olympic tournament.

Egbert Swensson (GDR)

Yachting
Born: May 24, 1956, Eggesin,
East Germany.
Height: 177cm/5ft 9in.
Weight: 72kg/159lb.
Career Highlights
Olympic Games: *470 class* silver
1980.
World Championships: *470 class*
gold 1982.

An electronics engineer, Egbert Swensson began yachting at the age of 12. In 1969, when only 13, he finished third in the German National 470 Championships, but he had to wait until 1976 for his first national title.

Since then, his international career has flourished, culminating in winning the silver medal at the Moscow Olympics with team-mate Jorn Borowski. Two years later he won the world 470 title, again with Borowski.

Jean Claude Vuithier (SUI)

Yachting
Born: January 19, 1951,
Neuchatel, Switzerland.
Height: 174cm/5ft 9in.
Weight: 65kg/143lb.
Career Highlights
Olympic Games: *Star class*
seventh 1976.

Switzerland is not one of the world's leading nations when it comes to nautical sports, but in Jean Claude Vuithier, they have their best prospect of winning an Olympic yachting gold medal — it would be their first ever.

Jean Claude started yachting in 1971. He used to compete in the Fireball class, but changed to the 470 class in 1975. He changed to the Star class for the 1976 Olympics. During 1983 he has been racing in the Soling class.

He competed in the 1976 Montreal Olympics finishing in a creditable seventh place in the star class. Unfortunately, he could not match this in Moscow and finished 13th — and last. Undaunted by that performance, he will be competing in Los Angeles, now armed with many years' experience.

Reg White (GBR)

Yachting
Born: Brightlingsea, England.
Height: 179cm/5ft 10in.
Weight: 83kg/183lb.
Career Highlights:
Olympic Games: *Tornado class*
gold 1976.

At the 1976 Games, Reg White and his brother-in-law, John Osborn, maintained Great Britain's high standard in the Olympic yachting competition, when they won the gold medal in the Tornado class — Britain's 14th Olympic yachting gold.

Having missed the 1980 Olympics for political reasons, Reg will be back in 1984 hoping to add to Britain's impressive list of Olympic yachting successes.

Reg White . . . gold in the Tornado class in 1976 ▼

Birgit Fischer (GDR)
Canoeing
Born: February 25, 1962, Brandenburg, East Germany.
Height: 173cm/5ft 8in.
Weight: 68kg/150lb.
Career Highlights
Olympic Games: *K1, 500 metres* gold 1980.

Birgit Fischer is the world's outstanding female canoeist, and an odds-on favourite to retain her K1 title in Los Angeles — particularly as she goes to the Games as the reigning World Champion.

She started canoeing in 1975 at the age of 13, and that year won the K1 title at the Spartakiad. In 1979 she won her first national and world titles — both in the 500 metres K4 event.

Jutta Hampe (GDR)
Rowing
Born: January 13, 1960, Weissenfels, East Germany.
Height: 180cm/5ft 11in.
Weight: 72kg/158lb.
Career Highlights
World Championships: *single sculls* gold 1983.

East Germany's Jutta Hampe first hit the headlines in 1977 when she won the single sculls title at the Spartakiad, and in 1983 she won her first world title, beating the USSR's defending champion Irena Fetisova into second place.

Beryl Mitchell (GBR)
Rowing
Born: June 26, 1950, London, England.
Height: 173cm/5ft 8¼in.
Weight: 70kg/155lb.
Career Highlights
Olympic Games: *coxless pairs* tenth 1976: *single sculls* fifth 1980.
World Championships: *Single sculls* silver 1981.

A teacher, Beryl Mitchell represents Britain's best chance of an Olympic medal in 1984. This will be her third successive Olympics, having first appeared in the coxless pairs in 1976, finishing tenth, and in Moscow in 1980 she finished fifth in the single sculls. A silver medal followed in the 1981 World Championships, and in the 1983 World Championships, she slipped to seventh, but won the consolation final.

East Germany's single sculls world champion Jutta Hampe ▶

Cycling

Cycling has always featured in the modern Olympic Games, although today's programme bears little resemblance to the inaugural 1896 series in Athens which involved just 19 riders from five countries contesting six races.

Athens produced the first triple winner in Olympic history, Frenchman Paul Masson who finished first in the one-lap (333.3 metres), 2000 and 10,000 metres events.

Yet just consider the work that went into winning the other three gold medals – Austrian Felix Schmal covering $195\frac{3}{4}$ miles (315km) to win the 12-hour race; Leon Flamond pedalling a dizzy path around 300 laps of the velodrome to score another success for France in the 100 kilometres; and Greek hero Aristidis Konstantinidis winning the road race from Athens to Marathon and back by a 20-minute margin despite wrecking his first bike, riding full tilt into a brick wall on another, and finally finishing on one borrowed from a spectator.

It was an extraordinary start, but indicative of the drama to follow after a track-only programme in Paris in 1900 when Georges Taillandier was recorded as winner of the one recognized event, the sprint.

The name of American Marcus Hurley does not appear on the official roll of honour, although he remains the only cyclist to have won four gold medals at the same Games. Ignorant of the Olympic rules on amateurism, the organizers of the 1904 programme in St Louis caused an uproar by inviting professionals to compete. After lengthy arguments the professionals left to stage their own meeting and amateur Hurley was left to claim track victories over the unusual distances of a quarter, a third, a half and one mile.

In 1908, Britain, the host nation, was extremely successful: home riders won everything except the newly introduced tandem sprint, which went to France, and the individual sprint which was declared void when the time limit expired. Nearly 100 riders took part on a 660-yard (770 metre) track built at London's White City, but the meeting was marred by rain and punctures.

The 1912 programme in Stockholm comprised just one event – a 320-kilometre (199-mile) road race which remains the longest ever. There were 121 starters, despatched at two-minute intervals from 2 o'clock in the morning until early dawn. Winner Rudolf Lewis, of South Africa, took nearly $10\frac{3}{4}$ hours to complete the course.

Harry Ryan and Thomas Lance scored the only British victory still recorded in the official lists when they won the tandem at the 1920 Antwerp Games.

The 1924 road race in Paris was notable for the most convincing winner of the century, Frenchman Armand Blanchonnet who came in nearly 10 minutes clear.

Harry, Percy and Frank Wyld became the first brothers to win medals in the same race when Britain took the team pursuit bronze at Amsterdam in 1928. Frank Southall completed the line-up and also finished second in the road race.

Italy completed a hat-trick of team pursuit golds and extended the sequence to four at Los Angeles in 1932. But four years later their monopoly was ended by France.

Allegations that officials showed favour to the home German riders in Berlin seemed justified after Arie van Vliet, winner of the 1000 metres time trial, was obstructed in the sprint final by German Toni Merkens. The Dutch team lodged a protest which was upheld – but Merkens kept the gold medal and the German federation was fined 100 marks instead.

By the time the 1948 Games came round in London, Reg Harris was world sprint champion and a household name in Britain but he failed to win an Olympic gold. How this came about is part of Olympic legend. Harris almost didn't get to the Games at all. In March of 1948 he suffered a broken neck when his car overturned, and he had only just returned to training – confounding the medical experts – when he crashed and broke an arm. On top of that, he was excluded from the team for refusing to train with his colleagues and was only reinstated at the last moment. In the end, Italy's Mario Ghella proved too fast for Harris and won the sprint final in two straight rides.

A bicycle built for two . . . 1908 tandem champions Maurice Schilles and André Auffray of France

The 4 kilometre pursuit race in Amsterdam 1928 ▶

Reg Harris . . . a broken neck cost him Olympic gold ▼

The tandem also held centre stage in Helsinki in 1952 when bespectacled Australian Russell Mockridge, who had retired two years earlier to join the Church and then returned to win a sprint silver medal at the 1951 World Championships, teamed up with Lionel Cox for the first time ever and promptly won the gold. Mockridge, killed in a road accident at the age of 30, also won the 1000 metres time trial.

Italian all-rounder Leandro Faggin was the personality of the Melbourne Games in 1956, winning the 1000 metres and also leading his country to victory in the team pursuit.

A shadow was cast over the sport by events in Rome four years later. Knud Jensen, a 22-year-old Danish rider, died during the inaugural 100-kilometre team time trial and although the official report cited sunstroke, it was later confirmed that drugs – nicotinyl tartrate, a mild vasociliator used to aid blood supply to muscles – had been a contributory factor. Italy won every event except the road race in which Viktor Kapitonov beat Livio Trape by inches to win the USSR's first cycling gold.

Czechoslovakia won a first gold at Tokyo in 1964, through Jiri Daler in the individual pursuit, introduced for the first time.

Contrasting Frenchmen Daniel Morelon, lean and slender, and Pierre Trentin, a broad, stocky figure, dominated the Mexico track programme in 1968. Morelon won the first of his two sprint gold medals, Trentin set a world record of 1:03.91 sec in the 1000 metres, and the two won the tandem.

West Germany finished a clear first in the team pursuit final against Denmark and were then disqualified for an illegal push, given – in a costly act of exuberance – by Karl-Heinz Henrichs to team-mate Jurgen Kissner in the closing stages when the race had been won.

On the road the remarkable Pettersson brothers – Eric, Gosta, Sture and Tomas – won a silver medal for Sweden in the team time trial.

In Munich in 1972, Norway won a first cycling gold, through Knut Knudsen in the individual pursuit. The same event produced the man of the 1976 Montreal Games, 20-year-old West German, Gregor Braun, who added a second gold in the team race. The tandem, considered too dangerous by many countries, was taken out of the programme.

Moscow's super-fast indoor wooden arena at Krylatskoye witnessed a first gold for Switzerland when Robert Dill-Bundi won the individual pursuit and a string of records, headed by the 1:02.955 1000 metres time trial of East German Lothar Thoms. He won by almost two full seconds, while Sergei Soukhoroutchenkov, of the USSR, finished three minutes clear in the road race.

And so to 1984 when two new events are added to the programme, a 50-kilometre points race for men and a road race for women who make their first appearance in Olympic cycling.

But for sheer drama, nothing has ever matched the Britain versus Italy tandem final, Harris and Alan Bannister against Ferdinando Teruzzi and Renato Perona. The programme overran to such an extent that the deciding third ride – Harris and Bannister winning the first match, the Italians the next – was run in near darkness. With no floodlights at the Herne Hill track, the white of the British jerseys was all that could be seen across the track from the home straight. Coming off the final bend, the British pair might have been ahead – but by the line it was the Italians first by less than half a wheel. Journalists used matches and torches to file their dramatic copy from unlit booths.

Craig Adair (NZL)
1000m time trial
Born: January 31, 1963,
  Christchurch, New Zealand.
Height: 183cm/6ft 0in.
Weight: 82kg/180lb.
Career Highlights
World Championships: *1000m
  time trial* fifth 1983.
Commonwealth Games: *1000m
  time trial* gold 1982.

He made his international entry at the 1981 Junior World Championships, finishing sixth, and won the Commonwealth title in Brisbane by the convincing margin of almost a second. His enormous potential was again underlined at the 1983 World Championships when, unsettled after a puncture, he

Bernd Drogan of East
Germany . . . went it alone
to the world title ▼

came back for a re-run and covered the last 333m lap faster than anyone else in the field.

Mark Barry (GBR)
Sprint and 1000m time trial
Born: May 13, 1964, Leeds,
  England.
Height: 168cm/5ft 6in.
Weight: 69kg/154lb.
Career Highlights
Junior World Championships:
  sprint seventh 1982; *1000m
  time trial* seventh 1982.
Commonwealth Games: *sprint*
  quarter-finalist 1982; *1000m
  time trial* seventh 1982.

Regarded as Britain's best sprint prospect since the golden era of Reg Harris, Barry won his first senior British title within days of returning from the 1982 Junior World Championships — where he

was the only rider to score a win over the USSR's eventual gold medallist Nikolai Kovche — and retained his title in 1983.

Steven Bauer (CAN)
Road race and points race
Born: June 12, 1959, St
  Catharines, Ontario, Canada.
Height: 172cm/5ft 8in.
Weight: 71kg/156lb.
Career Highlights
World Championships: *points race*
  fourth 1981; *points race* eighth
  1982.
Commonwealth Games: *road race*
  silver 1982.

One of the few riders of genuine world class both on the track and on the road, he missed out to England's Malcolm Elliott by inches in a sprint finish to the Commonwealth Games road race in Brisbane.

Falk Boden (GDR)
Road race and team time trial
Born: January 20, 1960,
  Elsterwerda, East Germany.
Height: 183cm/6ft 0in.
Weight: 74kg/162lb.
Career Highlights
Olympic Games: *team time trial*
  silver 1980.
World Championships: *team time
  trial* gold 1981, 1979.

A double Junior World Champion for the team time trial, Boden has been developing his solo talents in the last three seasons and won the 1983 Prague-Warsaw-Berlin Peace Race before finishing eighth in the world championship road race.

Bernd Drogan (GDR)
Road race and team time trial
Born: October 26, 1955, Dobern,
  East Germany.
Height: 181cm/5ft 11½in.
Weight: 71kg/156lb.
Career Highlights
Olympic Games: *team time trial*
  silver 1980.
World Championships: *road race*
  gold 1982, bronze 1979; *team
  time trial* gold 1981, 1979.

Racing internationally for over a decade, Drogan has been a prolific winner. He gambled on a lone break in the 1982 World Championship road race at Goodwood, and although tiring in the last few miles, judged his effort perfectly to hold off the closing pack by a few seconds.

Rolf Golz (FRG)
Pursuit and team pursuit
Born: September 30, 1962, Bad
Scussanried, West Germany.
Height: 176cm/5ft 9½in.
Weight: 70kg/155lb.
Career Highlights
World Championships: *team
pursuit* gold 1983; *pursuit*
silver 1982.

Golz reversed the usual pattern of
progress in 1982 – moving from
the road, where he finished second
in the West German Championships, to the track where he was a
surprise silver medallist at the
World Championships. He saved
his best for the team pursuit in
1983 and was the strong man of
his country's successful bid for
gold over the might of Eastern
Europe.

Mark Gorski (USA)
Sprint
Born: January 6, 1960, Itasca,
Illinois, USA.
Height: 185cm/6ft 1in.

Weight: 84kg/185lb.
Career Highlights
World Championships: *sprint* fifth
1983.

One of the new breed of American
male cyclists coming to the fore as
the sport's popularity increases on
the other side of the Atlantic,
Gorski beat then world champion
Sergei Kopylov on home ground
early in 1983 and overcame early
tactical errors at the World Championships to finish well up the list.

Lutz Hesslich (GDR)
Sprint
Born: January 17, 1959, Ortrand,
East Germany.
Height: 185cm/6ft 1in.
Weight: 82kg/180ib.
Career Highlights
Olympic Games: *sprint;* gold
1980.
World Championships: *sprint* gold
1983, 1979, silver 1982,
1981, bronze 1977.

Hesslich against Sergei Kopylov, a

rematch of the 1980 sprint final in
Moscow, is a mouth-watering prospect. The East German won that
one, then had to play second fiddle
to his friend and rival for two seasons before winning the 1983
World Championship. He also won
a junior world title and is a popular
figure on the Grand Prix circuit.

Juri Kashirin (URS)
Road race and team time trial
Born: January 20, 1959
Storozhevoye, USSR.
Height: 182cm/6ft 0in.
Weight: 78kg/171lb.
Career Highlights
Olympic Games: *team time trial*
gold 1980.
World Championships: *team time
trial* gold 1983, silver 1981,
bronze 1982.

The anchor man of the USSR's
time trial quartet is also an accomplished solo rider and British fans
well know his capabilities from
overall Milk Race victories in both
1979 and 1982.

The strong man of West ▲
Germany, Rolf Golz

Sergei Kopylov (URS)
Sprint and 1000m time trial
Born: July 29, 1960, Tula, USSR.
Height: 175cm/5ft 9in.
Weight: 77kg/169lb.
Career Highlights
Olympic Games: *sprint* bronze 1980.
World Championships: *1000m time trial* gold 1983, bronze 1981; *sprint* gold 1982, silver 1983.
Record
World indoor: *flying start* (1:0.249secs) 1982, *100m* (1:0.279) 1982.

If he wasn't a champion cyclist the flamboyant Kopylov would surely be a circus star. A superbly compact and powerful rider, he has entertained crowds everywhere with his repertoire of trick riding — usually to celebrate a victory.

Viktor Koupovets (URS)
Pursuit
Born: 1964, Moscow, USSR.
Height: 175cm/5ft 9in.
Weight: 70kg/155lb.
Career Highlights
World Championships: *pursuit* gold 1983.
Record
World indoor: *4000m pursuit* (4:37.687) 1983; *outdoor 4000m pursuit* (4:37.31) 1983.

He was unknown until he arrived in Switzerland for the 1983 World Championships and destroyed the opposition in the individual pursuit. Slight of build but a superbly fluent rider, Koupovets appears unstoppable.

Alexandr Krasnov (URS)
Pursuit and team pursuit
Born: April 7, 1960, Leningrad, USSR.
Height: 176cm/5ft 9½in.
Weight: 70kg/155lb.
Career Highlights
World Championships: *team pursuit* gold 1982, silver 1981.

The most experienced member of Russia's team pursuit squad, he is also an accomplished individual rider and gold medallist at the 1983 World Student Games.

Dainis Liepinch (URS)
Pursuit
Born: August 13, 1962, Riga, USSR.
Height: 184cm/6ft 0½in.
Weight: 78kg/171lb.
Career Highlights
World Championships: *pursuit* silver 1981, bronze 1983.

Junior world pursuit champion in 1980, the stocky Soviet hasn't fulfilled his promise at senior level yet, although he is on the fringe of a gold medal performance.

Olaf Ludwig (GDR)
Road race and team time trial
Born: April 13, 1960, Gera, East Germany.
Height: 182cm/6ft 0in.
Weight: 75kg/165lb.
Career Highlights
World Championships: *team time trial* gold 1981; *road race* sixth 1983.
Olympic Games: *team trial* silver 1980.

Ludwig was the world junior road race champion in 1977 and 1978. He cost East Germany their medal chance when he blew up in the 1983 World Championship time trial, but came back three days later to produce a fine ride in the solo race.

Detlef Macha of East Germany . . . greatness spoiled by inconsistency ▼

Detlef Macha (GDR)
Pursuit and team pursuit
Born: December 13, 1958, Greize, East Germany.
Height: 184cm/6ft 0½in.
Weight: 71kg/156lb.
Career Highlights
World Championships: *pursuit* gold 1982, 1981, 1978; *team pursuit* bronze 1982.

Whatever Macha's qualities as a three-time world champion, consistency isn't one of them. The year after winning his first gold he could only finish tenth. He did not ride at the Moscow Olympics, and in 1983 he failed to qualify for the last 16 after dominating the 1982 pursuit series at Leicester.

◀◀ *Dainis Liepinch of the USSR . . . yet to fulfil his youthful potential*

Michael Marcussen (DEN)
Points race
Born: January 9, 1955,
    Copenhagen, Denmark.
Height: 185cm/6ft 1in.
Weight: 80kg/176lb.
Career Highlights
World Championships: *points race*
    gold 1983, silver 1982, bronze
    1981, fifth 1980.

Denmark's Michael
Marcussen . . . Olympic
gold before professional
cash
▼

He has refused several tempting offers to turn professional in order to ride in Los Angeles, and will be a clear favourite to win the points race, which is included in the programme for the first time. He has an early morning cleaning job to help meet training expenses, and survived a mid-race crash to win the world title in 1983 and complete a set of medals.

Uwe Raab (GDR)
Road race
Born: July 26, 1962, Wittenberg,
    East Germany.
Height: 178cm/5ft 10½in.
Weight: 72kg/158lb.
Career Highlights
World Championships: *road race*
    gold 1983.

Best of the new breed of East German road men to enter the international scene, he proved too strong for Swiss rider Niki Ruettimann — now professional — in a two-up sprint to win the World Championship 1983 road race.

Fredy Schmidtke (FRG)
1000 time trial
Born: March 1, 1961, Cologne,
    West Germany.
Height: 191cm/6ft 3½in.
Weight: 88kg/193lb.
Career Highlights
World Championships: *1000m*
    time trial silver 1981, gold
    1982; *sprint* seventh 1981,
    eighth 1982.

The tallest of the leading track riders, Schmidtke was Junior World Champion in both the sprint and 1000 metres time trial in 1979. He made steady progress as a senior before ending the reign of seemingly invincible kilometre king Lothar Thoms at Leicester in 1982.

Sergei Soukhorouchenkov (URS)
Road race
Born: August 10, 1956,
    Trotsnaya, USSR.
Height: 175cm/5ft 9in.
Weight: 72kg/158lb.
Career Highlights
Olympic Games: *road race* gold
    1980.

He was a clear favourite to win the road race in Moscow four years ago and justified the tag with a brilliantly efficient ride to the gold medal.

He dominated amateur racing to the extent that cycling magazines were full of stories comparing him with the leading professional riders of the time and how he would fare if allowed in the Tour de France.

Alex Stieda (CAN)
Pursuit
Born: April 13, 1961, Belleville,
    Ontario, Canada.
Height: 180cm/5ft 11in.
Weight: 79kg/173lb.
Career Highlights
Commonwealth Games: *pursuit*
    bronze 1982.

He finished fifth in the 1979 Junior World Championship pursuit, but, although obviously capable, has yet to show his best and has been erratic.

Alexandr Panfilov (URS)
1000m time trial
Born: October 11, 1960,
    Leningrad, USSR.
Height: 175cm/5ft 9in.
Weight: 75kg/165lb.
Career Highlights
Olympic Games: *1000m time trial*
    silver 1980.

Tall in the saddle . . . West
Germany's giant Fredy
Schmidtke ▶ ▶

Of strikingly similar build to Sergei Kopylov who won the 1983 world kilometre title, Panfilov wasn't far away from gold in Moscow and will be an excellent number two.

Lothar Thoms (GDR)
1000m time trial
Born: May 18, 1956, Guben, East
　　Germany.
Height: 179cm/5ft 10½in.
Weight: 77kg/169lb.
Career Highlights
Olympic Games: *1000m time trial*
　　gold 1980.
World Championships: gold 1981,
　　1979, 1978, 1977, silver
　　1982, bronze 1983.
Records: *1000m time trial (indoor
　　standing start)* (1:02.955)
　　1980.

One of the all-time greats of track
racing, the balding East German
dominated the kilometre for five
years from his first gold medal
success in 1977. And he is still a
force to be reckoned with despite
defeat at the last two World
Championships.

Richard Trinkler (SUI)
Road race and team time trial
Born: August 22, 1950,
　　Winterthur, Switzerland.
Height: 176cm/5ft 9½in.
Weight: 68kg/149lb.
Career Highlights
World Championships: *team time
　　trial* silver 1982, bronze 1978,
　　fourth 1978.

*East Germany's swooping
bald eagle . . . Lothar Thoms*
▶ ▶

There will be no more experienced
competitor in the Olympic cycling
events than Trinkler, who has had
his opportunities to turn professional but opted to stay an
amateur.

Kenrick Tucker (AUS)
Sprint
Born: December 6, 1959,
　　Rockhampton, Queensland,
　　Australia.
Height: 182cm/6ft 0in.
Weight: 92kg/202lb.
Career Highlights
Olympic Games: *sprint* seventh
　　1980.
World Championships: *sprint*
　　seventh 1981, *1000m time
　　trial;* fifth 1981.
Commonwealth Games: *sprint*
　　gold 1982, 1978; *1000m time
　　trial* silver 1978.

Hit by illness and injury last season, Tucker also had to climb off
his sickbed to win the 1982
Commonwealth sprint title in front
of an enthusiastic home crowd.

Michael Turtur (AUS)
Pursuit

Born: July 2, 1958, St Agnes,
　　South Australia.
Height: 178cm/5ft 10in.
Weight: 76kg/168lb.
Career Highlights
Commonwealth Games: *pursuit*
　　gold 1982.

He beat England's Shaun Wallace
by less than half a second to win
the Commonwealth gold in Brisbane. The Adelaide carpenter disappointed at the 1983 World
Championships, but is so determined to reach the top at world
level that he has spent time training in East Germany with their top
coaches.

Shaun Wallace (GBR)
Pursuit
Born: November 20, 1961,
　　Christchurch, Hampshire,
　　England.
Height: 171cm/5ft 7½in.
Weight: 65kg/143lb.
Career Highlights
Commonwealth Games: *pursuit*
　　silver 1982.

He rode a personal best at the
1983 World Championships without managing to survive the first
round. But the British champion is
a fighter, leading the final of the
Commonwealth Games pursuit
until the very last 200 metres, and
follows Tony Doyle, Hugh Porter
and Ian Hallam in an event where
Britain is traditionally strong.

David Weller (JAM)
1000m time trial
Born: February 11, 1957,
　　Kingston, Jamaica.
Height: 186cm/6ft 1in.
Weight: 81kg/180lb.
Career Highlights
Olympic Games: *1000m time trial*
　　bronze 1980.
Commonwealth Games: *sprint*
　　bronze 1978; *1000m time trial*
　　fourth 1982.

He will be riding in his third Olympic Games. A surprise medallist in
Moscow, Weller has been quiet
since, as his studies — in America
— have taken preference, but his
ability is beyond doubt.

Marianne Berglund (SWE)

Women's road race
Born: July 23, 1963 Skelleftea,
    Sweden.
Height: 160cm/5ft 3in.
Weight: 52kg/114lb.
Career Highlights
World Championships: *women's
    road race* gold 1983.

Having competed in world championships since the age of 16, Berglund became Sweden's first ever women's cycling world champion in Switzerland in 1983. She should feel perfectly at home in Los Angeles, as she did much of her training in the US before her gold medal success last year.

Connie Carpenter-Phinney

(USA)
Women's road race
Born: February 26, 1957,
    Madison, Wisconsin, USA.
Height: 178cm/5ft 10in.
Weight: 55kg/120lb.
Career Highlights
World Championships: *pursuit*
    gold 1983, silver 1982; *road
    race* silver 1977, bronze 1981.

The absence of women's track racing from the Olympic programme

◄
*Sweden's first woman world
champion . . . Marianne
Berglund*

means that the tall American girl must bid for gold in her number two event. But she will be one of the most experienced and consistently successful road racers in the field.

Rebecca Twigg (USA)

Women's road race

Born: March 26, 1963, Seattle,
    Washington, USA.
Height: 171cm/5ft 7in.
Weight: 57kg/125lb.
Career Highlights
World Championships: *road race*
    silver 1983; *pursuit* gold 1982,
    sixth 1982; fifth 1981.

She missed the 1983 World Track Championships in order to concentrate on the road race – with the Olympics the main reason – and only missed a gold medal by inches.

*Connie Carpenter-Phinney
of America . . . confined to
the roads*
◄ ◄

Catherine Swinnerton

(GBR)
Women's road race
Born: May 12, 1958,
    Stoke-on-Trent, England.
Height: 167cm/5ft 6in.
Weight: 53kg/115lb.
Career Highlights
World Championships: *women's
    road race* ninth 1977, tenth
    1983.

She takes over from now retired Mandy Jones, the 1982 world champion, as Britain's gold medal hope in the first ever Olympic women's race. Experienced, Catherine rode her first World Championships in 1975 and has performed at a consistently high level since; winning British championship medals at will on the road and track.

She comes from a cycling family well versed in the art of winning and, but for crashes in both 1981 and 1982, could already have been a World Championship medallist.

Equestrianism

Big sister, rather than big brother, could be the dominating force in 1984. Britain, which has a proud record of galloping away with medals from major competition, has an equestrian task force for the Los Angeles Olympics which is spearheaded by a formidable line up of femmes fatale. While Cram, Ovett and Coe chase glory on the track, three day eventers Lucinda Green, Rachel Bayliss and Virginia Holgate can help make it a golden summer. All have the right pedigree — and horse power — to succeed at the top. Lucinda is the current world champion, taking the title on *Regal Realm* at Luhmuhlen in 1982 when Britain (Rachel and Virginia included) also won the team gold. This tough, talented trio were again in stunning form in 1983 with Lucinda winning Badminton for a record fifth time, Rachel the European championships at Frauenfeld in Switzerland and Virginia taking Burghley.

An Olympic medal is the only honour to elude Lucinda who will have the added spur of family support. Her husband David, who formerly rode for Australia, has been granted British citizenship and is eligible for the team. Both are sponsored by John Burbidge, an ambitious London businessman whose company, SR Direct Mail, is backing them with £150,000 over three years.

Richard Meade, the fourth member of the team that won the world championships, is one of Britain's finest Olympians. He already has three gold medals, having appeared in four Olympics since Tokyo in 1964. He won team gold in 1968 and again in Munich in 1972 when he also rode *Laurieston* to individual victory.

For various reasons, Britain's show jumpers have a considerably tougher assignment although, here too, the squad is graced by a woman capable of keeping the flag flying when the medals are handed out. Lesley McNaught, only 20 in February 1984, is a girl for the big occasion and the Olympics have been her target since she exploded onto the scene in 1981. That year she became European junior champion on *One More Time,* won the British Ladies' championship and became the youngest amateur champion. But in the summer of 1983 she surprisingly left the powerful Ted Edgar stable in Warwickshire after five successful years. Ted and his wife Liz, one of Britain's top professional show jumpers, first spotted Lesley when she was a 14-year-old schoolgirl riding a pony at a small show. *'It was obvious she had an outstanding talent,'* said Edgar who has also guided the brilliant career of Nick Skelton.

Skelton turned professional in 1982 after helping Britain win a team silver at the 'Alternative Olympics', staged after most of the equestrian world boycotted the Moscow Games in 1980.

John Whitaker, who was also in that team, has remained an amateur, however, and he and his brother Michael will instil much needed experience into a squad deprived of the professionalism of David Broome, Harvey Smith and Malcolm Pyrah. Broome and company have been declared ineligible for Olympics, although the top riders of other nations, who are in a similar position, will be at Los Angeles. *'We take a somewhat stricter line than other countries over the distinction between amateur and professional,'* admitted Major-General Jack Reynolds, director general of the British Equestrian Federation.

Britain's chances of winning their first show jumping medal since Ann Moore pocketed silver in Munich 12 years ago, are also affected by the limited choice of available horses. Team captain Ronnie Massarella declares that: *'To win gold we need to buy the right horses and have them and the riders trained by the best people in the country.'*

John Whitaker has an invaluable horse in *Ryan's Son* but the bay is now 15 and has been travelling the world's circuits for eight years. He showed no signs of staleness last year, carrying John to triumph in the Hickstead Derby and silver in the European Championships. Whitaker finished leading international prize winner, netting over £40,000. But an Olympic medal remains his priority and has been for the last eight years. He was also leading money winner in 1976 when he was shortlisted for the Olympics but was dropped, humiliatingly, after *Ryan's Son* refused in the final trial. Britain returned from Montreal empty handed.

The competition in Los Angeles will be fierce with America, West Germany and France all in with golden chances. Home advantage to the Americans will be substantial. Time and again, horses forced to travel long distances have failed to adjust. The Americans also have proven riders, a fact highlighted by their astonishing success in the annual World Cup.

Since Austrian Hugo Simon won the inaugural Cup in 1979, the United States have dominated, winning with Conrad Homfeld, Michael Matz, Melanie Smith and Norman dello Joio in successive years.

West Germany can boast Paul Schockemohle, who won the Euro-

Raimondo d'Inzeo of Italy whose career spanned eight Olympics ▶

Harry Llewellyn and Foxhunter, *who clinched Britain's lone gold medal of the 1952 Games in the Grand Prix jumping team event*

pean championship from John Whitaker on the great *Deister,* and current world champion Norbert Koof, the young farmer who took the title ahead of Pyrah in Dublin in 1982.

Whitaker again had to settle for silver at the 'Alternative Olympics' where Simon took the gold with Canada winning team gold and Britain the silver. France posted their Olympic challenge, winning team gold at the world championships to supplement the triumph of their three day event quartet, which included the Touzaint brothers Jean-Yves and Thierry, at the 1980 compensatory event before a crowd of 80,000 in Fontainebleau.

Sweden has also emerged as a force in eventing, winning the team gold at the European championships in Switzerland in 1983. Whatever the outcome one thing is certain. The Soviet Union won't ride away with gold as she did in Moscow in 1980. Response to the invasion of Afghanistan left only three non Iron Curtain countries involved in equestrianism at the Olympics — Mexico, Italy and India — and the Soviet team swept the board, winning in show jumping, eventing and dressage. With all the great equestrian nations staging their own breakaway competition — there were more countries at the alternative than in Moscow — never was an Olympic gold won so cheaply.

Equestrianism first entered the Olympics as chariot races, when individual horses and riders appeared in 648 BC. The first gold medallist of the modern era was Belgium's Aime Haegman and his outstanding horse *Benton II,* who triumphed in the Paris show jumping of 1900.

The competition has since attracted some great names. West Germany's Hans-Gunter Winkler captured five gold medals, a silver and a bronze in five Olympics from 1956-1972 and Italy's Raimondo d'Inzeo graced eight Games from 1948-1976 winning a gold, two silvers and three bronzes.

Stockholm, 1956, was the only Games in which the equestrianism

▲
▲
Top: Britain's Pat Smythe,
first woman to win
a medal in Olympic
equestrianism (with Tosca)

▲
Above:
Austrian Hugo Simon,
winner of the inaugural
World Cup, on Sorry

events have been held separately from the other sports. The break was necessary because the Olympics were being held in Melbourne and Australia has stringent quarantine rules. It was in these 1956 equestrian games that Britain's Pat Smythe won a bronze. Britain claimed another record in 1972 when Lorna Johnstone, competing in the dressage, became the oldest Olympic female participant of all time at the age of 70 years and five days.

Rachel Bayliss (GBR)
Eventing
Born: April 28, 1950, Bewdley,
    Worcestershire, England.
Height: 168cm/5ft 6in.
Weight: 59kg/129lb.
Career Highlights
World Championships: *team* gold
    1982.
European Championships:
    individual gold 1983, silver
    1979; *team* gold 1981.
Midland Bank Open: champion
    1976.
Burghley: runner up 1978.
Badminton: third 1982.

Rachel Bayliss, competing as one
of Britain's two individual entries,
took the silver medal in the 1979
European Championships in
Luhmuhlen and in 1983 went one
better. Against all the odds she
captured the gold at Frauenfeld in
Switzerland to stake her claim for
Los Angeles. The previous year she
was third at Badminton with *Mystic Minstrel* and it earned her a
place in the team which took the
gold medal in the World Championships in Luhmuhlen.

Goran Breisner (SWE)
Eventing
Born: July 1, 1954, Malmo,
    Sweden.
Height: 177cm/5ft 9½in.
Weight: 61kg/136lb.
Career Highlights
Badminton: third 1980, fourth
    1981.
Burghley: fifth 1979.
Boekelo: third 1982.
European Championships: *team*
    gold 1983.

Goran Breisner has been based
with fellow countryman Lars
Sederholm, a leading show jumping and event trainer, at the Water-
stock training centre in Oxfordshire
since 1978. Partnering *Ultimus* he
was fifth at Burghley in 1979 and
the following year was third at
Badminton. The horse developed a
chill a few days before the 1982
World Championships but last year
Breisner made up for that disappointment, helping Sweden to the
gold medal in the European
Championships at Frauenfeld,
Switzerland.

Cottier made an impact in 1978 as
a dashing member of the young
French Nations Cup team that won
in Rome. He captured the French
title in 1980 and featured in five
winning Nations Cup teams in
Rome, Aachen, Liége, Paris and
Toronto. In 1982 — with Patrick
Caron, Michel Robert and Gilles
Bertran de Balanda — he won team
gold at the World Championships
in Dublin.

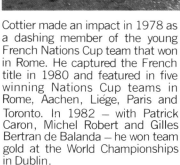

Frederic Cottier (FRA)
Show jumping
Born: February 5, 1954, Paris,
    France.
Height: 170cm/5ft 7in.
Weight: 68kg/148lb.
Career Highlights
World Championships: *team* gold
    1982.

Bruce Davidson (USA)
Eventing
Born: December 13, 1949,
    Massachussetts, USA.
Height: 183cm/6ft 0in.
Weight: 74kg/162lb.
Career Highlights
Olympic Games: *team* gold 1976,
    team silver 1972.

World Championships: gold 1978,
    1974; *team* gold 1974.
Badminton: runner-up 1982.
Pan American Games: *team* gold
    1975.
US Open: champion 1981, 1975.

▲
*American Bruce Davidson
with* Might Tango

▲

▲
Rachel Bayliss with Mystic
Minstrel

Bruce Davidson, a mainstay of the American eventing team, is the only rider to have won the World Championship twice. Selected as a 20-year-old, he was in the team which took the silver in Munich.

In 1974 he won the first of his world titles with *Irish Cap*, beating fellow American Michael Plumb into second place. On the same horse he helped the States take team gold at the 1976 Montreal Olympics and two years later retained his world title in his own country.

David Green (AUS)
Eventing
Born: February 28, 1960, Brisbane, Australia.
Height: 180.5cm/5ft 11in.
Weight: 65.5kg/143lb.
Career Highlights
Badminton: sixth 1982.
Punchestown: champion 1982.
Burghley: eighth 1983.

David is beginning to emerge from the shadow of his world champion wife, the former Lucinda Prior-Palmer. He finished a promising sixth at Badminton in 1982 and the following year was up with the leaders. He also impressed at Burghley last year when he partnered *Super Salesman*, competing in his

A Royal pupil... Niels Haagensen of Denmark ▼

first major international, to eighth place.

Lucinda Green, MBE (GBR)
Eventing
Born: November 7, 1953, London, England.
Height: 173cm/5ft 8in.
Weight: 61kg/135lb.
Career Highlights
World Championships: gold 1982: *team* gold 1982.
European Championships: gold 1977, 1975; *team* silver 1975.
Badminton: *champion* 1983, 1979, 1977, 1976, 1973; *runner-up* 1980, 1978; *third* 1977.
Burghley: *champion* 1981, 1977; *runner-up* 1982, 1976.

Lucinda Green confirmed her reputation as the outstanding woman in eventing when she won the individual World Championship at Luhmuhlen in September 1982 with *Regal Realm.* She followed it up seven months later with a record-breaking fifth victory at Badminton, the three day event Spring classic. Her triumph put her one up on Captain Mark Phillips who has won Badminton four times. Her first major success abroad came in 1975 when she rode *Be Fair* – a fifteenth birthday present from her parents – to victory in the 1975 European Championships with Princess Anne finishing second.

Lucinda had to withdraw during the 1976 Montreal Olympics when *Be Fair* injured a hock, but the following year she won the European title for a second time and became the first rider to win Badminton and Burghley in the same season.

Niels Haagensen (DEN)
Eventing
Born: May 20, 1955, Haestved, Copenhagen, Denmark.
Height: 180.5cm/5ft 11in.
Weight: 73kg/160lb.
Career Highlights
Alternative Olympics: gold 1980.
European Championships: gold 1979.

Niels Haagensen switched from specialized dressage – he was in Denmark's 1976 Olympic team in Montreal – to eventing with stunning success. Riding *Monaco* he won the European title in Luhmuhlen only thirteen months after taking up his new sport.

In the Spring of 1980 he continued the learning process and stayed with Mark Phillips and Princess Anne at Gatcombe Park while competing in trials around the

country. Haagensen followed up his European victory with an even finer achievement, taking the gold in the Alternative Olympics at Fontainebleau on the 13-year-old *Monaco*, who was then retired.

Virginia Holgate (GBR)
Eventing
Born: February 2, 1955, Malta.
Height: 168cm/5ft 6in.
Weight: 59kg/130lb.
Career Highlights
World Championships: *team* gold 1982.
European Championships: *team* gold 1981.
European Junior Championships: *individual* gold 1973; *team* gold 1973.
Mini-Olympics: three-day event champion 1975.
Midland Bank: champion 1982, 1981.
Badminton: fourth 1982.
Burghley: champion; 1983; fifth 1982; third 1981.

Virginia Holgate was a member of Britain's gold medal winning teams at the European and World Championships in 1981 and 1982. But she gained her greatest individual success last September when winning Burghley for the first time. She led from start to finish on her talented horse *Priceless* – highlighting a remarkable comeback by both rider and animal.

Miss Holgate broke her left arm in 23 places after a fall in 1977 and two years ago *Priceless* contracted a rare infection and was out of action for several months before fighting his way back to health.

Andrew Hoy (AUS)
Eventing
Born: February 8, 1959, Cukairn, NSW, Australia.
Height: 170cm/5ft 7in.
Weight: 64kg/141lb.
Career Highlights
Alternative Olympics: *team* bronze 1980.
World Championships: ninth 1982.
Burghley: champion 1979.

Andrew Hoy came to Britain as a 20-year-old unknown eventer in 1978 and was a guest of Captain Mark Phillips and Princess Anne. In 1979 he upstaged his hosts and surprised everyone by winning Burghley on his own horse *Davy*. The following year he was a member of the Australian team which came third at the Alternative Olympics in Fontainebleau.

Norbert Koof (FRG)
Eventing
Born: September 13, 1955,
    Dusseldorf, West Germany.
Height: 188cm/6ft 2in.
Weight: 71kg/156lb.
Career Highlights
World Championships: gold 1982.
European Championships: *team*
    gold 1981.
European Junior Championships:
    individual bronze 1973.
German Championships:
    runner-up 1977.
German Junior Championships:
    champion 1972.

Norbert Koof set show jumping alight when he won the individual gold medal at the 1982 World Championships in Dublin on a horse called *Fire*. Koof, a farmer, was the newcomer in the star-studded West German team and was a 66-1 outsider. But on the giant nine-year-old *Fire* he gave a superb display of horsemanship to relegate Britain's Malcolm Pyrah to second place with Frenchman Michel Robert taking the bronze.

Koof was the third West German in succession to win the world title following Hartwig Steenken in 1974 and Gerd Wiltfang in 1978.

Mark Laskin (CAN)
Show jumping
Born: 1952, Edmonton, Canada.
Height: 178cm/5ft 10in.
Weight: 73kg/160lb.
Career Highlights
Alternative Olympics: *team* gold
    1980.
Rothmans Equestrian of the Year
    Award: 1981, 1980, 1979,
    1978.

Laskin, who also enjoys skiing and playing hockey, was the youngest Canadian rider at the Alternative Olympics in 1980 and led his team to the gold medal with two clear rounds. He won two World Cup Grand Prix in 1979 in Vancouver and Toronto plus the New York World Cup qualifier.

Michael Matz (USA)
Show jumping
Born: January 23, 1951,
    Pennsylvania, USA.
Height: 183cm/6ft 0in.
Weight: 70.5kg/155lb.
Career Highlights
Olympic Games: *team;* fourth
    1976.
World Championships: bronze
    1978.
World Cup: champion 1981.
Pan Am Games: *team* gold 1979,
    1975; *individual* gold 1979.

Matz's career took flight when he gained the ride on the American thoroughbred *Jet Run* from Mexico's Fernando Senderos. They were bronze medallists at the 1978 World Championships at Aachen and the following year captured the individual gold at the Pan Am Games in Puerto Rico.

Matz was among the favourites to win the Olympic gold at Moscow before America pulled out in protest at the Soviet invasion of Afghanistan. He gained some compensation in 1981 by winning the World Cup in Birmingham (England) on *Jet Run* in front of compatriot Donald Cheska.

Matz followed in the footsteps of another American, Conrad Homfeld, who won the 1980 final in Baltimore. Americans continued to dominate the World Cup with Melanie Smith winning in Gothenburg in 1982 and Norman Dello Joio in Vienna a year later.

▲
*World Champion Norbert
Koof of West Germany*

*Michael Matz achieves lift
off with* Jet Run
◄

Lesley McNaught (GBR)
Show jumping
Born: February 10, 1964,
    Leicestershire, England.
Height: 168cm/5ft 6in.
Weight: 60kg/132lb.
Career Highlights
European Junior Championships:
    gold 1981; *team* gold 1981.
BSJA Ladies' National
    Championships: champion
    1981.
Benson and Hedges Amateur:
    champion 1981.
Royal International: *Daily Mail Cup*
    1982; *Radio Rentals
    Champion Horseman* 1982.
Horse of the Year Show: *Norwich
    Union Puissance* joint winner
    (with Harvey Smith) 1982.

Lesley McNaught rocketed to recognition in 1981 when she won the British Ladies' Championship and became the youngest Amateur Champion at the age of 17. She kept up the good work in 1982, winning the Daily Mail Cup and the Radio Rentals Champion Horseman. In the latter event she outrode world champion Norbert Koof to become the first female winner. But in 1983, when still a teenager, she shook the show jumping world by splitting from Ted Edgar, her guide and mentor. Lesley left her Hinckley home at 16 to live with Ted and Liz Edgar at their Warwickshire farm after the top showjumping couple had spotted her at a local Midlands show.

Brian McSweeney (IRL)
Eventing
Born: April 15, 1958, Baldonnel,
    Co. Dublin, Ireland.
Height: 178cm/5ft 10in.

Weight: 70kg/154lb.
Career Highlights
European Championships: bronze
    1981.
Irish National three day event:
    champion 1980.

Lieutenant McSweeney gained Ireland's first individual medal in a European Championship since Eddie Boylan's gold in 1967, when he piloted *Inis Meain* to third place in the 1981 championships in Horsens, Denmark. McSweeney, who joined the Irish Army in 1976, won the Irish National Championships in 1980 at Punchestown with *Glenannaar.*

Richard Meade OBE (GBR)
Eventing
Born: December 4, 1938,
    Chepstow, Gloucestershire,
    England.
Height: 183cm/6ft 0in.
Weight: 72.5kg/159lb.
Career Highlights
Olympic Games: *individual* gold
    1972; *team* gold 1972, 1968.
World Championships: *team* gold
    1982, 1970; *team* silver 1974;
    individual silver 1970, 1966.
European Championships: *team;*
    gold 1981, 1971, 1967.
Badminton: champion 1982,
    1970; runner-up 1973, 1972.
Burghley: runner-up 1981,
    champion 1964.

Richard Meade, at the age of 45 is one of Britain's most experienced and successful Olympic sportsmen. He has won three gold medals and competed in four Olympics. He made his Olympic debut in Tokyo in 1964 and four years later, with *Cornishman,* helped Britain to team gold. In Munich in 1972 he struck double gold, riding *Laurieston* to individual victory and also helping the team retain their title. He was just outside the medals again in Montreal where he finished fourth.

Meade, who also has two gold medals from World Championships, was awarded an OBE in the 1974 New Year's Honours.

Katie Monahan (USA)
Show jumping
Born: 1954, Bloomfield Hills,
    Michigan, USA.
Height: 170cm/5ft 7in.
Weight: 59kg/130lb.
Career Highlights
World Championships: silver 1979.
Washington Grand Prix: *leading
    international rider; 1982.*

New York Grand Prix: *leading
    international rider 1982.*

Katie Monahan announced her arrival by finishing runner up on *The Jones Boy* to Austria's Hugo Simon at the 1979 World Championships in Gothenburg. A year later, riding *Silk Exchange,* she was pipped for top honours again when she finished second to Harvey Smith in the Dublin Grand Prix; although the US team won the Nations Cup event there for the Aga Khan Cup

She had a successful autumn season in 1982 on the American circuit with *Noren,* a stallion bred in Normandy and bought in 1981 from Dutch rider Johan Heins. She won an event of the 1983 World Cup meeting on *Corniche.*

Gerry Mullins (IRL)
Show jumping
Born: December 29, 1953, Co.
    Limerick, Ireland.
Height: 170cm/5ft 7in
Weight: 63.5kg/140lb.
Career Highlights
World Championships: fourth
    1982.
European Championships: *team*
    bronze 1979.
Irish National Championships:
    champion 1976.

Mullins joined the Irish Army Equitation School in 1973, where he started as a successful three day event rider. His show jumping career took off in front of his home crowd at the 1982 World Championships in Dublin. With a faultless display on *Rockbarton,* he rocketed from thirteenth place to qualify for the four-man final. With the riders having to partner each other's horses, Mullins finished out of the medals, but *Rockbarton* did him credit and had the best record of the quartet. He also has a useful mount in *Inis Mor* with which he won a speed class in the 1983 World Cup in Vienna.

Michael Plumb (USA)
Eventing
Born: March 28, 1940,
    Chesapeake City, Maryland,
    USA.
Height: 178cm/5ft 10in.
Weight: 73kg/160lb.
Career Highlights
Olympic Games: silver 1976; *team*
    gold 1976; *team* silver 1972,
    1968, 1964.
World Championships: silver 1974;
    team gold 1974.

Plumb has competed in five successive Olympics up to and including the 1976 Games in Montreal where, riding *Better and Better,* he took the individual silver and team gold. He has also competed in three World Championships, winning team gold in 1974 and individual silver behind his fellow countryman Bruce Davidson.

*Sixth Olympics coming up
for America's Michael
Plumb* ▼

Hansueli Schmutz (SUI)
Eventing
Born: 1950, Switzerland.
Height: 181cm/5ft 11in.
Weight: 70kg/154lb.
Career Highlights
European Championships: gold
    1981; *team* silver 1981.

Hansueli Schmutz, a rank outsider, snatched the 1981 European Championships gold medal with the Dutch bred *Oran* in Horsens, Denmark. The Swiss farmer also helped his team win the silver medal. But tragedy prevented him from pursuing his target of a World Championship following at Luhmuhlen in 1982 when he withdrew *Oran* following the death of his team-mate Ernst Baumann who fell on the cross-country.

Paul Schóckemohle (FRG)
Show jumping
Born: March 22, 1945, Muhlen,
    West Germany.
Height: 181cm/5ft 11in.
Weight: 70.5kg/155lb.
Career Highlights
Olympic Games: *team* silver
    1976.
World Championships: *team* silver
    1982.
European Championships:
    individual gold 1981, 1983;
    team gold 1981.
Hickstead Jumping Derby:
    champion 1982.

Schockemohle can improve on the silver medal he won at the Montreal Olympics. With *Deister* an 11-year-old bay gelding, he has a horse to match the best. He won individual and team golds at the European Championships in Munich in 1981 and retained the title at Hickstead last year. *Deister* also won £12,000 and the Jumping Derby at Hickstead in 1982 after miraculously escaping serious injury when his horse-box overturned in a motorway crash.

A millionaire businessman with interests in engineering, Paul has followed in the footsteps of his elder brother Alwin who won the Olympic title in 1976 after becoming the first man to jump a double clear round in the Games.

Following brother's footsteps, Paul Schockemohle ▼

Hugo Simon (AUT)
Show jumping
Born: August 3, 1942, West
  Germany.
Height: 170cm/5ft 7in.
Weight: 68.5kg/150 lb.
Career Highlights
Alternative Olympics: gold 1980;
  team bronze 1980.
Olympic Games: equal fourth;
  1972.
World Championships: equal third
  1974.
World Cup: champion 1979; equal
  third 1982; runner-up 1983.

Simon originally rode for Germany, but to compete in the 1972 Olympics he changed his passport and allegiance to Austria, who had fewer top riders. On the supercharged *Gladstone,* a Hanoverian chestnut gelding, Simon won the inaugural World Cup in Gothenburg in 1979. The following year he took the individual gold medal at the compensatory Olympics in Rotterdam. Nothing that competed in Moscow would have touched him.

Melanie Smith (USA)
Show jumping
Born: September 23, 1949,
  Germanstown, Tennessee,
  USA.
Height: 170cm/5ft 7in.
Weight: 68.5kg/150lb.
Career Highlights
Alternative Olympics: *individual*
  bronze medal 1980.
World Cup Final: third 1983;
  champion 1982; runner-up
  1980.

Melanie broke all records in US Grand Prix Series history in 1978 when she won five classes on *Val de Loire,* to be named Rider of the Year. She again set the pace the following year, winning over $45,000, and was a member of America's gold medal winning team at the Pan Am Games.

She struck up an equally successful partnership with *Calypso,* taking the individual bronze at the 1980 Alternative Olympics in Rotterdam. The same year she was runner-up to her team-mate Conrad Homfeld in the World Cup at Baltimore. In 1982 she went one better, winning the World Cup in Gothenburg, and was third in the event last year in Vienna.

Richard Walker (GBR)
Eventing
Born: August 16, 1950,
  Johannesburg, S. Africa.
Height: 168cm/5ft 6in.
Weight: 60kg/133lb.
Career Highlights
European Championships: silver
  1969; *team* gold 1969.
European Junior Championships:
  gold 1969.
Badminton: champion 1969.
Burghley: champion 1982, 1980.

Richard Walker, who came to Britain from South Africa in 1960, became the youngest rider to win Badminton when he took the 1969 classic at the age of eighteen. The same year he won a team gold at the European Championships and individual silver.

Walker, who pilots his own plane, has won the Midland Bank Open — the official British Championship — three times, and Burghley twice.

John Whitaker (GBR)
Show jumping
Born: August 5, 1955,
  Huddersfield, Yorkshire,
  England.
Height: 175cm/5ft 8in.
Weight: 63.5kg/140lb.

Career Highlights
Alternative Olympics: silver 1980;
  team silver 1980.
World Championships: *team*
  bronze 1982.
World Cup: equal third 1982; fifth
  1979.
Hickstead Jumping Derby: runner
  up, 1981, 1980; champion
  1983.
European Championships:
  individual silver 1983.

John and the colourful *Ryan's Son,* a 15-year-old bay, have been a winning combination for the last eight years. Although leading money winner in 1976, that same year he suffered a cruel blow when he was shortlisted for the Olympics but controversially dropped after *Ryan's Son* refused in the final trial. He was the star of the British team in the alternative Olympics four years later when he won two silver medals.

He helped Britain to a team bronze in the 1982 World Championships in Dublin and was equal third in the World Cup, the highest-placed British rider. Although still an amateur, he and *Ryan's Son* enjoyed a memorable 1983, scooping over £40,000 to top the international winnings league.

Their triumphs included the Hickstead Derby and individual silver in the European Championships, also on the Sussex course.

Michael Whitaker (GBR)
Show jumping
Born: March 17, 1960,
  Huddersfield, Yorkshire,
  England.
Height: 175cm/5ft 8in.
Weight: 63.5kg/140lb.
Career Highlights
Hickstead Jumping Derby:
  runner-up 1983,
  third 1982,
  champion 1980.
European Junior Championships:
  team gold 1978.
Royal Windsor: leading rider 1982.
Royal International: *King George V
  Gold Cup* 1982; *Grand Prix*
  1982.

Michael emerged from the shadow of his elder brother John by dominating the 1982 Royal International Show. He enjoyed a fairytale week on *Disney Way,* winning the King George V Gold Cup and the Grand Prix. In 1980 he became the youngest winner of the Hickstead Jumping Derby on *Owen Gregory.*

Team Sports

The five team sports contested at the Olympics could hardly be split more definitely, both in terms of tradition and attraction.

Soccer and hockey are the long-standing games played on open fields and boasting great names among their medallists. Basketball, handball and volleyball are the more recent inclusions, still seeking to establish themselves as part of the Olympic fabric.

Soccer, no doubt, has the most romantic past as the Olympic competition was truly the World Cup before FIFA organized their own professional tournament in 1930.

The first soccer tournaments in 1900, 1904 and 1906 were considered unofficial, although the honour of scoring the first goal — unofficial or otherwise — fell to Great Britain in the guise of Upton Park FC who beat France 4-0 in 1900.

Fittingly, England, the cradle of the sport, hosted the first official tournament in London, 1908. Domestic strife prevented the emergent Hungarians from taking part, but the increasingly powerful Danes were there along with the Dutch, the Swedes and two French teams. The Danes were remarkably good and, playing a brand of straightforward soccer they had learned from touring British club sides, thrashed France 17-1 in the semi-final before losing 2-0 to Great Britain in the final, mainly because of poor finishing. That 17-1 remains the record score and Danish centre forward Sophus Nielsen hit ten of them.

Britain's team of leading amateurs included Vivian Woodward, an outstanding inside forward, who also represented Spurs, Chelsea and the full England team.

Woodward was in the team four years later when Britain again beat Denmark in the final in Stockholm. This time Britain won 4-0 against a Danish team reduced to ten men for much of the 90 minutes.

Denmark's left half was Nils Middleboe, who went on to captain Chelsea after World War I. So strong were Middleboe's amateur ideals that he turned down a move to Newcastle United and a job in the Danish Consulate in Newcastle because the Geordie club had secretly agreed to pay part of his wages at the Consulate.

Elsewhere, however, the spectre of shamateurism grew and by 1924 Britain were so concerned that they refused to send a team to the competition.

Uruguay emerged victorious from a tournament of 22 countries and went on to prove their global supremacy by retaining the title four years later — and lifting the first World Cup in Montevideo.

Uruguayan goalkeeper Antonio Mazzali, an Olympic hero with two gold medals, was involved in a scandal before the World Cup started. He escaped a curfew at the team's monastic headquarters but was caught creeping home, shoes in hand, and was immediately banished in disgrace. However, Uruguay still won the competition with nine of their Olympic team in the line up. Three other players, all Italians, claimed a similar 'double' winning the Olympics in 1936 and the World Cup in 1938.

Britain again declined to take part in 1928 and the vexed question of amateur/professional became even more difficult to answer in 1952 when the State-backed Eastern Europeans entered for the first time.

Since then teams from Eastern Europe have dominated the football tournament. Only two non-Eastern European sides have reached the final in all that time — Sweden, winners in 1948, and Denmark, the 1960 runners-up.

Gold medallists in Moscow were Czechoslovakia. But though the Czechs are automatically placed in the 1984 finals, they are unlikely to be favourites.

Peru's goalkeeper punches clear during an Austrian attack in the 1936 Berlin Games ▼

USSR ... favourites in Los Angeles ▶

The 1948 Olympic hockey final at Wembley. Grahanadan Singh, the Indian centre forward, scores in the 4-0 defeat of Great Britain

That label should belong to the Soviet Union. But it is an odd fact that, despite pioneering the state-amateur pattern for Eastern European sport, the Soviets have reached the Olympic football final only once.

In 1956, in Melbourne, the Soviet team captained by the great left-half Igor Netto beat Yugoslavia in the final. Now the Soviets placed third in Moscow, are fancied perhaps to repeat that 1956 triumph.

Their hopes rest on the successors of Netto at his old club – Moscow Spartak. Chief among them is Fyodor Cherenkov, the current Soviet Footballer of the Year. Aged 25 with more than 20 full international caps to his credit, Cherenkov is an outstanding attacking player.

A member of the third-placed team in Moscow in 1980, he was deliberately held out of the 1982 World Cup finals in Spain so as not to infringe the strict eligibility code applied to European players. They are not allowed to play in the Olympics if they have appeared in the World Cup or European Nations Championship.

Cherenkov was particularly outstanding for Spartak during the 1983-84 UEFA Cup, scoring the two goals which saw them to victory after an inspired display against Aston Villa in England.

Spartak team-mates, such as defender Boris Pozdnyakov and midfielder Eduard Kuznetsov, have also been regular members of the Soviet team which duelled for a place in the Los Angeles finals with qualifying rivals Hungary, Bulgaria and Greece.

Czechoslavakia, as holders, have been spared the qualifying battle. That is both an advantage and a disadvantage for they have had less chance to put together their team.

It seems likely, however, that to overcome this handicap they will lean heavily on the Sparta Prague men who proved so talented in the 1983-84 UEFA Cup.

Players such as defenders Frantisek Straka and Julius Bielik and midfielder Vlastimil Calta gained a wealth of international experience in their victories over the likes of Real Madrid, Watford and Widzew Lodz. A goalscorer against both Madrid and Widzew was the dangerous Stanislas Griga, another Czech Olympics probable.

Griga joined Sparta from Zilina three years ago and was their top league scorer in 1983 with 15 goals. Now he's setting his sights on higher targets!

The Soviets and Czechs lead the European challenge. But what of South America – and, more specifically, Brazil?

The Brazilians have never been the force in the Olympics which they are in the World Cup. Also, they go to the finals in the aftermath of a major row over player eligibility between their football confederation and domestic Olympics committee.

But you need only look at the Brazilian team which finished fourth in 1976 to understand what vast potential their comparative unknowns will carry. That 1976 team included two future World Cup men now starring in Italy – defender Edinho and midfielder Batista – as well as leftback Junior, one of the game's most skilled players, and a World Club Cup winner in 1981 with Flamengo of Rio.

Coach Cleber Camerino is hoping that world-class talent will emerge this time. Could it be the 26-year-old Fluminense goalkeeper Paulo Vitor, the 22-year-old right winger Gersinho from Pele's old club, Santos, or perhaps the centre forward from unfashionable Nautice, whose name is Francisco Ernandi Lima da Silva, but who is known throughout Brazil by his nickname, Mirandinha.

Europe and South America represent football's elite. But their hegemony is coming under increasing threat from Africa and Asia.

The 1976 finals brought clear signs when Israel, South Korea and Iran all reached the Olympic quarter finals. Four years later and that movement was reinforced by the arrival of Kuwait, Cuba, Iraq and Algeria in the last eight.

If any member of football's developing nations is to go a stage further, and reach the last four, it just might be Cameroun. The Africans created an immense stir in the 1982 World Cup finals with their skilful exuberance. Now they could make that experience count.

In the decisive qualifying ties Cameroun looked to Ernest Ebongue to deliver the goods and the goals. He went to the 1982 World Cup as an untried reserve, but now this 22-year-old from a club called Tonnerre has proved he does carry thunder in those boots.

▼ *Action between England and Pakistan in the 1982 World Hockey Championship in Melbourne*

◄ ◄ *Basketball during the 1936 Berlin Games*

He rocked Ethiopia with two devastating goals in the last round of the qualifying competition and could be a handful for anyone in the finals . . . even for those dominating and disciplined stars of Eastern Europe.

Hockey was dominated by the home countries when the sport made its Olympic appearance in 1908 in London. Four of the six competing sides came from England, Ireland, Scotland and Wales, with England beating Ireland in the final.

Hockey was dropped from the Olympic curriculum between 1908 and 1920 and again in 1924. Britain, displaying the kind of isolationism which also afflicted its football administrators of the time, declined to take part in 1928, 1932 and 1936 leaving the way open for India, who had learned the game from their Colonial masters.

When the two countries did meet, in London 1948, the pupils showed how well they had learned by caning Britain 4-0. It was one of eight gold medal triumphs enjoyed by India, and with Pakistan winning the competition twice, the sub-continent has been rightly regarded as hockey's supreme exponent.

Apart from the most wins, India hold two other Olympic records. The highest score was their 24-1 defeat of the United States in 1932 and the biggest winning margin in the final was their 11-1 trouncing of Japan in 1932. A women's competition, introduced for the first time in 1980, produced a famous victory for the newly independent Zimbabwe and provided a personal triumph for their 35-year-old player/coach Anthea Stewart.

All Olympic hockey finalists are selected by their international body. There is no qualifying competition and that has caused great controversy this time as Great Britain have been excluded from both the men's and women's events.

Great Britain's men, who some experts believed were medal contenders, have been chosen as first reserve, however, and there has never yet been an Olympic hockey tournament where all the original teams competed.

At present, the men are divided into two squads of six: Squad A: Australia, West Germany, India, Spain, Malaysia and USA; Squad B: Holland, Pakistan, USSR, New Zealand, Canada and Kenya or Egypt.

Of those, Pakistan are the current World Cup holders, Australia the best all-round team and the USSR the emergent black horses, who could emulate the exploits of their Winter Olympics ice hockey team.

Australia's captain Rick Charlesworth seems certain to be a star of the Games. A former opening batsman for Western Australia he would probably have made the Test team, but for his passion for hockey where he plays as a brilliantly creative inside right. He is also a member of the Australian parliament.

Pakistan have a mecurial inside left in Hannif Khan and Holland have a tearaway centre forward in Roderick Baumann, plus the sportsman who has twice won international Superstars, Ties Kruize. Kruize was badly hurt in a car accident, suffering concussion and breaking his knee, yet has since refashioned his career. Baumann and Kruize are lethal short corner men in the mould of Paul Litjens.

West Germany, too, have a real crowd pleaser in 191cm/6ft 3in Stefan Blocher a giant striding midfield player with sublime ball control.

The six teams in the women's competition do not include the Moscow champions, Zimbabwe. Instead they are Holland, Australia, West Germany, USA, Canada and New Zealand.

West Germany possess the outstanding player in the world in goalkeeper Suzanne Schmidt. But the Dutch, who will start favourites, have two superb performers in midfielder Marjolein Eysuogel and defender Fieke Boekhorst, an Amazon of a girl who tackles like a tank and hits shots like a howitzer.

Basketball provided the Olympic Games with one of its greatest controversies in 1972. Three seconds from the end the USA seemed to have clinched their final against the USSR when two free throws put them 50-49 ahead.

With one second remaining, the crowd mistakenly believed the match was over and invaded the court. The referee cleared them off, restarted the match and played out the final second.

But then Britain's Dr William Jones, secretary general of the *Federation Internationale de Basketball Amateur,* stepped in to decree that three seconds more should have been played, rather than one. The clock was reset and this time Aleksandr Belov scored the winning basket for the Soviet Union. The Americans made furious protests to no avail and in the end flew home without their silver medals.

The defeat ended a staggering US sequence of 63 victories between 1936 when the sport was introduced and 1972, during which period they won seven team golds.

The USSR have dominated the women's event, introduced in 1976, with Iuliana Semenova (218cm/7ft 2in) towering head and shoulders above the rest.

Handball had one Olympic outing as an eleven-a-side outdoor game in 1936 before returning as a seven-a-side indoor sport in 1972. Again it is mainly controlled by Eastern European countries with East Germany, the USSR and Romania taking the 1980 men's medals.

The women's competition, introduced four years later in 1976, has produced a double success for the USSR and few would back against them completing a hat-trick in Los Angeles.

In volleyball, the story is similar. Since it came into the Olympic programme in 1964 the Soviet men's and women's teams have lost only six matches between them and are the reigning champions.